Muslim Reformers in Iran and Turkey

MODERN MIDDLE EAST SERIES, NO. 25

Sponsored by the Center for Middle Eastern Studies (CMES)

The University of Texas at Austin

Muslim Reformers in Iran and Turkey

THE PARADOX OF MODERATION

GÜNEŞ MURAT TEZCÜR

UNIVERSITY OF TEXAS PRESS ◆ AUSTIN

Requests for permission to reproduce material from this work
should be sent to:
    Permissions
    University of Texas Press
    P.O. Box 7819
    Austin, TX 78713-7819
    www.utexas.edu/utpress/about/bpermission.html

∞ The paper used in this book meets the minimum requirements
of ANSI/NISO Z39.48-1992 (R1997) (Permanence of Paper).

Library of Congress Cataloging-in-Publication Data
Tezcür, Güneş Murat, 1979–
  Muslim reformers in Iran and Turkey : the paradox of moderation /
Güneş Murat Tezcür. — 1st ed.
      p. cm. — (Modern Middle East series ; no. 25)
  Includes bibliographical references and index.
  ISBN 978-0-292-72883-7
  1. Jabhah-ʾi Islahat (Iran) 2. AK Parti (Turkey) 3. Islam and
politics—Iran. 4. Islam and politics—Turkey. 5. Liberalism—Iran.
6. Liberalism—Turkey. 7. Iran—Politics and government—1997–
8. Turkey—Politics and government—1980– I. Title.
  JQ1789.A8J348 2010
  322'.10955—dc22
                                                    2009032295

CONTENTS

LIST OF TABLES AND FIGURES

LIST OF ABBREVIATIONS

AE   Assembly of Experts (Majles-e Khobregan-e Rahbari), Iran

AMAI   Army Mutual Assistance Institution (Ordu Yardımlaşma Kurumu), Turkey

CDU   Christian Democratic Union of Germany (Christlich Demokratische Union Deutschlands), Germany

DP   Democratic Party (Demokrat Parti), Turkey

DSP   Democratic Society Party (Demokratik Toplum Partisi), Turkey

EC   Expediency Council (Majma-ye Tashkhis-e Maslehat-e Nezam-e Eslami), Iran

ECHR   European Court of Human Rights, France

ECP   Executives of Construction Party (Hezb-e Kargozaran-e Sazendegi), Iran

FMI   Freedom Movement of Iran (Nehzat-e Azadi-ye Iran), Iran

FP   Felicity Party (Saadet Partisi), Turkey

GC   Guardians Council (Shura-ye Negahban-e Qanun-e Assasi), Iran

GIAU   Gendarmerie Intelligence and Antiterrorism Unit (Jandarma İstihbarat ve Terörle Mücadele), Turkey

IAF   Islamic Action Front (Jabhat al-Amal al-Islami), Jordan

IIDC   Islamic Iran Developers Council (Etelaf-e Abadgaran-e Iran-e Eslami), Iran

IIPF   Islamic Iran Participation Front (Jebhe-ye Mosharekat-e Iran-e Eslami), Iran

IISP   Islamic Iran Solidarity Party (Hezb-e Hambastegi-ye Iran-e Eslami), Iran

IRDS   Islamic Revolution Devotees Society (Jamiyyat-e Isargaran-e Enqelab-e Eslami), Iran

IRI   Islamic Republic of Iran

ISI   Import-substitution industrialization

JDP   Justice and Development Party (Adalet ve Kalkınma Partisi), Turkey

JP   Justice Party (Adalet Partisi), Turkey

MCA   Militant Clergy Association (Jamee-ye Ruhaniyyat-e Mobarez), Iran

MCL   Militant Clerics League (Majma-ye Ruhaniyyun-e Mobarez), Iran

MP	Motherland Party (Anavatan Partisi), Turkey
NAP	Nationalist Action Party (Milliyetçi Hareket Partisi), Turkey
NCP	National Confidence Party (Hezb-e Etemad-e Melli), Iran
NOP	National Order Party (Milli Nizam Partisi), Turkey
NSC	National Security Council (Milli Güvenlik Kurulu), Turkey
NSP	National Salvation Party (Milli Selamet Partisi), Turkey
OEIR	Organization of Endeavourers of Islamic Revolution (Sazeman-e Mojahedin-e Enqelab-e Eslami), Iran
PKK	Kurdish Workers Party (Partiya Karkerên Kurdistan), Kurdish nationalist insurgent movement
PPP	Purchasing power parity
RAD	Religious Affairs Directory (Diyanet İşleri Başkanlığı), Turkey
RF	Reform Front (Jebhe-ye Eslahat or Jebhe-ye Dovom Khordad), Iran
RFE/RL	Radio Free Europe/Radio Liberty
RPP	Republican People's Party (Cumhuriyet Halk Partisi), Turkey
SCC	Special Court for Clerics (Dadgah-e Vizhe-ye Ruhaniyyat), Iran
SDP	Social Democratic Party (Sozialdemokratische Partei Deutschlands), Germany
TAF	Turkish Armed Forces (Türk Silahlı Kuvvetleri), Turkey
TCC	Turkish Constitutional Court (Anayasa Mahkemesi), Turkey
TPP	True Parth Party (Doğru Yol Partisi), Turkey
VP	Virtue Party (Fazilet Partisi), Turkey
WP	Welfare Party (Refah Partisi), Turkey
WVS	World Values Survey

My interest in the subject of this book has its roots in my high school years in the mid-1990s, when the Welfare Party emerged as the most popular and dynamic force in Turkish politics. I became curious about this force, which remained very enigmatic for me. My college years in Istanbul introduced me to a relatively cosmopolitan atmosphere where I met people for whom the Welfare Party had something to offer. Those interactions deepened my curiosity. Meanwhile, the Welfare Party rose and went down; the Islamist movement lost its orientation with the 1997 military intervention; ex–Welfare Party cadres regrouped under a new party that suddenly became an enthusiastic supporter of the European Union (EU). Turkey experienced its worst economic crisis since World War II shortly after I went to graduate school in the United States. That crisis generated a golden opportunity for a relatively younger generation of politicians who abandoned their old mentor, Necmettin Erbakan, the leader of the Welfare Party. They claimed to rebuild the center in Turkish politics. When I was visiting the offices of their party in the summer of 2002, Recep Tayyip Erdoğan and his companions were full of enthusiasm and promises. They turned out to be very successful and became the predominant political force in the country after the November 2002 elections. Studying electoral processes when politicians compete to appeal to hearts and minds was very productive learning that helped me develop a better sense of how and why people act politically. Nonetheless, I realized that an exclusive focus on Turkey would leave my understanding too parochial and captive to domestic polemics. In late 2002, I decided to expand my research into Iran, where a Muslim reformist movement had recently achieved unprecedented popularity under the leadership of Mohammad Khatami. The center-periphery relations at a global level greatly shaped this decision. It was more feasible for a Turkish citizen based in the United States to conduct research in Iran than either a Turkish citizen based in Turkey or a U.S. citizen based in the United States. For many Turkish citizens, the Islamic Republic of Iran remains

"Turkey's Orient," the "essential other" against which the Turkish republic defines its spirit and achievements. Perplexingly for them, my travels to Iran have greatly informed my understanding of my own country's cultural and historical heritage and politics that have much in common with its eastern neighbor. I still consider myself a novice as a student of Iranian politics after many travels, interactions, and readings. At the same time, I feel confident that I gained some unique insights into the dynamics of Iranian politics that enable me to offer an interesting narrative of the contemporary evolution of Iranian Muslim reformers.

My research in these two countries mostly satisfied my original curiosity of learning how Muslim political actors believe, strategize, and act. The more I study Iranian and Turkish Muslim reformers, the more I become critical of the term "moderation" that has been central to scholarly and public debates about the progress of democracy in the Muslim Middle East. Muslim political actors are encouraged to be more moderate; moderation has been perceived as conducive to democratic openings. I tend to disagree. Muslim reformers in Iran and Turkey have not been lacking in moderation; on the contrary, they are often shown as the most prominent examples of "Muslim democrats." Yet they have not necessarily been agents of democratic change. In fact, moderation that entails compromise, commitment to electoral rules, and reconciliation may actually hinder the expansion of political rights, the establishment of a culture of human rights, and the making of political power accountable and transparent.

Writing a comparative narrative based on an analytical framework with the purpose of addressing multiple audiences always entails difficult trade-offs between theoretical parsimony and consistency on the one hand, and empirical accuracy and richness on the other. I strive to strike a balance between these two worthy goals. It remains the reader's right to judge.

I did not always feel comfortable writing this book, as scholarship does not free one from passing judgment on the objects of the study. Being aware of this inevitability, I have very self-consciously adopted a teleological bias that prioritizes individual-level freedoms. Partially because of my life experience and partially because of my reading of human affairs, I tend to treat individual autonomy and creativity as being indispensable for a good society. This emphasis naturally leads me to appreciate liberal democracy as an admirable political system (not necessarily as an economic system, though) in spite of the fact that liberalism and democracy do not always coexist in harmony. The preference for liberal democracy thoroughly characterizes this work and provides the basis of my positive and negative evaluations of Muslim reformers in Iran and Turkey. I hope my normative judgments remain solid and do not deviate from this framework. In any case, I remain solely responsible for all errors.

I would like to express my gratitude to the United States Institute of Peace (Grant #SG-112-06S), the National Science Foundation (Grant #0213790), Loyola University Chicago, and the University of Michigan for supporting my field research in Iran and Turkey. I have benefited from the collective wisdom of many scholars while working on this book. I would like to thank my dissertation committee members, Ronald Inglehart, Mark Tessler, Arlene Saxonhouse, Ann Lin, and Juan Cole, for their mentoring during my graduate years in Ann Arbor. Jillian Schwedler's feedback enabled me to significantly improve and clarify my analytical approach. Ted Jelen was kind enough to read an earlier version of this manuscript and provide useful feedback. Peter Schraeder, Mohammadreza Jalaeipour, Mirjam Künkler, Ted Jelen, Veit Bader, and Michelle Angrist read and commented on individual chapters. I very much appreciate their critical comments. Participants in seminars at Boğaziçi University, Koç University, Dartmouth College, and Northwestern University provided me valuable feedback that sharpened my arguments. Encouragement from Dale Eickelman and Raymond Tatalovich helped me preserve my determination. Nazeer Lotfi-Fard provided me with competent assistance regarding several written materials in Persian. It was a pleasure to work with my editors at the University of Texas Press, Wendy Moore, Jim Burr, and Sarah E. Hudgens, during the publication process. Finally, I would like to thank Nancy Warrington for her meticulous copyediting.

My fieldwork was a liberating experience and took me to remote corners and frontier areas of Iran and Turkey where geography reigns supreme over human will. I met with many individuals whose perspectives broadened my intellectual horizons and constantly reminded me of the eternal human aspiration for universality. At the same time, I came to realize the fragility of this aspiration and the common bonds that define our shared experience of the world. The mythical story of the Tower of Babel has much to offer in this regard. I managed to ward off cynicism as friendships continued to materialize in the most unexpected settings and times. There have been many individuals in Iran and Turkey whose help made my fieldwork a much richer experience. I cannot mention all of them here. I am especially indebted to Taghi Azadarmaki, Hossein Laleh, Babak Rahimi, Hadi, and Mohammad in Iran and Ali Aksoy, Cevdet Canan, Vahit Esmer, Fevzi Kangal, Zübeyir Nişancı, Mahfuz Nazar, and Fadıl Ülgen in Turkey.

The transliteration of Persian words generally follows the system suggested by the *International Journal of Middle Eastern Studies*. At the same time, my priority is making this work accessible to non-Persian and non-Turkish speakers. Hence, I have avoided most diacritical marks and used English spellings of common names and terms such as "sharia," "Shiite," "Khomeini," and "Tehran." I have reviewed my transliterations for consistency and accuracy. I hope native readers of Persian are willing to overlook any remaining errors. In addition, I use English acronyms of Iranian and Turkish organizations to simplify the language in this comparative study, such as JDP instead of AKP or AK Parti and IIPF instead of Mosharekat.

G.M.T.

March 2009

Chicago

Muslim Reformers in Iran and Turkey

CHAPTER 1

Introduction

In the summer of 2002, the headquarters of the Justice and Development Party (JDP; Adalet ve Kalkınma Partisi) was hardly a well-known address. Visitors to the newly constructed building located in the Balgat district of Ankara were few in number and had easy access to leadership cadres. The relationships were personal within the party; all divisions worked closely with one another. The party, led by Recep Tayyip Erdoğan and founded by a group of politicians who split from the Islamist[1] movement, had around fifty parliamentarians and was in the opposition. The party leadership had an ambitious political vision. The JDP would have a democratic governance structure, establish rigorous ethical standards for its members, actively fight against corruption, realize social justice by redressing income inequalities, and become a leading actor of Turkish democratization, which gained new impetus with the increasing prospects of Turkey's membership in the European Union (EU). The public was receptive to the JDP in the aftermath of Turkey's worst post–World War II economic crisis. The tripartite coalition government, which had ruled the country since the April 1999 elections, started to unravel and called for early elections. The JDP fully capitalized on this golden opportunity and swept the polls just fifteen months after its foundation. Erdoğan became prime minister in March 2003 after the ban on his political activity was revoked. The once-quiet headquarters was soon swarmed by people from all over the country who had their own expectations, requests, and hopes. Meanwhile, in the eyes of many outside observers, the JDP was a perfect example of "moderate Islam" demonstrating the compatibility of Muslim faith with democratic and peaceful governance in the post–September 11 era of tensions and conflict.

Another "moderate face of Islam" was already in "power" to the east of Turkey, in a rather unexpected setting, the Islamic Republic of Iran. Mohammad Khatami, a middle-ranking cleric and former minister of Culture and Islamic Guidance, was the underdog candidate in the 1997 presidential elections. He

1

had few financial and organizational resources at his disposal; he was not the preferred candidate of the Islamist guardians, who controlled key positions of the political regime. Yet he emerged triumphant from the 1997 presidential elections, a victory that took many observers by surprise. Khatami adopted a modest posture, toured the provinces in hopes of reaching the ordinary voters during his campaign, and developed a discourse integrating themes of civil society, popular participation and rule, and rule of law. He seemed to offer a genuine choice to many Iranians who enthusiastically went to the polls. President Khatami set up a new platform called the "Dialogue of Civilizations" and repeatedly expressed his desire to improve Iran's relationship with the West, including the United States. His presidency inaugurated a new period in which demands for democratic reform were voiced and found public following. Less than three years after Khatami's victory, his followers loosely organized as the Reform Front (hereafter RF; Jebhe-ye Eslahat or Jebhe-ye Dovom Khordad) and gained the control of the parliament after defeating their rivals in the 2000 elections. For many, these two victories revealed the widespread discontent with the Iranian regime and public desire for substantial political change. The Islamic Republic of Iran, which came into existence following the Revolution of 1979, would be reformed from within. For the first time in the modern history of the Middle East, popularly elected politicians who promised to synthesize democratic governance with Islamic principles gained political prominence.

Ironically, the two countries that hosted the rise of the strongest reformist Islamic oppositions in the Middle East were the secularist Turkish regime and the Islamist Iranian regime. Whereas the secularist worldview restricted public expressions of religion, the Islamist worldview established the hegemony of a particular version of religion over the public sphere. This chapter first defines the historical puzzle of Muslim reformism in these two countries. After summarizing plausible explanations that focus on either Iran or Turkey, I offer a comparative explanation informed by moderation theory. I then introduce a revised version of theory that contributes to a better scholarly understanding of the evolution of Iranian and Turkish Muslim reformers. In the last two sections of the chapter, I discuss the methods used and provide an overview of the book.

2

does this book accomplish this?

The Historical Puzzle

This book follows the trajectory of the RF in Iran and the JDP in Turkey from the early 1990s to the last half of the first decade of the twenty-first century (see Figure 1.1). The RF in Iran and the JDP in Turkey represent the forces of Muslim reformism. They share certain common characteristics. The RF and the JDP, the Muslim reformers, accept the inviolability of political pluralism, competitive elections, and human rights while seeking a political role for Islamic symbols, norms, and faith.[2] Meanwhile, they represent diverse positions on issues such as gender equality; the application of Islamic law; the sociopolitical status of vulnerable groups, including non-Muslims and ethnic minorities; and relations with Western countries.[3] Hence, their espousal of rights is often more restrictive and more inconsistent than that of political actors fully committed to liberal democracy. Second, they reflect the rise of postideological thinking among Islamic cadres.[4] Many Iranian and Turkish Islamists who had previously denounced democracy as culturally inauthentic and institutionally redundant emerged as staunch advocates of democratic reform. A prominent activist and intellectual in the Turkish Islamist movement put this transformation in perspective:

> The core idea of modernization in Iran and Turkey has been the state's engineering of social consciousness and transformation of social relations. . . . Islamism adopted this authoritarian tendency in both countries. Islamists aimed to capture the state and reorganize society. Only in the early 1990s did Islamists start to develop a liberal and rights oriented reading of Islam.[5]

The primary focus of the book is on groups of political elites who formed powerful organizations, occupied key governmental positions, and articulated visions of common good that often put them at odds with the nonelected guardians (discussed in detail in Chapter 5), who command considerable political power. Other political actors are included in the analyses as long as they affect the ideas, interests, and behavior of these political groups. The book primarily addresses a historical puzzle (see Table 1.1): Why did the strongest Muslim political reform movements in the contemporary Middle East emerge in Iran and Turkey, which substantially differ from each other in terms of political rule, religious establishment, socioeconomic structure, cultural past, and international linkages? Also, why did the evolution of Iranian and Turkish Muslim reformers follow a similar trajectory?[6]

Iran and Turkey have many differences. First, the historical evolution of Islam in Iran and Turkey has followed substantially different paths. Canonical differences and the historical rivalry between the Hanafi school of Islam—dominant in Turkey since the Ottoman times—and the Jaafari school of Twelver Shiite Islam—the state religion of Iran since the sixteenth century—are tremendous. However, Islam being Sunni in Turkey and historically lacking an autonomous clerical establishment has not necessarily made religious movements in this country less or more democratic than in Iran, where Shiite Islam, with its powerful clerical establishment, is the predominant religious denomination. Second, since 1923 Turkey has been a secular republic in which the role of religion in public life is highly regulated, whereas Iran since 1979 has been an Islamic republic with state enforcement of Islamic morals in public life. Politics are expressed within the limits of a secularist paradigm in Turkey; in Iran, Islamist principles usually determine the parameters of

Figure 1.1. The Evolution of Muslim Political Actors in Iran and Turkey

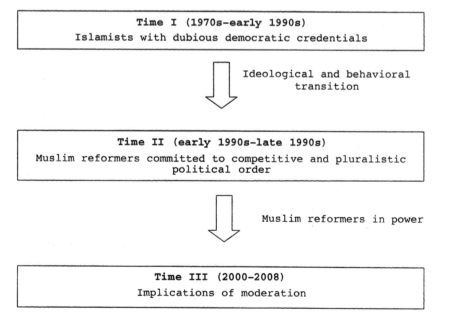

Time I (1970s–early 1990s)
Islamists with dubious democratic credentials

Ideological and behavioral transition

Time II (early 1990s–late 1990s)
Muslim reformers committed to competitive and pluralistic political order

Muslim reformers in power

Time III (2000–2008)
Implications of moderation

Table 1.1. The Historical Puzzle

	Legacy	Regime Type	Recent Political History	Economic Structure	Foreign Relations	
IRAN	Safavid-Shia	Islamist	Autocratic rule	Regulated, oil-based rentier	Antagonism with the United States	**Muslim Reformism**
TURKEY	Ottoman-Sunni	Secularist	Competitive elections since 1950 interrupted by coups	Open, liberalized/ privatized	NATO member; EU aspirant	

political discourse. Third, Turkey has had more than fifty years of parliamentary democracy, albeit interrupted by military interventions; Iran's brief experiences with parliamentarism, starting in 1906 and repeating again in 1951 and 1979, were followed by the consolidation of autocratic rule. Fourth, Turkey since the late 1940s has been allied with the United States, whereas the Iranian regime since the revolution has been the main antagonist of the U.S. government in the region. Turkey currently seeks membership in the EU; the Iran-EU relationship has been characterized by tensions and uncertainty. Yet these political differences have not prevented the almost simultaneous rise of Muslim reformers in both countries in the late 1990s. Finally, Iran and Turkey have little in common in the way their economies are structured and how that impacts regime stability. The Iranian economy is highly regulated, oil based, and characterized by heavy state involvement in all aspects of production. The business sector has no autonomous capacity to push for political and economic liberalization. In contrast, Turkey has an open and diversified economy that was beset by erratic growth rates during the 1990s. The business interests have organizational independence and in the past often advocated democratic reforms as necessary to limit arbitrary state intervention.[7]

The simultaneous rise of Muslim reformism in Iran and Turkey also defies the expectations of theoretical perspectives that exclusively focus on the relationship between political and religious authority and political theology, which involves religious justifications for legitimate political authority.[8] Differentiation implies that religious and political entities are mutually autonomous from each other and independently govern their own affairs. Additionally, the relationship between these two entities can be characterized by either consensus or conflict. Political theology either espouses liberal-democratic ideas or backs authoritarian regimes. Liberal democracies tend to have high levels of differentiation and consensual relationships between religious and political authority. In contrast, in the Muslim world, the states have been mostly integrationist and political theology has had strong authoritarian tendencies. In fact, the integrationist and repressive regimes in the Middle East and Central Asia "have radicalized already conservative Muslim movements by suppressing their legal, nonviolent participation . . . and sequestering them from the *moderating* influences of democratic competition, compromise, and public argument."[9] In this sense, liberal democracy is more likely to be achieved in regimes with high levels of differentiation between religious and political authority. Similarly, religious actors are more likely to become agents of democratization in differentiated regimes. Whereas the Turkish regime is categorized as having conflictual differentiation, the Iranian regime is classified as consensual integrationist, like Saudi Arabia's.[10] Hence, they are anathemas to each other. While this theoretical perspective plausibly expects the growth of a strong Muslim political reform movement in Turkey, it does not offer any insights regarding the rise of the most ambitious Muslim political reform in Iran. After all, Iran and Saudi Arabia have a similar type and degree of differentiation. Moreover, the predominant political theology in Iran, *velayat-e faqih* (guardianship of the jurists), is not more hospitable to liberal democracy than that in Saudi Arabia, Wahhabism. The fact that Iran has some institutional features in common with Turkey and different from Saudi Arabia may provide a more satisfactory understanding.

Country-Specific Explanations

Before laying out the explanatory framework developed in this book, it is instructive to briefly discuss narratives that aim to explain the rise of Muslim reformers in either Iran or Turkey. Three such narratives exist for each country. Iran is the only country where Islamists were able to lead a mass uprising and establish a theocratic regime. However, with the advent of the 1990s, signs of popular discontent with state policies and of public apathy toward the ruling ideology increased. The regime's enforcement of Islamic morals; failure in dealing with high levels of unemployment, especially among the youth; and inability to transform oil wealth into economic prosperity all contributed to public discontent. In these respects, Iran was not very different from many other Middle Eastern regimes where incompetent governance fueled support for Islamist movements. Opposition movements in Arab countries often perceived further Islamization as a panacea to sociopolitical problems. Different from these countries, however, in Iran, Islamists were not ruled but ruled. Ex-revolutionaries who were disillusioned with the Islamist experiment formed the backbone of the nonviolent and loyal opposition to the Islamic Republic. Islamists in other countries would not undergo a similar metamorphosis because they did not achieve their ideal of an Islamic state. The shortcomings of the Islamic state are a primary cause for the popularity of Muslim reformist platforms. This is a valuable perspective that well captures the transformation of revolutionaries, who had been believers in the notion of an Islamic state, into the dissidents of the Islamic Republic. Yet this perspective does not tell anything about the rise of a new generation of believers who remained adherent to the Islamic state and rose to power with the 2004 parliamentary and 2005 presidential elections.

Another perspective focuses on the historical evolution of Shiite traditions. Ruhollah Khomeini's theory of *velayat-e motlaq-e faqih*, the absolute rule of the clergy, which became the blueprint of the constitution of the Islamic Republic, represented a radical innovation in Shiite theology. Shiite tradition defined the role of the clergy as a collective guardianship in the social and legal sphere, not in the political sphere. The Islamic Republic set this tradition aside and institutionalized the rule of politically committed clergy. However, clerics and religious intellectuals who were discontent with the Islamic Republic challenged this departure from tradition.[11] They were concerned with the corruptive influence of politics on clerics and on public religiosity and the exploitation of Shiite Islam as a justification for authoritarian rule. Because of their religious credentials, they effectively threatened the regime's monopoly over Islamic discourse. Sunni countries would not have a similar intellectual movement because clerical authorities in these countries were historically subordinated to the state. As a result, they would not be in a position to actively support or lead democratic opposition movements. This perspective accurately identifies the inherent tension between Shiite traditions and the notion of an Islamic state ruled by the *faqih*. However, neither the disillusionment with ideology nor traditional Shiite perspectives can be the *necessary* conditions for the rise of Muslim reformism, as they were completely irrelevant to the similar developments in Turkey.

Yet another perspective focuses on the rise of the RF as a powerful opposition movement by specifying institutional factors that distinguish Iran from more stable authoritarian countries. According to this viewpoint, the lack of a single ruling party undermined elite cohesion and made institutional mediation of elite disputes very difficult in the Islamic Republic. "Ruling parties thus resolve conflicts in a positive-sum fashion . . . When parties have declined or disappeared, intra-elite conflicts escalate, and leaders polarize into competing factions. . . . The realignment of previous supporters of authoritarianism with the opposition presents *a structural opportunity for democratization*" (italics added).[12] While this perspective rightly focuses on how political opportunities inherent to the factional nature of political rule in Iran facilitated the rise of the RF, it has two shortcomings. First, it just asserts that the RF failed to take full benefit of these opportunities because the movement preferred "accommodation over confrontation."[13] It does not offer any explanation for why the RF made the choice of "accommodation." Additionally, the viewpoint does not adequately discuss the ideological trends that were mostly autonomous from political opportunities and accompanied the rise of the RF. Hence, analytical focus should also include the organizational resources and ideological worldview of the RF. Next, it can be disputed whether factionalism inherent to the Islamic Republic generated a "structural opportunity for democratization." After all, it can be argued that electoral factionalism actually hindered the development of a mass-based opposition movement, limited the scope of elite defections, and prevented distribution of targets of public discontent and blame.[14]

It is also possible to identify three influential perspectives that seek to explain the emergence and rise of Muslim reformers in Turkey. The first focuses on Turkey's rather unique secular heritage. Turkish secularism not only limits religion's role in public life; it represses parties and social movements that politicize the public's religious sentiments,[15] and bans political parties that defy the restrictions on the public roles of Islam. Consequently, according to this point of view, the "moderation" of Islamists in the 1990s can best be explained as a product of the secularist character of the regime. The founders of the JDP who had previously been members of the Islamist parties banned by the Constitutional Court realized the infeasibility of Islamist goals in Turkey. They decided to reinvent themselves as centrists to avoid repression. Hence, Turkish Islamists became more democratic than their counterparts elsewhere in the Middle East because the secularist guardians disciplined them.[16] The fundamental weakness of this perspective is that it misreads the Islamist response to state repression. In fact, Islamists had already become quite "moderate" before the state crackdown. Moreover, reformists who had emerged from within the Islamists continued to challenge the Turkish version of secularism.

A second viewpoint, which also underlines the uniqueness of Turkish experience, argues that the rise of Muslim reformers occurred in spite of secularism.[17] According to this view, Anatolian Sufism informed how Muslim Turks and Kurds made sense of sociopolitical affairs and contributed to social stability and cohesion.[18] While Sufi beliefs and practices showed great variety, they generally shunned Islamist platforms. The pious middle class practicing Sufi Islam greatly benefited from economic liberalization and Turkey's increasing integration into the global economy with the advent of the 1980s. The JDP leaders established strong networks with the pious middle class and recruited its members to leadership positions. The rise of Muslim reformers in Turkey in the 1990s can best be understood as an effect of the tolerant, pluralistic, and civic characteristics of Anatolian Sunni Islam. The JDP's leadership cadres generally adhere to Sufism, and the party's rise represented continuity with Turkish Islamic traditions.[19] The main problem with this perspective is its assumption of a direct connection between Sufi beliefs and political behavior. The effects of organizations and institutions on behavior are ignored. Furthermore, the viewpoint depicts a quixotic portrayal of Turkish Sufism and ignores its more authoritarian characteristics.

A third approach focuses on the effects of EU-induced democratization in Turkey. Since the beginning of the twenty-first century, Turkey has achieved considerable progress in fulfilling the EU's Copenhagen criteria, which include democratic reforms, respect for human rights, the rule of law, and the protection of minorities. The JDP, which has formed the Turkish government since November 2002, actively pursued a reformist agenda and undertook major policy initiatives to augment the chances of Turkey being admitted to membership in the union. Consequently, the EU decided to open up formal negotiations with Turkey in December 2004. The JDP realized that EU reforms would weaken the secularists, including the military, and solidify civilian control of the armed forces. Besides, the success in achieving progress toward EU membership would translate into intense public support for the party. While the JDP became an advocate of Turkey's membership to the EU out of self-interest, it also unintentionally came to accept the EU rules and norms that severely limit the scope of Islamist influence. Hence, the EU's extensive leverage over and linkages with Turkey were the primary causes of "moderation" of the Islamists.[20] It is clearly true that pursuing the EU membership process reinforced the reformist tendencies of the EU, restrained military involvement in politics, and contributed to Turkey's democratization. At the same time, this perspective conflates the causal sequence between the EU process and the JDP's moderation. The EU process did not "moderate" the JDP; the party was already moderate enough to pursue an energetic EU policy, albeit temporarily. In summary, none of these three factors peculiar to Turkey can qualify as the *necessary* conditions for the rise of Muslim reformers, as they are not pertinent to developments in Iran.[21] So it would be misleading to talk about either *Iranian* or *Turkish exceptionalism.*

A Theory and a Comparative Explanation

Conventional explanations that focus on the characteristics unique to Iran and Turkey fail to offer a satisfactory answer to this comparative puzzle. An explicitly comparative perspective based on an elaborate theoretical framework would identify causal dynamics that were at work in both cases. This book draws on moderation theory to develop a comparative understanding of the evolution of Muslim reformism in Iran and Turkey.[22] Moderation theory was originally developed to explain the democratic evolution of Socialist parties in Western Europe. According to this theory, Socialist parties would, over time, accept democratic processes and norms, since they remained an electoral minority and would have to compromise with non-Socialist parties in order to become part of governments.

The book revisits moderation theory and offers a more nuanced analysis of its causal mechanisms. Moderation can be defined on two analytical levels. *Ideological moderation* can be defined as a *process* through which political actors espouse ideas that do not contradict the principles of popular sovereignty, political pluralism, and limits on arbitrary state authority.[23] In most cases, it entails the continuous expansion of boundaries of internally consistent and justifiable political action. *Behavioral moderation* concerns the adaptation of electoral, conciliatory, and nonconfrontational strategies that seek compromise and peaceful settlement of disputes at the expense of nonelectoral, provocative, and confrontational strategies that are not necessarily violent but may entail contentious action. Moderation theory, as articulated in this book, has three distinct causal mechanisms: (1) the effects of free electoral competition; (2) the effects of state repression; and (3) the effects of organizational resources (see Chapter 2 for an extensive discussion). The theory primarily analyzes how these three effects shape political *behavior*.

The basic idea, which is similar to the median voter theorem,[24] is that once radical political groups, who are committed to the overthrow of the political system, are organized as vote-seeking parties, electoral considerations would make these groups abandon revolutionary goals. This is because revolutionary and extremist platforms usually fail to mobilize pluralities, not to mention majorities. Radical groups organized as electoral parties need to appeal to the greatest number of voters to remain politically viable and win elections. Second, radicals remain suspicious in the eyes of the regime elites who command superior coercive mechanisms. Radicals need to pursue cautious and conciliatory policies toward these elites to avoid their wrath. The logic of political survival necessitates that radicals avoid openly confronting the elites. These two mechanisms are well established in moderation theory and are supported by examples from Europe and Latin America. The third mechanism, the effects of organization, is less articulated. This is rather surprising because the origins of moderation theory can be traced at least back to Robert Michels' analysis of the German Social Democratic Party, the first mass party that inspired all other Socialist parties. The effects of organizational resources on party behavior are central to Michels' analysis. An organizational perspective suggests that the maintenance of the organization and its authority structure becomes the priority overriding all declared goals. In the case of radical groups organized as electoral parties, revolutionary goals become unreachable simply because of the lack of organizational resources. An electoral party, by definition, is a very unlikely candidate to challenge the political regime and bring about its fall. Electoralism, defined as the strategy of exclusively pursuing votes to achieve and sustain political power, requires professionalism, expertise, and competency in certain kinds of political action, such as campaigning and patronage distribution, rather than in others, such as civil disobedience and participatory decision making.[25] Furthermore, the way in which authority is distributed and produced within the organization greatly shapes its behavior. Organizations with centralized and hierarchical decision making or with fragmented and loose linkages do not necessarily foster democratic forms of political participation.

These three effects of moderation theory have great relevance for a scholarly understanding of the evolution of Muslim reformers in Iran and Turkey. The relatively competitive nature of politics in these two countries in comparison to Arab countries, with the partial exception of Lebanon, has been critical to the rise of Muslim political movements with strong democratic dispositions. While many countries have Muslim movements that can be characterized as moderate, the latter *flourish* under relatively pluralistic and free political circumstances. In other words, moderates become more visible and effective in regimes with relatively high degrees of political inclusion. This is how the first mechanism of moderation theory works in Iran and Turkey.[26] Turkey has a long history of free multiparty elections dating back to 1950. Since 1969, the Islamists have participated prominently in public debates and every parliamentary election except in 1983. While they challenge the secular character of the regime, they prioritize legality over illegality, subversion, and violence. Since the early 1970s, electoral commitment has been a characteristic of the Turkish Islamists and has facilitated the rise of Muslim reformers, that is, pious politicians who espouse public expressions of Muslim identity and are committed to electoral competition and political pluralism. Similarly, parliamentary and presidential elections have introduced a degree of uncertainty and change to Iranian politics that is absent in authoritarian Arab regimes. The advocates of Muslim democracy are faced with the daunting task of challenging the regime's monopoly over Islam and articulating more democratic and liberal versions of Islam. Elections do not involve only competition for votes but also competition for the mastery of public opinion. In a competitive political environment, citizens have easy access to different sources of political information and opinion through mass media such as newspapers, radio, and the Internet, and official interpretation of events can be challenged and even ridiculed.[27] The relatively high levels of electoral competitiveness in both countries offered a suitable environment for the rise of Muslim reformers. Iranian and Turkish Muslim reformers mobilized public support and occupied positions of power as a result of electoral competition. They developed platforms that had mass appeal, and their responsiveness to

popular demands made them victorious at the ballot box. While Muslim political actors are capable of moderating their goals and strategies no less than
Socialist or Catholic parties, reformist trends are more likely to become predominant and persuasive in pluralistic political settings.

Meanwhile, the threat of state repression has been a constant source of
anxiety for Muslim reformers in both Iran and Turkey. Despite their ideological differences, the Iranian and Turkish regimes are both characterized by a
guardianship of bureaucratic elites that restrains the activities of popularly
elected political elites. The RF has to appear more Islamist than it actually
is, the JDP more secularist, because their survival depends on their ability to
portray themselves in the image of ruling regimes. Yet the RF's caution did not
spare it from repression. The RF candidates were systematically disqualified
from running in elections. The RF-affiliated press and civil-society organizations remained under constant pressure and were banned in many instances.
The JDP barely escaped the fate of the Welfare Party (WP; Refah Partisi) and
the Virtue Party (VP; Fazilet Partisi) from which its leadership cadres came
when, in July 2008, the Constitutional Court warned but did not dissolve the
party on the grounds that it was a focal point for antisecular activities. Muslim
reformists had to appease the regime elites who remained deeply suspicious
of the "real intentions" of the RF and the JDP. The fear of state repression and
the logic of organizational survival considerably restricted the range of policy
choices available to Muslim reformists even if they came to power through
popular elections. Yet state repression did not necessarily generate radicalization, as opportunities for political inclusion were not completely missing. In
Iran, the RF remained the legal and loyal opposition after it lost the control of
the presidency and the parliament. In Turkey, the JDP consolidated its power
by sweeping the polls in the 2007 parliamentary elections, and it remains the
predominant political actor.

Finally, the way in which the RF and the JDP organized had substantial implications for their decisions at critical junctures. The RF remained an amalgam of factions rallied behind Khatami and lacked a strong organizational
framework to channel and direct mass discontent and participation. The factions did not necessarily coordinate their actions and often pursued strategies
that made collective planning impossible. In sharp contrast, the JDP rapidly
crystallized into a highly centralized and hierarchical party dominated by its
leader, Erdoğan, who had the ultimate say in all important party decisions.

The JDP had an impressive and professional organization that reached even the most remote areas of Turkey. Yet, in both cases, organizational resources did not support democratic forms of autonomous political participation and greatly restricted policy choices available to the RF and JDP leaderships. Once these organizational structures were established, neither the RF nor the JDP was capable of developing strategies that would have reformed the political system they had been highly critical of.

Ideological Moderation

Moderation theory assumes that ideological change follows behavioral change. This assumption has great appeal, as it implies that extremist political worldviews based on binary distinctions between good and evil do not necessarily block the establishment and consolidation of pluralistic politics. Hence, even enemies of democracy may unintentionally develop strong democratic commitments once they are allowed to participate in the democratic process. The best protection of democracy is found in democratic practices that allow for inclusion of undemocratic actors, not in "militant democracy," which restricts political participation. This book tends to adopt a more skeptical position regarding the claim that ideological transformation follows once strategic interests are altered. The relationship between ideological and behavioral moderation appears to be more complicated than recognized by moderation theory for three reasons.

First, moderation theory is likely to misidentify the causal sequence between ideological and behavioral change. Radicals' decision to participate in legal political process (i.e., contesting elections, dismantling clandestine organizational frameworks, etc.) is unlikely to happen without extensive internal deliberation, discussion, debate, and conflict. Even the decisions that are primarily driven by strategic interests need to be ideologically justified. Otherwise, they would not be sustainable and would be likely to generate internal splits and crises of authority. Radicals' political inclusion succeeds only when they are willing and ideologically ready to make the compromise with the ruling regime. They should have *already* had a relatively moderate worldview to be able to justify their participation in a legal political system in their ideological discourse. The "declared goals" of radical transformation may remain the same on paper, but "real goals" have already changed before the decision to participate. The participation decision requires ideological justification that would not emerge from a worldview that rejects any relationship with the regime as ideologically blasphemous and unacceptable. Hence, groups that decide to participate are usually not that radical in the first place. For instance, social democracy differed from Communism in twentieth-century Europe in that the former accepted the rules of electoral competition, the supremacy of parliamentary rule, and the necessity of cross-class alliances.[28] These choices were very different from the Leninist theory that dismissed parliament as an impotent institution, preferred a vanguard party model over a mass party, and predicted the imminent collapse of the capitalist order.[29] Most importantly, these differences were not just ideological adjustments to changes in strategic interests and structural opportunities. Social democracy was built on extensive and deep theoretical controversies, starting with the disagreement between the "orthodoxy" of Karl Kautsky and the "revisionism" of Eduard Bernstein.[30] Similarly, the question of why revolutionary Communism continued to arouse deep passions and commitments among so many political activists in post–World War II democratic France and Italy, which offered very strong institutional and socioeconomic incentives for ideological moderation, cannot be explained by moderation theory.[31] In this sense, moderation theory may not be immune to the trap of tautology, that is, arguing how institutional incentives moderate political actors who already abandoned radical worldviews. Moderation, by definition, implies ideological change. Yet that change is not necessarily generated by dynamics identified by moderation theory. Moreover, ideology maintains the identity of the group in the eyes of its members and supporters.[32] Any political action that cannot be justified in ideological terms would alienate members and supporters.

Second, the roots of ideological change are often found in factors that are not captured by moderation theory. Ideological change may take place in diverse political settings as a result of a combination of factors that are not analyzed by moderation theory. A variety of intracountry and international factors may be conducive to it. Countries with vast differences, from Egypt to Indonesia, have witnessed the formation of the Muslim reformist phenomenon since the 1990s. In particular, political inclusion has been neither a necessary nor a sufficient condition for ideological moderation in Iran and Turkey.[33] In both countries, the expansion of a pluralistic public sphere that spurred debates among Islamists and disagreements between Islamists and other political groups enabled ideological change and contributed to the emergence of Muslim reformers. Institutional incentives reinforced and accelerated, but did not cause, ideological moderation.

A third and related reason concerns behavioral moderation in the absence of strong institutional incentives and a lack of behavioral moderation in the presence of strong institutional incentives. Neither of these developments would be expected by moderation theory. Two recent and important works demonstrate that moderation of Islamists takes place even under continuing authoritarian rule. Carrie Wickham argues that the leaders of the Wasat Party engage in "democratic learning" in response to their continued repression.[34] This learning was also a result of participation in autonomous associations, collaborative interaction with secular opposition, and travels abroad.[35] Similarly, Jillian Schwedler rightly criticizes moderation theory for not explaining "why some political actors become moderate while others in similar circumstances do not."[36] She argues that public political space became more pluralistic and offered new opportunities for activism and interaction in both Jordan and Yemen in the 1990s despite the fact that both regimes remained authoritarian. She explains why Jordanian Islamists became ideologically more moderate while the Islah Party in Yemen did not by highlighting the differences in political opportunity structures (monarchy vs. presidency), internal group structure (democratic vs. fragmentary), and ideology (justification of new political practices vs. no such justification). Both Schwedler and Wickham conceptualize ideological moderation as a process distinct from behavioral moderation, which can be caused by factors that are beyond the scope of moderation theory. This book builds on their conceptual approach.

The RF was formed by left-leaning revolutionaries who had been politically marginalized in the Islamic Republic in the early 1990s, following the death of Ruhollah Khomeini. They found sanctuary in official and semiofficial think tanks and research institutes, universities, bourgeoning civil-society associations, and media outlets. They gradually abandoned the ideological rigidity of their revolutionary years and became critical of what they called absolutism and ideological excessiveness. They were influenced and joined by a group of intellectuals who increasingly became critical of the ideological worldviews that were predominant in prerevolutionary and early postrevolutionary years. These intellectuals questioned the notion of revolutionary struggle in the name of social justice and reconstruction of societal relations by the all-powerful state. The East European revolutions and disillusionment with the outcome of the Iranian Revolution stimulated these intellectual trends that increasingly engaged with the democratic notion of popular sovereignty and the liberal-democratic notions of rule of law, human rights, and political pluralism.[37] The presidency of Ali Akbar Hashemi Rafsanjani (r. 1989–1997) inaugurated an era of socioeconomic reconstruction, partially lifted the siege mentality that dominated Iranian public life during the war with Iraq (1980–1988), and contributed to the formation of a more pluralistic public sphere. The intellectual trends, which formed the reformist-religious discourse, became more pronounced and influential in the late 1990s and actually outlasted the RF. The core of this discourse has been the difference between "Islam as a revealed religion and the hermeneutics of Islam as popularly understood over time."[38] When the revolutionaries-cum-reformists eventually experienced a political revival in the late 1990s, they were already ideologically moderate. The electoral victories of Mohammad Khatami and the RF basically popularized, electrified, and reinforced the reformist discourse.[39] Hence, ideological moderation did not simply follow behavioral moderation as moderation theory would expect. There was no simple process of ideological adjustment following changes in strategic interests. Rather, ideological transformation has accompanied, if not preceded, behavioral change and had its sources in political developments that are not identified by moderation theory. In fact, ideological moderation was taking place in public discussions and debates when the leftist revolutionaries were excluded from the political system. Moderation theory, with its limited focus on institutional and organizational factors, would miss the critical dimension of political change in contemporary Iran.

Turkish Islamism as represented by the National Order (Milli Görüş) political parties since 1969 was not that revolutionary to begin with. The overthrow of the state authority through violent means was never central to the ideological worldview of Turkish Islamism. Moreover, Turkish Islamism was primarily organized as electoral parties seeking votes and participating in the legal political order. The Islamist parties had parliamentary representation, joined coalition governments, and won municipal elections even before the victory of the WP in the 1995 parliamentary elections. Nonetheless, the Islamists' notion that democratic governance was majoritarian was hardly compatible with liberal-democratic notions of limits on state power and inviolable individual liberties. Islamist intellectuals and activists gained increasing public visibility and a greater following in the early 1990s when the Turkish public sphere was expanding. Private media channels that offered critical alternatives to the official regime line flourished; associational life that had been destroyed by the 1980 coup was revitalized; political views proliferated. Just like their counterparts in Iran, they engaged with liberal-democratic ideas and gradually shunned the goal of an all-encompassing Islamic state.[40] By the time the WP reached the peak of its political power, it hosted a variety of political positions ranging from illiberal sharia rule to liberal criticisms of restrictions on public expressions of religious and ethnic identities. The WP's ideological worldview was ambivalent and flexible enough to simultaneously support conflicting positions. Interestingly, and unlike the effects of military rule on Islamists in the early 1980s, military repression in the second half of the 1990s did not radicalize the already moderating Islamist movement. Rather, it sharpened the ideological divisions within the Islamist movement and accelerated the marginalization of uncompromising Islamist positions. The WP's successor, the Virtue Party (VP), became an advocate of the EU, expansion of human rights, and popular political participation. Electoral opportunities clearly favored and reinforced the reformist trend, which was independently organized under the rubric of the JDP in 2001 and swept the 2002 elections. The reformists, who generally belonged to a generation that reached maturity in the 1970s and 1980s, collectively decided to adopt more moderate positions that justify a greater range of political action as a result of debates and discussions. Their strategic interests coincided with their ideological preferences, which had been becoming more moderate since the early 1990s. Consequently, moderation theory would misread the transformation of Muslim politics in Turkey for two reasons. First, ideological moderation was not simply an unintentional by-product of behavioral modification in Turkey. Second, the Islamists who were less willing to abandon rigid ideological worldviews failed to capitalize on electoral opportunities and increase their popular support. The Felicity Party (FP; Saadet Partisi), established by Islamists in 2001, remained true to its ideological commitments at the cost of staying in the margins of politics.[41] As this example shows, political inclusion has not been sufficient to engender ideological moderation.

The Paradox of Moderation

This book also engages with the implications of moderation for the advancement of democratization: In what ways did moderation of the Islamists contribute to the democratic opening-up in Iran and consolidation in Turkey? The conventional assumption is that the rise of moderate Islamic forces is a necessary if not sufficient condition for the establishment and sustainability of democratic rule in the greater Muslim world. The rise of Muslim reformists as the centrist political forces is often interpreted as having the potential of neutralizing the "Islamist threat" in the broader Muslim world.[42] They are also portrayed as strong evidence for the compatibility of Islam and democracy.[43] These moderate Muslim actors are promoted as a force that can block the expansion of Islamic radicalism and establish good relations with Western governments.[44] In particular, the JDP is portrayed as the "moderate force" representing "Muslim Democracy," which "offers the whole world its best hope for an effective bulwark against radical and violent Islamism."[45] Similarly, moderation induced by inclusion is thought to foster democratic commitments. "Political participation under normal conditions indeed appears to favor moderation and strengthen the commitment to the democratic process."[46] I disagree with these sweeping conclusions that associate "moderate Islam" with democracy and call for a more nuanced approach. Moderation turns out to be a double-edged sword that may not be conducive to democratic transition or consolidation. The implications of moderation are not necessarily conducive to democracy for two reasons. First, there is no convincing empirical evidence that the rise of Muslim reformers is inevitably accompanied by the decline of Islamists. Both groups simultaneously may expand their sphere of influence in certain historical periods, as happened in Turkey in the early 1990s. In Iran, the rise of popular radicalism represented by Mahmoud Ahmedinejad immediately followed the demise of the RF's popularity. Besides, Muslim reformers may prefer to enter into coalitions with the Islamists at the expense of secular and liberal political forces. Second and more important, the *process of moderation* may entail strategic decisions and a preference for certain tactics over others that stall or even impede the *process of democratization*. In this sense, moderation at the behavioral level implies that risk-aversive strategies and electoral tactics are given priority over bold strategies and nonviolent but contentious tactics such as grassroots mobilization and civic disobedience. Political legality and recognition by the regime involve trade-offs. Once Islamists are integrated into the political system by moderating, they are likely to implement platforms that seek to compromise with, if not appease, the guardians of the regime and avoid tactics that would increase political tensions. Ironically, they are unwilling to challenge authoritarian practices as long as these practices do not harm them. Electoral calculations, fear of state repression, and organizational constraints all make them politically risk aversive. Yet democratization calls for less compromising positions and more confrontational tactics, especially at crucial junctures when opportunities for political change are unprecedented. Pragmatism and a willingness to compromise that emanate from political inclusion are not always conducive to democratization.[47] Popular mobilization that involves mass demonstrations and building coalitions with political forces demanding change is central to democratic achievements.[48] Radical political forces that effectively challenge the rulers may be the agents of democratization.[49] In fact, moderate political actors may miss crucial opportunities for democratization, given their myopic group interests and organizational considerations. Their failure to take advantage of these opportunities stems not from their ideological worldviews but rather from strategic interests, which prioritize organizational survival, and a dearth of organizational resources and tactics, which can sustain contentious action.[50] Hence, the critical task for Muslim reformers is developing organizational capacity and political alliances to make political power more accountable, more equally distributed, and less hegemonic. The *paradox of moderation* is that a willingness to make political compromises, the ability to organize as electoral parties, and a preference for conciliatory tactics over confrontational ones do not necessarily facilitate and enable democratization. Under certain conditions, moderation actually undermines democratic achievements. Besides, as Cihan Tuğal shows, moderation of Islamic radicals, who have been absorbed into the existing political system, in Turkey entails their embracing of hegemonic forms of neoliberal economic policies in place of platforms prioritizing social justice.[51]

This emphasis on the implications of behavioral moderation distinguishes this book from previous research on the process of moderation. Both Schwedler and Wickham focus on ideological moderation, a process they normatively find positive. Schwedler defines moderation as "movement from a relatively closed and rigid worldview to one more open and tolerant of alternative perspectives."[52] Similarly, Wickham talks about ideological moderation as a process that entails "abandonment, postponement, or revision of radical goals that enables an opposition movement to accommodate itself to the give-and-take of 'normal competitive politics.'"[53] As stated above, this book offers a similar understanding of ideological moderation. However, it also analyzes the dynamics of behavioral moderation, which ultimately influence the outcome of political struggles and decide on policy choices. Such an analytical emphasis is missing in Schwedler's and Wickham's works primarily because the IAF (Jabhat al-Amal al-Islami) in Jordan, the Islah in Yemen, and the Wasat in Egypt remained opposition parties with no direct influence on governmental policymaking. The RF and the JDP provide a better pair to test the expectations of moderation theory, as both political parties won elections and actually formed governments. Furthermore, this comparative study of these political actors demonstrates that sustainable democratization often requires cross-cutting linkages and alliances between state and societal actors. Conceptual frameworks that are based on rigid state-society dichotomies fail to appreciate the importance of these linkages and alliances for the expansion of rights.[54]

A distinguishing characteristic of both the RF and the JDP was their rise to power shortly after their foundation. This had the unintended consequence of hampering the process of institutionalization that would have taken place in parties that remained in opposition during long years. This observation is consistent with the theoretical expectation that "parties that gain national power immediately after their formation—thus undergoing organizational consolidation while in power—[tend] to become weak institutions."[55] When the RF gained control of both the presidency and the parliament, it was composed of more than a dozen factions loosely connected to each other in their common opposition to the asymmetrical distribution of political power in Iran. Furthermore, these factions had very fragile linkages with the populace. With partial exceptions, they lacked nationwide grassroots organizations and a collective identity. Their main source of power emanated from newly gained elected public offices and media outlets. These offices gave them influence over policymaking and public opinion, public visibility, and international connections. They were very willing to compromise with the regime guardians and their hard-line allies so that the RF actors would be allowed to keep these offices and remain included in the political system. Compromises, back-door negotiations, and measured complaints soon transformed into appeasement of the guardians, who quickly realized that the RF was very vulnerable. The guardians suppressed the reformist media outlets, disqualified RF candidates from running in the elections, and increased repression on the RF's societal allies, including the student, women's, and union movements, and the dissident clerics. The RF could not help these actors pursuing rights agendas lest its delicate relationship with the guardians be irreparably damaged. When the RF realized that it had no leverage over the guardians other than its perceived popularity, it was too late to pursue a more contentious and broad-based popular strategy. The RF simply lacked the organizational resources to initiate it. Once it fell from political power, the RF had no strong civil-society associations to mobilize sustainable public support and push for political change. Behavioral moderation proved to be costly and brought about the demise of one of the most promising Muslim reformers in the world. Besides, the growing tensions between the United States and Iran in the post–September 11 geopolitical context and Iran's looming suspicions of a regime change sponsored by the United States did not help the RF, which was continuously hard-pressed to prove its loyalty to the Islamic Republic.

The JDP found itself in government in a much more favorable environment. The relationships with the EU were progressing and promised to liberalize Turkey's political governance. Meanwhile, the regime guardians led by the military command decided to tolerate the JDP government and did not take an uncompromising stance, as they had done vis-à-vis the WP. Later, some groups, including high-ranking military figures, unsuccessfully tried to dislodge the JDP from power by employing a strategy of tension.[56] Yet these groups never received support from the military high command, which partially explains their failure. The JDP government also achieved sustainable high levels of economic growth that contributed to its popularity. Meanwhile, the JDP gradually matured into a leader-dominated, highly centralized, patronage-distributing party that encouraged a culture of corruption and discouraged democratic forms of political participation. As a result, the JDP leadership was not accountable to its grassroots base, most of whom were seeking selective incentives (i.e., material benefits, status, and power). These "careerist" party members were willing to tolerate the leadership's compromises and deviations from its declared positions.[57] The lure of political office and the desire not to provoke the ever-suspicious regime guardians soon made the JDP more interested in perpetuating its power than in consistently pursuing an agenda of reform at a time when the structural opportunity for democratization was unprecedented in Turkey. The party consolidated its power over state institutions and exerted increasing control over the media, unions, business, and professional associations. Instead of reforming the state institutions, such as the authoritarian Higher Education Council, the party aimed to dominate them. It was also unwilling to expand political opportunity structures that would help societal actors with rights agendas, which came to play a more influential role in the twenty-first century. Like the RF, the JDP was not eager to establish confidence-based strategic alliances with these actors, including liberals, marginalized identity groups seeking greater political representation, labor unions, and social movements and rights associations. The times when the JDP was willing to redress political injustices (e.g., Kurdish demands for ethnic rights or Alevi demands for religious rights) were for electoral reasons, and it failed to translate its promises into consistent policies. At critical junctures, the JDP leadership wavered and preferred to adopt a risk-aversive, cautious, and pragmatic strategy that aimed to make compromises with the regime guardians. Most astonishingly, the JDP quickly abandoned its declared goal of enacting a new constitution in the aftermath of the 2007 elections. A new constitution would be a major contribution to the consolidation of democratic rule and would facilitate the formation of a human rights culture. The JDP leadership circulated a draft constitution but soon withdrew it. A new constitution would directly defy the interests of the regime guardians, and the JDP decided not to take that risk. The party barely survived when the Constitutional Court was just short of the qualified majority decision that would bring about the JDP's dissolution.[58] Moderation was a safe route that the JDP leadership did not want to leave. It was just not a good way to expand rights.

Methods

The data collected herein come from a variety of original sources that include ethnographic observations, interviews, electoral results, printed material in local languages, public opinion surveys, and macro-level socioeconomic and demographic data. The data collection started in spring 2002 and was completed in spring 2009. Combining qualitative and quantitative methods has two primary benefits in the study of Muslim reformers. The effective use of qualitative methods, such as participant observations and in-depth interviews, enables the identification of the micro-level processes that characterize decision making at the elite level.[59] These methods illuminate the dynamics by which actors form preferences, articulate interests, and make decisions. It would be unrealistic to claim that this methodological orientation fully identifies causal process and mechanisms. Preferences and interests may remain unobserved.[60] Still, the focus on *how* actors perceive their preferences and articulate their interests generates a mutually informing process between theory building and empirical study. It makes the theory more sensitive to empirical observations and refines it.[61] The value of quantitative methods lies in presenting an objective depiction of the context that is independent of the perceptions of the actors. For example, party elites might develop a new platform in response to their perception of the electorate's preferences. However, this perception might be out of touch with the actual voting behavior and public opinion. This study analyzes available electoral results, public opinion surveys, and demographic data to describe the actual existing circumstances under which Muslim reformers operate. Consequently, the study aims to present a compelling causal story informed by theoretical debates while being sensitive to the particular characteristics of each case.[62]

The data collection efforts in Iran started in early 2003 and continued until spring 2009. I visited Iran on six different occasions: in winter and spring 2003, summer 2005, summer 2006, spring 2008, and spring 2009. I collaborated with the Social Science faculty at Tehran University to conduct surveys of a representative sample of Tehran residents in August 2003 and December 2007. The surveys asked questions about political attitudes, orientations, religiosity, and cultural norms of the citizens. I designed the survey instrument and supervised the fieldwork of the public opinion polls. Additionally, I was a participant observer in the 2005 presidential elections and 2008 parliamentary elections. I interviewed campaign workers, journalists, and ordinary citizens; observed the campaigns; and systematically followed printed and electronic Persian news sources, especially during the elections. They provided useful information about RF strategies and the general composition of Iranian politics. I also obtained official statistics on electoral results and socioeconomic and demographic indicators.

I conducted ethnographic work on the JDP from summer 2002 to spring 2003. During this period, I had the opportunity to closely observe the JDP as it evolved from a nascent opposition party to the strongest party of Turkish politics. I was a participant observer in the November 2002 elections and March 2003 by-elections in the southeastern province of Siirt. I interviewed leading party politicians, party members, and ordinary people from diverse social backgrounds. During the campaigns for the November 2002 elections, I visited thirty-five provincial capitals (Turkey has eighty-one provinces) and attended twenty party rallies (fifteen of them being JDP rallies) and various party meetings. I conducted a similar study during the July 2007 elections focusing on the JDP's campaign. I joined vote-canvassing efforts of several parties, observed political rallies and meetings, and interviewed politicians, party activists, and voters. I continued interviewing politicians in the aftermath of the elections. As in Iran, I obtained official statistics on electoral results and socioeconomic and demographic indicators and compiled a huge archive of printed and electronically published material in Turkish. I also used ecological inference analysis to generate voter transition tables in Turkey. Finally, I used the World Values Survey (WVS) to investigate the social and cultural context from which Muslim reformers emerged in comparative perspective.

An Overview of the Book

The remainder of this book is divided into eight chapters. Readers who are primarily interested in moderation theory and how this theory is applied to the Iranian and Turkish cases may want to concentrate on Chapters 2, 6, 7, and 8. The next chapter discusses moderation theory, introduces the theoretical framework, and applies it to the Iranian and Turkish cases. It also discusses how the Christian Democratic experience can be relevant in understanding Islamic political actors. Chapter 3 first surveys the literature on the relationship between Islam and democracy from a methodological perspective. It then discusses Muslim political attitudes in some detail. It also briefly explores the historical processes through which Muslim reformers emerged and identifies the basic characteristics of Muslim reformers. Chapter 4 offers a theoretically guided and historically informed discussion of Muslim engagement with secularism and democratization, and the ambiguities of Muslim reformism.

Chapter 5 describes the institutional environment within which Muslim reformers operated in Iran and Turkey. Two defining features of the regimes were guardianship and the dynamics of electoral competition. The postrevolution and postcoup constitutions, in Iran and Turkey respectively, empowered guardians at the expense of elected governments. While the guardianship set the parameters of the Muslim democratic experience, popular elections defined new opportunities for Muslim reformers.

Chapters 6 and 7 offer analytical narratives that discuss the evolution of Muslim reformers in Iran and Turkey, using the guidance of the theoretical framework developed in Chapter 2. Chapter 6 serves three purposes. The rapid rise and just as rapid fall of the Iranian reformist movement were equally unpredicted. The election of Khatami to the presidency in 1997 was no less surprising than the election of Ahmedinejad in 2005. First, it narrates the ideological transmutation experienced by the leftists after their political defeat and disillusionment with the result of the revolution in the 1990s. Next, it analyzes the rise of the RF and its dilemmas as a legal opposition movement in the Islamic Republic. Finally, the chapter explains the demise of the RF as a consequence of these dilemmas. The electoral strategy of reform pursued by the RF ultimately undermined its organizational capacity and eroded its public standing.

Chapter 7 studies the rise of the JDP as the main center-right party in Turkish politics. The JDP came to power in 2002, just a year after its establishment. The chapter has three goals. It first sheds light on the factors that contributed to the foundation and rise of the JDP. Particularly important were the divisions within the Welfare and Virtue Parties, state repression, and the dynamics of electoral competition. The chapter then continues with a discussion of the JDP's organizational basis and its evolution into a leader-dominated, vote-maximizing, patronage-distributing centrist party. The chapter concludes with an analysis of the JDP government policies on issues critical to democratization in Turkey and an explanation of its declining reformist orientation.

Chapter 8 analyzes the results of the July 2007 elections in Turkey and the March 2008 elections in Iran on the basis of ethnographic research. It focuses on campaign issues and strategies and sheds unique light on the dynamics of electoral competition in both countries. It also engages with the question of how these elections affect strategies and evolution of Muslim reformers. Chapter 9 concludes with an analytical summary of the experience of Muslim reformers in Iran and Turkey and reflections on recent developments in these two countries.

CHAPTER 2

From Islamists
to Muslim Reformers

A Theory of

Political Change

Moderation Theory

An influential body of scholarship argues that radical parties become increasingly moderate if they are integrated into the legal and electoral system. The origins of this idea, which can be called moderation theory, are found in the work of Robert Michels, who is most well known for his "iron law of oligarchy." He argues that Socialist parties, committed to bringing about working-class democracy, are characterized by highly authoritarian practices.[2] In fact, the very essence of the party organization does not allow for democratic decision making. Parties are controlled by a small group of leaders who develop their party's strategies with minimum input from the members and followers.[3] Another significant but more obscure aspect of his work discusses the external behavior of revolutionary Socialist parties. He identifies two causal mechanisms through which these parties lose their radical orientations: (a) pursuit of votes, and (b) organizational survival.

Michels defines the modern political party as the "organization of the electoral masses."[4] Radical parties aspire to the greatest number of votes to gain strong parliamentary representation and replace the ruling elites. However, espousal of ideological and revolutionary policies alienates large segments of the electorate. Consequently, radical party leaders are faced with an inescapable dilemma: they have to eschew the pursuit of radical ideological principles to attract more votes. Radical parties gradually transform into pragmatic, vote-maximizing electoral parties to remain politically viable. Michels argues that the evolution of the German Social Democratic Party (SDP; Sozialdemokratische Partei Deutschlands) at the dawn of the twentieth century exemplifies this process.

27

A key assumption in his theoretical framework is that vote maximization entails developing "centrist" political platforms. If the majority of voters evaluate radical political platforms as "extremist," then these parties must develop less ideological platforms to remain competitive in elections. Alternatively, radical parties will have no electoral incentives to pursue conciliatory policies if their ideological platforms have public appeal. Another assumption is that, beyond their core constituency, which is small in number, radical parties draw support from voters who are disaffected with mainstream parties. These protest votes are sustainable as long as radical parties deliver economic prosperity and political stability. Conversely, confrontation with the regime and other parties will eventually jeopardize the voter base of radical parties. As a result, radical parties have strong incentives to develop moderate platforms and to avoid political tensions. The party might enter into government coalitions or foster political alliances to end their isolation. All these factors will tarnish the party's radical characteristics.

The second mechanism specified by Michels that tames radical parties is the fear of state repression. They become particularly vulnerable to state repression when they engage in electoral competition. As electoral parties, they can no longer retain clandestine networks. Their organizational structures are exposed to state authorities. Party leaders increasingly become concerned with state repression. As a result, the greater a party's electoral organizational capacity, the more timid its policies are. The fear of state repression reinforces conservative tendencies of the party. To quote Michels: "The party doctrines are, whenever requisite, attenuated and deformed in accordance with the external needs of the organization."[5] The party organization acquires a life of its own at the expense of revolutionary principles. The pursuit of legality replaces the pursuit of legitimacy—the struggle against the repressive sociopolitical order.

These two reinforcing mechanisms—electoral calculations and survival instincts—transform the revolutionary party into a parliamentary party that pursues accommodative policies toward the state. Under the dynamics of electoral competition and the constant threat of state repression, revolutionary parties modify their original ideological commitments and affirm their revolutionary credentials only in theory and on paper, "not on lines which interest the police."[6] Consequently, a process of substitution of ends takes place whereby an organization's survival prevails over the official ends as the party becomes institutionalized.[7] In the words of a perceptive observer of political parties:

> A permanent gap opens between official aims and organizational behavior. The relation between aims and behavior never completely disappears; it attenuates. The correspondence of a party's behavior to its official aims is constantly reaffirmed by its leaders, but only these courses of action—amongst the many possible that the party may choose to achieve its official aims—which are compatible with the organization's stability will be selected.[8]

Other prominent scholars of twentieth-century European politics make similar arguments. Joseph Schumpeter rejects the notion that parties can be defined by their principles. A party's overriding priority is winning the competitive struggle for political power by appealing to the greatest number of voters. He gives the example of how Socialist parties abandon Marxist internationalism when they realize that adherence to its maxims would be costly in elections.[9] Along similar lines, Seymour Martin Lipset argues that obtaining electoral majorities requires the abandonment of exclusivist platforms and organizational strategies.[10] Otto Kirchheimer observes that ideological platforms have been counterproductive, as they deter potential voters.[11] In general, "parties of integration," which espouse radical ideologies and exert significant influence on all aspects of their members' lives, failed to remain competitive in post–World War II European elections.[12]

Adam Przeworski and John Sprague identify the dilemma facing electoral Socialism: "Participation in electoral politics is necessary if the movement for Socialism is to find mass support among workers, yet this participation appears to obstruct the attainment of final goals."[13] Socialist parties had initially participated in electoral politics to subvert democratic competition. As a result of their failure to obtain an electoral mandate for radical change, they were forced to develop platforms that cut across existing cleavages and to dilute their ideology to attract more votes.[14] They believed that they would win a majority of the votes and hence achieve the ultimate goal of establishing the Socialist state through popular support. However, the goal of winning "an electoral mandate for socialism" was a mirage.[15] Workers who were most receptive to Socialist messages were not in the majority, and the road to electoral victory hinged on the ability of Socialist parties to mobilize diverse groups such as students, retirees, and members of the middle class. As long as Socialist parties chose to tailor their messages and platforms to appeal to these groups—and many did—their image of the party of revolutionary workers was diluted and eventually disappeared. Moreover, as these parties became strongly immersed in electoral politics, the tactics for achieving the Socialist state were reduced to a choice between different electoral strategies.[16] The completely unintended consequence of the decision of Socialist activists to participate in democratic politics was the transformation of these radical movements into parties that contributed to the welfare of the working classes and the discontented sectors of society through democratic policies. They became the primary institutional vehicles through which peripheral groups were integrated into the democratic system. Elections are not helpful for radical goals. They are inherently conservative, as they are designed to represent the heterogeneity of interests in the society.[17] Furthermore, the Socialists' experience in governance softened their ideological outlook and resulted in their "domestication" by the system.[18] In the end, the ballot box revolutionized the Socialist parties.

Samuel P. Huntington generalizes these observations about the Socialist experience in Western Europe as the third wave of democratization. He identifies a trade-off between participation and radicalism. As previously excluded groups participate in competition for power and win elections, they also moderate their tactics and policies.[19] Even in unstable Pakistani electoral politics, the radical platforms of the Islamic Community Party (Jama'at-e Islami) never attracted large public support, and the dynamics of open politics made the party leadership adopt more pragmatic stances while compromising the party's ideological commitments.[20] Christian Democrats in Latin America played a similar dual game characterized by pursuit of votes and threat of military repression; they had to position themselves against other parties in the electoral arena while sending signals to the military and other veto players. These signals may either indicate willingness to support the end of democratic regime or support for it.[21]

This vast and rich literature on how radical parties—parties whose ideological platforms are fundamentally at odds with one or several aspects of the ruling regime—evolved in Europe has a common thread: the *inclusion* of these parties in parliamentary systems brought about their *moderation*. Once organized as an electoral party aiming to maximize their vote share, radical parties prioritize electoral calculations over ideological goals.[22] They have strong incentives to comply with democratic rules even if they do not hold deep democratic convictions.[23] Electoral concerns and fear of state repression check their radical tendencies. Revolutionaries become moderates not as a result of ideological metamorphosis or civic learning but because of strategic interests.[24] Their beliefs are not thought to have any significant influence on their behaviors. Consequently, democratic systems were consolidated even in the absence of committed democrats.[25] Additionally, these parties now facilitate the incorporation of the marginalized and underrepresented societal groups into democratic politics. In this sense, increased competition is paralleled with increased participation in politics.[26]

Figure 2.1 illustrates the three main causal components of moderation theory: state repression, dynamics of electoral competition, and resources of the groups organized as vote-seeking parties. These three factors are mutually reinforcing and create strong incentives for the integration of radicals into the political system. Moderation theory builds on the premise that vote-seeking parties become more risk aversive and vulnerable vis-à-vis publicly nonaccountable state elites. *Behavioral moderation* involves accommodative and nonconfrontational strategies instead of more confrontational and con-

Figure 2.1. Unpacking Moderation Theory: Causal Factors

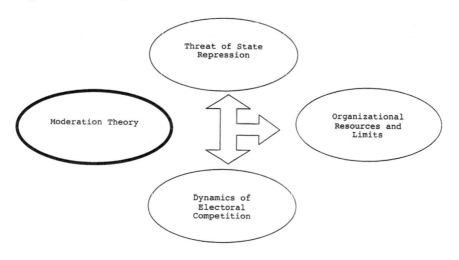

tentious ones. It is followed by *ideological moderation,* which entails incorporation of democratic symbols and respect for political pluralism.

The Christian Democrat Experience

Moderation theory is also employed to analyze the trajectory of Christian Democrats in Continental Europe throughout the twentieth century. A few years after the defeat of Nazism, Gabriel Almond wrote a monograph about the importance of the Christian Democratic parties for the survival of democracy in Western Europe.[27] In that work and another article published in the same year, he categorized the Christian Democrats who were powerful in Austria, Belgium, France, Italy, Germany, and the Netherlands as an essential part of the moderate democratic center, along with the Socialists who stood against Communist assaults.[28] With the exception of Germany, where a significant number of Protestants joined the Christian Democratic Union (CDU) after the catastrophic years of the Third Reich, Christian Democratic parties mostly appealed to Catholic voters and were inspired by various forms of Catholic teachings.

The Christian Democratic parties of Western Europe emerged in the late nineteenth and early twentieth centuries when mass politics were coming into maturation.[29] Stathis N. Kalyvas argues that the formation of Catholic parties was the unintentional result of the Church's response to the anticlerical attacks of the modern states aiming to curb the power of the Church in the realms of education and the family. The Church was initially very reluctant to sponsor Catholic political parties because the existence of separate parties would have weakened the unchallenged position of the Church.[30] Moreover, direct participation in electoral politics would have tarnished the image of the Church as being above political factionalism.[31] In the end, Catholic parties emerged because of the existence of independent Catholic activists and the success of these parties in the elections.

Until the aftermath of World War II, these Catholic parties were not very receptive to democratic and liberal principles, with the partial exception of the Catholic Center Party in Germany.[32] In most cases, the Christian Democratic commitment to liberal democracy developed after World War II. The Christian Democrats in Austria, Belgium, Germany, Italy, and the Netherlands became the pillars of the newly established secular democratic system.

In these countries, center-right politics became synonymous with Christian Democrats. When the bitter memories of the war years were still fresh, Christian Democratic parties acted as responsible parties that favored social conciliation and played a critical role in the successful consolidation of democracy in the Western European countries.[33]

Christian Democrats built their political platforms on the notion of personalism, which was set against both liberal individualism and Socialist communalism.[34] In the personalist view, society is composed of morally interdependent individuals who are members of the natural units of family, church, and nation. This notion entails the solidarity-based understanding of social relations rather than the competition-based understanding of liberalism. As a result, Christian Democratic politics generated policies favoring the welfare state, the role of religion in education, and the traditional nuclear family structure.[35] Consistent with their image of being centrist parties, Christian Democrats' electoral appeal cut across class differences and mobilized people from quite heterogeneous backgrounds. In this sense, Christian Democrats have exhibited the characteristics of catchall parties with great flexibility and moderation.[36] They eschewed the imposition of religious faith upon society and showed sincere devotion to the principles of religious tolerance and popular sovereignty. They tended to be more popular among religious voters, and they have provided institutions through which religious demands can be raised in secular politics. Perhaps their greatest contribution to European democracy was that they made religious identities fully compatible with secular democratic attitudes and behaviors.

The crucial question regarding democratic consolidation in post–World War II Western Europe is, how did these religious parties with dubious democratic credentials come to be the pillars of the new democratic system in the postwar years? Kalyvas suggests that the dilemma confronting religious parties in Europe in the age of mass politics was not quite distinct from the dilemma confronting the Socialist parties in the same period. As Catholic confessional parties entered into democratic competition, the ultimate criterion that guided their behavior became the number of votes they collected in the elections. The inability of these parties to obtain sustainable electoral victories by relying only on pure confessional appeals forced the leaders to rethink their electoral strategies.[37] The dynamics of electoral competition created strong incentives for these parties to mobilize a broader segment of the population by moderating their platforms and being more inclusive. In addition, the necessity of negotiating and entering into coalitions with other parties in parliamentary politics tamed the antisystem stance of the religious parties. Gradually, Catholic parties were integrated into the system, and they ensured the stability of democracy by occupying the center-right position of the political spectrum. Kalyvas concludes:

> In many ways, Christian Democratic and Social Democratic parties are mirror images of each other. Both parties were initially to subvert liberal democracies; both evolved into mass parties and decided to participate in the electoral process after painful and divisive debates. Their decision had tremendous consequences: both parties integrated masses of newly enfranchised voters into existing liberal parliamentary regimes, and both were deradicalized in the process . . . democracy in Europe was often expanded and consolidated by its enemies.[38]

The single most important insight that can be derived from the studies of the Christian Democrats in Europe is that electoral constraints and incentives shape the political behavior of these parties. When religious movements decide to participate in electoral competition as parties, they are faced with unprecedented opportunities and limitations. The dictates of the political competition become more important than the dissemination of the religious truth. The historical trajectory of Christian Democrats demonstrates that religiously inspired political identities and demands do not necessarily threaten pluralistic and competitive politics. Organized as political parties, religious groups adapt to the dynamics of political competition and might be instrumental in the orderly incorporation of marginal groups to the democratic system.

A Reappraisal of Moderation Theory

Based on the summary above, five theoretical expectations can be derived from moderation theory: (1) Radicals, once they organize as electoral parties, are likely to develop centrist and vote-maximizing platforms that contradict their original goals under the dynamics of political competition (*Proposition I*); (2) these parties behave moderately—that is, they avoid confrontation, make compromises, and negotiate with their political opponents—especially when the threat of state repression is a recurrent concern (*Proposition II*);

34

(3) as parties founded by radicals grow and institutionalize, priorities of organizational survival gain priority over programmatic goals and ideological lines (*Proposition III*); (4) ideological moderation—that is, commitment to democratic pluralism—naturally takes place after strategic interests and organizational resources change (*Proposition IV*); (5) ideological and behavioral moderation are conducive to democratic transformations (*Proposition V*).

I agree with Propositions I and II but argue that Proposition III needs to be refined, Proposition IV is misleading, and Proposition V does not hold true under certain historical circumstances (see Table 2.1). First, Proposition III conceptualizes parties as organizations concerned for survival and growth, which ignores the role played by ideological goals in motivating party members and supporters. The organizational priorities of survival and growth may often shadow ideological goals, but the latter are not necessarily empty rhetoric with no influence over party identity and behavior. Following Panebianco, it can be argued that party ideology has two functions. It maintains "the identity of the organization in the eyes of its supporters" and "conceals the distribution of selective incentives," which "would weaken the credibility of the party as an organization dedicated to a 'cause,' and therefore adversely affect its distribution of collective incentives."[39] He also offers a simple classification of party members: believers who are motivated by collective interests, which focus on gains of solidarity, self-identification, and ideological achievement that come with participation in the organization, and careerists who are primarily motivated by selective interests such as status, power, and material inducements.[40] Parties not only need to appeal to broad electoral constituencies and alienate powerful state elites but also to satisfy believer and careerist members whose contributions are essential for the functioning of the organization.[41] On the one hand, parties that completely disregard their identity and ideological goals run the risk of losing the loyalty of believers.[42] On the other, parties that stick to official and ideological goals at the expense of electoral opportunities and benefits of participating in coalitions run the risk of losing the attachment of careerists.[43] Hence, Proposition III can be modified in the following way: as parties founded by radicals grow and institutionalize, priorities of organizational survival gain priority over programmatic goals and ideological lines as long as party members are primarily motivated by selective incentives and believers have no alternative to turn to or lack substantial influence over party leadership (*Proposition IIIr*).

Second, behavioral moderation does not always contribute to democratic transition and consolidation. Behavioral moderation implies that a party prefers electoral strategies over contentious tactics and compromises over confrontation when dealing with the state elites. Yet these preferences may not be the best choices when the state elites are unwilling to give up unaccountable power and expand the scope of political participation, which would alter the hegemonic institutional structure. These elites exist in democratic regimes as much as in nondemocratic regimes. As Nancy Bermeo argues, in these situations, popular social movements that employ radical tactics, such as mass demonstrations and civic disobedience campaigns, may be more instrumental in bringing about democratic change than electoral parties.[44] Moderation may entail pro-change actors losing their leverage over the hegemonic state

Table 2.1. Moderation Theory Revised

Theoretical Expectations of Moderation Theory	A Reappraisal of Moderation Theory
Proposition I—Electoral Effect: Radicals, once they organize as electoral parties, are likely to develop centrist and vote-maximizing platforms that contradict their original goals.	
Proposition II—Repression Effect: These parties behave moderately, especially when the threat of state repression is a recurrent concern.	
Proposition III—Institutionalization Effect: As parties founded by radicals grow, priorities of organizational survival gain priority over programmatic goals and ideological lines.	*Proposition IIIr*: Priorities of organizational survival gain priority over programmatic goals and ideological lines as long as party members are motivated by selective incentives and believers have no alternative to turn to or lack substantial influence.
Proposition IV—Dynamics of Moderation: Ideological moderation naturally takes place after strategic interests and organizational resources change.	*Proposition IVr*: Ideological moderation precedes, facilitates, or accompanies behavioral change.
Proposition V—Moderation-Democratization Nexus: Ideological and behavioral moderation are conducive to democratic transformations.	*Proposition Vr*: Behavioral moderation may be pernicious for democratic transformations under certain historical conditions.

does This chart hold true w/
his explanation, is there adequate
support?

elites that resist the expansion of rights and pursue policies that discriminate against certain social groups. In fact, Michels, who studies the SDP in imperial Germany, recognizes this counterintuitive result and avoids using the term "moderation." As a formerly radical party becomes more institutionalized, its ability to transform the undemocratic characteristics of the regime fades away. Hence Proposition V is reformulated: behavioral moderation may be pernicious for democratic transformations under certain historical conditions (*Proposition Vr*).

Finally, moderation theory exclusively focuses on how institutional and organizational factors shape the behavior of party leaders and assumes that ideological moderation follows change in strategic interests. While this focus makes the theory applicable to a variety of historical and cultural contexts with similar institutional frameworks, the causal story it offers may be incomplete. A better specification of the institutional factors, such as electoral rules, may explain some variation in party behavior.[45] In any case, an exclusive focus on the behavioral dimension is unlikely to provide a satisfactory account of political change in many cases. As Jillian Schwedler eloquently argues, a comprehensive theory of political change should specify whether and how "the inclusion in pluralist political processes may lead political actors to gradually adopt a more open and tolerant worldview than the one they held prior to such participation."[46] Political elites may respond differently to similar institutional constraints and opportunities.[47] The observation that political leaders tend to have more elaborate belief systems and are more likely to be guided in their actions by their beliefs than ordinary people supports this argument.[48] For instance, the French Communist Party preserved its radical orientation for decades despite the looming threat of electoral marginalization. Not all Turkish Islamists who were faced with electoral incentives and institutional constraints evolved in a way that would be predicted by moderation theory. After the split of Erdoğan and his friends, the old guard organized under the rubric of the FP, which is exclusively based on collective interests and experienced no ideological adaptation. Given these cases, it is essential to conceptualize ideological change as separate from behavioral change. Participation in elections will not moderate a radical party unless party leaders have enough intellectual resources to develop an ideological reorientation. Furthermore, the source of ideological change can be the result of political learning even in the absence of institutional incentives and constraints. Consequently, ideological moderation is not a simple adjustment to changes in strategic interests and organizational resources. As Douglass C. North argues, the response of actors in unprecedented situations "depends on how novel they are and on the cultural heritage of the actors. Their cultural heritage will, in many instances, determine the success or lack of success of the actors to adapt their behavior to changing circumstances."[49] In fact, behavioral moderation may not be sustainable if not sanctioned and justified by a permissive ideology. Ideological moderation precedes, facilitates, or accompanies behavioral change (*Proposition IVr*).

Conceptualizing Ideological Influence and Change

The relationship between ideology and behavior requires some clarification. There are primarily two ways by which beliefs and ideas affect behavior. They can either directly inform behavior by specifying its goals or indirectly influence behavior by defining acceptable forms of action. The idea that certain religious beliefs, practices, and institutions are more likely to result in certain social, economic, and political outcomes has a long tradition in social science.[50] Such cultural-historical explanations include arguments that religious heritage independently shapes behavior (e.g., the Protestant belief of a "calling" giving rise to capitalist accumulation, or the Islamic notion of jihad promoting imperialistic violence)[51] and certain critical points in history set the direction of future developments (e.g., Mohammed's dual rule as the prophet and the political leader, making the separation of politics and religion unthinkable in Islamic societies).[52] The direct impact of beliefs and ideas on behavior is more likely to occur in situations where "institutionalized guides for behavior, thought, or feeling are weak or absent."[53] In these "unsettled situations," ideologies, defined as consistent and crystallized sets of ideas about how a good society ought to be, have the potential of directly guiding behavior.[54]

However, beliefs and ideas often do not directly influence action by determining its ends. Actors are not imprisoned in their cultural traditions. Rather, they make some types of behavior more thinkable than others. They *predispose* actors to behave in certain ways and *discourage* them from acting in other ways.[55] Cultural symbols, which enable actors to communicate, perpetuate, and develop their knowledge about and attitudes toward life,[56] provide them with multiple strategies to achieve their goals. Actors are unlikely to behave in ways that defy their cultural norms and cannot be justified within their cultural frameworks. The level of ideological rigidity determines the parameters of behavioral adaptation. As a result, certain types of behavior are more appropriate in some cultures than others, even if actors perceive their interests and formulate their goals in similar fashion. The "logic of appropriateness" proposes that actors avoid practices that violate institutionally and culturally established norms.[57] As actors are most likely to ignore strategies of action that are alien to indigenous institutional and cultural settings, certain types of beliefs and ideas become more thinkable than others, regardless of consequences.

It is also important to realize that beliefs and ideas forming the core of cultures are prone to change. Explanations that emphasize long-term continuities usually tend to underestimate the constant evolution of seemingly stagnant cultures.[58] Naturally, cultures and institutions differ in their ability to adapt to changing external conditions. This difference might be the decisive factor in the rise and demise of civilizations, regimes, and organizations.[59] Over time, actors may internalize new habits and practices, which replace older metanorms and gain almost universal acceptance within the community.[60] Beliefs and ideas evolve as actors engage in "meaning-making practices" that create a dynamic relationship between social reality and culture.[61]

This conceptual framework allows us to approach the questions of how beliefs affect behavior and how beliefs evolve in a systematic manner. Cultural traditions can be classified according to (1) their repertoire of tolerated behaviors and (2) their adaptability in response to changing structural conditions. Particularly interesting and relevant for the purposes of this book are great religious traditions, including Islam. Max Weber argues that "salvation by faith," which characterizes certain forms of Islam and Christianity, entails a "sacred inner religious state that may sanction different maxims of conduct in different situations, and which is thus elastic and susceptible of accommodation."[62] Pious believers may deliberately reject the immediate past of their religious heritage in favor of an ideal sociopolitical order that is imagined to be the essence of the faith.[63] They would be receptive to a variety of alternative strategies of action as long as they are able to justify those strategies in terms of their faith, which has a rich and complex history. Following Weber, it can be argued that Islamic traditions potentially sanction a wide range of behaviors and generate innovative responses in the face of socioeconomic and political changes.[64]

This conceptualization—the effects of ideology on behavior by setting boundaries of justification and elasticity for religiously inspired political behavior—leads to three insights that are directly pertinent for understanding the dynamics by which Muslim reformers arose in Iran and Turkey. First, Islamist politicians are not necessarily driven by rigid religious ideologies that dictate their behavior. Theoretically speaking, Islamic traditions draw the boundaries of behavior without defining goals. Second, sea changes in international and domestic politics, formation of pluralistic public spaces that contribute to exchange of and exposure to new ideas, new life experiences that come with political maturity, and disillusionment with leadership all affect the boundaries of religiously inspired political mindsets. These developments, which may take place in the absence of any strong institutional incentives affecting strategic interests, result in the formation of new sets of preferences and change the boundaries of justifiable political behavior. Finally, ideological change may accompany behavioral change as Muslim political actors discard prevailing norms in favor of alternative culturally acceptable norms that are more compatible with their evolving strategic interests.[65] In summary, ideological change, which may have its origins in factors that are not identified by moderation theory, needs to be treated as an autonomous process that may precede, accompany, facilitate, or undermine behavioral change. Given differences in institutional opportunities, organizational resources, and ideological worldviews, political actors are more likely to behave in certain manners than in others.[66]

Revisiting the Historical Puzzle

As stated in Chapter 1, this book addresses the question, why did the contemporary evolution of Iranian and Turkish Muslim reformers follow a similar trajectory? It aims to clarify the mechanisms through which beliefs and behavior of Muslim reformers in Iran and Turkey have evolved in institutionally defined political contexts.[67] The methodological approach in this book follows the logic of "method of agreement" and presents a comparative historical analysis of Iranian and Turkish Muslim reformers.[68] The method of agreement is particularly suitable for explaining similar or common outcomes in two or more cases with few common characteristics.[69] It focuses on factors that are common to all cases and are relevant for explaining similar outcomes.[70] The analysis demonstrates that the factors that are unique to either Iran or Turkey are not necessary for the rise of Muslim reformers.[71] Thus, it augments the applicability of the theory to diverse historical and cultural settings.

Neither in Iran nor in Turkey did ideological moderation take place as a result of political inclusion, as would be suggested by Proposition IV of moderation theory. In the Islamic Republic, the rise of a Muslim reformist discourse and mindset coincided with political marginalization of the leftist faction. Even if Turkish Islamists had been included in the political system and had taken part in the government since the 1970s, the rise of Muslim reformism did not happen until the 1990s. The death of Khomeini in 1989 transformed factional differences into an open struggle for power in the Islamic Republic. The leftists who were in favor of state control of economic production, demanded redistributive policies, and espoused revolutionary foreign policy suffered a heavy defeat in the 1992 parliamentary elections after many of them were disqualified from running by the Guardians Council (GC). This defeat was a milestone in Iranian politics. Deprived of a platform through which they could effectively influence policymaking, many leftists took shelter in civil-society organizations. After the end of war with Iraq in 1988, Iran entered into an era of socioeconomic reconstruction under the presidency of Rafsanjani. The private sector's share of economic production grew considerably, women's literacy and university enrollment rates increased significantly, the intellectual life was revitalized, and a younger generation with no experience of the revolution came of age politically. Meanwhile, Marxism, the major competitor of Islamism during the 1970s and 1980s, lost its appeal and credibility after the fall of the Communist bloc. All these changes produced demands for greater social liberties and political democratization.[72] The leftists were joined by individuals with little previous political experience and incorporated the themes of popular participation, civil society, free elections, rule of law, and opening up in foreign relations to their discourse. They now criticized the Islamic regime for subverting the ideal of the revolution and demanded political reform.

In the case of Turkey, Islamists had participated in electoral politics since the 1970s. The demise of the Turkish left in the aftermath of the 1980 coup and the collapse of the Soviet Union provided a unique opportunity for the Islamist movement. Islamism emerged as a credible force that carried to the center of the Turkish political spectrum the demands of the socioeconomically marginalized urban poor and the culturally marginalized provincial and pious middle classes who benefited from the economic liberalization of the 1980s. The expanding public sphere also contributed to the Islamist discourse characterized by lively debates and competing perspectives. The WP (1983–1998), the primary agent of the Islamist project, was far from being a monolithic entity and hosted radical as well as more liberal voices. As a result of the party's expansion, two factions with clear differences emerged within the party ranks. The reformist faction, led by relatively young figures, played key roles in increasing the party's popularity among the pious middle classes and urban peripheries. The rise of the WP came to an abrupt end when the Turkish Constitutional Court banned the party in January 1998 and its successor, the VP, performed poorly in the 1999 elections. State repression and electoral defeat crystallized ideological divisions within the party ranks. The reformers tried to end the hegemony of the party old guard and offered a dramatically new political project. A leading Islamic writer sympathetic to them captured the essence of their project:

> The project of re-creating the VP as the new center-right has two components: First, it involves neutralizing the old guard and making reformers the leading force in the party. Second is the emergence of a conciliatory periphery [on the assumption that the VP leads the forces of the periphery]. Reformers are putting forward the need for a long-desired and justified change. Their support among the VP grassroots, the media, and power holders is a consequence of this.[73]

As suggested by Proposition I of moderation theory, Muslim reformers capitalized on electoral opportunities by developing centrist platforms that were very different from radical discourses they had employed until the early 1990s. Reorganized as electoral parties, they adopted centrist strategies that aimed to make them acceptable to large segments of society. The advocates of reform banded together and supported the candidacy of Khatami in the 1997 Iranian presidential elections. Khatami's landslide victory heralded the birth of the reformist movement in Iranian politics. The RF swept the 2000 parliamentary elections and for a while presented a viable and popular alternative to the authoritarianism of the Islamic Republic. These elections, conducted under relatively free circumstances, provided a unique opportunity to the RF to mobilize public support and challenge the hard-liners' control over public opinion. The RF and its allies shaped political discourse by popularizing the themes of civil society, popular rule, and human rights in their newspapers and magazines. These were remarkable achievements, given the authoritarian history of the Islamic Republic. Even people who were disappointed with the reform movement conceded that his legacy was lasting:

> Mr. Khatami started with big promises but failed to fulfill them. However, it would be unrealistic to overlook what he achieved. If nothing else, he changed the style and substance of political discourse in the country. Now all presidential candidates adopt his discourse. Even Ahmedinejad cannot definitively stop the process of change.[74]

While the Muslim reformers in Turkey were unable to dislodge the old guard, they were ultimately successful with the establishment of the JDP and its electoral victories. The JDP, established by Erdoğan in 2001, suddenly rose to power with the 2002 early elections. The party explicitly claimed the legacy of the Turkish center-right and aimed to develop a mainstream image with some success. With the backing of the European Union, the JDP engaged in an ambitious reform program that significantly overhauled the country's administrative, political, and legal systems. The JDP also seemed to pursue a progressive policy that might improve Turkey's highly problematic relationship with its Kurdish minority. In fact, the JDP's rule introduced the dual blessing of political stability and sustainable economic growth to Turkey after more than a decade of unstable coalition governments and highly erratic economic performance. The party consolidated its power by emerging triumphant from the 2004 local elections and 2007 parliamentary elections.

Muslim reformers had to contend with the ever-aggravated state elites who were deeply suspicious of the RF's and the JDP's motives. As suggested by Proposition II of moderation theory, Muslim reformers generally preferred negotiations over confrontation, compromises over principled positions, and electoralism over mass demonstrations, as well as social movements based on broad alliances of pro-change forces. Their fear of state repression and concerns with political legality induced Islamic political actors to develop politically cautious and risk-aversive strategies. At the same time and as suggested by Proposition IIIr, the growth of electoral organizations and the control of public offices gain priority over programmatic and pro-reform goals. Preserving the newly won privileges became more important than redressing the authoritarian and corrupt practices engrained in the political system. This was because neither the RF nor the JDP had strong internal democratic practices. A small number of elites made final decisions and were hardly accountable to their supporters. The RF lacked strong organizational capacities and robust vertical links with citizens. In general, factions-cum-parties forming the RF had little influence as an organized force in shaping public opinion. Believers in political reform simply abandoned the RF at critical times, such as in the 2004 parliamentary and 2005 presidential elections. Erdoğan had absolute control over his party's grassroots and the party's parliamentary group; filled the bureaucracy with his followers; and cultivated his own media, business, labor union, and civil associations. This situation inevitably contributed to political polarization, as his opponents remained extremely suspicious of the concentration of power in his hands. Despite the party leadership's original goal of fostering democratic practices, power distribution was very asymmetrical and fostered patron-client relations. As the party grew, its ranks were filled with careerists pursuing selective incentives. A Turkish politician who was one of the leading figures of the JDP expressed how earlier commitments were soon forgotten:

> When we established this party, our goal was to make collective reasoning supreme. We hoped to institutionalize party democracy and protect the rights of the opposition within the party. . . . We hoped to have free and participatory primaries for electing candidates who would run for office under the party's ticket. All these ideals were soon abandoned.[75]

By 2003, it became clear to most observers that Khatami and his allies in the parliament could not overcome the institutional power of the guardians. Khatami preferred constant negotiation and consultation over open confrontation, regardless of the ineffectiveness of the former strategy. Most members of the RF had no faith in contentious politics, given the legacy of the chaotic and bloody revolutionary years and the war with Iraq. Ultimately, the RF's goal of democratizing the Islamic Republic through legal means was frustrated. When Iranian Muslim reformers *deliberately* committed themselves to a legal and nonconfrontational strategy and pursued reforms within the existing constitutional framework, they were confronted with two distinct problems. First, their integration into the political system reduced their ability to form and lead a popular opposition movement that might have forced the guardians to make substantial concessions. They were gradually transformed into a bunch of factions engaging in squabbling while lacking strong linkages with the populace. Public frustration with the performance of the RF fueled widespread apathy and caused believers of political reform to discredit and desert the RF. In the words of an Iranian journalist:

> Optimism about Khatami and reform was not well founded. The power structure of the Islamic Republic does not allow for reform, as the power circle remains narrow. Some people change positions, but there has been no real opening up. Elections will not change anything.[76]

Second, they remained oblivious to nonelectoral oppositional strategies and became highly risk aversive lest they provoke even more repression. When the guardians blocked the legal ways of reform and eliminated the reformists from the parliament, the latter were organizationally and ideologically incapable of pursuing alternative strategies such as mass civil disobedience or continuous street demonstrations. The RF failed to grow as a popular democratization movement. The 2005 presidential election was the nail in the coffin of the RF when reformist candidates were eliminated in the first round. Many groups from the RF threw their support behind their ex-archenemy Rafsanjani, whom they had previously criticized as the most visible symbol of the corrupt, authoritarian, and clandestine nature of the regime.[77] Meanwhile, Rafsanjani aimed to reinvent himself as the savior of reform. In the words of a supporter, "Mr. Hashemi [Rafsanjani] is the only person who can pursue *conciliatory* and *centrist* politics. Iranian people are aware of his unique status" (italics added).[78] It turned out that Rafsanjani was no match for Mahmoud Ahmedinejad, who rapidly cultivated popular support with his puritan and pious style and social justice–focused platform. In a candid self-criticism, a leading journalist noticed how the reformers' defense of Rafsanjani was wrong.[79] In any case, the RF failed to develop a strategy that would overcome the institutional deadlock of Iranian politics.

The JDP achieved more success in implementing its agenda than its Iranian counterpart. The Turkish political system was much more pluralistic and liberal than the Iranian system. Moreover, the JDP had more latitude vis-à-vis the state elites. In particular, the increasing ties between the European Union and Turkey initially emboldened the JDP to take historical initiatives.[80] Yet its pursuit of democratic consolidation was inconsistent and half-hearted. Further

did this have an effect on the ability to reform, does he give enough credit to this advantage?

democratic progress in Turkey needed decisive and bold political action that would surely invite opposition from the forces of the status quo. As in Iran, behavioral moderation was not an effective strategy of democratization. Yet the party attempted, without much success, to avoid open political conflict with the president (until the party's candidate became president in August 2007), the armed forces, and the judiciary that were highly skeptical of the party's agenda. Instead of pursuing a strategy of democratic expansion that would entail alliances with politically marginalized groups seeking rights—such as the Alevi and the Kurdish organizations—and increasingly influential liberal media and associations, and a new constitution promising more freedoms, the JDP preferred to preserve the political status quo lest it provoke the state elites. That risk-aversive strategy was most clear in the aftermath of the 2007 elections when the party won a fresh and overwhelming popular mandate. Most importantly, the party lacked a consistent and comprehensive strategy to address Kurdish demands for political representation, cultural rights, and security. It missed several crucial opportunities to increase civilian control over the armed forces and create a political environment conducive to fully restoring Turkey's relations with its Kurdish minority. Besides, the JDP rapidly became a party of careerists who benefited from the vast selective incentives emanating from the party's control over government and municipalities. These careerist members were in no position to make the party leadership accountable and ask for greater internal party democracy and pursuit of political reform.[81] Recurring corruption scandals seriously tarnished the popular image of the party.

> The party [JDP] was not sincere and serious about rooting out corruption. . . .
> My initial discomfort was caused by the party's stance toward corruption. . . .
> When I expressed my opposition and documented corrupt practices, I was isolated. With few exceptions, I found no allies within the party.[82]

As suggested by Proposition Vr, behavioral moderation of Islamist politicians in Iran and Turkey was a double-edged sword. Moderation of Islamists did not necessarily increase the prospects for democratic transition in Iran and consolidation in Turkey. The Iranian Reform Front lost its *legal struggle* with the guardians and was eliminated from positions of power. The electoral strategy of democratization in Iran appears to be a very remote possibility. The JDP matured into a leader-dominated, vote-maximizing, patronage-distributing center-right party. Its reformist agenda has remained unfulfilled, especially with regard to issues critical to democratic consolidation in Turkey, such as minority rights, freedom of expression, and public accountability of government. Yet the prevailing geopolitical context was much more favorable to the JDP than to the RF. Turkey's strong linkages with the EU and the considerable leverage of the Western governments and public opinion over Turkey prevented a total breakdown of the electoral and pluralistic order. In particular, the guardians exercised self-restraint, as when the Constitutional Court decided not to ban the JDP in July 2008 and the General Staff of the army resisted demands for a coup from senior generals in the early years of the JDP government. It seemed that the guardians were seriously concerned with negative international repercussions of overthrowing a popularly elected government. The JDP enjoyed exceptionally positive relations with the EU and to a certain extent with the United States. The party's "moderate Islamic" image was a huge asset in the eyes of the Western policymakers who were concerned with the rise of radicalism in the Muslim world. In contrast, the escalating tensions between Iran and the United States contributed to the marginalization of the RF and the concentration of power in the hands of hard-liners. The hard-liners accused the RF of pursuing a policy of appeasement toward the United States and sacrificing Iran's national interests. The RF was unable to overcome the siege mentality characterizing Iranian politics.

Muslim Reformism
in Comparative Perspective

The "Islam and Democracy" Debate

The idea that Islam by its very nature is inhospitable to democracy and pluralism continues to have some broad appeal.[1] It is based on the assumption that Islamic religion, with its distinctive historical self-consciousness and value patterns, is a world set apart from Western civilization, with which it often engages in violent confrontations.[2] Islam is argued to be antisecular by definition, and this implies that Muslims cannot support political secularism because of their religious identity. Bernard Lewis writes, "In such a society [Islamic], the very idea of separating church and state is meaningless, since there are no two entities to be separated."[3] The nature and composition of Islam has not, since its beginning, given any room to the development of the idea of the secular polity, which is indispensable for democracy. The sovereignty of God, which is central to Islamic political thought, stands in sharp contrast to the idea of the rule of popular will, the linchpin of democracy.[4] The logical offshoots of this argument are the necessary exclusion of Islam from public life for democracy to flourish and preferably an enlightened and progressive statesman to provide leadership.[5] The absence of such a visionary figure may justify the continuation of authoritarian rule in Muslim societies. While Fareed Zakaria avoids characterizing Islamic or Arab cultures as hindrances to liberalism, he argues that the current economic, political, and social crises of the Arab countries prepare the ground sufficiently for the rise of extremist and illiberal Islamism. The analogy he has in mind is the rise of fascism and Nazism in the interwar years in European countries. He concludes:

> The Arab rulers of the Middle East are autocratic, corrupt, and heavy-handed. But they are still more liberal, tolerant, and pluralistic than what would likely replace them . . . The Arab world today is trapped between autocratic states and illiberal societies, neither of them fertile ground for liberal democracy.[6]

The arguments implying the incompatibility of public expressions of Islam and democracy often point to the lack of democratization in the Middle East, the core of the Muslim world. In fact, the sweeping democratic waves emanating from the collapse of the Soviet-controlled Socialist bloc only tangentially affected the Middle East. Not only did the Middle Eastern brand of authoritarianism appear to be built on stronger foundations than anywhere else, but opposition movements in the region did not have strong democratic credentials. The collapse of the authoritarian governments as a result of mass disobedience in Serbia in 2000 (the Bulldozer Revolution), in Georgia in 2003 (the Rose Revolution), and in Ukraine in 2004 (the Orange Revolution) has no Middle Eastern counterparts.[7] The only successful mass movement in the region resulted in the establishment of the Islamic Republic of Iran, a theocratic republic. Elsewhere, Islamist opposition movements were brutally repressed by ruling autocracies, as in Egypt in 1954, Iraq in 1980, Syria in 1982, and Algeria in 1992. Yet the strongest opposition movements that commanded mass followings remained mostly religious in nature. These groups were often perceived as having dubious democratic and liberal credentials: the Muslim Brotherhood in Egypt, the Islamic Salvation Front in Algeria, and the Welfare Party in Turkey. In Egypt, Jordan, Kuwait, Morocco, and Yemen, rulers used limited political and economic liberalization to prolong their rule and divide the opposition forces.[8] In Turkey, an Islamic-led coalition government was forced to dissolve under intense pressure from the military in 1997. Elsewhere, hereditary succession became the most common and stable means of transferring power. Power was smoothly transferred from father to son in Bahrain, Jordan, Morocco, Qatar, Syria, and the United Arab Emirates by the end of 2000. Muslim-majority states that seceded from the Soviet Union were ruled by ex-Communist apparatchiks who established personalized autocracies.[9] Large-N analyses indicate a robust relationship between the Islamic religion and authoritarian governance.[10]

At the same time, the developments were more encouraging for the prospects for democracy in other parts of the Muslim world.[11] The decision by the Bangladeshi army to withdraw from politics reinvigorated multiparty democracy in that country in 1991. The 1997 Asian financial crisis brought the end of Suharto's dictatorship in Indonesia. His regime's austerity measures that cut government spending and subsidies led to massive elite defections and triggered public unrest. Since then, Indonesia has held six free and competitive national elections.[12] The 1990s also witnessed the demise of authoritarian governments in several Muslim-majority countries in Africa. Mass protests brought the end of military regimes in Niger and Mali in 1991.[13] A democratic government was established in Niger in 1993. A coup derailed the democratic process in 1996, but free and fair elections were reestablished by 1999. Democracy has functioned in Mali since 1992 without any interruption. Years of military rule ended in Nigeria in 1999. Since then, Nigeria has been enjoying the longest period of civilian rule in its history, although the elections in April 2007 were marred by fraud and inconsistencies. More than thirty years of de facto single-party rule ended in Senegal in 1992 with citizens voting for a parliament and a president in free and fair elections. Multiparty democracy was further consolidated in elections in 1997, 2002, and 2007.[14]

Western scholars, Muslim reformers, and intellectuals vigorously argue that Islam is not inherently undemocratic and point to the proliferation of nonviolent and moderate expressions of Islamic faith.[15] Muslim believers constantly interpret their faith and generate novel understandings of sacred texts.[16] Rather than timeless, eternal Islamic values motivating action, values are molded by agency.[17] The recent intellectual trends demonstrate the vibrancy of the Muslim quest for rule of law, human rights, popular sovereignty, separation of powers, and ruler accountability.[18] The Islamic state is not associated with democracy but with free elections, consultation, and rational decision making.[19] The framing of democratic messages in Islamic language may make democratic principles intelligible and plausible to a broader Muslim public.

While this debate has been intellectually productive and has generated a considerable amount of public interest, it is not very helpful in understanding under what conditions interpretations of Islam that are hospitable to liberal democracy gain wide acceptance among Muslim political activists and publics. Textual analyses, which cherry-pick phrases from canonical texts and Muslim intellectuals, do not provide solid grounds for making sweeping generalizations about Islam. Studies that go beyond textual analyses and offer more analytical perspectives that seek to understand the resiliency of authoritarianism, especially in the Muslim Middle East and Central Asia, are more informative. Macro-level studies suggest that the Arab world rather than Muslim countries in general has a democratic deficit. They argue that the prevalence of conflict, more specifically the Arab-Israeli conflict, is responsible for the lack of sustainable democratization in the Arab world.[20] Alternatively, the survival of authoritarian regimes in the Middle East is explained by their robust coercion capacities and abundant revenues from nonmineral resources.[21] Authoritarian governments in the region are characterized by neopatrimonial practices that hinder institutionalization and protect the ruler from elite defection.[22] Neopatrimonial practices entail the ruler's control over every aspect of government, thereby providing him absolute control over subordinates.[23]

The Muslim Public

Another realm of study that has attracted scholarly focus has been the relationship between belief systems and political attitudes of the Muslim public. This approach, which considers the effects of Islamic religiosity on political attitudes and behavior, emanates from scholarly studies that assign "political culture" an independent, causal role, and one of their earliest representations is Gabriel Almond and Sydney Verba's eloquent *Civic Culture*.[24] Their argument is that democracy becomes sustainable only when its fundamental principles are associated with the psychological orientation of the majority of citizens. Along similar lines, scholars have argued that cultures characterized by self-achievement and ethos and thrift are more likely to have sustainable rates of economic growth;[25] cultures promoting parochial self-interest over community interest are doomed to backwardness;[26] cultures fostering religious beliefs in hell and heaven contribute to economic growth;[27] cultures deprived of interpersonal trust provide an unstable, "quicksand" basis for democratic consolidation;[28] cultures begetting social capital tend to produce more effective public institutions;[29] and some cultures are more prone to inter- and intracommunal violence than others.[30] Especially in the last two decades, political-culture-based explanations were catapulted from second-order, residual-theory status to major contenders in structure-, institution-, and rationality-based explanations.[31]

At the same time, cultural explanations based on the "*Civic Culture* tradition" are also subject to a plethora of criticisms that point to the conceptual, theoretical, and measurement problems inherent in the approach.[32] Cultural explanations tend to construct concepts that are too broad, difficult to measure, and too ambiguous to allow for solid causal relations.[33] For instance, a study that aims to test the "clash of civilizations" thesis on the basis of survey data simply assumes that all countries with a Muslim majority can be considered as having "Islamic culture." These countries include Albania and Azerbaijan, which have much more in common in terms of history, politics, and socioeconomic structure with Bosnia, Bulgaria, Macedonia, and Georgia (all belonging to the Orthodox Christian zone).[34] Besides, culture is usually defined as a set of values that motivate and shape attitudinal and behavioral characteristics of individuals or groups. This definition assumes that values that vary across different cultures causally affect how and why individuals and groups reason and act in political settings.[35] Yet it also isolates individuals from their environment, hence from the "cultural" setting in which they adapt these strategies.[36] Survey studies that focus on individual-level expressions of Islam ultimately ignore the great historical and sociological diversity within Islamic traditions.[37] It also often remains unclear how culture measured at an individual level causally affects institutional-level outcomes.[38] Levels of interpersonal trust and commitment of citizens to democracy may be irrelevant for understanding the structural and institutional factors that make democracies more enduring and sustainable.[39] Besides, cultural explanations rarely specify the mechanisms through which enduring value, attitudinal, and behavioral patterns decide types of political institutions.[40] A productive way to overcome the problem of causal underspecification is combining survey analysis with meticulous historical narrations and ethnographic work.[41] Cultural explanations should also attempt to explain how deeply rooted value orientations come into existence and to specify their dynamics of change.[42] Naturally, if culture is proposed as an explanation, it should be made clear how culture comes into existence and how durable it is in a given society.[43]

Given these conceptual and theoretical problems affecting even some of the best work in the *Civic Culture* tradition, it is surprising to note that culture-based explanations have wide circulation in studies of democratization in Muslim-majority countries. This may reflect the lasting legacy of the ways in which Western knowledge of Islam and the Middle East has developed since the nineteenth century.[44] Nonetheless, these studies show that Muslim denomination and beliefs do not necessarily translate into an authoritarian or theocratic worldview. Recent survey findings from Muslim-majority countries provide empirical evidence that Islamic beliefs do not necessarily negatively affect attitudes toward democracy.[45] At the same time, survey questions do not generally provide any insights into how citizens understand democracy and what they expect from it. Several examples from World Values Surveys (WVS) conducted in fourteen Muslim-majority countries between 2000 and 2005 demonstrate the difficulty of interpreting survey findings.[46] In general, positive attitudes toward democracy as an ideal and its preference over alternative methods of political rule are not necessarily accompanied by widespread opposition against authoritarian rule. Despite their preference for democratic rule, heavy majorities are still satisfied with incumbent performance in authoritarian Egypt, Iran, and Jordan. For instance, only 8 percent of Egyptian respondents are dissatisfied with the way government manages the country's affairs, and 95 percent are satisfied with the manner in which democracy is developing. It should be remembered that Egypt has been ruled by the same person under emergency rule since 1981. In sharp contrast, only 24 percent of Turkish respondents are satisfied with the manner in which democracy is developing in their country, and 72 percent are either very dissatisfied or completely dissatisfied with the incumbents. This is despite the fact that Turkey has a history of free and competitive multiparty elections going back to 1950 and the highest prospects for democratic consolidation in the Muslim Middle East. ✱ good evidence

Although it seems that democracy, as an idea and as a practice, is enormously popular among the Muslim public, it is not always clear if respondents understand democracy to mean popular sovereignty, competitive and pluralistic politics, and civil liberties. When respondents are asked if a good government would enact laws in line with popular wishes, not all of those respondents who view democracy as better than any other regime agree. While 98 percent of Egyptian respondents think democracy is better than any other regime, only 74 percent agree that the government should enact laws in line with popular wishes. Similarly, in Jordan, 90 percent find democracy desirable, yet only 63 percent say that governmental laws should be in accordance with popular wishes. In Pakistan, even fewer respondents (60 percent) claim that popular laws should be enacted by the government, whereas 82 percent prefer democracy to any other regime. It is hard to say what democracy means to respondents who do not favor the idea of popular sovereignty. Given the fact that even the staunchly authoritarian regimes in the Muslim world make some reference to democracy in their pursuit of legitimacy, democracy may have multiple and often contradictory implications in the eyes of citizens in the Muslim-majority countries.

It can be surmised that democracy may very broadly stand for a "common good" that involves economic prosperity, social justice, political stability, and lessening of economic inequality in the eyes of the Muslim public. In this regard, it would be interesting to look at the relationship between support for popular sovereignty and sharia, which has symbolized just rule in Muslim societies for centuries. Survey results demonstrate an ambiguous relationship between sharia and popular sovereignty. The fourth wave (1999–2004) of World Values Surveys asked respondents in eight Muslim-majority countries whether they agree that only laws of the sharia should be implemented. The notion of sharia-based law enjoys the support of majorities with the exceptions of Bangladesh, Indonesia, and Iraq. In Algeria, 56 percent; in Pakistan, 60 percent; in Jordan, 75 percent; in Egypt, 79 percent; and in Saudi Arabia, 83 percent either agree or strongly agree with the statement that only laws of the sharia should be implemented. Meanwhile, majorities in all eight countries prefer that laws should be made according to popular wishes. Not many people see a contradiction between sharia-based laws and popular will. It remains unclear how the public will respond if popularly elected authorities enact legislation perceived to violate the fundamentals of sharia.

These results attest to the multidimensional meaning of sharia.[47] The concept has deep roots in history, and it is usually associated with a good, uncorrupted political order in the public vernacular. In the twentieth century, it became the rallying cry of the Muslim modernists who were rejecting the immediate Islamic cultural past as corrupt and articulating a political vision in which Islam as religion became a blueprint for a social order.[48] In this sense, it would be misleading to equate all demands for the implementation of sharia with radicalism. What is more important is how sharia is interpreted. In a recent survey in Turkey, when respondents were asked if they would like to have sharia rule, around 25 percent answered positively. However, when asked about the specific applications of sharia rule, such as the mutilation of thieves' hands, positive responses decreased to the low teens.[49] Moreover, the percentage of respondents saying yes to the establishment of a sharia-based religious state dropped to 15 percent in 2003, despite the fact that a party that is controlled by ex-Islamists came to power in November 2002.[50] In countries where support for sharia rule is high, the crucial question remains whether interpretations of Islam that are compatible with democratic competition and individual rights are espoused by opinion leaders and influential politicians.

Figure 3.1 visualizes the astonishing relationship between regime type and popular views regarding respect for human rights in fourteen Muslim-majority countries for which WVS data is available. With the exception of Bangladesh and Jordan, the relationship between political rights and civil liberties and public perceptions of respect for human rights seemed to be inversely related. Less than 20 percent of Turkish respondents thought that human rights were respected in their country in 2001. In contrast, 66 percent of Iranians in 2000, 68 percent of Saudi Arabians in 2003, and 71 percent of Egyptians in 2000 responded that there was either a lot or some respect for human rights in their countries. Ironically, ruling regimes in these three countries have repeatedly

Figure 3.1. The Relationship between Regime Type and Public Perception of Human Rights

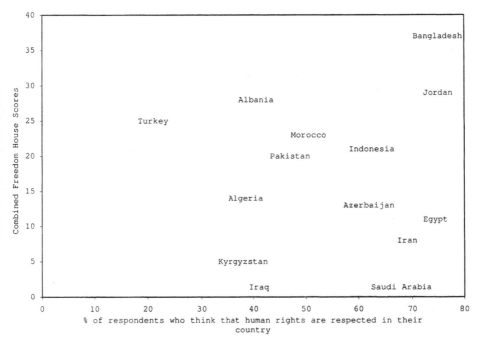

Source: Combined Freedom House scores are the aggregation of political rights and civil liberties scores for the five years before the survey year. Scores were subtracted from 70, so higher scores represent greater levels of political rights and civil liberties. Data were obtained from www.freedomhouse .org and www.worldvaluessurvey.org. Data from the fourth wave of the WVS that was conducted between 1999 and 2004 are used.

committed gross human rights violations and are more authoritarian than the Turkish regime. In Jordan, which is similar to Turkey in terms of the scope of political rights and civil liberties, more than two-thirds of the respondents thought that human rights were respected in 2001.

It appears that the meaning of human rights varies across different regimes and historical circumstances. It may be argued that respect for human rights is ingrained in the popular conscience in Turkey. For instance, ordinary Turkish citizens may feel that human rights are not respected in their country if they are treated rudely and unfairly penalized by police. Likewise, pious Turks may think that human rights are not respected in the country because veiled women are banned from university campuses and public employment. The Turkish press often treats the troubles of the health care system or the embezzlement of public funds as violations of human rights. Hence, human rights are not just viewed as irrelevant issues that concern only dissidents and repressed minorities but are considered indispensable for the decent treatment of citizens by the government. In contrast, human rights in Egypt and Iran do not seem to have broad connotations for the public despite the relative strength of reformist opposition movements.

This discussion of Muslim public opinion serves two purposes. Primarily, it would be completely misleading to assume the existence of an encompassing "Islamic culture" that is characterized by fixed political belief and value orientations. There are no theoretical or empirical reasons to expect that Islamic denomination and Muslim beliefs have strong influence on people's attitudes toward democratic ideals and evaluations of democratic performance. While the intensity of Muslim belief may affect political ideology and partisan affiliation in some contexts, it does not seem to influence how people make sense of democracy. Hence, public attitudes are not obstacles for the formation and rise of Muslim reformist parties and movements. Second, survey results leave many questions regarding political attitudes of the Muslim public unanswered. This is partially because survey research is still in an infant stage in most of the Middle East and broader Muslim world. Additionally, the ways in which democracy is understood and perceived by the Muslim public are characterized by ambiguities and, often, inconsistencies. People may have unrealistic expectations for democratic governance or associate it with everything they find desirable. Abstract questions involving the concept of democracy are not very helpful in shedding light on the existence of democratic culture among citizens. It would be more productive to focus on public attitudes on salient political issues that may prove to be litmus tests of democracy. One may investigate whether Turkish citizens are willing to give full political rights and civil liberties to the Kurds; Iranian citizens endorse state imposition of religion and the GC's screening of candidates; or Egyptian citizens approve limits on presidential terms. It would also be more illuminating if survey studies were combined with focus groups or participant observations that may reveal how pious Muslims articulate their political opinions. Nonetheless, support for democracy and refusal of alternatives such as military rule are encouraging in Muslim-majority countries with free and competitive elections—such as Indonesia and Turkey. It can be expected that citizens have a more realistic and sound understanding of democracy in such countries.

Muslim Political Groups

Muslim political organizations have been the major actors challenging the status quo in many of the Muslim-majority countries in the last quarter century. They represent a wide variety of positions ranging from advocacy of global jihad to establishment of democratic and pluralistic rule. Despite this diversity, it can be argued that Islamic political activists have been developing stronger commitments to democratic governance since the early 1990s.[51] By the mid-1990s, Communism had collapsed, the euphoria of the Iranian Revolution had waned, the authoritarian Arab states had thwarted Islamist challenges, and the discourse of democracy—free elections, protection of individual rights, limits on state power, the rule of law—had globally circulated and become prestigious.[52] Their experience of state repression, questioning of the state-centric nature of the Islamist ideology, and disagreements with the older generation of Islamists made them more receptive to democratic ideas. They had become more interested in participating in electoral contestation and had come to respect electoral results.[53] As a general rule, Muslim political actors in more open and liberal states tend to be more moderate and develop relatively conciliatory platforms.[54]

The origins of Islamism as an ideology have their roots in the late nineteenth century, when a group of intellectuals articulated the notion of "Muslim unity" and claimed that Islam is inherently compatible with modern science and political governance.[55] However, ideologies of authoritarian and secular modernization overshadowed Islamism until the last quarter of the twentieth century. The most successful example of secular-authoritarian modernization was led by Mustafa Kemal Atatürk (1881–1938), who established the Turkish Republic in 1923. A national parliament in Ankara, an impoverished town in barren Central Anatolia, were powerful enough to abolish the caliphate and to destroy the most important symbol of Islamic unity.[56] That was a solid testimony to the weakness of the notion of "Islamic unity and state" in the early twentieth century.[57] From the 1920s to the late 1960s, modernizing strongmen appealed to the hearts and minds of citizens in the nascent states of the Muslim world. Reza Pahlavi (r. 1925–1941) and his son Mohammad Reza Pahlavi (r. 1941–1979) in Iran, Sukarno (r. 1949–1966) in Indonesia, Habib Bourguiba (r. 1957–1987) in Tunisia, Gamal Abdel Nasser (r. 1954–1970) in Egypt, and Houari Boumedienne (r. 1965–1978) in Algeria were leaders committed to achieving speedy development through large-scale cultural and material modernization projects. In their vision, Islam did not have much of a role to play in the future of their societies and in international competition. Yet the energy and mass appeal of secularist modernization did not prove to be lasting; its limits became clear by the early 1970s. Almost every state in the Islamic world, with the exception of the Gulf monarchies sitting on vast oil reserves, was overburdened under the morass of extensive commitments to their citizens. Economic policies based on import-substitution industrialization (ISI) were in disarray.[58] Welfare states promising careers, status, housing, and basic luxuries to aspirant young citizens were no longer capable of delivering their intended goals. In the Arab Middle East, Israel's victory in the Six-Day War of 1967 was a decisive point that exposed the hollowness of the ideals of pan-Arabism.[59] From then on, secular Arab nationalism no longer had the dynamic spirit to inspire a vision of good society for millions.

The rise of Islamism coincided with the increasing problems of secular-authoritarian modernization. Until the mid-1990s, it could hardly be said that democratic ideas were very popular among Islamic cadres. The predominant discourse was the idea of establishing the "Islamic state," which was much influenced by the founder of the Muslim Brotherhood, Hasan al-Banna (1906–1949), found its earliest expression in the work of the Pakistani journalist Abul Ala Mawdudi (1903–1979), was highly inspired by Sayyid Qutb's (1906–1966) discussion of vanguard Muslims, and was galvanized by Ruhollah Khomeini's (1902–1989) overthrow of the Pahlavi monarchy. These men exerted great influence on the formation of Islamic politics in the second part of the twentieth century in many parts of the Muslim world. The thought of these major figures of Islamism has remained controversial and been open to opposing interpretations. The texts they produced have been interpreted in multiple ways, reflecting changes in political circumstances and needs. Nowadays, it is not rare for an Iranian democracy activist to read and understand Khomeini as an advocate of unconditional popular government. Still, their political vision can hardly be characterized as being hospitable to liberal democracy. They generally perceived democracy as a set of institutional rules devoid of intrinsic values and that serve the domination of particular classes over others. They simply rejected the idea that democratic governance as practiced in the West might serve some desirable normative goals such as freedom and social justice. In their eyes, Western political systems are far from achieving social justice and have failed to eradicate oppressive rule. Democracy is just another type of political institution and not appropriate for Muslim societies. All secular regimes are illegal, and thus no significant difference exists between democracy, Socialism, or monarchy. Political institutions were no help when people's morals were corrupted. For them, a sociopolitical system based on Islamic principles represents complete rupture with corrupt and secular orders.

Mawdudi suggested that only the establishment of an Islamic state emulating the example of the rule of the first caliphs would restore power and dignity to Islam.[60] He formulated Islam as a revolutionary force in opposition to the existing political order and rejected political pluralism. Although Mawdudi's vision failed to construct a mass-based Islamist political identity led by a single movement in Pakistan,[61] his ideas were popularized and provided a firm basis for the idea of an Islamic state in the modern age. For the Egyptian Qutb, all societies that compromised the sovereignty of God with "man-made laws" were corrupt and had to be fought against. Qutb called these societies *jāhiliyya*, a term he borrowed from the Qur'an, where it was used to describe pre-Islamic Arabic society.[62] Whether democracies or not, these societies, he believed, subdue noble human ideals to material interests and institutionalize humankind's slavery to its base instincts.[63] Qutb advocated the overthrow of these societies by any means necessary.[64] The task of true Muslims was simply to wage a long war, jihad, against these societies and disseminate the message of Islam for achieving human dignity and freedom.[65] While Qutb's disciples developed various readings of his central concepts of *jāhiliyya* and jihad, the Islamic state envisioned by Qutb was never fully realized in any Arab country.[66]

The man who achieved that ideal for the first time in modern history came from an unexpected part of the Middle East. The theme of Islamic government that would become the core element of Khomeini's political thought was already in its embryonic form in 1941.[67] Khomeini developed the notion of the rule of the religious jurist, which became the building block of the Islamic Republic of Iran, only in the early 1970s. In a series of lectures delivered in Najaf in 1971, Khomeini forcefully argued for the necessity of the most learned and just religious clergy to defend Islam against imperialism and its local collaborators.[68] In Khomeini's political vision, rulers would be constrained only by the divine law revealed to humans in the Qur'an. For Khomeini as well as Qutb, it was indeed an insult to Islam to talk about Islamic democracy, because Islam provides an immaculate understanding of sociopolitical life and does not need any qualifiers.[69]

Muslim political organizations that were heavily influenced by either of these thinkers/activists had initially tended to assign no value to democratic rule. They were ardently against what they perceived as Western cultural infiltration and the erosion of social moral fabric. Western societies were morally corrupt and promoted materialistic values at the expense of spiritual and religious values. In contrast, Islamists called for the prohibition of liquor, the end of the public financing of cultural institutions such as ballet, increasing the role of religious teaching in public education, the restriction of tourism, and the implementation of policies that were thought to make society morally upright and Islamic. The state would enforce these policies so that society did not deviate from the right path. However, the goal of establishing the Islamic state proved to be an illusion except in Iran. Authoritarian Sunni Arab regimes skillfully played the sectarian card to contain the revolutionary fervor of the Shia in Iran.[70] Most of the Arab states, with the exceptions of Syria and Libya, actively supported Saddam Hussein's war against the nascent Islamic Republic in the 1980s. These Arab states, as well as Pakistan and even secular Turkey, enhanced their religious credentials by co-opting agendas of the conservative Islamic groups while suppressing the radicals. The revolution did not create a snowball effect, and all authoritarian Arab regimes survived, becoming more vigilant against the Islamic opposition.[71] The Islamist experiment in Sudan, led by the National Islamic Front under Hasan Turabi, also turned into a failure.[72] The Taliban in Afghanistan ruled for five years in desolate conditions; their regime was hardly a source of emulation.[73] Meanwhile, Western scholars started to announce the failure of the Islamic state as an ideological project and argued that Islamists were losing momentum.[74] The defeats of Islamists in domestic political arenas ultimately created rifts and paved the way for the rise of the global jihad movement that attacked Western targets.[75]

Meanwhile, a considerable number of second-generation Islamic activists engaged in a critical and productive dialogue with democratic concepts and practices. Generations of activists who had spent their youth working for Islamist promises of social justice and religious order in the 1970s and 1980s experienced disillusionment when those promises remained unfulfilled in the 1990s. Some of these Muslim activists realized that the "Islamic solution" actually was not free from the social and political malaise associated with the authoritarian regimes of the Muslim world. Correspondingly, they increasingly came to a perceptive analysis of how the ideal of an Islamic state was not immune to the problems of repression, corruption, nepotism, economic inefficiency and waste, and intellectual and cultural stagnation. They argued that the concepts of human rights, rule of law, and political participation were already deeply rooted in the Islamic canon and traditions. They increasingly recognized the importance of making rulers institutionally accountable; curbing the arbitrary power of the state; respecting basic freedoms of expression, faith, and assembly; and promoting free electoral competition for achieving a better society. Partially as a result of their suffering and humiliation at the hands of state authorities, these Muslim politicians became advocates of the right to dissent.[76] Most importantly, they challenged radicals for being revisionists and not representing the *authentic* face of Islam.[77]

Public support for Islamic political organizations mostly came from urban peripheries and not from the least backward regions, as modernization theory would argue.[78] Islamic movements or parties articulated the grievances of the working poor and lower-middle classes in an accessible and local language, successfully exploited the discontent with the political status quo, and provided extensive social services.[79] They formed effective and resilient alliances between the pious middle class and the urban poor.[80] The notion of moral community, in which the faithful are mutually responsible to and for each other, was instrumental in preserving this alliance.[81] Activists articulate hybrid, flexible, and often ambiguous understandings of Islam that appeal to multiple audiences rather than simply revitalize an already existing Islamic culture or espouse a coherent Islamic ideology.[82] The leadership cadres often come from the socially and politically marginalized, educated middle class in pursuit of social status and recognition.[83] These individuals are not ideologically committed and would be satisfied if they gained effective political representation. They often became the moderate face of political Islam and outmaneuvered more radical Islamist forces. Being products of the public university system and having professional careers, including law, journalism, and administration, they emerged as the leading voices of a nonviolent political Islamic vision.[84]

Muslim Reformers

In Turkey, the Justice and Development Party established by a group of ex-Islamists won the 2002 parliamentary elections and inaugurated one of the most persistent political and economic reform periods of modern Turkish history. In Iran, the Reform Front led by ex-leftist Islamists dramatically altered the political landscape in the late 1990s and early part of the twenty-first century before being repressed by the guardians of the Islamic regime. In Egypt, a group of younger members of the Muslim Brotherhood expressed their open displeasure with the leadership and left the Brotherhood to form an independent political party (the Wasat Party) in 1996. They were committed to electoral competition as the only legitimate means of acquiring and staying in political power and embraced political pluralism and moderation as their guiding principles. While avoiding both cultural defeatism and the uncritical nativism that glorify a particular interpretation of Islamic culture, they struggled to define Islam as a force that had the ability to speak in persuasive terms to a broad audience in an increasingly globalized world.[85] In Indonesia, Muslim reformers such as Abdurrahman Wahid (b. 1940) and Amien Rais (b. 1944) played pivotal roles in bringing about the end of Suharto's oppressive rule in 1998 and subsequently in the emergence of an electoral democracy.[86] Followers of "Civil Islam"—to borrow a term used by Hefner to describe the dominant Muslim view on politics in Indonesia[87]—resisted the last attempts of Suharto to play on Muslim sensibilities by igniting ethnoreligious hatred toward the non-Muslim minorities of Indonesia and shunned the radical Islamists. In the parliamentary elections of 1999, following the collapse of the authoritarian regime, reformist groups, including Muslim parties who fought for democracy, captured around 60 percent of the vote. They have remained key actors for democratic consolidation in Indonesia. In Tunisia, Rashid al-Ghannushi (b. 1941) has emerged as an opposition leader who articulates an Islamic understanding of democratic values and procedures. While being critical of Western liberalism, he perceives free electoral contest and fundamental freedoms as the only viable mechanisms for resisting despotism.[88]

The rise of Muslim reformers offers a more complex picture of politics in the Muslim world and depicts richer possibilities than either authoritarian secularism or Islamic radicalism.[89] Muslim reformers perceive elections as the only source of legitimate political power that also prevents its corruption.[90] They view democracy as a set of institutions and a value system independent of Western lifestyles and morals. They often justify their support for democracy in reference to traditional Islamic or national sources. From a Muslim reformist view, religious mobilization is a mixed blessing, since the politicization of Islamic identity may lead to the corruption of Islamic beliefs and bring repression. In most cases, they make attempts to appeal to constituencies who do not share the pious lifestyle of their core supporters. This strategy of broadening their appeal often takes place under the dynamics of electoral competition.

Muslim reformers' political view involves pragmatism, flexibility, and accommodation and departs from the neofundamentalist vision of reducing political problems to a lack of morals.[91] It is true that sharia, with the exception of the JDP of Turkey, most often occupies a central place in the political platforms of Muslim reformers. They are usually in favor of the implementation of sharia in civic and family affairs. Even the JDP, which rarely makes references to sharia, tried to criminalize adultery in September 2004 but without success. However, it should not be assumed that preference for sharia necessarily stems from a belief in the supremacy of God-given laws over parliamentary legislation. As argued above, revival of sharia was central to Islamic reformism in modern times. What is crucial is whether interpretation and application of sharia contradict fundamental individual rights. In particular, sharia-inspired laws may jeopardize or further marginalize the social and civic rights of vulnerable groups such as women and non-Muslim minorities. Muslim reformist positions usually remain ambiguous and unclear regarding this issue.

CHAPTER 4

Muslim Reformism

Engagement with

Secularism and

Liberal Democracy

Muslim reformism has its origins in the nineteenth century when superior Western firepower and technological advances began to achieve dominance over Muslim societies. The reformist response involved a comprehensive attempt to identify the causes of Western dominance and Muslim weakness. It sought to reestablish the relevance of Islamic identity in a rapidly transforming and modernizing world. The current trend of Muslim democracy may be conceptualized as representing a high point in this reformist lineage that encourages a self-critical yet confident perspective and a systematic engagement with Western achievements such as political pluralism and human rights. The appeal of Muslim reformism in countries such as Indonesia, Iran, and Turkey indicates that the lasting importance of Islam does not necessarily signify a negation of secularism understood as neutrality of religion. Besides, many Muslim politicians and intellectuals refuse to endorse authoritarian versions of Islamic political identities on the basis of their Islamic identity and readings.

This chapter starts with a conceptual and historical discussion of secularism and a comparative narrative of Western and Muslim experiences of secularism. A central contention is that Islamic political movements of the twentieth century were defensive efforts in an increasingly secularized sociopolitical environment. The Islamic revival of the twentieth century was not necessarily a stubborn resistance to modernity and secular trends. Rather, it represented Muslim believers' attempts to reinvent their religion as a force capable of guiding action and defining political vision in the age of secularism. These endeavors were heterogeneous and gave rise to thinkers and organizations that competed with each other to be the authentic representative of Muslim belief. They had various forms, ranging from clandestine cells with violent goals to intellectual outlets preaching the message of religious and political pluralism.

The chapter then provides an analytical discussion of Muslim reformism in Iran and Turkey with regard to their democratic commitments. An uncritical acceptance of the term "Muslim democrats" is misleading and obscures the fluid and constantly evolving nature of the Muslim political identity. While Muslim reformism clearly represents a rupture with the premises of the Islamist ideology, it is not yet at ease with all the premises of liberal democracy. In particular, Muslim reformism, like Christian political groups in the United States, seems to have a dismissive sense of the threats of *religious conformism* to social pluralism and individual liberties. Despite its decisive turn toward popular rule, political pluralism, and human rights, Muslim reformism in Iran and Turkey is still characterized by ambiguity and confusion on issues that are crucial for protection of basic rights. Important indicators show that Muslim reformists may discriminate against, or at least fail to offer full protection to, groups such as non-Muslims or nonpious Muslims, and that they have a shallow sense of democratic participation and the linkage between transparency and good governance. This does not necessarily mean that Muslim reformers are singularly defective in this regard, since many political groups in Western democracies have similar issues. Additionally, Iranian and Turkish Muslim reformers are products of specific historical and cultural conditions and constantly evolve as prevailing political conditions change and new leadership cadres emerge. Their evolution is not a deterministic process.

Muslim Political Experience in the Age of Secularism

The meaning of secularism continues to be highly contested and is subject to a variety of competing interpretations. Regardless of which definition of secularism is employed, many informed observers would argue that Muslim societies are far from being secularized. The available survey data show that Islam continues to be essential to the self-identification and moral imagination of hundreds of millions of people. Social and political movements with Islamic orientation and goals have been very active and often enjoy mass support. Issues related to public expressions of Muslim identity are central to political debates in societies with Muslim majorities and sizable minorities. At the same time, the intellectual trajectory of Muslim reformism cannot be fully grasped without an understanding of how global diffusion of secular practices affects Islam. In fact, Muslim reformism can be defined as an ongoing process that aims to redefine and reinvent Islamic belief in "the age of secularism." In its most contemporary versions, it aims to come to terms with this secular condition rather than to deny or eliminate its existence.

The Canadian philosopher Charles Taylor offers an innovative and sophisticated conceptualization of secularism in a recent and important book.[1] He suggests that secularism can be thought of as three distinct processes: (1) the retreat of religion from public space; (2) the decline in religious beliefs, commitments, and participation; and (3) the emergence of a social imagination in which belief in God is no longer taken for granted and only remains one option among many. He defends the idea that secularization does not necessarily imply the privatization of religion or the decline of religious commitments.[2]

Taylor convincingly refutes the "subtraction theories" that describe secularism as the end of a religious yoke on human nature and rationality.[3] He argues that the third process remains the core aspect of secularism in the contemporary age. He observes that belief in God is no longer the default position and has ceased to be axiomatic in Western societies. The gist of his historical and philosophical discussion of secularism involves the widespread acceptance of an immanent sort of human flourishing that categorically rejects a higher sense of time and existence. His ambition is to examine how an exclusive humanism that accepts no higher beings becomes a "live option for large numbers of people." In the secular age, a purely self-sufficient humanism that involves no final goals beyond human flourishing (i.e., transcending visions) becomes a widely available option.[4]

A crucial aspect of Taylor's narrative is his conceptualization of secularism as a new and unprecedented form of human experience that followed the religious reform movements of early modern Europe. In his view, the advent of the modern age, which entailed great changes such as urbanization, industrialization, class differentiation, and the rise of a scientific worldview, not only destabilized religious belief and practice but also generated new religious forms.[5] The process of disenchantment, through which magic and supranatural expectations were detached from religious belief, is central to his conceptualization of secularism.[6] In this sense, he does not conceive the process of secularization as a linear decline of religion but as a process characterized by increasing fragmentation and pluralism of human experience, which generate alternative forms of belief and unbelief. For instance, the emergence and spread of new forms of religiosity that reinforced belief in God and involved voluntary solidarity societies followed the rise of the Enlightenment. Taylor labels this period, which lasted approximately from 1800 to 1960, as the Age of Mobilization.

Secularism understood as the decline of religious belief and practices has been a limited development in most Muslim societies, with the exception of countries that were under Communist rule during the twentieth century, such as Albania and Azerbaijan. Citizens in Muslim societies tend to have a resilient belief in God and strong religious identifications, describe themselves as being pious, and report frequent attendance at mosques (at least among males).[7] Few individuals profess complete disbelief, or at least, prevailing social norms discourage individuals from openly denouncing belief. Nor has the second understanding of secularism, the privatization of religion, been very helpful for making sense of contemporary Muslim societies either, because secularization understood as the decline or privatization of religion has not really occurred in Muslim countries.[8] Muslim identities struggle for greater public representation and visibility even in regimes such as Tunisia and Turkey that marginalize Islam's role in public rituals, symbols, and discourse. Popular Islamic symbols and practices, such as veiling, gender segregation, and no-interest banking, demand public legitimacy and recognition. Furthermore, the sense of sharing a common faith has been essential to the collective capacity of Muslims. Islamic nongovernmental organizations, social movements, and brotherhoods have increasingly been developing new forms of social services, redefining acceptable boundaries of political action, and regenerating religious patterns. By all accounts, Islam remains a very *public religion*.[9]

Taylor explicitly notes that his account of secularism is based on the historical trajectory of the Western civilization "whose principal roots lie in what used to be called 'Latin Christendom.'"[10] Furthermore, he maintains that the secular condition defined as the impossibility of a naïve acknowledgement of the transcendent, is largely absent in Muslim societies.[11] While the United States may be as religious as most Muslim societies in terms of religious belief and attendance, the former clearly belongs to the secular age in which unbelief becomes very plausible.[12] One tends to disagree with Taylor, given the interconnectedness of the human experience since the early twentieth century. From the cartoons of Prophet Muhammad published by a Danish newspaper

A religious procession visiting the Shrine of Fatima Maʿsuma (Qom, March 2008)

in September 2005 to the increasing presence of Muslims in Western societies, Muslim experience is no longer that separable from the reach of secularism. Traditional Muslim beliefs can no longer be assumed to be the only viable alternative that would ultimately prevail over other faiths or unfaiths. Heresy, blasphemy, and even apostasy have increasingly become more common and open than ever. Geographical, technological, and political boundaries that insulated an overwhelming majority of Muslims from Western trends have become increasingly porous. The traditional distinction between *dar-al Islam* (the land of Islam) and *dar-al harp* (the land of war) is no longer sustainable. Muslim societies are deeply enmeshed in global technological, cultural, political, and economic webs. The condition of secularism as the irreversible pluralism of religious and nonreligious experience deeply affects Muslims. Muslims are now required to express and explain their faith to diverse, questioning, and skeptical audiences as never before. In fact, the predominance of the secular condition à la Taylor in the West has had great repercussions for Muslim self-perceptions and engagement with modernity.

A complete account of the historical process of how secularism generated by Western civilization made inroads into Muslim societies and elicited responses is beyond the purposes of this discussion. Muslim societies have been extremely diverse and home to a great variety of political regimes and socio-religious practices. It is still possible to identify three patterns that characterize Muslim encounters with secularism: (1) Western imperialism and technological superiority; (2) state-imposed modernization; and (3) the proliferation of lifestyles, social practices, and intellectual trends that deviate, or are perceived to deviate, from Islamic norms. These three encounters define the dynamics of Muslim reform and the promises and limits of Muslim democracy.

In the Muslim world, the initial rise of nonreligious and areligious ethics, norms, and regulations usually followed confrontations with the West and subsequent defeats. The global reach of secularism achieved by Western expansionism and imperialism generated a deep crisis in Muslim societies. Western secularism, as perceived by Muslims, represented an ideological outlook of supreme self-confidence. It carried the mantle of scientific truth and technological superiority that dismissed alternative civilizational perspectives as being inferior.[13] Consequently, Muslim believers have had to come to terms with the technological and scientific superiority of the Western world at least since the nineteenth century.[14] A typical response, which rapidly became popular among political and intellectual elites, was the rejection of "tradition" in favor of Western norms, practices, and institutions. The adoption of Western methods started as defensive measures in the realm of the military and quickly spread to other fields such as education, administration, law, literature, and art. The rise of the nation-states and the modernizing elites who were convinced of the superiority and desirability of the Western norms in the first half of the twentieth century meant that secularism was mostly a state-dictated process in Muslim societies. The modernizing elites imposed secular visions that often failed to evoke popular enthusiasm and imagination.[15] Their secular visions did not involve freedom of belief but rather freedom *from* religious forms that were conceived to beget dogmatism, backwardness, despotism, and superstitions. Islam, in its traditional forms, had no role in inspiring and informing public action. The reform of Islam meant its *privatization* and becoming a matter of personal conscience. The modernizing elites were also fearful of challenges to their rule by religious hierarchies and leaders who could mobilize masses on the basis of sacred Muslim values and sensibilities. They aimed to concentrate power in their own hands while emasculating autonomous religious entities. They reasoned that their survival hinged on the effective neutralization of Islam's influence on sociopolitical life.

The modernizing elites had different degrees of success in imposing their vision. The paradigmatic case was that of Turkey, where war hero Mustafa Kemal Atatürk minimized the political role of Islam, destroyed its autonomy, and heavily regulated public expressions of the religion. A man who was either irreligious or did not wear his faith on his sleeve, Atatürk established a cult of personality that has survived until now. He did not bother to attend the Friday prayers, a symbol of ruler-people unity, and did not seek any religious legitimacy after consolidating his rule. The pace and scope of political change that affected the population under his rule was unprecedented in the modern history of Muslim societies. The Pahlavi regime (1925–1979) in Iran followed a similar policy but ultimately collapsed as a result of a mass rebellion led by the religious opposition. Nonetheless, a lasting legacy of the state-imposed modernization was the formation of social classes, mostly but not exclusively the urban middle class that pursued secular lifestyles. These classes were most established in countries ruled by ambitiously modernizing regimes for extended periods of time, such as Iran, Tunisia, and Turkey. The resulting societal pluralism was unprecedented and challenged the centuries-long dominating role of Islam in the public sphere in Muslim-majority countries. Practices that hurt traditional Muslim sensibilities, such as mixed-gender gatherings, liberal changes in public dress code, consumption of alcohol in the public sphere, and open denouncement of sharia as an archaic set of rules, became widespread. Cultural preferences and lifestyles have been extensively politicized in these societies. Consequently, secularism defined as the marginalization of religion's public role was no longer an externally or state-imposed force but became a societal force that was internalized by a considerable number of nominal or pious Muslims.

Secularism associated with Western dominance over Muslim societies has led to a crisis in Muslim self-perceptions and some soul-searching since the mid-nineteenth century. Islam as a set of beliefs and regulations was under threat. It could no longer automatically be taken as *the* superior mode of life that enabled stability and order. It had to be redefined, rearticulated, and defended in an increasingly interconnected and globalized world. Muslim responses to these three waves of secularism exhibited considerable temporal and spatial variance. Furthermore, Muslim reformist intellectuals and movements that were critical of the traditional forms of Islam offered competing visions, ranging from calls for a return to a purified Islam[16] to reinterpretations that argued for the compatibility of Islam with modern science and practices.[17] In any case, secularism, regardless of how it was conceptualized, did not find fertile soil in Muslim reformist thought. It was often associated with political suppression of Islam or the proliferation of societal practices that were not compatible with Muslim sensibilities. For Muslim political thinkers, secularism was closely associated with the attempts of elitist modernizers to transform society in an authoritarian way.[18]

Islamism as a political ideology was a relative latecomer that reached its prime with the Iranian Revolution of 1979. Several general reflections are necessary to develop a better understanding of the relationship between Islamism and Muslim reformism in the last decade of the twentieth century. First, Islamism was primarily an intellectual and organized response to the actual or perceived threats posed to the Muslim way of life by the ascendancy of modernist, secularist, and leftist ideologies. In particular, religious intellectuals and scholars were concerned with the growing appeal of Marxism and its variants among the young and active segments of the society in the 1950s and 1960s. They were aware that traditional forms of Islamic education and organizations were incapable of mobilizing masses on the basis of religious commitments against the onslaught of what they perceived as Godless ideologies. Thus, it is not surprising that Islamists often imitated Marxist strategies (i.e., forming vanguard organizations à la Lenin) and regularly engaged with Marxist literature. Nor was it uncommon for Marxists to convert to Islamism.[19] The anxiety to contain and eradicate leftist forces was a common experience for Islamist activists in settings as diverse as Egypt, Indonesia, Iran, Iraq, Lebanon, Syria, and Turkey. In an international system characterized by ideological and geopolitical competition between the West and the East, Islamism waged a zero-sum game against leftist influences and often found alliances in conservative and status quo forces whose primary enemy was "Communism."

Second, Islamist movements of the twentieth century usually had hegemonic ambitions and aspired to regulate all aspects of social affairs and political governance according to a set of *idealized* religious norms. The capture of the state and the reorganization of the society according to some preset Islamic criteria were their driving goals. The state enforcement of the Islamic principle of commanding right and forbidding wrong (*amr bil ma'ruf wa-nahy an al-munkar*) was central to the Islamist mission.[20] These holistic understandings of Islam left little space for individual autonomy and despised the notion of freedom of religion. They had a difficult time coming to terms with the notion of secular spheres where religious regulations and institutions would be irrelevant.

Finally, the Islamists had a complex and often conflict-ridden relationship with the Islamic scholars.[21] The Islamist aspiration of establishing an encompassing Islamic state made the scholars uneasy for three reasons. First, the scholars cherished the autonomy that sustained their authority, and they feared that an Islamic state would completely erode their independence. "The possibilities that the ʿulama see in the state as the instrument of Islamization, then, are often counterbalanced by the dangers that it represents to a religious tradition that the ʿulama seek to maintain as relatively independent."[22] Next, the Islamists threatened the privileged position of the scholars as the custodians of the tradition and interpreters of the canonical sources of Islam. For the Islamists, "One does not *necessarily* need that tradition to understand the 'true' meaning of Islam, and one certainly does not need the ʿulama to interpret Islam to the ordinary believers. That authority belongs to everyone and to no one in particular."[23] The codification of sharia would have many pitfalls and be dramatically different from historically evolving understandings of sharia as a specialized *process* associated with legal and educational institutions.[24] Third, scholars, especially the ones who espoused a measured distance from direct political activism, were worried that the politicization of Islam would bring the corruption of faith. For all of these reasons, scholars entered into tactical alliances with the rulers who offered them extensive patronage and increased the scope of their authority in educational, legal, and societal affairs. Ironically, "This has enabled the ʿulama not only to challenge the Islamists on behalf of the state, but also to challenge the state itself on behalf of Islamism."[25]

Muslim Reformers and Secularism

Muslim reformism represented a rupture from Islamism with regard to the conceptualization of the political sphere and the notion of the Islamic state.[26] While Muslim reformers politically articulate demands inspired by their faith and religious lifestyles, they comply with democratic manners and justify their demands in references to common values and the public good.[27] They do not claim that their version of Islam is the only true version and that all other political discourses are blasphemous. The collapse of the Soviet Union and the end of the Cold War generated new political spaces and opportunities that had previously not been available. Marxism and its variants ceased to be competitive ideological forces in most parts of the Muslim world. Moreover, the failure of authoritarian states in delivering performance in the Middle East discredited the modernist platforms. At the same time, democracy, defined as a set of institutions including elections, achieved a global status of ascendancy. The Islamist participation in elections became a defining element in political struggles in countries such as Algeria, Jordan, Lebanon, and Turkey in the early 1990s. Regardless of the ultimate consequences, electoral participation made Islamists familiar with the pluralistic nature of politics and exposed them to the practical challenges of mobilizing public support. Next, voices criticizing the notion of the Islamic state have been more vocal and significant. From a reformist point of view that is often shared by traditionally oriented scholars, the establishment of the Islamic state is likely to erode the true spirit of religion. Muslim reformist reaction to the Islamic state has produced leading thinkers in a very unexpected place, in an Iran ruled by the Islamists since 1979.[28] It is worth quoting Mohsen Kadivar, who became one of the most articulate and outspoken critics of the Islamic state:

> When a religious government adopts a totalitarian or dictatorial attitude, the private sphere sustains even more damage than in nonreligious environments since the totalitarian leaders are worldly gods literally creating hell for their citizens, but religious governments do the same in the name of a divine paradise. . . . Determination of exigency (*maslahat*) must not be the prerogative of the state for it would mean that religion has become a handmaiden of political power . . . centralizing power in a fallible individual . . . beget corruption and will have the end result of obliterating religious principles. . . . Deceit, duplicity, and maintaining appearances are only some of the pitfalls of imposed religiosity.[29]

This is an explicit refusal of Khomeini's *velayat-e faqih* and his argument that state interests (*maslehat*) are more important than sharia itself. This denunciation of the Islamic state from a Muslim point of view is crucial, for it develops an internal critique of the core principle of the Islamist mission. The state should not impose Islamic norms and practice because that would undermine the principle of freedom that is central to Islam. A recent work by the Sudanese Muslim thinker Abdullahi Ahmed An-Na'im takes this argument further and asserts that secularism, defined as religious neutrality of the state, is "a necessary condition for Muslims to comply with their religious obligations."[30] The gist of his argument is that "the secular state is more consistent with the inherent nature of *sharia* and the history of Islamic societies."[31] In his view, the state is a political institution by definition and therefore cannot be Islamic.[32] Given the fact that sharia principles represent a diverse body and are subject to competing interpretations, the enactment and enforcement of Islam by the state inevitably represents "the political will of the ruling elite, not the normative system of Islam as such. Yet such policies and legislation are difficult to resist or even debate when presented as the will of God."[33] In fact, he argues that the Islamic state is a postcolonial innovation that promotes a "European, positivistic view of law and totalitarian model of the state that seeks to transform society into its own image."[34] This is not acceptable from an Islamic point of view because religious belief needs a free space and a process of contestation and reformation to remain vibrant. He calls for a secular state that is religiously neutral but simultaneously "includes a public role for religion in influencing public policy and legislation, subject to the requirement of civic reason."[35] This means that religiously inspired and informed policy proposals are acceptable as long as they are presented on nonreligious grounds (not as immutable religious truths) and respect basic human rights. Tariq Ramadan, a prominent Muslim intellectual residing in Europe, espouses a similar view. He argues that secularism means a neutral public space in which faiths and unfaiths can coexist peacefully.[36] Such a position is compatible with certain versions of Western liberalism.[37]

It can be argued that Muslim reformism in the twenty-first century takes a clear and unambiguous intellectual and political position against the Islamic state.[38] This position, which is justified with reference to both Islamic sources and faith and universal values, has the potential of convincing large segments of the Muslim public that the Islamic state does not represent their authentic self and is not in their best interests. The RF in Iran and the JDP in Turkey were the manifestations of this position. The ideological orientation of the RF had several characteristics that set it apart from ideological trends that had been dominant in Iran throughout the second half of the twentieth century.

Ali Mirsepassi identifies the three phases of Iranian political thought as (1) an uncritical embracing of Western practices and norms, (2) a leftist modernist approach critical of both Islam and dominating aspects of the West such as imperialism and capitalism, and (3) an Islamist discourse of authenticity.[39] The discourse of authenticity that reached its zenith during the revolution of 1979 defined politics as a constant struggle between the forces of good and evil and made nonnegotiable truth claims.[40] Thinkers such as Jalal Al-e Ahmad, Murtaza Mutahhari, and Ali Shariati, who dominated the Iranian intellectual scene before the Islamic Republic, exemplified this posture. Mehrzad Boroujerdi labels their political thought as nativist, which implied a call for "the resurgence, reinstatement, or continuance of native or indigenous cultural customs, beliefs, and values." It resisted "acculturation," privileged "one's own authentic" ethnic identity, and longed for a return to "an unsullied indigenous cultural tradition."[41] It assumed irreducible ontological differences between the West and the East. While critical of Orientalism, it uncritically reproduced Orientalist assumptions and shared its epistemological axioms in inverse manners.[42] In a sense, Orientalism and nativism were enemies in the mirror. Consequently, nativism was incapable of coming to terms with globalization, pluralism, and democratic governance that entails competition.[43] The intellectual legacy characterizing the RF and articulated by figures such as Hasan Yousefi Eshkevari, Mohsen Kadivar, Mostafa Malekian, Mojtahed Shabestari, and Abdolkarim Soroush overcame this nativist stance and adopted a more self-critical approach toward Iranian and Islamic identity. These intellectuals and clerics questioned the categorical demeaning of the West and shallow glorification of Iran and Islam. They were instrumental in popularizing democratic and even liberal interpretations of Islam among Iranian citizens and were catalysts of political change. For instance, Mohammad Khatami's calls for "dialogue of civilizations" represented a sincere attempt to open up a channel of cross-cultural discussion and understanding.[44] Regardless of its shortcomings and unfeasibility, given the intensity of geopolitical competition in the Middle East, Khatami's position was dramatically different from the xenophobic and ever-distrustful Islamist perception of world politics. Furthermore, the RF developed an intellectually sound critique of the Islamic state. From the RF's perspective, the state enforcement of Islam was at best ineffective and at worst counterproductive. In the words of Kadivar:

Religion in Iran has two very different faces: public and authentic. There is a huge difference between the two at the moment. In public, people act religiously. Yet many people, especially the younger generation, are now turning against the religion because of their anger with the government. Being against the government makes people be against the religion . . . I think freedom of religion will promote voluntary and authentic religiosity.[45]

The religious patterns of the generation that did not experience the monarchical rule demonstrated considerable deviation from the religiosity promoted by the Islamic Republic. Attitudes toward religion among this generation involved unexpected positions, such as rejection of any religious legitimacy for political action and a complete rejection of religion itself for being irrelevant to modern life.[46]

In a similar vein, the JDP promoted a moderate and engaging understanding of Islam that was accommodative and tolerant of differences. Necmettin Erbakan's National Order movement, which preceded the JDP, promoted an uncompromising political vision that claimed superiority over all other

[handwritten margin note: It probably demonstrates climate for JDP allowed for JDP success]

A group of young males dropping pieces of paper with their demands written on them into a well. The popular belief is that the Mahdi will respond to these demands. (Jamkaran Mosque, March 2008)

political platforms. This vision was based on a binary division of the world into enemies and friends that left little room for pluralism and free political competition. The JDP leadership explicitly rejected the notion of the Islamic state and the binary distinctions that were associated with Erbakan's political stance. The JDP perceived Islam as a source of an ethical code and moral obligations that directed individual behavior and provided social cohesion. It made no explicit references to Islam as a legal code that had to be implemented in social affairs. Religious reform had also gained speed under the JDP government. The party actively promoted reformist interpretations of the Islamic canon, and conceptualized religious faith as a free choice.[47] The party's approach had a lot in common with the platforms espoused by the Fethullah Gülen community since the late 1990s. While the Gülen community and the JDP did not have any organic linkages, many members of the community took leadership positions (i.e., ministerial positions, seats in the parliament) within the party. Fethullah Gülen (b. 1941), who was an ethnic Turk from the eastern province of Erzurum, formed an effective network of disciples who became very active in education, welfare provision, state bureaucracy, business, and NGOs by the late 1980s.[48] The community established around five hundred schools in more than ninety countries around the world. Its activities became visible also in the United States, especially in the aftermath of the September 11 attacks. The community denounced terrorism committed in the name of Islam, actively sponsored interfaith dialogue—an obvious similarity with Mohammad Khatami's "dialogue of civilizations"—and engaged with representatives of non-Muslim religions. It actively supported the JDP government in Turkey. For both entities, the supremacy of national will and consolidation of multiparty competition unfettered by external interference (i.e., guardians regulating political sphere) were the ultimate goals. They adopted a discourse on rights and limits on arbitrary state authority and opposed the ban on the headscarf not on the basis of religious truths but with references to civic reason and individual rights.[49] They argued that young women should not be deprived of their right to education. Furthermore, the JDP's pro-EU stance that aimed to diminish the power of the guardians in Turkey was in line with the community's preferences. Both the JDP and the Gülen community espoused a public understanding of Islam that entailed conspicuous religious symbols and religiously inspired policy platforms. Not surprisingly, the "moderate" Islam represented by the JDP and the Gülen community were "the best partners to help the United States foster an enlightened form of Islam" in the post–September 11 era.[50] Notwithstanding their espousal of Muslim reformism, authoritarian practices characterized both the party's and the community's internal affairs. The community had a hierarchical internal structure that promoted strict gender segregation and subordination of women, and stifled dissent and individual autonomy.[51] This caveat aside, Muslim reformers in Turkey were successful in developing discourses that were compatible with democratic aspirations, human rights, and political pluralism.

It would be difficult to reach a similar conclusion regarding Muslim reformers' engagement with the global reach of secularism defined by Taylor as the inevitable questioning of religious faith and the permanency of the condition of disbelief. Muslim reformers perceive Islam as more than just a belief system; Islam provides a normative guide that informs their social behavior and understanding of the common good. While Muslim reformers unambiguously reject the idea of the Islamic state, their views on individual choice and freedom of expression in Muslim societies are much more ambivalent and problematic from a liberal point of view. The key question is, how do Muslim reformists in Iran and Turkey conceptualize the scope of societal and religious pressures on individuals? In other words, do Muslim reformists perceive *religious conformism* as a force that should be checked and contained or a natural aspect of Muslim societies?[52]

Religious conformism entails norms and practices that regulate the public and occasionally the private sphere, according to some preconceived Islamic rules, and that are morally or physically enforced by the society (not the state). It does not mean that Islam, by its very nature, is a *fundamentalist religion* that envisions a holistic understanding of religion according to which believers are required to obey the laws of the religion in all aspects of their life.[53] Furthermore, religious conformism is not a problem peculiar to Muslim majority societies. Powerful Christian groups in the United States and secularist majorities in Western democracies and elsewhere also exercise social control inimical to individual choice. The crucial issue is the predominant popular understanding and practice of religion, whether or not it involves a notion of a transcendent world, rather than the content of religion per se. The examples of religious conformism would include intolerance of individuals who openly express their unfaith and are critical of certain Islamic practices, individuals who do not fast during the holy month of Ramadan or for Friday prayers, individuals who sell or consume alcohol, individuals who violate gender segregation, women who are perceived not to dress "properly," couples who are perceived not to behave "properly," homosexuals and lesbians who are perceived not to "fit" a Muslim society, and anybody who is perceived to hurt Muslim "sensibilities." These individuals are very vulnerable to the intimidations of the religious majority, as they do not share the priorities of the majority and disagree with conventional interpretations of the religion. From a liberal perspective, individuals who fall under these categories should be given equal rights, respect, and freedom in Muslim societies as long as they do not threaten the rights of others. After all, "some of the most persistent threats of tyranny over individuals—sometimes over members of the group and other times over nonmembers—have come from groups entrusted with both spiritual and political authority."[54] The establishment of democratic rule in Muslim-majority countries does not necessarily guarantee the rights of dissidents, women, and religious minorities.[55] The tyranny of the religious majority is a particularly acute concern in an era when mobilization on the basis of religious, sectarian, and ethnic identities threatens the social fabric of many countries, such as Iraq, Lebanon, and Pakistan. For the sustainability of liberal democracy, organized religious groups or communities should not wield the equivalent of political power over their members and society at large.[56] This means that a form of secularism that assigns the state a passive role vis-à-vis the society may not be sufficient to ensure freedom of belief and freedom *from* religion in Muslim-majority societies.[57] In the absence of strong institutional and legal protections, freedom *of* religion may threaten freedom *from* religion and independent thought. In this sense, democratic rule may undermine basic premises of liberalism. While respecting the public expressions of religious belief and display of religious symbols, a state based on liberal constitutionalism and pluralistic civil society should assertively ensure that individuals who deviate from the societal norms do not remain vulnerable to religious conformism and intimidation.

Muslim reformism has not yet fully come to terms with the pluralism inherent in societal life in the early twenty-first century. In this regard, the ideas of the progressive Iranian cleric Mohsen Kadivar are instructive. Kadivar argues that Islamic jurisprudence "fully acknowledges the sanctity of the private domain."[58] A sin committed in private is not a concern for the state. Even so, there are certain rules that should be observed by Muslims in the public sphere according to sharia. The principle of commanding good and forbidding wrong is repeatedly emphasized in the Qur'an, and Islamic canonical texts imply that "Sharia does not tolerate individuals who do not respect Islamic rules in the public sphere."[59] In a society based on sharia, committing a sin in public is a crime that must be punished. According to Kadivar, Muslims should express their disapproval of individuals who behave "improperly" in public. There are several steps that include vocal objection and physical action. "The third phase, meaning physical objection, is considered the religious preroga-tive of the government . . . and in the absence of a religious government, it is apparently everyone's religious duty."[60] While Kadivar thoroughly respects freedom of opinion and religion, such a position can easily lead to public vigi-lantism that stifles individuality, suppresses any action considered heresy, and results in the imposition of a certain understanding of religiosity over society. This is a major danger to individual rights, especially in Muslim societies where traditional or radical interpretations of Islamic canon have been influ-ential or predominant. In fact, Sudanese Muslim reformer An-Na'im is aware of this Tocquevillian danger of society over individual. He notes that there are several realms where sharia and human rights seem to be incompatible: "Con-flicts between Shari'a and human rights include issues of the rights of women and non-Muslims . . . [and] the third main area of conflict [is], namely, the freedom of religion and belief."[61] He argues that as the Qur'an neither defined nor imposed punishment for charges of apostasy, blasphemy, or heresy, sharia should reconsider these notions in terms of the freedom of religious belief. He optimistically calls for reinterpretation of sharia in realms of gender rela-tions, non-Muslims, and violently aggressive jihad.[62] The obvious problem is that liberal interpretations of sharia are not necessarily the default positions in many Muslim societies. Many contemporary interpretations of Islam have hegemonic tendencies.

While the JDP's approach to individual liberty in a Muslim-majority so-ciety tended to be more liberal and accommodative than its reformist coun-terpart in Iran, there were certain limits to the party's conceptualization of freedom of (un)belief. It was an article of faith among the core supporters of the party that the Turkish secular state establishment sided with citizens with secular lifestyles against citizens pursuing a pious lifestyle.[63] The JDP leadership agenda on rights was selective and discriminative. The party de-liberately prioritized the ban on free public expressions of Muslim piety (e.g., the ban on the headscarf in university campuses) over other rights issues such as the restrictions on Kurdish culture and language and Alevi beliefs. Instead of pushing for a complete overhaul of the illiberal 1982 Constitution, the party, in alliance with Turkish and Kurdish nationalistic parties, changed two articles of the Constitution to revoke the ban on the headscarf in February 2008. A month later, the public state prosecutor submitted an indictment to the Constitutional Court calling for the dissolution of the JDP on the grounds that it had become a focal point of antisecular activities. The self-appointed guardians of the republic decided to remove the JDP from power by undemocratic means. It was basically a decapitation strike aiming to temporarily ban the JDP leader Erdoğan from political activity and paralyze his movement. The JDP would have preempted such a strike if it had pursued a truly liberal agenda that would have ended official discrimination against all vulnerable groups, not just the young women who don the headscarf. Additionally, the party was hardly tolerant of individuals and practices that were considered improper from a Muslim point of view. In particular, the party had a very low tolerance of criticisms of religious dogmas, which were often labeled as attacks against the "sacred values" of the society. The following excerpt from a speech by Hüseyin Çelik, the former minister of education, sheds some light on his understanding of freedom *from* religion:

> Laicism [secularism] is a system in which the pious can freely practice his/her religion while the nonreligious is able to pursue a nonreligious life and is not held accountable for his/her nonreligiosity . . . If Aziz Nesin has a right to live and die nonreligiously in this country, pious people have a right to believe and practice what they believe in.[64]

The self-contradiction and bitter irony in these words is hard to miss if one remembers the life story of the great Turkish writer and satirist Aziz Nesin. Born in 1915, Nesin was one of the most perceptive and brilliant critics of the societal practices and state regulations in Turkey. Having had a strong Islamic education in his childhood, Nesin later became a self-convinced atheist. He espoused that none of the historical figures can be considered infallible and penetratingly criticized blind and uncritical religious faith. His writings since the 1940s often brought the wrath of the successive governments upon him. In July 1993, a governor of the Central Anatolian city of Sivas invited him to an annual festival honoring the famous Alevi poet Pir Sultan Abdal, who lived in the sixteenth century. Abdal's heterodox beliefs and protest platforms led to his execution by the Ottoman governor of Sivas, who belonged to the Sunni sect. Sivas continued to have a substantial Alevi population and witnessed communal clashes in the late 1970s. Nesin earlier had become the target of vituperative attacks because he had translated excerpts from Salman Rushdie's novel *The Satanic Verses* into Turkish and published them in his newspaper. His visit to the town created a big uproar, and local newspapers accused him of provoking the "sacred sentiments" of the population.[65] On Friday, July 2, a mob formed after the Friday prayers. After attacking various places in the city, the mob surrounded the hotel where Nesin and other guests were staying and set it on fire. Thirty-seven people, including thirty-three poets, intellectuals, and writers who were attending the festival, were killed. Nesin somehow managed to survive the inferno. Subsequent investigations revealed that the disaster could have been avoided if the security forces had been properly and effectively deployed. Three days later, an armed group stormed a Sunni village east of Sivas and massacred thirty-three villagers. The attack was officially blamed on the insurgent PKK, the Kurdish Workers Party, but the assailants and motives of the attack remain unidentified.

The burned hotel was later restored and was still in use in early 2009. The JDP government refused the proposals that the hotel should be closed down, declared it a memorial, and transformed it into a museum.[66] Nesin died from natural causes in July 1995. In accordance with his will, his remains were buried without a ceremony in the garden of the Nesin Foundation, which supports poor and orphaned children. The minister of education was right: Nesin did indeed live and die as a nonreligious person. The minister just omitted a minor detail; Nesin narrowly escaped a very brutal death at the hands of a fanatical religious mob.

A similarly dismissive or antagonistic attitude toward impiety and unbelief was also evident in the thought of Fethullah Gülen. In an interview given to the pro-Gülen community newspaper *Zaman* in 2004, he remarked that atheism is the corruption of people's hearts and minds and emanates from ignorance. He added that an infidel (atheist) is as despicable as a murderer, according to the Qur'an and Islamic tradition.[67] He later announced that he was misunderstood and always stood for dialogue and cooperation among people from different faiths and unfaiths.[68]

These examples do not necessarily mean that Muslim reformism is incapable of coming to terms with societal pluralism as defined by Taylor. Muslim reformism has been rapidly evolving and may develop a more inclusive approach toward impiety and unbelief in the near future. It has the potential to effectively counter Islamophobia, which came into full public view in instances such as the Danish cartoons or Dutch parliamentarian Geert Wilders' *Fitna* movie, by encouraging civic engagement and protests. The existence of social classes that adopted secularism as a way of life in Muslim societies such as Iran and Turkey and the growing number of Muslims in Western societies make religious pluralism and public expressions of impiety and disbelief a perennial condition for pious Muslims. Besides, Muslim religiosity has been characterized by increasing internal differentiation and pluralism with the rise of more individualistic and secular forms of piety. Still, there is much room for critical engagement with Muslim reformism, as it does not fully accommodate pluralism in societal affairs nor protect individuality. It has not yet convincingly argued against hegemonic forms of Islam that leave little space for individualism and societal plurality. This is the central challenge for Muslim political identity in the age of global secularism.

Muslim Reformers and Democratization

A central characteristic of the third wave of democratization that took place between 1970 and 1990 was the active role played by the Catholic Church in promoting popular struggles against authoritarian regimes and withdrawing support from them.[69] During this period, Catholic-majority countries in Southern Europe, Latin America, Eastern Europe, and the Pacific embraced regimes legitimated by popular mandate and characterized by electoral competition. The two crucial stages of this remarkable transformation were the Second Vatican Council in 1962–1965 that recognized the principle of religious freedom, and the liberation theory with its emphasis on social justice that gained ground in 1968.[70] The national churches that enjoyed greater autonomy from the state, had extensive transnational ties, cultivated strong bonds with nationally organized movements, and embodied national identity were in a better position to promote democratization.[71] The churches with greater autonomy came to accommodate the basic contours of secularism defined as the emancipation of life spheres—such as economy, political rule, scientific inquiry, or legal affairs—from religious institutions and norms. The more the Catholic Church is capable of recognizing the limits of its interference, the more successful it becomes in defending civic liberties and political rights.[72]

Muslim reformers have developed strong and sustainable commitments to electoral competition, political pluralism, and limits on arbitrary state action. Hence, it is now redundant to ask whether Islam is compatible with democracy on the basis of Muslim reformist experience. Islamic political actors are not less capable than their Catholic counterparts of embracing electoral competition, political pluralism, and human rights. Notwithstanding its problematic relationship with secularism, the rise of Muslim reformism in Iran and Turkey demonstrates that democratic interpretations of Islam are gaining popularity in diverse settings characterized by significant differences in sectarian affiliation and regime type. The main challenge for Muslim reformism is not necessarily to develop readings of Islam that are compatible with democracy, political pluralism, and human rights. Muslim reformists have achieved considerable progress in these areas. But they have had a poor record in designing institutions, developing organizational capacities, and making constitutional changes that would facilitate democratization. In particular, Muslim reformers' understanding of how power relations should be managed in a democratic order remains underdeveloped and is characterized by ambiguities. Democracy can be conceptualized as a conflict-management system in which power is checked and constrained so that it does not become hegemonic and dominating.[73] Democratization involves, among other things, reducing the autonomy of unaccountable power centers.[74] The institution of free and competitive elections is a necessary but not a sufficient step in making power accountable and less hegemonic. The institutionalization of the separation of powers, the development of less hierarchical forms of social and political participation, the empowerment of civil-society actors, and the achievement of political transparency are also central to sustainable democratization. Nevertheless, Muslim reformers in Iran and Turkey have focused exclusively on the electoral aspect of democratization at the expense of other processes.

Political power remains highly concentrated and publicly unaccountable in Iran and to a lesser extent in Turkey. As delineated in previous chapters, the guardians preserve their autonomy, and Muslim reformers have been unsuccessful in minimizing their political influence. In Turkey, the counterinsurgency campaigns against the Kurdish insurgents begot a culture of impunity and sustained enclaves of authoritarianism that undermine parliamentary democracy. The assassination of a Catholic priest in the Black Sea coast city of Trabzon in February 2006, the attack against the secularist *Cumhuriyet* newspaper and the attack against the Council of State in May 2006, the assassination of the Turkish-Armenian intellectual and journalist Hrant Dink in January 2007, and the massacre of Christian missionaries in the Eastern Anatolian town of Malatya in April 2007 were all related to the clandestine and violent groups that enjoy shadowy linkages to the elements in state security forces.[75] Their goal was to foster a culture of fear and destabilize the parliamentary rule in the country. These groups and their affiliates, organized as "nongovernmental organizations," also fostered xenophobic and illiberal trends in Turkish politics. As I argue in Chapter 7, the JDP government missed a golden opportunity to end the culture of impunity and contain these forces in the Şemdinli incident in November 2005. At the same time, power distribution within the JDP remains very hierarchical and asymmetric. In fact, political power was concentrated in the hands of a single person, Prime Minister Erdoğan. He was the undisputed leader of the JDP without any mechanism of party democracy. He decided on all candidates running on the party ticket in local and parliamentary elections, and on members occupying top positions in the party. He tolerated no dissent within party ranks. He also had absolute control over the JDP's parliamentary group, which has held an absolute majority in the parliament since November 2002. This enabled him to control the legislative and executive organs of the state. Furthermore, he had the last word on who would be Speaker of Parliament and President, as the JDP majority in the parliament elected both positions. In addition, he actively cultivated pro-JDP media organs, business associations, and labor unions and attempted to increase the government's power over the judiciary. Fearful of Erdoğan's powers, the guardians hoped that the JDP would be weakened in the 2007 elections. When the party received an even stronger popular mandate and attempted to broaden the scope of its power, the guardians sought the dissolution of the JDP on the grounds that it had become a focal point of antisecular activities.

The concentration of political power at two opposing poles, in the hands of the guardians and the JDP leader, has greatly contributed to political polarization since early 2007. The guardians justified their power on the grounds of being the ultimate defenders of republican values, while the JDP leader made constant references to national will. As long as two sides opposing each other monopolized power, political struggles had the characteristics of a Gramscian "war of positions."[76] Both sides tried to undermine each other in a zero-sum struggle that entailed mutual domination.

The JDP's main challenge was not that of promoting liberal or moderate interpretations of Islam, as is often assumed. Turkish Muslim reformers had a pragmatic approach to politics with a rather shallow intellectual basis. This stood in sharp contrast to Iranian Muslim reformers, who clearly distinguished themselves from the Islamists and articulated political ideas developed by formidable and innovative intellectual figures. Nonetheless, the JDP successfully popularized an inclusive and pluralistic understanding of Islam by developing the Sufi heritage of Anatolia as a reference point. The litmus of the JDP's democratization agenda was making power accountable and dispersed, increasing the scope of rights in a comprehensive manner through institutional, administrative, and legal changes. In this regard, the JDP's records remained weak. In critical junctures such as the Şemdinli incident of November 2005 and the e-memorandum of April 2007, the party had the unwavering and full support of the Turkish liberals. The latter had a disproportionate influence over public opinion compared to their relatively small numbers. The liberals' backing of the JDP bestowed the party with considerable legitimacy at a time when the party was under fire from the guardians. The liberals saw no viable alternative other than to be the party that would energetically pursue membership in the EU and diminish the political power of the guardians. They hoped that the JDP would expand civic spaces and establish firm foundations for political liberties. Yet the JDP failed to ride this liberal momentum, which would have unraveled Turkey's entrenched guardianship, and vacillated at critical moments when it had unique opportunities to accomplish a democratic breakthrough.

One factor considerably limited the ability of Muslim reformers in Iran and Turkey to adopt more liberal platforms. The political culture in which Muslim reformers operate has not been very conducive to the rise of a self-assured liberalism. Muslim reformers in both countries were always under pressure to prove their loyalty to the ruling regimes. They were constantly faced with charges of being unpatriotic and having weak commitments to the foundational principles of the ruling regimes. In this sense, they suffered a legitimacy crisis and remained ideological pariahs even if they were in command of the government. This inevitability affected the political language they developed. They had to adopt the key aspects of the regime's discourse and appear to be like their opponents for the purposes of political survival. In Iran, the hardliners harshly accused the reformers of betraying the revolutionary tradition and deviating from Khomeini's path. In Turkey, the guardians charged the JDP with being uncommitted to the secular nature of the Turkish republic. While constantly assuring the public that they were committed to secularism, the JDP leadership developed a discourse of victimization and argued that the party represented the national will of the silent masses. This discourse represented continuity with the center-right tradition that incorporated themes of victimization at the hands of the elitist guardians.[77] The JDP was better positioned to counter the charges of the guardians than the previous center-right parties because it had reliable allies. The EU and the Turkish liberals sided with the JDP and contributed to the political legitimacy of party.

Their opponents also accused the RF and the JDP of being unpatriotic. The notion of martyrdom has been central to both Iranian and Turkish political discourse since the early 1980s. This is not because of some unchanging radical characteristics of Islam.[78] The nascent Islamic regime in Iran commanded the largest mobilization in the history of Iran when confronted with the better-armed armies of Saddam Hussein in 1980. The regime achieved that "by producing and promoting a culture of martyrdom based on the religious themes found in Shi'i Islam and in Sufism."[79] This culture was based on a binary understanding of politics as being between friends and enemies. It prioritized the sacred duty of serving the state over individual rights. It defied a culture of human rights and constantly suspected foreign conspiracies and sedition. Consequently, it did not provide a fertile ground for the proliferation of liberal arguments that promote the inviolability of human choice and dissent. The regime-sustained effort of glorifying self-sacrifice for the sake of the state and community had lastingly shaped the parameters of political platforms. As discussed in the previous chapters, Ahmedinejad claimed to represent the generation that fought in the war and suffered the worst for their country. His supporters argued that they were the real guardians and true followers of the revolutionary spirit, and they accused their opponents (e.g., reformists) of violating the basic premises of the culture of martyrdom as being central to the Islamic regime's self-perception. Coupled with the current tensions with the United States that generate a siege mentality, this attack put the reformists, many of whom actively participated in the war efforts, on the defensive.[80] The RF's success in effectively addressing "the legacy of the failure and the tragedy of the war and the culture of martyrdom that was born of it" would have great influence on the prospects for democratic change in Iran.[81]

For a long time, the Turkish Armed Forces heavily relied on conscripts to confront the threat presented by the Kurdish insurgents, a practice that resulted in heavy casualties.[82] Correspondingly, the Turkish state promoted a political culture that glorified self-sacrificing service and tolerated no alternative discourses. As in Iran, this culture was internalized by large segments of the society and restricted the number of policy positions that could be considered publicly legitimate. Politicians and public figures who questioned the integrity and consistency of the culture of martyrdom risked public ostracism and legal persecution. Even the most mainstream public figures were not immune from persecution if they contested the basic premises of the culture of martyrdom. In a recent case, a public prosecutor prepared an indictment against Turkish diva Bülent Ersoy, who expressed on a TV show that she would not send her child to serve in the military, if she had one, because young conscripts meet a meaningless end. The prosecutor argued that Ersoy deliberately alienated the public from military service and undermined the morale of the army.[83]

Not surprisingly, the JDP's Kurdish policy was heavily constrained by the parameters of the culture of martyrdom. The opposition accused the JDP of being lenient on Kurdish separatism and giving concessions to the "terrorists." The JDP leadership was also accused of having a cavalier attitude toward the sacrifices of citizens who lost their lives fighting against the PKK. On several occasions in 2007, the public booed the JDP members who were attending the funerals of the martyrs. In fall 2007, the PKK attacks that killed more than two dozens Turkish soldiers generated an overwhelming wave of nationalist resistance that increased the pressures on the JDP, which was inclined to pursue a nonmilitary solution to the Kurdish question. Thousands of citizens marched in the streets in many cities, protesting the PKK attacks. The JDP was at pains to reassure the Turkish public of its nationalistic credentials. It was unable to counter and contain the rising xenophobic discourse with a discourse of equal citizenship and human rights, as the party leadership was unwilling to take any political risks. Shortly thereafter, the JDP-controlled

Crowds protesting the PKK in an Eastern city (Elazığ, October 2007)

parliament and government authorized military strikes against suspected PKK hideouts in the Kurdistan region of Iraq. The strikes were highly unpopular among the Kurdish citizens of Turkey that formed an important segment of the JDP's constituency. Consequently, for both the RF and the JDP, the prevailing culture of martyrdom increased the political costs of their efforts to develop a sustainable and consistent liberal discourse.

CHAPTER 5

The Guardians
and Elections
in Iran and Turkey

This chapter describes the institutional and ideological basis of guardianship and the dynamics of electoral competition in Iran and Turkey. According to the conventional wisdom, the Iranian and Turkish regimes are located
on opposite ends of the relationship between the state and religion. While the
former embodies the complete fusion of religious and political authority, the
latter derives its legitimacy from nonreligious sources and severely restricts
public expression of Islam. The *faqih* (jurist, or expert in Islamic law) who
holds the supreme power in Iran is responsible for guiding the religious community during the occultation of the Twelfth Imam and acts as his deputy (Article 5 of the 1979 Constitution). Political rights are conditioned on religious
obligation, and the state enforces religious morality in public life in Iran. In
Turkey, sovereignty exclusively belongs to the Turkish nation, and religion has
no role in state affairs and politics (Preamble of the 1982 Constitution). None
of the rights and freedoms enshrined in the constitution shall be exercised in
a way that endangers the secular order of the state (Article 14).

Despite their competing ideological stances on the political role of Islam,
the Iranian and Turkish regimes share a fundamental institutional feature.
Government by guardians, identified by Robert Dahl as a perennial alternative to democracy, characterizes both the Islamist Iranian and the secularist
Turkish regimes. The notion of guardianship is based on the assumption that
the ruling elite has the right to govern by reason of its unique knowledge,
wisdom, and virtue.[1] It directly challenges the ascending theory of power that
subjects political rule to popular consent and underlies the modern notion of
representative democracy. The Iranian and Turkish regimes have elements
of guardianship that coexist with institutions of popular sovereignty. Both
regimes claim popular legitimacy and hold regular and competitive elections
for public offices. However, the authority of these public offices is restricted by

nonelected and publicly nonaccountable institutions controlled by the guardians. The guardians justify their political involvement based on suprademocratic notions of sovereignty enshrining the revolutionary ideals. Democratic politics are by definition unpredictable and may bring groups to power that have at best dubious loyalty to the regime in the eyes of guardians. These groups may be unwilling to fight against the external and internal enemies of the regime, or worse, may betray the revolutionary principles. Hence, in both regimes, guardianship is characterized by the fear of majority rule, and it draws the parameters of popular rule and dissent. These parameters are more permissive in Turkey than in Iran, reflecting the more than half-century legacy of multiparty competition and greater pluralism and the extensive linkages with and leverage of the European Union in the former. Nonetheless, the evolution of the Iranian and Turkish Muslim reformers is fundamentally shaped by their struggle with the guardians for political legitimacy and power.

While electoral dynamics provided the main vehicle for Muslim reformers in both countries to mobilize popular support, the nature of electoral competition was dramatically different in the two countries. In Iran, parties are loosely organized groups with little organizational capacity. The electoral system encourages individualistic competition and serves the purpose of allocating power among rival factional groups. In contrast, Turkey has the longest history of electoral election among Muslim-majority countries. Major political parties receive substantial state aid and are strongly organized all over the country.[2] The electoral system reinforces the hierarchical nature of the parties and has been characterized by fierce competition and a high degree of fragmentation and volatility. Consequently, the Muslim reformist experience in Iran and Turkey reflects the impacts of peculiar electoral competition in each country.

Guardianship in the Islamic Republic

The Islamic Republic of Iran (IRI) is the only regime in the Muslim world that is directly ruled by the clergy. The justification for clerical rule derives from the clerics' status as the interpreters of the divine law and guiders of the religious community during the occultation of the Twelfth Imam. The 1979 Constitution explicitly states that the new regime is founded on the belief in "One God's exclusive sovereignty and right to legislative" and "divine revelation and its fundamental role in setting forth the laws" (Article 2).[3] All laws in the country must obey Islamic criteria (Article 4), and the ultimate political power lies in the hands of the *faqih* (Articles 5 and 110). Originally, the *faqih* was entitled to rule by virtue of his superior religious knowledge and ability to be the ultimate guide (*rahbar*) in the absence of the imam. However, after the amendments of 1989 that took place a few months before the death of Khomeini, the requirement for the *faqih* to be a *marja-e taqlid* was dropped from the constitution (Article 109). *Marja-e taqlid* describes the most prominent and learned members of the Shiite clergy who have many followers who imitate their teachings and deeds.[4] Only a handful of clerics reach this status during their lifetimes. This constitutional amendment was necessary to make Ali Khamenei, whose religious credentials were relatively weak, the *faqih*. The Assembly of Experts (AE; Majles-e Khobregan-e Rahbari), a body of eighty-six clerics who are popularly elected every eight years (Article 107), selects and supervises the *faqih*. In practice, the *faqih* has tenure for life and is not publicly accountable.

The other key institution is the Guardians Council (GC; Shura-ye Negahban-e Qanun-e Asasi), which has twelve members. Six of these members are clerics directly appointed by the *faqih*. The other six are jurists who are selected by the parliament from among the candidates nominated by the head of the judiciary, who is in turn appointed by the *faqih* (Article 91). Hence, the GC is responsible only to the *faqih*. The members serve for a period of six years. The GC is entitled to supervise all parliamentary legislation on the basis of its compatibility with Islam and the constitution (Articles 94 and 98). The six religious members of the GC determine if legislation under consideration is compatible with Islam, and all members decide whether legislation violates the constitution (Article 96). The Expediency Council (EC; Majma-ye Tashkhis-e Maslehat-e Nezam-e Eslami) was established by the 1989 amendments and adjudicates the disagreements between the parliament and the GC. All members of the EC are appointed by the *faqih,* and the council meets on his request (Article 112). The EC has usually sided with the GC.[5] Meanwhile, all constitutional amendments depend on the consent of the *faqih* (Article 177). Article 99 empowers the GC to supervise all popular elections, including the presidential and the parliamentary ones. The GC used its constitutional authority to interpret this vaguely worded article to dominate the electoral process. Currently, the GC screens all aspirants and disqualifies ones who are deemed to lack the required technical, moral, and political credentials.

The way in which clerical power is exercised in the IRI is not necessarily compatible with the theory of *velayat-e faqih*.[6] After the 1989 amendments, political qualifications of the *faqih* were given decisive priority over his religious credentials and status in the clerical hierarchy. The *faqih* can no longer claim legitimacy by virtue of his unique religious standing. The dissociation of *faqih* from *marja* was approved by Khomeini himself, who argued that a simple *mujtahid* can serve as the *faqih* if he is selected by the popularly elected religious experts.[7] However, Khomeini earlier explicitly stated that "since Islamic government is a government of law, knowledge of the law is necessary for the ruler . . . he [the ruler] must surpass all others in knowledge."[8] Thus, after the dismissal of his designated successor, Hossein Ali Montazeri, who was a *marja*, Khomeini was obliged to forsake his original notion of the *faqih* for the purposes of political expediency. A year before his death he also declared that the state interests (*maslehat*) had absolute priority over the application of religious law (sharia) in cases of conflict between them.[9] "The governance is among the primary Islamic rules and takes precedence over the whole secondary rules, including the prayers, fasting, and hajj . . . The government can unilaterally revoke a Shar'i contract that it has itself signed with people when it is understood to be against the interest of the country or Islam."[10] Finally, increasing politicization of Shiite clergy undermines the clerics' historical autonomy from the state. For these reasons, it would be misleading to perceive clerical rule as a natural end point of the historical evolution of Shiite theology.

The consolidation of clerical power at the expense of traditional Shiite theology and clerical hierarchy generated dissent among the clerical ranks, who are excluded from political power and resent Khamenei, whom they do not perceive as their equal, much less their superior.[11] Khamenei's claim to rule is much more precarious, given his lack of charisma and *marja* status.[12] In his official biography, he refers back to Khomeini's strong endorsement of him for the position of *faqih*. He also argues that the responsibility of being a *faqih* is qualitatively different from and higher than the responsibility of a *marja*. His claim to *marjayat* extends only to Shia living abroad. This compromise was likely intended to secure the support of Iranian *marja* and silence their opposition to Khamenei's rule.[13] Additionally, Khamenei used the vast state resources to contain clerical opposition to the *velayat-e faqih*. First, he extended the state's control over the clerical establishment in Qom by putting clerics directly on payroll, supervising their writings and sermons, and marginalizing the senior clerics who oppose him.[14] Next, Friday prayer leaders in all sizable towns are directly appointed and supervised by the *faqih*. While Friday prayers are important avenues for regime propaganda, politicization of Friday prayers resulted in declining rates of attendance. Attendance at prayers has come to be an indicator of loyalty to the ruling regime rather than religiosity.[15] Finally, the Special Court for Clerics (SCC; Dadgah-e Vizhe-ye Ruhaniyyat), established in 1987, has become an effective tool to persecute clerics who challenge the *velayat-e faqih*.[16]

Still, for several reasons, it would be an exaggeration to claim that the IRI suffers a "legitimacy crisis" that jeopardizes the very existence of clerical rule.[17] First, the regime sponsors an extensive network of patronage-client relationships that involve an important section of the clerical class.[18] The beneficiaries of these networks have a vested interest in the continuation of the prevailing political system. The enormous economic foundations (*bonyad*) that are controlled by the clerics directly reporting to the *faqih* are exempt from taxation and receive preferred treatment, credit subsidies, and governmental concessions.[19] They are in charge of vast economic assets and are the biggest employer in the country after the state.[20] They operate companies in a wide range of fields, from soybean production to tourism. These foundations and groups with connections are given preferred treatment in contracts and become the primary beneficiaries of privatization schemes.[21] Massive amounts of public funds are transferred and redistributed for political purposes without public accountability.[22]

Second, the regime claims to derive its legitimacy from the popular revolutionary struggle and war against Iraq in the 1980s. It managed to demoralize the opposition and bolster its public legitimacy by broadcasting and publicizing self-condemning confessions by its prisoners, obtained through torture, especially in the first half of the 1980s.[23] These public recantations were effective as long as the attentive public remained ignorant of torture and threats that forced prisoners to surrender their will, and did not question the constant reference to foreign plots and internal subversive elements.[24] Regime-sponsored ceremonies at anniversaries of the revolution and war effort against Iraq, public spaces dedicated to the martyrs of the revolution and the war, programs broadcast in the state-controlled media, ideological doctrines taught in schools, and public respect shown to veterans of the revolutionary struggle and war efforts continue to be central to social life under the Islamic Republic. Public participation in pro-regime demonstrations is generally widespread. It can rightly be argued that the expressions of loyalty to the regime in officially staged events may be misleading. The weakness of an authoritarian regime is exposed only when it starts to crumble, as citizens falsify their preferences until the last moment.[25] At the same time, a study based on a public opinion survey conducted in 2003 demonstrates that religious Iranians living in Tehran adhered to the principles of Islamic rule that involve clerical rule, supremacy of sharia, and state enforcement of Islamic norms even if they were politically dissatisfied.[26] Their support for the regime seems to be anchored in their religious beliefs rather than being contingent on the regime's performance.

Another important mechanism the regime employs to keep citizens politically content is the huge subsidy system. Iran has the typical characteristics of a rentier state.[27] Rentier states derive a substantial portion of their income from their possession of a valuable resource, such as hydrocarbon products, strategically important geographical passes, remittances from exported labor, or politically motivated external aid. Iranian rents emanate from the country's vast oil and natural gas fields. More than three-fourths of Iranian exports and around half of state revenues come from petroleum. According to the World Bank, Iran earns 50 billion of its 55 billion U.S. dollars in export revenues from fuel exports. In contrast, the manufacturing sector, dominated by inefficient industries catering to heavily protected domestic markets, generated only 1.6 billion U.S. dollars in export revenues. As a result, the Iranian economy is highly vulnerable to fluctuations in oil prices, especially to decreases in oil prices. Both positive and negative changes in oil prices augment inflationary pressures. Positive oil price shocks lead to appreciation of the domestic currency and hurt nonoil exports; negative oil price shocks increase the price of imports. Yet government expenditures are only marginally affected by oil price fluctuations.[28]

Figure 5.1 shows the relationship between GDP growth rate and oil prices in Iran from 1980 to 2005. The pattern is unmistakable. Since the early 1980s, the higher oil prices are, the higher the Iranian GDP growth is. Only in the

Figure 5.1. GDP Growth Rate in Iran and Oil Prices (1980–2005)

Sources: GDP growth rates (in %) were obtained from IMF World Economic Outlook. Oil prices are from BP publications.

last several years have rapidly increasing oil prices not translated into higher growth rates. When oil prices decline, Iranian economic performance also slows down. On the basis of this information, one can expect that the Iranian regime would be weaker in bust periods. However, Figure 5.2 tells a different story. It shows the relationship between GDP per capita (PPP) and oil prices from 1980 to 2007. Unlike the trend shown in Figure 5.1, Iranian GDP per capita, adjusted for inflation, is not dependent on oil prices and has been steadily increasing since the early 1990s. It appears that the Iranian regime keeps the cost of living artificially low regardless of the performance of its economy. Prices of essential consumption goods, gasoline, and electricity are heavily subsidized in Iran.[29] The state provides generous welfare benefits such as cheap housing and health services. Poverty sharply declined in the last five years and lower-income citizens now have better access to basic services.[30] Consequently, the Iranian public is not exposed to shocks in oil prices. This observation is compatible with the generalizations that oil wealth increases the durability of regimes, and bust periods do not exert any significant influence on regime survival.[31]

However, the subsidy system unintentionally hurts Iran's economy and environment.[32] Because of subsidized petroleum prices, domestic consumption has been increasing at a rapid rate. Given the limits of Iran's refinery capacity and the unprofitable nature of refining gasoline for the domestic market, Iranian gasoline imports have been steadily increasing. As a result, the decline in the exportable fraction of oil production threatens the sustainability of the subsidy system.[33] Domestic consumption levels reached 40 percent of oil production in 2005.[34] It is estimated that Iran spent 25 billion of 44.6 billion U.S. dollars it earned in oil exports on subsidies.[35] After coming to power in summer 2005, the Ahmedinejad government increasingly relied on funds from the Oil Stabilization Fund established by the Khatami government to finance the subsidies. Meanwhile, parliament reduced the government's gasoline subsidy allocation, and the Iranian government considered partially cutting gasoline

Figure 5.2. GDP (PPP) per Capita in Iran and Oil Prices (1980–2007)

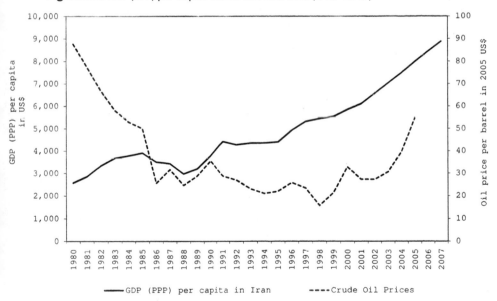

Sources: GDP (PPP) per capita figures were obtained from the World Bank. Oil prices are from BP publications.

subsidies and introducing gasoline rationing despite the windfall from oil revenues in 2006. However, cutting subsidies would generate a backlash against the government, especially since President Ahmedinejad ran on a populist platform that promised to distribute Iran's oil wealth to the people. His election slogan was "Bring the oil revenues to the people's dining tables." In his campaigning, he sharply criticized the previous governments for failing to deal with corruption and nepotism and decreased income inequality. During his tenure, he has increased the salaries of teachers, provided cheap credit to newly married couples, and offered housing subsidies for low-income citizens. All these policies have contributed to higher inflation rates and increased governmental expenses.[36]

Finally, the Islamic Revolutionary Guard Corps (Pasdaran) is the clerical regime's version of the Praetorian Guard.[37] They are separate from, and parallel to, the regular conscripted army and consist of ground, naval, air, and intelligence forces. The chief commander of the Pasdaran is directly responsible to the *faqih*. The political influence of the Pasdaran has increased since the 1997 presidential elections.[38] It has established monopoly-type economic ventures that provide access to large funds independent of governmental control.[39] Many former members were elected to the parliament in 2004, and they command influential positions in the state bureaucracy. President Ahmedinejad, for example, is a former member of the Pasdaran.[40] The Islamic Iran Developers Council (IIDC; Etelaf-e Abadgaran-e Iran-e Eslami) and the Islamic Revolution Devotees Society (IRDS; Jamiyyat-e Isargaran-e Enqelab-e Eslami), which dominated the Seventh Parliament (2004–2008), are led by a younger group of regime loyalists with backgrounds in the Pasdaran and the Iran-Iraq war. Alongside its defensive task against external threats, the Pasdaran is responsible for suppressing any "counterrevolutionary activity." The paramilitary organization Basij is organized under the Pasdaran.[41] In addition to Basij, several layers of vigilante groups also operate against internal dissidents. These groups enjoy official patronage, are quickly mobilized, and engage in violent behavior with impunity.[42]

In summary, the guardians of the IRI are entrenched in a network of social, economic, political, and military institutions. They have constitutionally sanctioned veto power over popularly elected institutions, control far-reaching patronage resources, possess robust coercive capacity, and largely co-opt the traditional clerical establishment.

Guardianship in the Secularist Republic

Guardianship is less entrenched in Turkey than in Iran. Still, the guardians, especially the armed forces, are the major veto players in Turkish politics. They are primarily concerned with what they perceive as threats to national integrity and the secular character of the regime. The preamble of the Turkish Constitution defines the purpose of the republic as reaching the status of modern civilizations and applying Atatürk's principles and revolutions.[43] It states that sacred religious beliefs are absolutely excluded from state affairs and politics by reason of Atatürk's laicism principle.[44] The laicism principle has primarily implied two policies: (1) the marginalization of Islam in public affairs, and (2) state co-optation of Islamic organizations.[45] The notion of "defensive modernization," characterizing the mindset of reformist figures of the late Ottoman period, entailed the emancipation of legal, educational, financial, and political spheres from religious tutelage.[46] The clergy's authority and influence had gradually been receding since the mid-nineteenth century.[47] The secularism of the Turkish Republic offers continuity with this tradition.[48] The second dimension of the laicism principle has implied state control over popular religion.[49] While the implementation of these policies varied over time, reflecting the priorities of the ruling governments and changing geopolitical conditions, they have defined the parameters of Islamic political activism in Turkey.

The Turkish Armed Forces (TAF; Türk Silahlı Kuvvetleri) have historically had strong political autonomy and have justified their intervention in politics on the grounds of protecting the integrity and secular character of the republic.[50] The 1980 coup was a watershed in civilian-military relations for two reasons.[51] First, the 1982 Constitution established the constitutional channels through which the TAF influence policymaking. Second, the coup solidified the public image of the military as the savior of the regime from civil war and significantly contributed to its political prestige. In fact, the coup was welcomed by a substantial section of the population.[52] Other factors also facilitate the military's independence from civilian control. The civilian governments have only symbolic control over the tenure, appointment, and dismissal procedures of the TAF. Soldiers can be put on trial only in military courts that have very broad jurisdiction. The military also exerts enormous pressure on the civilian judiciary.[53] The military is significantly involved in economics through the companies controlled by the Army Mutual Assistance Institution (AMAI; Ordu Yardımlaşma Kurumu). The compulsory deductions from salaries of the officers of the armed forces have provided a steady flow of capital to the AMAI, established in 1961. The institution also benefits from significant tax immunities and favorable legal treatment. Consequently, the AMAI has become one of the country's major companies in the aftermath of the 2001 economic crisis.[54] Most significantly, the autonomy of the military extends to law enforcement. The doctrine of *posse comitatus* that prohibits military forces from engaging in law enforcement has not been applicable in Turkey. The General Command of the Gendarmerie, which is directly responsible to the Turkish General Staff, is responsible for law enforcement in all rural areas, which make up 92 percent of Turkey's landmass.[55] Additionally, the Gendarmerie has its own intelligence-gathering networks and has engaged in extralegal counterinsurgency operations since the early 1990s. The existence of the Gendarmerie Intelligence and Antiterrorism Unit (GIAU; Jandarma İstihbarat ve Terörle Mücadele)[56] is officially denied, but all available evidence points to the fact that GIAU is responsible for a wide range of activities, including executions of hundreds of Kurdish nationalists.[57] The military pursued its own policies independent of the civilian governments, especially in the Kurdish-majority provinces from the late 1980s to the early years of the twenty-first century, when these provinces were under the "State of Emergency."[58] The TAF also classified the media outlets according to their news coverage and editorial line and boycotted the ones that were perceived to be hostile to the military.[59]

The National Security Council (NSC; Milli Güvenlik Kurulu) has served as the primary channel through which the military has influenced civilian governments (Article 118 of the 1982 Constitution).[60] Its members have been the chiefs of the armed forces, the president, and selected members of the cabinet. For two decades, it was usually the military that determined the republic's security policies in realms ranging from responses to the Kurdish insurgency to the role of Islam in public education. The NSC Secretariat General was controlled by the military and supervised the implementation of the NSC's "advisory" decisions. The secret regulation of the Secretariat General gave the institution enormous prerogatives in formulating and implementing state policies. The Secretariat General was responsible for defining internal and external threats, developing and implementing defensive strategies, and supervising the implementation of these strategies. It also gathered intelligence on whether the NSC decisions were being complied with by the civilian government. Furthermore, the Secretariat General designed, coordinated, and governed psychological warfare plans.[61] The institutional power of the NSC and the Secretariat General was curbed as a result of the seventh reform package demanded by the EU in August 2003.[62] The NSC Secretary is now chosen from among civil servants; civilians make up a majority of the Council; the frequency of NSC meetings is reduced to once every two months; the implementation of NSC decisions is assigned to elected governments; and most importantly, governments are no longer required to prioritize the Council decisions.[63] However, the institutional reforms have not reduced the military's informal political influence or visibility.[64]

The military's decisive influence on the formulation of the state's security policy has become public knowledge with the revelation of the National Security Document (Milli Güvenlik Siyaseti Belgesi), which is prepared by the NSC Secretariat General in secrecy and approved by the NSC. The parliament has no role in the writing of the document that defines the security priorities of the regime. According to national press reports, this document is regularly updated to reflect changes in the regime's security concerns.[65] The document was updated in fall 2005 for the last time before it was leaked to the public. It is a widespread assumption in Turkish politics that civilian governments are required to comply with these priorities. In fact, the civilian governments formally approve the document. The earlier versions of the document reflected the Cold War geopolitics and identified the threat of Communism as a matter of regime survival. The current version (2005) identifies four groups as internal threats: Kurdish separatists, Communists, Islamic radicals, and religious minorities. A remarkable aspect of the document is its characterization of nonviolent demands for greater political representation of Kurdish, Islamic, and non-Muslim entities as extensions of activities threatening the national integrity and secular character of the republic. The "recommended" policies to be implemented against internal threats include educating the public about the true nature of laicism and Islam, supporting antimissionary activities, and neutralizing the influence of Kurdish nationalism and Islamic radicalism in social, cultural, and economic spheres. Naturally, civilian governments are strongly expected to agree with and to implement these recommendations.

The Religious Affairs Directory (RAD; Diyanet İşleri Başkanlığı), which is mainly under the control of elected politicians, is the principal state organ regulating Islam. The explicit purpose of the RAD, established in 1924, was the governance of public worship and direction of religious beliefs. In essence, the RAD was entrusted with the task of promoting a regime-friendly version of Sunni Islam among the populace.[66] Legislation dating to 1965 currently specifies the functions and organization of the RAD, and Article 136 of the 1982 Constitution defines it as an apolitical institution that aims to ensure "national solidarity and integration."[67] Its director is responsible to the prime minister and is appointed by the president on the basis of the prime minister's suggestion. The importance of the RAD in state bureaucracy has increased since the 1980 coup. The military reasoned that pious people would be less likely to engage in disruptive political activity and saw in Islam an antidote against leftist appeals among the populace. Religious classes were made mandatory in public education, more schools were opened with extensive religious curricula, the budget of the RAD was greatly augmented, Sufi brotherhoods were increasingly tolerated and seen as a remedy to Kurdish separatism, and the public was generally encouraged to attend mosques. For example, the number of mosques rose from 47,645 in 1981 to 57,060 in 1985. In contrast, less than 5,000 new mosques were constructed from 1971 to 1981.[68]

Historically, the main responsibility of the RAD has been the governance of mosques. By 2004, more than seventy-six thousand mosques existed in Turkey. The RAD is required to appoint imams (religious personnel whose main task is leading communal prayers) and to supervise each of these mosques. However, around 30 percent of the mosques did not have a state-appointed imam because of the lack of personnel.[69] The RAD espouses the Hanafi legal school of Islam and centrally issues religious edicts that are read by imams in mosques during Friday prayers.[70] This practice results in an open discrimination against the Sunni Muslims who are not followers of the Hanafi school and the non-Sunni Muslims such as Alevis.[71]

The judiciary has taken a very active role in Turkish politics, especially since the early 1990s. Particularly important are the decisions of the Turkish Constitutional Court (TCC; Anayasa Mahkemesi). Articles 147–153 of the 1982 Constitution specify the current nature and authority of the TCC, established by the 1961 Constitution. The president selects its eleven permanent and four auxiliary members from among candidates nominated by various state institutions and high-ranking bureaucrats and lawyers. The TCC reviews parliamentary laws and bylaws on grounds of procedural and substantial compatibility with the constitution. It also reviews constitutional amendments on procedural grounds. However, governmental decrees enacted during states of emergency, martial law, and wars are beyond the scope of the court's authority. Lower courts, the president, political parties with at least twenty members in the parliament, and one-fifth of the members of the parliament are the only groups with rights to appeal to the court. The court is required to provide written explanations for its decisions, which are final.

Articles 68 and 69 enumerate the principles that the political parties have to abide by. Article 69 states that the Constitutional Court may ban a political party if its program and bylaws violate the principles stated in the fourth paragraph of Article 68 or the party has become a center of activities that violate the same principles. The court has dissolved almost two dozen parties, most of them representing Kurdish nationalism.[72] Particularly controversial was the dissolution of the Islamic WP and VP and the Kurdish parties. In a case brought by the Welfare Party politicians to the European Court of Human Rights (ECHR), the court ruled in favor of the Turkish state.[73] Several changes to Article 69 in October 2001 made the dissolution of parties more difficult. The Constitutional Court may now ban a party on the grounds of its activities violating Article 68 only if these activities are fully endorsed by the party leadership or are continued with determination by party organs. Moreover, the court may now opt for the partial or complete end of state aid to a party instead of banning it. Finally, all decisions outlawing political parties now require a three-fifths majority in the court. These changes ensured that the JDP narrowly escaped dissolution in July 2008, by a vote of six to five, when the TCC decided that the party had become the center of antisecular activities. The TCC eventually decided to partially cut state aid to the party.

The TCC has prioritized the republican notions of secularism and national integrity over liberal-democratic principles of political participation and pluralism. Furthermore, the court has been very selective in its interpretations of civil and political rights and has not generally advocated the expansion of these rights.[74] The performance of the court contradicts the perception of judicial review as a force that consolidates liberal democracy. As Ran Hirschl argues, the global trend toward the "judicialization of politics" has not necessarily been conducive to democratization. Rather, it has been supported by elites whose political hegemony is threatened by popular forces.[75] More specifically, secular elites in Middle Eastern countries have found it in their best interest to transfer political power to the courts, which are impervious to popular religious and ethnic demands.[76]

The ban on the headscarf (*başörtüsü* or *türban*) in public institutions such as university campuses and bureaucracies represents another dimension of the state's regulation of public expressions of Islam. Since the 1980s, the Provincial Administrative Courts, the High Administrative Court (Danıştay), and the TCC have decided to uphold the ban. More recently, the High Administrative Court upheld the administrative decision that disciplined a K–12 schoolteacher who occasionally dons the headscarf.[77] The courts reasoned that in a Muslim-majority country, freedom *from* religion is sustainable only if the state regulates public expressions of Islamic symbols and rituals. Hence, they argued that the donning of the headscarf challenges the republican secularism principle and violates the 1982 Constitution. The preamble of that constitution explicitly states that "no action that contradicts Atatürk nationalism, principles, revolutions, and civilization may be extended protection."[78] In reaction, a female university student donning the headscarf appealed to the European Court for Human Rights. The ECHR ruled that the Turkish state's ban on the headscarf is legitimate, as it pursues the aim of "protecting rights and freedoms and maintaining public order." It basically deferred to the Turkish courts in deciding whether the headscarf poses a threat to individual freedoms and public order.[79]

Guardianship in Turkey has differed from that in Iran in three respects. First, the influence of the guardians on popularly elected legislative and executive organs is restricted to issues that primarily involve state security concerns. As long as the civilian politicians do not trespass the lines drawn by the guardians, they have the power to formulate, legislate, and implement state policies. At the same time, these security concerns are very broadly defined and include a diverse set of issues ranging from public expressions of Islam and ethnic identities to foreign policy making. Second, since the early 1980s, the guardians have often been in alliance with civil-society organizations that enthusiastically support their agendas. Opinion survey pools continuously reveal that the military enjoys a very high standing among the populace. As discussed in the seventh chapter, powerful media, business, and civil organizations either tacitly or openly supported the military intervention in 1997, which resulted in the fall of the WP. Finally, external pressures to reduce the power of the guardians have been important in Turkey since the early years of the twenty-first century. The EU officially recognized Turkey's candidacy in 1999. In December 2004, it decided to open up membership negotiations with Turkey, which started in October 2005. Constitutional amendments in October 2001 and May 2004 were based on liberal-democratic principles. Successive Turkish governments since 2001 have passed nine reform packages that aim to bring the country's legal system in harmony with the EU standards. While the reform process has eroded the institutional basis of guardianship, it has not yet substantially reduced its influence in Turkish politics. Meanwhile, the EU-induced reform process lost its steam by early 2006.

Electoral Competition in the Two Republics

The Islamic Republic of Iran holds popular elections for four different bodies: presidency, parliament, the Assembly of Experts, and local councils. A general characteristic of these elections is the intensity of factional conflict and the lack of mass political parties. They serve to legitimize the ruling regime, determine the balance of power among factions, and prevent factional conflict from destabilizing the regime and turning violent. In fact, elections in the IRI, by their very nature, discourage the formation of hierarchical mass party organizations. Elections do not undermine the continuity of clerical rule, as the guardians decide who can be included in the electoral competition and the power of elected representatives remains highly constrained. The nomination process is far from being democratic, since all aspirants have to be approved by the GC.[80]

The IRI has had eight parliamentary elections since 1980. The parliament had 270 members until 2000, when the number was raised to 290. Iran has 207 electoral districts. According to the electoral law of 1980, the elections take place in two rounds. Initially, a candidate had been required to acquire more than 50 percent of all valid votes to be elected in the first round. Later this threshold was reduced to 33 percent, and then to 25 percent by the 2000 elections. In the runoffs, the two candidates with the highest number of votes vie for each remaining seat. The Parties Law of 1981, which regulates political parties, associations, societies, and Islamic and religious minorities' societies, requires all groups to register and apply for a license at the Interior Ministry.[81] Articles 9 and 10 establish a commission in the ministry, known as the

Article 10 Commission, for the purpose of issuing licenses to these groups and supervising their activities. Article 16, which describes forbidden activities, includes very vaguely defined clauses such as "making efforts to create and intensify the division within the ranks of the nation," and "violating Islamic standards and the basis of the Islamic republic." If a group is found to violate Article 16, the commission can cancel its license and request its dissolution by the court. Furthermore, all groups need to obtain written authorization from the Interior Ministry before they can hold assemblies and deliver speeches. By February 2007, 223 groups were registered with the commission and were subject to the Parties Law.[82] Many of them can be considered advocacy or interest groups with no involvement in parliamentary politics.

Political parties do not currently receive state aid and tend to be loose elite associations with little vertical linkage with the voters.[83] The citizens directly vote for candidates in parliamentary elections, and the parties are not represented on the ballots. Voters express their choices by writing their favored candidates on a piece of paper. They may vote for as many candidates as there are seats to be filled in their districts. While the parties circulate lists of their candidates among voters, a single candidate may simultaneously appear on multiple lists. Parties cannot run ads on the state-controlled television or radio or in its publications or use sermons at Friday prayers for propaganda purposes.[84] Negative campaigning is forbidden. Candidates usually sponsor their own campaigns.[85] The campaign period lasts for seven days and ends twenty-four hours before the ballot day. The individualistic nature of the parliamentary elections discourages the formation of strong party structures and undermines party hierarchy. Furthermore, as a result of the GC's screening of the candidates and the weakness of parties, membership in parliament has been very volatile, and incumbents do not enjoy strong advantages over challengers. For instance, fewer than sixty parliamentarians from the Fifth Parliament (1996–2000) retained their seats in the Sixth Parliament.[86]

Nine presidential elections took place in the IRI between 1980 and 2008. Only three of these elections could be considered competitive in practical terms: the races won by Bani-Sadr in 1980, Khatami in 1997, and Ahmedinejad in 2005. Candidates favored by the guardians secured landslide victories from 1981 to 1997. This trend was upset with the victory of reformist Khatami in 1997, who also easily won a second term in 2001. Voter turnout was a record 80 percent in 1997. The 2005 presidential elections were very unpredictable, and none of the seven candidates received a majority of the votes required for victory. The winner in the runoff was Ahmedinejad, the mayor of Tehran. Although voter turnout was around 63 percent in the first round, it was particularly low in western regions inhabited by ethnic minorities such the Azeri Turks, Kurds, and Arabs. For instance, it was only 33 percent in the province (*ostan*) of Kordestan, 37 percent in West Azerbaijan, and 55 percent in Khuzestan.

The regime manipulates the elections in several ways. First of all, all candidates have to apply to the Interior Ministry, which sends their files to the provinces. In the provinces, these files are investigated by district committees, which communicate their decisions to the central committee. The GC makes the final decision and can disqualify any candidate. The GC does not provide a public rationale for its decisions. Furthermore, the GC also has the authority to invalidate electoral results. Many aspirants are disqualified on the grounds that they are not committed to the IRI and the institution of *faqih*, they served the monarchy, or they acted against the theocracy in the past.[87] The disqualification rates over the years have varied significantly.[88] While they were below 20 percent in 1984 and 1988, 34 percent of all applicants were disqualified when the GC applied a more selective criterion in 1992. The disqualification rate reached a peak in 1996, when the GC disqualified around 44 percent of the aspirants. A fundamental reason for the reformist victory in the 2000 parliamentary elections was the GC's relative noninterference in the candidacy process. Only 8 percent were disqualified. In contrast, the reformists lost control over parliament in 2004 when the disqualification rate rose to 29 percent. Interestingly, voter turnout is not consistently linked to the disqualification ratio.[89] For example, turnout was higher in 1996 (75 percent) than in 2000 (69 percent) despite the fact that the GC's disqualification ratio was substantially higher in 1996 than in 2000. In the 2004 elections, calls for a boycott partially resonated with the electorate, and turnout remained at 51 percent. In general, turnout tends to be higher in provincial towns and small districts, where personal connections and patronage promises are more important than in big cities. For example, turnout in Tehran in 2004 was around 33 percent, well below the national average. The guardians regularly exhort the public to participate in the elections and portray high electoral turnout as popular endorsement of the IRI. Exhortation also involves intimidation, however. Citizens receive a stamp in their identity cards when they vote, and citizens without a stamp are likely to experience various degrees of discrimination in their dealings with state authorities.[90] Furthermore, the reformist candidates accused the Basij of committing fraud and manipulating the results in the 2005 presidential elections.[91] In the absence of independent election monitors, these accusations were not substantiated.

In spite of their limitations, the elections introduce an element of pluralism and unpredictability to Iranian politics unprecedented in many authoritarian regimes. Major political actors take the elections seriously and commit their resources and energies to emerge victorious at the ballot box. The turnout rate rarely falls below 50 percent. Most important, the candidates favored by the guardians have been defeated several times. Unlike the hybrid regimes in the post-Communist world, however, electoral competition does not lead to changes in the fundamental distribution of power in Iran.[92] Electoral victories do not translate into effective legislative and executive power, for the guardians preserve their undisputed power over the elected politicians. It may be too bold to argue that the Islamic Republic has survived because of the fragmented nature of the Iranian state, not "*in spite of* elite fragmentation and contestation."[93] Nonetheless, undisputed hard-liner control of critical state institutions and powerful organizational resources ensures that elite fragmentation and contestation persist without leading to any change in the authoritarian character of the regime. Hence, opposition participation in electoral politics may not be the strategy that best serves the goal of political reform.

The Turkish Republic has held free and competitive parliamentary elections since 1950. The leader of the party with the largest parliamentary group forms the government. The president was elected by the parliament for a seven-year term until a constitutional amendment in 2007 instituted the popular election of the president every five years. Turkey has used a party-list proportional representation electoral system with a national threshold of 10 percent since the 1983 elections. It has eighty-five electoral districts with from one (Bayburt) to thirty (Istanbul I. District) members. The parliament has had 550 members since the 1995 elections. Major Turkish political parties tend to be very hierarchical, centralized organizations characterized by patron-client networks.[94] In most parties, leaders have absolute control over the decision making and the grassroots members. The closed-list proportional representation used since the 1995 elections reinforces the leaders' control over the nomination process. Voters identify parties with their leaders and do not directly vote for candidates running under party labels. Primaries are rarely held, and the grassroots members have little control over the formation of the party lists that are decided by the leadership. Party provincial organizations operate as patronage distribution centers, especially when the party is in government. The undemocratic practices characterizing the internal working of the parties reduce their representativeness and alienate citizens who value participatory decision making.

The center-right parties, which have had an uneasy relationship with the guardians, have been the predominant players in the elections. The center-right Democrat Party (DP; Demokrat Parti) won three successive elections and was in power from 1950 until the 1960 coup. Its successor, the Justice Party (JP; Adalet Partisi) won the 1965 and 1969 elections. The 1970s saw the rise of leftist and radical-right forces and coalition governments that were unable to establish public order and prevent street violence. In the aftermath of the 1980 military coup, the Motherland Party (MP; Anavatan Partisi) emerged as the major center-right party and dominated Turkish politics until the 1991 parliamentary elections. However, the center-right steadily lost its public appeal during the 1990s. The electoral strength of the main center-right parties, MP and the True Path Party (TPP; Doğru Yol Partisi), dropped from 55 percent in 1987 to 25 percent in 1999. The main beneficiaries of the center-right's erosion were the religious and nationalistic parties, which increased their vote share from 9 percent to 33 percent in the same period. The regrouping of the center-right under the banner of the JDP, founded by former Islamists, arrested the rise of the radical right.

The most distinctive pattern in Turkish politics during the 1990s was protest voting behavior. Voters tended to penalize governmental parties with poor economic performance in their last year in government and shift to parties that were in opposition.[95] The coalition governments between 1991 and 2002 largely proved to be incapable of coping with the mounting economic and political challenges. Turkey had its worst post–World War II economic crisis in 2001. Two other economic crises, in 1994 and 1999, were also painful. The ongoing armed conflict with the Kurdish insurgent organization PKK also drained the country's resources and polarized its political environment. Public confidence in the political parties and in politicians reached its nadir by the first years of the twenty-first century. In 2000, confidence in political parties was 2.1 points out of 10, whereas it was 3.9 for the parliament.[96] According to a comprehensive survey study of the electoral system and political parties in 2001, which was funded by the largest business association in Turkey, 84 percent of the respondents said that the political party system was functioning improperly.[97]

While protest-voting behavior explains the high levels of volatility and fragmentation in Turkish politics, it offers little explanation for why some oppositional parties were more successful than others. In particular, it does not explain why the center-left parties failed to capitalize on the erosion of the center-right as much as the radical-right parties did and later the JDP. A conceptual framework that combines a protest-voting perspective with a geographical and cultural understanding of Turkish politics is useful for making sense of the political circumstances and the evolution of Muslim reformers (i.e., the JDP) in Turkey.[98] Such a framework builds on the center-periphery paradigm that has been very influential among scholars of Turkish politics.[99] An implication of this paradigm is that religion has continued to be a major predictor of political orientation in Turkey.[100] While this binary division lost much of its value with the rise of the center-left and radical-right in the 1970s and the erosion of the center-right in the 1990s, it points to the existence of major party blocs in Turkish politics that have survived for decades. Voter transitions between these blocs tend to be very low, especially in certain geographical areas.

A geographical understanding of the Turkish electoral landscape identifies the regions that disproportionately affect electoral outcomes.[101] The center-right parties have been powerful nationwide, with the exception of the few provinces with idiosyncratic characteristics. This gives a strong advantage to a center-right party that is capable of winning in the regions where only rightist parties are running. If a center-right party manages to dominate the regions that overwhelmingly vote for rightist parties, it is most likely to win a plurality in the elections. The weakness of both center-left and radical-right parties in some geographical areas means that these parties are no matches for center-right parties in most elections.[102] However, the rise of radical-right parties in regions where leftist parties have no strong presence undermines the appeal of the center-right parties. Hence, the regions where the competition for votes is exclusively among the rightist parties are crucial for the electoral strategies of the center-right parties.[103] The center-right parties steadily lost their public support to the radical-right parties in conservative Central

Anatolian provinces during the 1990s. Whereas in the 1991 elections two center-right parties gained 40 percent of the parliamentary seats from twenty Central Anatolian provinces, their control was reduced to only 16 percent in 1999. In contrast, radical-right parties increased their share of parliamentary seats from 45 to 72 percent in the same period. Consequently, the rise of the radical-right parties reflected their increasing appeal in these culturally conservative and nationalistic provinces predominantly populated by Sunni Turks. The JDP emerged as the major center-right party by recovering the votes lost to the radical-right parties during the 1990s. The electoral triumph of the JDP in the 2002 elections was a result of its ability to mobilize voters in coastal regions and large cities and its strong appeal among the conservative Sunni voters of Central-Eastern Anatolia. In contrast, the JDP's appeal among the Kurdish provinces in Southeast Anatolia was rather limited in the 2002 elections. The party became the leading political actor in the Kurdish provinces only with the 2004 municipal and 2007 parliamentary elections. The geographical distribution of the JDP's vote considerably restricted the maneuverability of the party leadership, especially regarding the Kurdish issue. It simply cannot afford to be soft on "PKK terrorism" and make too many concessions to Kurdish nationalists. That would undermine the electoral base of the party, especially in Central Anatolia and coastal areas that attract immigrants from Kurdish regions. In fact, the leadership wavered in pursuing reformist agendas on critical issues because of electoral constraints as much as the guardians' objections.

CHAPTER 6

A Moment of
Enthusiasm
in the
Islamic Republic

The evolution of Islamic political activism in Iran, since the mid-1970s, has demonstrated the elastic influence of Shiite Islam over political thought and behavior. Shiite beliefs, norms, and rituals supplied the vernacular means through which revolutionaries articulated desire for social justice and freedom and mobilized public support. With the consolidation of Islamist rule in the early 1980s, rulers of the Islamic Republic demanded unconditional political obedience from citizens on the basis of their religious faith. However, clerics and lay intellectuals have increasingly criticized the regime's monopolization of the "religious truth" and have emphatically argued for political pluralism. The late 1990s saw the emergence of a vibrant Muslim reformist movement in Iran.

Unlike their counterparts elsewhere, Muslim reformers in Iran did not face a "secular" authoritarian regime that effectively blocked the goal of the Islamic state. They were ex-revolutionaries who were disillusioned with the Islamic state. While they remained loyal to the revolutionary heritage, they became vociferous advocates of moderation, rule of law, democratic governance, civil society, and political competition. Former Islamists have matured into seasoned politicians who believe in the essential reformability of the Islamic Republic. They aimed to create a public sphere free from regime control, and they achieved some success. Most importantly, they channeled their energies into winning elections and using the power of elected office to reform the political system. The electoral strategy failed in the face of stiff resistance from the guardians. In fact, it brought political marginalization and public discrediting of the reformers. This chapter narrates the emergence of the RF from the factional politics of the Islamic Republic, as well as its intellectual basis, electoral victories, and ultimate failure by 2004. It attempts to provide a convincing explanation for why public support for the RF was unsustainable and to delineate the organizational factors that severely constrained its public appeal.

The Revolutionary Heritage

The most serious challenge to political rule in the Middle East throughout the second half of the twentieth century was military coups. From the overthrow of the monarchy in Egypt in 1952 to Muammar Qaddafi's disposal of the Libyan king Idris in 1969, presidents and kings had been very vulnerable to conspiracies within armed forces. The increasing state power, the emergence of leaders with superior survival skills (e.g., Hafez Assad in Syria and Saddam Hussein in Iraq), and, most important, the flow of revenues from oil exports to state coffers in the early 1970s brought an end to the era of coups.[1] The surviving regimes were characterized by deep public apathy and exclusion of citizens from meaningful political participation. The Iranian Revolution was the only instance when street demonstrations and mass disobedience overwhelmed a Middle Eastern regime. From a modern perspective, revolution, which is the ultimate expression of the human capacity to create a brand-new political order, cannot and ought not to have any relationship with religion, which is thought to be the ultimate expression of human limitation and fallibility in the face of an otherworldly and omnipotent force.[2] The Iranian Revolution necessitated a serious and wholehearted rethinking of such descriptions of the relationship between religion and revolution. Like his fellow Shiite clerics Musa al-Sadr in Lebanon and Muhammad Baqir al-Sadr in Iraq, Ruhollah Khomeini fundamentally reinterpreted Shiite traditions that often espoused political quietism in the face of tyrannical rule and social injustice. However, only Khomeini was eventually triumphant. Musa al-Sadr organized Shia as a viable political force in confessional Lebanese politics before disappearing on a trip to Libya in 1978.[3] Muhammad Baqir al-Sadr was the leading intellectual figure behind the establishment of the Islamist Daʿwa Party in Iraq in the late 1950s. The Baʿth regime, which felt threatened by the Iranian Revolution, executed him in April 1980.[4] Has the historical evolution of Shiite Islam been a main cause of the revolution and the establishment of the Islamic Republic? This question has been a subject of lively and intense scholarly debate. It is also greatly pertinent to the emergence of factional competition in the post-Khomeini era.

Some scholars argue that the organizational structure of Shiite clergy and the nature of Shiite beliefs made unique contributions to the revolutionary struggle. According to one perspective, the clerical rule was a culmination of a centuries-long process that started with the occultation of the last Twelver Shiite imam in the ninth century.[5] The notion of occultation was a response to the crisis of the imamate when the Eleventh Imam died without a designated successor in AD 874.[6] During the occultation of the imam, the Shiite learned men (i.e., clergy) gradually increased the scope of their influence and authority over the community of believers, starting with the Hilla school in the tenth century. Under the sponsorship of the Safavid dynasty, the Shiite clergy was firmly established in the Iranian lands. Critical developments were the victory of the Usuli (methodological) school, which grants greater flexibility and prerogative to *mujtahid,* over the Akhbari (traditional) school in the eighteenth century, and the increasing autonomy of the Shiite clerics during Qajar times in the nineteenth century.[7] The clerics challenged the ruling Qajar dynasty and were pivotal in mobilizing public support during the Tobacco Boycott in 1891 and the Constitutional Revolution in 1905–1906.[8] Hamid Algar characterizes the revolution of 1979 as the ultimate result of the Shiite clergy's expanding power.[9] For Michael Fischer, reinterpreted Karbala symbolism and Shiite ideals united disparate interests into a mass movement that overwhelmed the monarchy.[10] Theda Skocpol maintains that mass rebellions overcame state repression because thousands of citizens "were willing to face death again and again in the recurrent mass demonstrations that finally wore down, demoralized, and paralyzed the army, the shah, and his U.S. supporters."[11] Said Amir Arjomand argues that religious symbols and rituals, such as the gatherings at forty-day intervals to commemorate the "martyrs," coupled with religious belief in otherworldly salvation, ensured the ultimate triumph of the revolutionary movement in Iran.[12] Shahrough Akhavi also underlines doctrinal aspects and the folk nature of the Shiite religion to account for the rise of revolutionary process.[13] Mansoor Moaddel identifies religious ideology as the principal causal factor of the Iranian Revolution.[14] Despite their differences, all these studies focus on factors that are thought to be *unique* to Shiite Islam.

Others downplayed the role of Shiite Islam in explaining the revolution by focusing on socioeconomic factors and class dynamics.[15] The Pahlavi regime could no longer claim legitimacy based on economic performance.[16] Moreover, the shah's policies alienated key social groups such as the commercial business sector and pushed them toward the opposition.[17] The shah also failed to build a loyal constituency among the peasants and the working class.[18] Social groups such as students, workers, and capitalists had different reasons for rebelling against the monarchical regime.[19] Radical Islamists lacked sufficient support and organizational power to demand an Islamic republic even in the most intense days of the revolution.[20] Yet Khomeini skillfully capitalized on the nativist, anti-imperialistic intellectual tradition that had a ready audience in the last years of monarchical Iran.[21] Khomeinism, as conceptualized by Ervand Abrahamian, is essentially a middle-class movement that mobilizes lower segments of society through vague promises of social justice while maintaining the preexisting modes of economic production and distribution.[22] Khomeini's theory of *velayat-e faqih* represents an innovation in Shiite political thought rather than being the culmination of the Shiite clerical tradition.[23] Khomeini benefited largely from the ideas of lay figures like Jalal Al-e Ahmad and Ali Shariati.[24] In summary, they do not assign a causal role to religious ideology in explaining the revolution.[25] They imply that any non-Shia-majority country with similar sociopolitical institutions and economic developments is prone to experience revolution.

More recently, Charles Kurzman argues that all existing accounts of the revolution fall short of providing a convincing causal story of the events.[26] He perceives the Iranian Revolution as a self-generating dynamic process that becomes impossible to contain by force or concessions after a certain threshold of viability, which remains unpredictable, has passed. He criticizes explanations that highlight the clerics' role and Shiite beliefs, symbols, and rituals as major causal factors of the revolution. The radical clerics' control of the mosque network was an end of the revolutionary process rather than its cause.[27] The radical Islamists also constructed new cultural meanings and practices that defy predictions based on cultural continuities.[28]

It can be concluded that the relationship between Shiite Islam and political action is far from being linear and unidimensional. Revolutionaries successively challenged the political quietism of the traditional clergy and constructed a Shiite identity that glorifies unconditional rebellion against "unjust" authority. However, Shiite Islam failed to be a self-sustaining revolutionary force against an even more repressive and isolated regime in Iraq than in Iran. While certain aspects of Shiite Islam *facilitate* political mobilization and self-sacrificing action, Shiite Islam by itself does not necessarily translate into certain types of political behavior or support doctrines. The transformation of Shiite beliefs, symbols, and rituals into anchors of Islamist or democratic platforms depends on a host of structural, institutional, organizational, and leadership factors. The postrevolutionary politics in Iran strongly support this argument.

Political Marginalization and Transformation of the Leftists

What was long ago said about Lenin may be equally true about Khomeini: Whatever he might be, he had an indomitable "political will" and the great "organizational skill" necessary to make the revolution come about.[29] Under the conditions of the extreme fragmentation of authority and disorder, Islamists were better positioned to capture state power. They gradually subdued more liberal and moderate groups that participated in the revolution. A leading liberal figure was Mehdi Bazargan, who was the leader of the Freedom Movement of Iran (FMI; Nehzat-e Azadi-ye Iran) and became the first prime minister of the revolutionary state. Bazargan and his associates had a pluralistic understanding of politics and believed in electoral competition as the ultimate arbiter of power.[30] Pious activists, such as Bazargan, did not envision a theocratic political government and opposed direct clerical rule. Furthermore, even revolutionary clerics were not uniformly supportive of a theocratic government. Mahmoud Taleqani, one of the most popular leaders of the revolution, had a progressive political worldview that allowed for pluralism.[31] When Khomeini appointed Bazargan prime minister in February 1979, the latter was confronted with a parallel authority that was utterly beyond his control.[32] Radical Islamists organized militias, social security networks, and local revolutionary courts that neutralized the governmental authority. Like the aftermath of the February Revolution of 1917 in Russia, the moderates lost to the superior organizational and leadership skills and political determination of the radicals.[33]

By 1982, all opponents of the clerical Islamic Republic were either eliminated or brought under control. During the 1980s, the immense war effort against Iraq and the international isolation of the country provided the regime with the necessary pretext to characterize all political dissent as the betrayal of the revolution and to thus eliminate the opposition. Yet Islamists themselves were not united and had substantial disagreements. Politics in the Islamic Republic gradually took the form of elite factionalism. There were irreducible differences between these factions on the issues of the state's role in the economy, the international dimension of the revolution, and the extent of state interference in the cultural aspects of life.[34] Until 1987, factions operated under the rubric of the Islamic Republican Party (Hezb-e Jomhuri-ye Eslami), established by Mohammad Beheshti in February 1979, and lacked robust vertical linkages with the public.[35] The rightist faction (rast), an amalgam of prominent revolutionary leaders and powerful organizations, was against the extensive nationalization of industry and comprehensive economic redistribution programs. The right espoused middle-class bazari (merchant) interests and argued for the sanctity of private property. It also favored pragmatism in foreign policy. In cultural matters, the rightists were for the state enforcement of a puritan understanding of Islam. In contrast, the leftists (chap) favored extensive state involvement in economics for redistributive purposes, supported large-scale land reform, espoused a revolutionary stance in international politics, and were more reluctant toward the state enforcement of religious morals.[36]

The revolution initially resulted in a narrowing of the income inequality gap, in land redistributions, and in real increases in the purchasing power of the working poor. The minimum wage was augmented, and changes in the rate of income tax made the taxation slightly progressive.[37] The institutionalization of populist practices also alleviated the harsh life conditions of the poor. The large foundations (bonyad) established by the revolutionary state provided extensive welfare assistance to the needy. State employment rapidly expanded at the cost of creating a largely ineffective bureaucratic system. Paralleling these developments was a huge increase in petty commodity production and self-employment activities in the urban areas.[38] The right strongly opposed redistributive policies entailing extensive state involvement in economics and violability of private property. It had the backing of the commercial and landowning classes, who were politically well organized and had a strong capacity for collective action.[39] With the end of war with Iraq in 1988, the elimination of the position of prime minister occupied by the leftist Mir-Hossein Mousavi, and the election of the pragmatist Ali Akbar Hashemi Rafsanjani to the presidency in 1989, the state mostly abandoned redistributive policies in favor of market-oriented reforms that aimed to boost private investment and attract foreign investors.[40] While populist policies such as keeping redundant public-sector employment, providing welfare assistance to the poor through foundations, and subsidizing essential consumer products and gasoline were not abandoned, the government gradually eschewed redistributive economic policies. The leftists who controlled the Third Parliament (1988–1992) continued to oppose Rafsanjani's economic agenda. The ever-pragmatic Rafsanjani solicited the support of the right.

Factional conflict gained an organizational basis with the self-dissolution of the Islamic Republican Party in 1987. The Militant Clergy Association (MCA; Jamee-ye Ruhaniyyat-e Mobarez) emerged as the leading rightist organization. This faction also had the support of Ali Khamenei, who replaced Khomeini as the *faqih* in 1989, and of the Guardians Council. In 1988, the left established the Militant Clerics League (MCL; Majma-ye Ruhaniyyun-e Mobarez). These two hybrid organizations never crystallized into political parties with concrete platforms and mass membership, but they reflected the irreducible intraelite divisions. Only after the death of Khomeini and the selection of Khamenei as the new *velayat-e faqih* did the tensions between factions erupt into open conflict; by the early 1990s, it resulted in the total marginalization of the leftists. The GC interpreted Article 99 of the constitution, which confers to that body the responsibility of supervising popular elections, in a very interventionist way. It disqualified 34 percent of all aspirants from running in the 1992 parliamentary elections.[41] Most of the disqualified were affiliated with the leftist faction. In contrast, the disqualification rate had been 15 and 19 percent in 1984 and 1988 respectively.[42] Moreover, Rafsanjani and his allies successfully portrayed the leftists as obstructionists who were blocking reconstruction efforts. The 1992 parliamentary elections were a total defeat for the leftists, whose parliamentary presence was reduced to a small minority. Overall, only 83 out of 270 members of parliament managed to preserve their seats.[43] A few years after the death of Khomeini, the leftists were effectively eliminated from politics, and all-important branches of the government were controlled by the Rafsanjani-rightist alliance.

Ideological moderation among the revolutionary elite in Iran has its roots in the early 1990s. Interestingly, this observation defies Proposition IV of moderation theory, which expects that political inclusion would generate behavioral modification that would be followed by ideological moderation. In the Islamic Republic, ideological moderation was the unintended consequence of the political exclusion and electoral defeat of the leftist revolutionaries and the sea changes taking place in world politics. Intellectuals and clerics, who had been actively involved in the revolution, started questioning its consequences and criticizing the theological basis and political structure of the Islamic Republic. The replacement of Khomeini with a relatively mid-ranking and uncharismatic cleric and the gradual transformation of revolutionary ideals into bureaucratic authoritarianism were major disillusionments. Furthermore, the global prestige and circulation of liberal democracy and human rights following the revolutions that took place in Eastern Europe in the late 1980s and the collapse of the Soviet Union had a strong impact on the ex-revolutionaries. Deprived of institutional power and the means to challenge the rightist dominance of the regime, they flocked to think tanks, newspapers, and magazines, where they articulated discourses on the rule of law, civil society, popular sovereignty, and human rights.[44] They gradually eschewed their revolutionary rhetoric and began to appreciate freedom of association, empowerment of civil-society organizations, and the limits on arbitrary state power. They capitalized on the ambivalent legacy of the revolution that combined elements of popular participation and pluralism with Islamic rule. Rather than being the negation of political modernity, the Iranian Revolution generated a complicated relationship between religious truth and democratic rule.[45] The dualistic nature of the revolution led to a situation where both democratic and authoritarian discourses claimed to represent the true legitimacy of the revolution. Individuals who had impeccable revolutionary credentials reinvented themselves as democrats without ceasing to be followers of Khomeini and loyal to the Islamic Republic.[46] They argued that Khomeini's support for absolute clerical rule was a strategic response to postrevolutionary instability. In their view, Khomeini was not inherently in favor of absolute clerical rule.[47] In several years, the evolution of the ex-revolutionaries would dramatically broaden the factional nature of Iranian politics.

The careers of many prominent figures of the reform movement illustrate the transformation of Islamist revolutionaries into advocates of popular sovereignty, political pluralism, and the rule of law. Mohammad Khatami (b. 1943), who served as the president from 1997 until 2005, had been an active participant in the revolutionary process and was elected to parliament in 1980 from the province of Ardakan. Later, he served as the director of the *Kayhan* newspaper and the minister of Islamic guidance in the cabinets of Prime Minister Mousavi from 1982 to 1986 and of President Hashemi Rafsanjani from 1989 to 1992. He also filled important governmental positions related to war propaganda and the command of the army during the war with Iraq. After he resigned from the post of minister under increasing pressure from the right, he became the director of Iran's National Library, a position he held until his presidency.

Mohammad Mousavi Khoeiniha (b. 1938), who published the leading reformist newspaper *Salam* from 1991 to 1999, was detained by the shah's secret police, SAVAK, in 1976. After the revolution, Khomeini appointed him as his representative to radio and television. He served as the guide for the revolutionary students who stormed the U.S. embassy in November 1979.[48] He had been the leader of the leftists in parliament but lost his seat in the 1984 elections. In the late 1980s, he led Iranian pilgrims to Mecca and served as the Prosecutor General. At that time, he was a staunch advocate of land redistribution and revolutionary foreign policy. His decision to publish *Salam* coincided with the gradual eclipse of the leftist faction. The newspaper became the leading platform for voices criticizing the rulers while advocating the rule of law and political equality. The Special Court for Clerics (SCC) found him guilty and fined him in 1999. The MCL selected Mousavi Khoeiniha as its secretary general in August 2005.

Mehdi Karroubi (b. 1937), who was the Speaker of the reformist-dominated Sixth Parliament (2000–2004) and one of the founders of the MCL in 1988, had also been the Speaker of the leftist-dominated Third Parliament. He also ran the Martyrs Foundation and the Imam Khomeini Relief Committee. After his defeat in the presidential elections of 2005, he established the National Confidence Party (NCP; Hezb-e Etemad-e Melli).[49]

Abdollah Nouri (b. 1949), Khatami's popular interior minister who was impeached and sentenced, had previously served as the interior minister in Rafsanjani's first cabinet and had been Khomeini's representative in the army. He published the reformist newspaper *Khordad* until 1999, when the SCC sentenced him to five years in prison. Khamenei pardoned him in November 2002.

Nonclerical figures of the RF also had impeccable revolutionary credentials. The leading figures of the RF, including Abbas Abdi (b. 1956), Ebrahim Asgharzadeh (b. 1955), Masume Ebtekar (b. 1960), Saeed Hajjarian (b. 1954), Mohammad Reza Khatami (b. 1959), and Mohsen Mirdamadi (b. 1956), had all been affiliated with the radical student organization that stormed the U.S. embassy in 1979. Abdi was a prolific writer and editor-in-chief of *Salam*. He was arrested several times, the last time being in 2002 on charges of espionage. He was released in 2005 and has kept a low political profile since then. Asgharzadeh had served in the leftist-dominated Third Parliament (1988–1992) and was the chief of the Islamic Iran Solidarity Party (IISP; Hezb-e Hambastegi-ye Iran-e Eslami) until recently. Ebtekar had been the spokeswoman of the hostage takers and became the vice president responsible for the environment in the Khatami government. Hajjarian, who was a founding member of the postrevolutionary Intelligence Ministry, is widely considered the architect of the RF. He was one of the individuals who relocated to the Institute for Strategic Research affiliated with the Presidential Office in the late 1980s and was instrumental in transforming the political discourse of leftist revolutionaries. Khatami appointed him as his advisor in 1997, and he narrowly survived an assassination attempt in 2000. Reza Khatami, the younger brother of the president, served as the secretary general of the Islamic Iran Participation Front (IIPF; Jebhe-ye Mosharekat-e Iran-e Eslami) from 1998 to 2006 and as the Deputy Speaker of the Sixth Parliament. Mirdamadi's newspaper, *Nowruz*, was banned by order of the judiciary in 2002, and he also resigned from his parliamentary post in 2004. He was elected secretary general of the IIPF in August 2006. Ataollah Mohajerani (b. 1954), who oversaw the flourishing of the press during his tenure as Khatami's minister of Culture and Islamic Guidance, had been elected to the First Parliament and served as the parliament's deputy to Prime Minister Mousavi. He remains an influential member of the pragmatist and centrist Executives of Construction Party (ECP; Hezb-e Kargozaran-e Sazendegi), which is closely affiliated with ex-president Rafsanjani. Behzad Nabavi (b. 1941) had negotiated on behalf of the hostage takers and served as the minister of Heavy Industry in the 1980s. He later acted as the Deputy Speaker of the parliament after 2000, and resigned from parliament in 2004 in protest of the GC's disqualification of reformist candidates.

This survey of some of the most influential figures of the RF demonstrates how moderate and nonviolent opposition to the current ruling system in the Islamic Republic is rooted in the revolutionary experiences of the ex-Islamists. Like their counterparts in Turkey, Iranian Muslim reformers were post-Islamists who gradually eschewed their ideological commitments to the monolithic Islamic state.[50] Unlike Turkish Muslim reformers, however, they had firsthand experience of Islamic rule. Their engagement with democratic ideas also reflected their political defeat and marginalization. They later successfully exploited the electoral opportunities offered by the Islamic Republic in the late 1990s. By that time, the intellectual climate was also conducive to the ideas of civil society, human rights, popular rule, and political pluralism. In this sense, their experience gives support to Proposition IVr, indicating that ideological moderation precedes and facilitates behavioral change. In Iran, ideological moderation was not simply a by-product of changes in political opportunities.

The Intellectual Roots of Reform

The rise of the reform movement in Iran was accompanied by a profound transformation of the predominant intellectual climate in the country.[51] Unlike their counterparts in Turkey, Iranian post-Islamists did not have a well-established tradition of electoral politics to build on. The formation of a democratic political discourse that effectively challenged the hegemony of the Islamist state in the 1990s was a remarkable development whose effects may prove to be longer lasting than the achievements of the RF.[52] The reformist intellectuals called for the inviolability of the private sphere, multiparty politics, and public accountability of the state.[53]

Leading intellectuals of the 1960s and 1970s were advocates of Iranian cultural and political authenticity vis-à-vis the West and had little taste for democratic institutions, which they perceived as tools of social inequality and domination. The thought of Jalal Al-e Ahmad (1923–1969), who wrote the popular book *Gharbzadegi* (Westoxification), became a manifesto for the rediscovery of the true meaning of the Shiite traditions that would resist the influx of Western consumerism and moral culture.[54] The most influential lay intellectual of the revolutionary period was Ali Shariati (1933–1977), who reconceptualized Shiite Islam as a force that inherently resists tyranny and injustice. He was sharply critical of contemporary expressions of Shiite Islam, which were characterized by docile and superstitious interpretations by the ineffectual and politically subservient clergy. In Shiite Islam, Shariati saw a great mobilizing force that would appeal to ordinary believers' sense of rightness and justice and urge them to political action. For Shariati, Shiite Islam was an *ideology* that guided and motivated collective struggle for the achievement of a better sociopolitical order. In his vision, individual liberties were subordinated to collective responsibilities and a desire for social justice.[55]

The revolutionary promises of justice and equality were soon overtaken by the rise of a bureaucratic authoritarian state characterized by repression, inefficiency, corruption, and patronage. The towering lay intellectual of the postrevolutionary era offered a dramatically different understanding of the relationship between religion and politics. The disillusionment with the results of the revolution fostered an atmosphere of soul-searching and engagement with liberal-democratic ideas previously dismissed as being inauthentic. Several philosophical figures developed systematic critiques of the ruling ideology, including Mostafa Malekian and Abdolkarim Soroush. Born in Tehran in 1945, and with a graduate degree from England, Soroush emerged as the most sophisticated and elaborate lay voice of the postrevolutionary intellectual conundrum. In the early revolutionary period, he was appointed to the Advisory Council on the Cultural Revolution, which aimed to purge the higher education system of all "un-Islamic elements" and reopen the universities. In 1983, he submitted his resignation and became a researcher at the Institute for Cultural Research and Studies. In the early 1990s, Soroush had increasingly become critical of the *velayat-e faqih* and publicized his ideas in a magazine called *Kiyan,* which he co-founded, and gathered a huge following, especially among the educated youth.

The most distinctive characteristic of his political thought is the distinction between religion and religious knowledge.[56] He argues that whereas the essence of religion remains constant and is absolute, the human understanding of religion evolves over time, and all religious knowledge is "time-bound."[57] His theorization of religious knowledge renders any human claim to absolute truth invalid. Every generation ought to generate new understandings of religion that are in accordance with the demands of the time. The secularization of religious knowledge entails "the belief in the fundamental truth of religion coupled with concern over its contamination and profanation by political concerns."[58] Thus, he argues that politicization of religion brings its decay, and dogmas presented as religious truths cannot form the basis of political decisions and obligations. A second significant dimension of his political thought is his conceptualization of religion as the language of duties, and modern politics as the language of rights. Believers are entitled to salvation only if they fulfill religious obligations. In contrast, modern political discourse involves human rights, protection from arbitrary state interference, popular rule, and pluralism.

The fusion of religious with political authority is problematic for two reasons. Primarily, in such a political system, believers are forced to obey political authority, which pursues its own parochial interpretations of religion, under threat of eternal damnation. The state enforcement of religious law transforms religion into an oppressive ideology. Under these circumstances, religion degenerates into "doctrinarian propaganda and intimidation."[59] Second, in the modern age, religious knowledge has to integrate the language of inviolable rights to be viable and acceptable in the political sphere. Rule in the name of otherworldly sources and the demand for political obedience on the basis of religious faith are incompatible with the modern language of rights. Soroush envisions the notion of religious democracy for societies in which the majority of the population remains pious and demands the application of religious laws. The democratic aspect is very inclusive and includes rationalization of governmental policies and deliberations, separation of powers, universal compulsory education, freedom and autonomy of the press, freedom of expression, consultative assemblies on various levels of decision making, political parties, elections, and parliaments.[60] Consequently, Soroush provides an explicit refutation of the *velayat-e faqih* embodied by the Islamic Republic of Iran.

Several mid-ranking clerics also played critical roles in challenging the regime's claim to absolute religious knowledge. These clerics include Hasan Yousefi Eshkevari (b. 1950), Mohsen Kadivar (b. 1959), and Mojtahed Shabestari (b. 1936). Eshkevari, who had been a political dissident before the revolution and a member of the first postrevolutionary parliament, gradually turned into a vocal critic of clerical rule. In the 1990s, he was a contributing editor to the magazine *Iran-e Farda* and director of the Ali Shariati Research Center. He argues that the clergy should be free from political interference because only if they are independent can they have a critical and respectable voice against political wrongdoings.[61] Instead, he advocates the idea of "Islamic democratic government," in which clerics are not directly involved in political governance.[62] The SCC had him arrested in August 2000 and sentenced him to seven years in prison. He was released in February 2005. Kadivar, who was arrested by the shah's regime because of his political activism, earned the prerogative of practicing *ijtihad* (reaching religiously binding

decisions through logical reasoning) in 1997 and a Ph.D. in Islamic
and philosophy from Tarbiyat Modarres University in 1999. The most
aspect of his political theology is the conceptualization of *velayat-e fa*
linchpin of the Islamic Republic, as just one of the nine types of gover
envisioned by Shiite religious scholars.[63] Hence, *velayat-e faqih* was neither
historically inevitable nor a required condition of Shiite Islam.[64] In his own
words:

saying the same thing?

> I wrote an introduction, around 30 pages, to a work by Mulla Mohammad Ka-
> zim Khurasani. Khurasani was a leader during the Constitutional Revolution of
> 1905–6 and was critical of the notion of the guardianship of the jurisprudent
> (*velayat-e faqih*). Subsequently, around 80 papers were published that were crit-
> ical of my introduction . . . In my other works, I have demonstrated that a large
> number of Great Ayatollahs do not endorse the notion of the guardianship of
> the jurisprudent. . . . Genuine forms of religiosity will flourish only if freedom
> of religion exists and the state does not force people to appear religious.[65]

Shabestari was another cleric who criticized the notion of religion as a holistic body of knowledge that substitutes for human reason and advancement.
Like Eshkevari, he was also elected to the First Parliament (1980–1984) before
leaving active politics to teach at the University of Tehran. Like Soroush, Shabestari is also critical of the claim that humans can possess absolute religious
truth. No individual or group can justifiably claim a monopoly over deciding
what is right and wrong in the religious sense. While human rights and democracy do not derive from the religious canon, they are perfectly compatible
with Islam because they lead to just and universally desirable rule.[66]

The intellectuals mentioned here were not necessarily active supporters of
the RF. Figures like Soroush and Shabestari generally avoided daily politics.
Neither did all reformers espouse the abolishment of *velayat-e faqih* and the
guardianship institutions. Reformist politics were characterized by fluidity,
multiplicity, and, often, conflicting tendencies. Yet the proliferation of reformist thinkers who developed powerful critiques of the ruling system increased
the self-confidence and religious legitimacy of the reformist politicians. The
democratic interpretations of Shiite Islam and the revolutionary legacy effectively ended the ruling regime's monopoly over political-religious discourse
and made the regime vulnerable to criticism by its own criteria. The reformist
thinkers made it possible to envision indigenous alternatives to the *velayat-e*

faqih and the authoritarian practices characterizing the Islamic Republic. The failure of RF in realizing these alternatives did not necessarily make them irrelevant to the future of Iran.

The Rise of the Reform Front

After their defeat in the 1992 elections, leftists-cum-reformers mainly boycotted the 1996 parliamentary elections. The elections produced a parliament dominated by hard-liner rightists content with the existing institutional division of power, but with a sizable minority of pragmatists and technocrats affiliated with Rafsanjani.[67] The increasing division between Rafsanjani and his supporters in the ECP and among the hard-liners led the former group to ally themselves with the MCL and other leftist-reformist organizations in the 1997 presidential elections.[68]

The GC permitted only 4 of the 238 applicants to run for the presidential elections on May 23, 1997. The favorite of the race was Speaker of the Parliament Natiq Nouri, who had the implicit blessing of the supreme leader Khamenei and was backed by the hard-liner rightists who controlled the legislative branch and the judiciary. In addition, he was widely perceived as the candidate who would win the elections. According to a poll conducted by the Public Opinion Studies and Survey National Center, Nouri had the support of 41 percent of the respondents, and 64 percent of the all respondents thought that Nouri would be the next president.[69] The regime mobilized its considerable sources to support Nouri's candidacy. Friday prayer leaders endorsed him, and he received immense coverage in the regime-controlled media.[70] His main competitor was Mohammad Khatami, a member of the MCL, who rapidly became the candidate supported by groups critical of the ruling regime. The key themes of the Khatami campaign were civil society, rule of law, and Islamic democracy. Khatami's success lay in his ability to appeal to many Iranians who were politically apathetic or disillusioned with the regime. In fact, voter turnout, which had been 51 percent in the 1993 presidential elections, skyrocketed to 80 percent in 1997. Many Iranians voted for the first time. On May 23, Khatami swept the polls by capturing 69 percent of the votes. Young voters overwhelmingly voted for Khatami. According to a survey conducted after the elections, more than 80 percent of the respondents cited opposition to the status quo, undesirability of other candidates, and a prevailing atmo-

sphere of political pressures as the main reasons for supporting Khat*
suggested by Proposition I, Khatami's appeal stemmed from his cent*
es that appealed to a large body of the electorate with different prio...

A cleric who thinks democracy represents one of the finest achievements of Western civilization[72] came to power as a result of popular elections in a regime founded by a cleric who dismissed democracy as being irrelevant.[73] Khatami's election provided a unique political opening. Civil society and student activism dramatically increased; reformist journals and magazines flourished; the state enforcement of religious morals became visibly less intense, especially in big cities; and Khatami's call for dialogue with the United States resonated well with the Iranian public.[74] Khatami had to walk a tightrope after his inauguration. His political vision accommodated the principles of freedom of expression and political pluralism with Islamic rule. For him, Islamic values were perfectly compatible with democratic norms and ideals.[75] The reform movement he headed was rooted in the democratic spirit of the revolution and the legacy of Khomeini.[76] He portrayed Khomeini as a benevolent leader who was against dogmatism and despotism in politics. Khatami emphasized the importance of people's participation in the revolution and maintained that the ultimate goal of the revolution and the 1979 Constitution was the empowerment of people.[77] Khatami defined the reform movement as a force that embodied the Constitutional Revolution of 1906, the nationalization of the oil industry in 1951, and the Islamic Revolution of 1979.[78] In a sense, he was exploiting the ambiguities and ambivalences inherent in the legacy of the revolutionary leader.

Yet there were limits to Khatami's strategy to reclaim the spirit of revolution and Khomeini's legacy. First, although Khomeini might have been a revolutionary populist, his political vision can hardly be characterized as inclusive of liberal-democratic principles. Nothing in the praxis and thought of Khomeini suggested even a lukewarm embracing of the liberal concepts of individual rights.[79] His politics were occasionally based on a binary division in which political opponents were treated as foes who have to be eliminated.[80] Not surprisingly, Khatami never openly challenged the legitimacy of *velayat-e faqih,* despite the inherently authoritarian nature of the institution.[81] Second, groups who unyieldingly opposed Khatami's reformist agenda and institutional change also had immaculate revolutionary credentials. They were both institutionally and rhetorically resourceful in frustrating the reform agenda of Khatami and his allies. Shortly after Khatami assumed the presidency, he was confronted with entrenched forces fiercely opposing his agenda, employing both violent and legal methods, despite his constant attempts to have "dialogue." The heads of the powerful *bonyads*, revolutionary guards, vigilante groups, well-connected and well-financed conservative-religious associations, and the GC were either openly or covertly hostile to Khatami's reform agenda.

"Rogue elements" linked to the Intelligence Ministry murdered a series of dissident intellectuals in late 1998 and early 1999 (chain murders, *qatale-ye zanjire-ye*).[82] While Khamenei accused foreign forces of conspiring against the Islamic Republic, Khatami established an investigatory committee. Several individuals working for the Intelligence Ministry were implicated, and the intelligence minister ultimately resigned. However, powerful groups behind the murders were never exposed. The closure of Mousavi Khoeiniha's *Salam* newspaper for its investigation of the murders sparked unprecedented student demonstrations that were brutally suppressed by police forces backed up by vigilante groups in July 1999. These events demonstrated the limits of the president's power over the state apparatus. However, Khatami's strong condemnation of the murders, widespread public reaction, and bold and investigative reporting by journalists such as Akbar Ganji[83] for the first time eroded the culture of impunity pervasive in the Islamic Republic. This was a significant step toward making the regime accountable and transparent to the public. In response, the guardians employed judicial means to suppress popular politicians and dissidents.[84] A key Rafsanjani ally, the mayor of Tehran, Gholamhussein Karbaschi (b. 1954), was arrested on corruption charges in April 1998 and sentenced to five years in prison in July of that year.[85] The SCC had Mohsen Kadivar arrested in 1999 for likening the Islamic Republic to the monarchical regime it replaced. He was sentenced to eighteen months in prison.[86] Another target of the SCC was Khatami's ex-interior minister, Abdollah Nouri, whose trial thrust him into the spotlight as an eloquent and bold critic of the ruling clerics.

Meanwhile, reformers, who were emboldened by Khatami's electoral performance, concentrated their energies on mobilizing public support in the upcoming elections. As Proposition I of moderation theory would expect, they developed an *electoral strategy* to appeal to the greatest number of voters and end their political marginalization. As discussed in the previous chapter, the

Iranian electoral system is characterized by fluidity and severe restrictions on campaigning. Political parties remain weakly organized and lack strong internal cohesion. Even so, the initial years of the Khatami era saw the proliferation of party activism.[87] The IIPF, established in 1998, became the main organization espousing a reformist agenda. The electoral strategy bore its first fruits with the 1999 local council elections: the reformers swept the polls. They promoted the first local council elections that had taken place since the revolution as an important step toward developing a bottom-up democratic organization. Public enthusiasm in the elections was relatively high, around 65 percent.

Since his election in 1997, Khatami had had to work with a noncooperative and often hostile parliament dominated by the principalists (osulgaran).[88] The real momentum of the reformist movement came with the 2000 parliamentary elections. The reformers formed a loose alliance before the 2000 parliamentary elections. The alliance, Dovom Khordad,[89] included the IIPF and seventeen reformist organizations such as the MCL, the pro-Rafsanjani ECP, the IISP, and the Organization of Endeavourers of Islamic Revolution (OEIR; Sazeman-e Mojahedin-e Enqelab-e Eslami).[90] The RF pursued a coordinated campaign and generated a joint list of candidates for electoral districts except for Tehran. The reformist newspapers galvanized public interest in the elections by emphasizing the importance of the reformist control of parliament.

An interesting aspect of the February 2000 parliamentary elections was the low ratio of aspirants disqualified by the GC. In sharp contrast to both the 1996 and the 2004 elections, the GC disqualified only about 8 percent of the 6,856 applicants.[91] Although the reasons for such a dramatic change in the GC's behavior are hard to elucidate, it can be argued that the guardians did not feel secure and confident enough to completely block the reformers from running in the elections. They might have reached the conclusion that it would be better to have the RF confined in the parliament where they would have only limited power rather than encouraging them to wage a popular campaign at the grassroots level. They might have anticipated that incorporation of the RF into the institutional framework of the regime would gradually undermine their agenda and publicly expose their vulnerabilities. If the guardians were such savvy political players, their strategy ultimately would work. Or they were concerned with the social reaction that might follow their decision to exclude the reformers from the electoral competition. Alternatively, they might have underestimated the appeal of the RF, especially in smaller towns and rural areas where patronage networks and personalities highly affect voting behavior. In any case, the elections were a landslide victory for the RF. The voter turnout was 69 percent. The RF's ability to mobilize large segments of young voters, some of whom had never voted previously, was likely a crucial factor in their victory.[92] The youth population, between ages fifteen and twenty-nine, made up around one-third of the total population.[93] Citizens who had been sixteen years old were eligible to vote in 2000, although the voting age was raised to eighteen in 2007.[94]

The candidates affiliated with the RF parties captured 150 seats in the first round, and controlled around 200 of the 290 parliamentary seats at the end of the second round. The IIPF, led by Mohammad Reza Khatami, had around 80 seats, and the MCL, led by Karroubi, around 60.[95] In addition, some of the independents were also sympathetic to the reformist agenda. The hard-liner right's parliamentary group was reduced to fewer than 60 seats.[96] The biggest loser of the elections was ex-president Rafsanjani, who did not receive enough votes to win a seat representing Tehran in the first round. The reformist press made him a symbol of corrupt, clandestine, and incompetent aspects of the ruling regime. Rafsanjani attempted to portray himself as a supporter of Khatami and his agenda, but to no avail.[97]

The central idea of the RF was the recovery of the democratic spirit of the revolution. Before the elections, the IIPF declared that the party followed Khomeini's path and would establish the rule of law (a reference to shadowy violent groups operating with official protection); decentralize the administration; make state enterprises and *bonyads* transparent; abolish the SCC; amend the press law to protect the freedom of expression; eliminate censorship of books, films, and theater; and promote the integration of the Iranian economy with the world economy.[98] Meanwhile, the IIPF developed a criticism of the religious government for failing to answer the needs of a modern society. The party's main power base was the urban middle class, who became disillusioned with the results of the revolution. The party had weak linkages with regular salary earners and workers. For the IIPF, the Islamic religion was turned into a tool in the service of power. An unintended consequence of the politicization of the religion was the corruption of societal values. The party's goal was to invite broad political participation and democratize the institutions of power through gradual reform.[99] As Proposition II of moderation theory would suggest, the RF eschewed head-to-head confrontation with the guardians and their hard-liner allies.

The Failure of the Electoral Strategy

The response of the guardians and their allies to the sweeping reformist victory in the parliamentary elections was swift and overwhelming. The GC changed the electoral results in several provinces to the disadvantage of reformist candidates, declared that Rafsanjani won a seat, and refused to certify the election results in Tehran, which jeopardized the opening of the parliament.[100] The assault on the RF was intensified in the aftermath of the elections.[101] Less than a month after the elections, the hard-liner cleric Mohammad Mesbah Yazdi denounced the Khatami government by characterizing its cultural politics as "trampling upon the blood of martyrs."[102] Two days later, Hajjarian, who was the chief reformist strategist, the director of the reformist daily *Sobh-e Emrooz,* and a member of the Tehran municipal council, was the target of an assassination attempt.[103] He barely survived his wounds but remained crippled. For the reformers, it was a clear warning that their popular mandate would not translate into effective political power.[104] In April, in his address to a Friday prayer congregation, Khamenei criticized the press for creating artificial divisions, which were then exploited by the enemy. He also made a distinction between "American-type reforms" and "Islamic reforms," and praised the president while vehemently criticizing his more "radical" allies.[105] This speech was followed by a full-scale attack on press freedom by hard-liners in the judiciary.[106] Before the end of April, sixteen reformist dailies had been banned. Meanwhile, the courts issued arrest warrants for various reformist figures, including Eshkevari and Ganji, for attending a conference in Berlin. In July, the Revolutionary Guards issued a statement denouncing the supporters of the RF as "the champions of American-style reforms."[107] By the end of the year, some twenty-five reformist newspapers had been closed and several journalists had been imprisoned.[108] Most importantly, the RF was also unable to overcome the veto power of the GC despite its control of the parliament. According to the Deputy Speaker, Nabavi, two-fifths of all parliamentary bills had been vetoed by the GC within the first six months of the new parliament.[109] Khamenei personally intervened in August to declare that a new bill easing the restrictions on the press would be against the interests of the nation.[110] The hard-liners were fearful that the RF's success in popular mobilization would bring about their downfall. In this sense, they were fighting for their survival.

> The reformists attempted to undermine the constitution by calling for the elimination of indirectly elected offices such as the Guardians Council. They attempted to illegally expand their power. They were following the ideas of Hajjarian. They pursued his strategy of "pressure from below, and negotiation at the top" to generate conflict and maximize their power. They insisted on civic disobedience. By promoting the idea of freedom of the press, they aimed to shape and control public opinion.[111]

WTF?

Public enthusiasm for the RF was gradually replaced by apathy and disenchantment. When Khatami declared that he would run for a second term, public reaction was guarded. There was an intense discussion about the merits of voting for him again. For many reformers, the elections were a referendum on Khatami's presidency.[112] Khatami easily secured a second term in the absence of a serious challenger by receiving 77 percent of the national vote. However, turnout dropped from 80 percent to 67 percent. Particularly striking was the low turnout in areas populated by minorities, such as Kurdistan (53%) and East and West Azerbaijan (53% and 64% respectively), Ardabil (58%), and Khozestan (59%).[113] Apparently, ethnic minorities no longer found Khatami's discourse of reform very credible.

The harassment of the RF continued after the elections. The judiciary persecuted outspoken members of parliament; the reformist press was under constant threat of closure; the GC and the EC effectively frustrated the government's and the parliament's ability to change the institutional distribution of power. Voter turnout in the local council elections held in February 2003 was a dismal 49 percent. In Tehran, turnout reached a nadir of 13 percent. The low voter turnout helped the hard-liners to capture seats previously held by the supporters of the RF. The electoral setback intensified the debate within the reformist ranks about the merits of their electoral strategy. A common assumption was that the hard-liners could win only if turnout was low.[114] However, public avoidance of the polls reflected not only reaction against the ruling regime but also lost confidence in the RF. According to a survey conducted in Tehran in August 2003, over 50 percent of the respondents found the political system either rarely or never responsive.[115] Around 45 percent thought that the state completely failed to serve the public interest. The public was also critical of the RF. Only a third of the respondents mentioned reformist figures or groups as being capable of solving the country's political problems. The RF was gradually losing its relevance in the eyes of the public.[116]

Consistent with the expectations of moderation theory (Proposition II), Khatami and his allies acted with moderation in the face of increasing repression. They continued to operate within the existing institutional and legal structure. The most critical aspect of their strategy was the drafting of two bills that would end the GC's approbatory supervision of the candidates and enhance the status of the president vis-à-vis other branches of the regime. The bills would give the president the power to call for a referendum on these two issues. The irony was that both bills needed the GC's approval before they could be passed. The GC rejected the twin bills several times, and despite reformist threats, no compromise was achieved.[117] Some members of the RF were in favor of radical actions and disagreed with the cautious style of Khatami.[118] For example, the IIPF-affiliated parliamentarians considered resigning en masse but could not convince the members of the MCL to join them and could not take decisive action.[119] A frustrated Khatami eventually asked parliament to withdraw the twin bills.[120]

The final nail in the RF's coffin was the 2004 parliamentary elections. The GC disqualified around 3,600 of the 8,000 registered aspirants from running in the elections. Among the disqualified were more than 80 current members of the parliament. About 90 reformist parliamentarians organized a sit-in in the parliament building in reaction.[121] In an open letter to the president, the regional governors threatened to resign en masse if the disqualifications were not revoked.[122] Less than a week later, more than 100 parliamentarians went on a hunger strike to protest the violation of constitutional rights.[123] Parliament passed an emergency amendment to the electoral law that would make all sitting parliamentarians eligible to run in the elections and decrease the GC's control over the candidacy process. The GC swiftly rejected the amendment.[124] Khatami and Karroubi criticized the GC's decision and called for a comprehensive review of all the disqualified candidates. They argued that 190 out of 290 parliamentary seats would be uncontested.[125] The GC eventually decided to decrease the number of disqualified candidates to 2,400 but increased the number of disqualified sitting parliamentarians from 83 to 87.[126] Following that, 125 parliamentarians submitted their resignations and declared that elections under these conditions would destroy the republican aspect of the regime.[127] The IIPF announced that it would boycott the elections unless the disqualifications were overturned. Khamenei criticized calls for a boycott and resignations as being *haram* (religiously forbidden) by arguing that elected officials were obliged to serve the people.[128] A few days later, the parliamentarians ended their sit-in protest. In a final act of open defiance, many parliamentarians sent a letter to Khamenei questioning his role in the process.[129] In a sense, these halfhearted and not very well coordinated acts of defiance came too late. Active public support for the reformers remained negligible. Fulfilling his ceremonial duty, Khatami exhorted the public to vote by arguing that low turnout would play into the hands of the hard-liners.[130]

The elections took place on February 20, and turnout was around 51 percent.[131] About twenty-three million of forty-six million eligible voters did not participate in the elections.[132] While some key members of the RF boycotted the elections, other reformist groups participated but performed poorly.[133] The winners of the 2004 parliamentary elections were a younger cohort of hard-liners, organized under the banner of the Islamic Iran Developers Council (IIDC). According to its charter, the IIDC believes in religious democracy and strives to effectively confront American globalization.[134] This group won 14 of the 15 council seats in the city of Tehran in 2003 and all 30 of the parliamentary seats in 2004. The group controlled around 170 seats in the parliament.[135] While being loyal to the *velayat-e faqih,* they avoided radical discourses on cultural issues, campaigned on themes of economic improvement, and co-opted the reformist strategy of appealing directly to the people.[136] The Speaker of the Parliament from 2004 to 2008, Gholam-Ali Haddad-Adel (b. 1945), hailed from this group and dreamed of transforming Iran into a developed nation enjoying social welfare, like an "Islamic Japan."[137] Overall, the principalists learned some lessons from the reformist victories. They realized the importance of newspapers and television in shaping public opinion and adopted some of the reformist slogans.[138]

The RF was in complete disarray in the aftermath of the 2004 parliamentary elections. The reformers accused the GC of betraying the republican promises of the revolution and Khomeini's legacy.[139] Yet the RF did not envision any strategy other than the legalistic-electoral one.[140] The IIPF Seventh Congress, held in July 2004, revealed the prevailing defeatist atmosphere. Secretary General Mohammad Reza Khatami confessed that they had no other option than legal political activism.[141] Being unable to generate change, the reformers now played the "fear card" and argued that hard-liner domination of the regime would undermine the Islamic Republic and lead to anarchy.[142] They apologetically pointed out that people had unrealistic expectations of the RF.[143]

The June 2005 presidential elections were unprecedented, given the high level of fragmentation and the intensity of competition. The reformers failed to reach a consensus on a single candidate despite the warnings of Hajjarian.[144] This time, 1,014 aspirants registered their candidacy, but the GC approved only 6, including Karroubi and Rafsanjani. Not only had reformist candidates been disqualified but also several well-known hard-liners.[145] The IIPF candidate, Mostafa Moin (b. 1951), who had served as the minister of culture and higher education in the Rafsanjani and Khatami cabinets, was among those whose candidacy was rejected. However, Khamenei intervened and reinstated Moin and another reformer, Mohsen Mehralizadeh.[146] The irony was hard to miss. Reformist candidates were eligible to run only because of the unilateral action of the *faqih* (*hokm-e hokumati*), which was devoid of any legislative or judicial sanctioning. A hard-liner candidate later withdrew, and 7 candidates competed. The ex-president Rafsanjani, who was busy reinventing himself as the savior of the reform movement, led the pack in campaigning.[147] Moin was calculating that a higher voter turnout would be the key to his victory, which turned out to be a complete miscalculation.

All candidates, with the exception of Tehran mayor Mahmoud Ahmedinejad (b. 1956), built their platforms on themes popularized by Khatami. The septuagenarian Rafsanjani portrayed himself as the only candidate who could achieve progress, and promised greater economic liberalization and social freedoms and normalized relations with the United States.[148] Mohammad Baqir Qalibaf (b. 1961), the former head of the police, reinvented himself as a component technocrat who was sensitive to the priorities and needs of Iran's younger population. However, the candidates who developed populist messages and focused on the plight of low-income Iranians performed well at the ballot box. Voter turnout was around 63 percent and 61 percent in the first and second rounds respectively.[149] Ahmedinejad, who emerged as the "antiestablishment candidate" with his strong social justice, equality, and anticorruption messages, received 19 percent of the national vote and secured a runoff against the frontrunner Rafsanjani.[150] His references to the promises of the 1979 revolution resonated well with the public.

Motorcyclists celebrating the victory of Ahmedinejad in an upscale Tehran neighborhood (Tehran, June 2005)

> Mr. Ahmedinejad represents a return to the essence of Islam and revolutionary ideals. Twenty years after the revolution, its ideals were forgotten. The monarchical system was almost reinstituted. Our goal is to rekindle the spirit of revolution and make Iran prosperous under the guidance of our leader [*rahbar*].[151]

Karroubi, who also adopted a populist platform by promising approximately $65 a month to every Iranian citizen over the age of nineteen, finished third with 17 percent. He cried foul play by accusing the Revolutionary Guards and the Basij of interfering in the elections on behalf of Ahmedinejad.[152] The newspapers that published his open complaint letter to Khamenei were temporarily banned.[153] While Rafsanjani and Moin joined Karroubi in questioning the fairness of the elections, accusations of rigging were not substantiated with evidence in the absence of independent electoral monitoring.[154] In any case, it remained unclear how the Basij was able to tilt the elections in favor of Ahmedinejad. It would be unrealistic to assume that Basij members could easily be mobilized for supporting a candidate. The organization has a loose structure. "I voted for Larijani in the first round and for Ahmedinejad in the second. I did not notice any centralized intervention to make Basij members support Ahmedinejad. There was no order coming from the top to vote for Ahmedinejad in 2005," remarked an ex-Basij member.[155] It seems more reasonable that the Basij higher command engaged in electoral fraud on behalf of Ahmedinejad in certain districts.

In an ironic twist, the RF threw its support behind Rafsanjani in the second round. The IIPF explicitly asked Iranians to vote for Rafsanjani to stop reactionary forces and fascism.[156] However, for many Iranians, Ahmedinejad represented a fresh and untested alternative to returning to the status quo, In his television appearance before the elections, he flatly rejected accusations of religious fanaticism and declared that social justice, ending corruption, and helping working-class families were his priorities. He won the second round with a landslide by capturing 62 percent of the national vote in contrast to Rafsanjani's 36 percent. The election of Ahmedinejad to the presidency effectively ended the first reform era in the Islamic Republic.

Vandalized posters of Rafsanjani, who was defeated by Ahmedinejad in the June 2005 presidential elections (Kashan, June 2006)

Posters of Khomeini, Khamenei, and Ahmedinejad in a village market (Kandovan, June 2006)

The Impasse of the Reform Front

Would the RF have been more successful if it had pursued a strategy of civil disobedience and grassroots mobilization? Would public pressure have ended the GC's involvement in the electoral process and increased the powers of elected offices? These are reasonable counterfactual questions, given the initial popularity of the RF and a variety of choices available to its leaders at several critical junctures, such as during the student demonstrations of 1999, the mass closure of the reformist press in 2000, the GC's vetoing of Khatami's twin bills in 2003, or the mass disqualifications of 2004.[157] The RF lacked decisive leadership and pursued an accommodative and moderate strategy regardless of the consequences, lest it increase the repression it faced. By 2001, it became clear to many that this strategy was not working. Despite its control of the presidency, the cabinet, and the parliament, the RF failed to overcome the veto power of the guardians and control the actions of their hard-liner allies entrenched in security forces, *bonyads*, and organizations directly reporting to the *faqih*, such as the Council of the Friday Prayers.[158]

As moderation theory would expect, the reformers preferred a moderate electoral-legal strategy to a radical strategy of grassroots mobilization and mass agitation. Being children of the revolutionary period, they were convinced that the 1979 Constitution was capable of generating a democratic system. They were also deeply concerned with the hard-liner accusations of treason and generally avoided confrontation. According to the IIPF, the main problem lay in the way the constitution was interpreted by the guardians.[159] Its secretary general argued that a clear and transparent interpretation of the constitution would contribute to the democratization of the regime.[160] While the IIPF identified the establishment of grassroots democracy as its principal goal, it insisted that no action outside the legal framework would be pursued.[161]

Fear of state repression and loyalty to the Islamic Republic were not the only factors that made the RF act with moderation. As Proposition III of moderation theory suggests, organizational constraints ultimately shaped the RF's behavior. The reformist organizations lacked the characteristics of mass parties and were unable to coordinate their activities. They remained a loose collection of influential individuals with little grassroots participation. In contrast to electoral politics in Turkey, the party meetings remained elite gatherings. The weak organizational structure of the parties reflected the rudimentary and highly restrictive nature of the Iranian elections. Citizens voted directly for individual candidates without party labels, the citizens themselves lacked strong party identification, the campaigning period was short and heavily regulated, and state aid to parties was nil. Moreover, the ruling clerics had little sympathy for parties and viewed them as alternative avenues of power that would undermine their hegemony.[162] However, institutional constraints only partially explain the elite-oriented nature and small membership base of the reformist organizations. Some of the reformers saw no role for the mass political parties. They explicitly concentrated their energies on striking deals among the elites rather than incorporating the public into their organizations.[163] They encouraged citizens to vote in the elections but did not envision more direct and engaged forms of public participation. They were more interested in preserving their elected offices and political access than in fighting for a more equal distribution of political power. The RF did not pursue the interests of its key constituencies nor did they build resilient linkages with the public. In the end, they alienated their core supporters, including the student and women's movements, and lost their political influence.[164] The reformist parliamentarians had little active support from the student and civil-society organizations when they staged a sit-in protest against the GC's disqualifications in 2004.[165] The RF's control of both the presidency and the parliament from 2000 to 2004 made it look inept and a part of the corrupt system in the eyes of many Iranians.[166] In a sense, it became a victim of its own electoral successes. As suggested by Proposition Vr, a strategy of democratic change based on moderation proved to be futile in the Islamic Republic.

The lack of coordination and unity also fatally undermined the RF's ability to confront the guardians' assault. They occasionally engaged in squabbling that both tarnished their public image and undermined their capacity for collective action. That was particularly evident during the disqualification crisis before the 2004 elections. Reformist parliamentarians whose candidacies were approved by the GC tended to avoid participating in the sit-in to avoid the ire of the guardians.[167] While the IIPF declared that the elections would be illegitimate and called for a boycott, the MCL decided to take part in the electoral contest.[168] As noted earlier, Khatami urged citizens to vote despite the fact that hard-liner candidates faced no serious opponents in many electoral districts. After the elections, IIPF Secretary General Mohammad Reza Khatami was highly critical of "moderate reformers," who participated in the elections under the terms of the hard-liners.[169] In contrast, Karroubi, then secretary general of the MCL, criticized the decision to boycott the elections as well as "radical" stances that made reconciliation with the GC impossible.[170] The same Karroubi openly challenged the GC and the *faqih* for conducting unfair elections in June 2005.

In the IIPF's Ninth Congress in August 2006, Mohammad Reza Khatami, who stepped down from the post of secretary general, lamented the heavy pressures on the RF and sharply criticized the Ahmedinejad government policies.[171] He drew parallels between the reform movement and the constitutional movement of 1906 and Mosaddeq's nationalization of oil in the early 1950s. Despite its shortcomings, the reform movement would be more successful than the previous experiences and break the vicious cycle of repression, he argued. He identified democratization of the government and bolstering the civil society as two priorities of the reform movement. However, he was mostly silent on how the IIPF would enlarge its membership base, increase its society-level activities, and restore the public confidence in the reform movement. In February 2009, former president Khatami announced that he would challenge the incumbent Ahmedinejad in the June 2009 presidential elections with the same promises he had offered in 1997.[172] Then he withdrew and declared his support for ex-prime minister Mousavi. It appeared that the electoral strategy was still the only game in town.

CHAPTER 7

Elusive
Democratization
in the
Secular Republic

Islamic political movements in Turkey have been primarily organized as electoral parties. In contrast to Islamic movements such as the Muslim Brotherhood (Al-Ikhwan al-Muslimun) in Egypt or the Islamic Daʿwa (Hezb-e al-Daʿwa al-Islamiyya) in Iraq, they have not had cell-based, clandestine, and vanguard-type organizational structures. The recurrent theme in forty years of Islamic party activism in Turkey has been the tension between religious party platforms, the dynamics of electoral competition, and secularist rule. Islamist politicians often pursued pragmatic policies at the expense of ideological consistency and integrity. They entered into coalitions and electoral alliances with parties they had previously condemned in the 1970s and 1990s. As strategic actors seeking votes and political office, Muslim politicians faced the dilemma of challenging the legitimacy of the secular regime while acting under legal constraints.

From a comparative perspective, the authoritarian conditions that played into the hands of radical Islamists in the late 1970s in Iran were absent in Turkey. Islamists failed to mobilize a broad coalition against the secular regime in the pluralistic and highly competitive Turkish political environment. A primary reason for this failure was the diversity of Muslim responses to Turkish secularist modernization, ranging from enthusiastic acceptance to passive resistance, from pragmatic accommodation to outright opposition. Islamists had to contend with this diversity, which often favored center-right parties, to mobilize a sustained and direct challenge to the modernity project by the republic. Another factor limiting the appeal of Turkish Islamists was the absence of an autonomous and popular clerical establishment in Turkey that might have led the opposition against the secular regime, as in the case of Iran. Turkish Islamists were led by lay people who could not claim mastery of religious knowledge and jurisdiction as did Khomeini and his associates. They had to constantly negotiate with popular Sufi sheiks and brotherhoods and state-appointed clergy in their quest for popular support. The fact that popular and Sufi religious identities did not always overlap with political identities propagated by the Islamists limited the appeal of Islamist political parties. Besides, a full understanding of the evolution of Islamic politics requires a focus on center-right parties in Turkish politics. Center-right parties contributed to the development of a competitive and pluralistic political environment in two ways. First, they were instrumental in the integration of marginalized conservative and pious citizens into the legal and electoral system in the 1950s and 1960s. Second, they limited the appeal of Islamists.

Center-Right: The Pivotal Player in Turkish Politics

According to an influential paradigm, the prevailing cleavage in Turkish politics was the struggle between center and periphery at least until the 1970s.[3] The forces of the center were the bureaucracy, the Turkish Armed Forces (TAF), the intelligentsia, the professional urban classes, and the Republican People's Party (RPP; Cumhuriyet Halk Partisi).[4] The center, which ruled the country until the first free elections in 1950, generally advocated a strict interpretation of secularist nationalism that limited public expressions of religion. In contrast, the periphery, which was led by elites who had defected from the RPP and represented rural peasants and nascent commercial and industrialist classes, had a more lax understanding of secularism and was more receptive to popular demands and tolerant toward religion. The Democratic Party (DP), representing the periphery and supported by the Turkish bourgeoisie, came to power in 1950 and won three consecutive elections before being overthrown by a military coup in 1960.[5] The DP leadership's understanding of democracy rested on the majoritarian notion of "popular will" and had little room for separation of powers.[6] The party advocated a more liberal understanding of secularism. According to Ali Fuat Başgil, who was an advisor to the DP government, secularism must not obscure religious freedoms. These freedoms include, among others, the unfettered dissemination of religious knowledge. Secularism does not involve the state's control of religion but the complete separation of the two.[7]

With the 1960s, the center gradually evolved into the center-left while the periphery became synonymous with the center-right. The RPP, which was closely associated with the status quo, assumed a new role as the party of social protest and change in the 1970s. The political dualism started to come apart with the rise of far-left and far-right forces in the late 1960s.[8] Figure 7.1 shows the rise of religious and national right parties at the expense of the center-right during the 1990s. Religious and nationalist right parties replaced the center-right as the main political force in the country in the late 1990s. Only the electoral victories of the JDP in 2002 and 2007 stopped this trend.

The value of the "center-periphery" paradigm lies in its powerful description of the main cleavage in Turkish politics in the post-World War II era. This paradigm conceptualizes political conflict between two equally "legitimate" groups, not between secularist-progressives and religious-reactionaries or Ja-

Figure 7.1. Turkish Electoral Landscape from 1987 to 2007

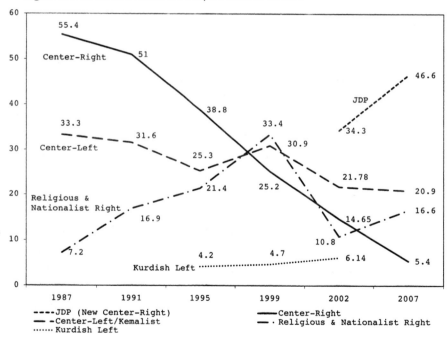

Note: The Kurdish left sponsored independent candidates in the 2007 elections to obtain parliamentary representation despite the 10 percent threshold, and twenty-two of these candidates gained seats in the parliament. The vote share of all candidates backed by the Kurdish left was around 4 percent.

cobin elites and authentic popular forces. It maintains that political tension emanates from the opposing agendas of groups that were pushing for broader political participation and groups that were defending the republican notions of restrictive political governance. The latter are the secularist-nationalists who oppose the corrosive effects of electoral politics on republican principles, while the former are populist-reformists who derive their legitimacy from the public support they enjoy.[9] What was religious fanaticism and reaction for the latter was religious freedom and sacred values for the former.[10] Yet the leadership of both camps supported Turkey's membership in NATO and the European Union. Most importantly, the center-right tradition never directly challenged the secular legal framework of Turkey.[11] For example, the Justice Party (JP), which was the main center-right party from 1961 to 1980, promoted a mode of secularism that is accommodating to popular religious demands and practices.[12]

According to a common view, the TAF's involvement in politics protects democratic accomplishments against the threat of "Islamic radicalism."[13] Accordingly, the political role of the TAF is not perceived as a pernicious influence.[14] This view ignores the decades-old Turkish center-right tradition with its more liberal understanding of the religion-and-politics relationship.[15] This stands in sharp contrast to Iran under the shah, where the weakness of liberal oppositional forces paved the way for mass mobilization under Islamist leadership. Antirepublican radicalism never enjoyed widespread public support in Turkey. Besides, not all military interventions in Turkey targeted "Islamic radicalism." While the purported goals of the 1960 and 1997 interventions were to defend secular republicanism against governments that encouraged or promoted religiously reactionary elements (*irtica*), the perpetrators of the 1980 intervention saw in Islam an integrative and pacifying force. Most prominently, the junta sponsored a school curriculum that advocated religious interpretations of nationalism and loyalty to the state on the basis of piety in its quest to reinvent a politically docile population.[16]

Consequently, the view of Turkey as a society divided between secular elites and religious masses is very misleading.[17] The vitality of center-right parties, which facilitate the political integration of pious Sunni citizens, has been crucial for the stability of Turkish democracy and has contributed to its longevity. From this perspective, the most remarkable development in recent Turkish politics has been the revitalization of the center-right. The rise of the

JDP in the 2002 and 2007 elections represents neither a new form of Islamic radicalism nor a model of Islamic democracy. Rather, it reconstructed the political tradition represented by the DP in the 1950s, the JP in the 1960s and the 1970s, and the Motherland Party (MP) in the 1980s.

Struggle for the Moral Order

Islamism as a political ideology arose as a response to the military defeats of the Ottoman Empire and the superiority of the Western world in knowledge and science.[18] For its proponents, rather than being an impediment to scientific and social progress, Islamic civilization provided an alternative to the West.[19] In this sense, it was a particular mode of incorporating Western science while refusing its cultural values. It envisioned a political unity built on the religious identity of Muslims.[20] Islamism lost its appeal in Turkey with the rebellion of Arabs against the empire and the rise of Turkish nationalism in Anatolia. After democratization in 1946, several proto-Islamist parties that catered to popular religious demands emerged, and Islamic publications critical of the state-imposed secularism experienced a revival.[21] The main thrusts of the Islamist criticism of the republican years were the severe restrictions on religious freedoms and a characterization of Turkish secularism as being antireligious. Democracy, understood exclusively as the will of a religious majority, was a vehicle for revoking the restrictions on religion.[22] In 1970, Necmettin Erbakan (b. 1926), a professor of engineering, founded the first party with an explicit Islamic message.[23] Small and medium business owners in conservative Anatolian cities, various Sufi orders, organized student movements such as the National Turkish Student Union (Milli Türk Talebe Birliği), and Islamic intellectuals were the main pillars of the new party. A common concern of these entities was the "threat of Communism," which remained the defining characteristic of the political right in Turkey until the early 1990s.[24] In particular, the İskenderpaşa Cemaati (Iskenderpasa Community) of the Nakshibendi Order, led by Mehmet Zahid Kotku (1897–1980), played an important role in the formation of the National Order Party (NOP).[25] The İskenderpaşa Cemaati experienced a remarkable transformation under Kotku and attracted young, well-educated, and aspiring middle- and lower-middle-class members who also became active in politics.[26] Kotku was a role model and an inspiration for Erbakan, who belonged to this ambitious generation.[27]

This close but tension-ridden relationship reveals the importance of officially banned Sufi orders in creating an Islamic political identity in Turkey.[28] The rigid ideological frameworks of the Islamist parties during the 1970s and 1980s were not effective in mobilizing broad public support and generating enough momentum to challenge the political system. The NOP presented itself as an alternative to the "liberal" view represented by the center-right JP and the "leftist" view of the center-left RPP.[29] While accusing all other parties of being the "imitators" of the West, the NOP claimed to be the only *authentic* voice of the nation.[30] Like Mawdudi's Jamaat-e Islami in Pakistan, the foundation of the NOP was expressed in terms of a reaction to the centuries-old decline of the Muslim world.[31] The quest for authenticity that is central to all Islamic revivalist movements in the twentieth century also defined the founding ideology of the NOP.[32] The party was founded on an apologist understanding of Islam. The world was perceived through a "clash of civilizations" perspective, and "Zionists" and "Masons" were accused of conspiracies.[33] In its founding statement and program, the party criticized Turkey's modernization project for ignoring the "moral development" of citizens. For the party, Turkey remained backward because the rulers had pursued a superficial model of development that was inattentive to national Islamic traditions and heritage. Japan was praised for its ability to achieve economic development while preserving its cultural identity and past. The NOP was fiercely opposed to the agents of Western influence such as tourism, ballet schools, lotteries, consumption of alcohol, birth control, and New Year's celebrations. The party was also very critical of Turkish secularism, which was considered to be inimical to religion.[34] It was committed to electoral democracy, but it criticized Western democratic systems for promoting unfettered freedom and anarchy.

The Turkish Constitutional Court (TCC) dissolved the NOP for being a center of antisecular activities and opposing the "revolutions of Atatürk" in May 1971.[35] The National Salvation Party (NSP), founded in October 1972, gained forty-eight parliamentary seats in the 1973 elections.[36] The NSP was most successful in the economically backward and culturally conservative Central Anatolian provinces and the Kurdish provinces of the east. It pursued a strategy of religious mobilization that was based on the conviction that true and pious Muslims would vote for the party. From a classic modernization perspective, the NSP was the party of social segments that were most resentful toward socioeconomic change. The party also had the support of a leading student union, the National Turkish Student Union, which adopted an increasingly Islamist platform during the 1970s. "Anti-Communism," which entailed intense hostility toward any leftist movement, and reordering of the society according to Islamic norms were main themes of the union.[37] Many leading politicians of the WP in the 1990s and the JDP in the 2000s, including Tayyip Erdoğan, Abdullah Gül, and Bülent Arınç, were active in the union. In the 1970s, the NSP entered into several coalition governments as the junior partner. This generated strong tensions between the party's ideological commitments and the logic of electoral politics. While participation in coalition governments put vast patronage resources at the party's disposal and reinforced its status as a legal party, it also tarnished the NSP's image as a serious alternative to the "system parties." As a result, the party suffered a serious setback in the June 1977 elections. Nevertheless, the party joined other rightist parties to form a coalition government that lasted until January 1978.[38]

The second half of the 1970s witnessed the formation of an Islamist activism and political mindset that was inspired by thinkers such as Mawdudi and Qutb and was more universalistic and ambitious than that of the NSP.[39] A young generation of Islamist activists organized around magazines such as *İslami Hareket, Şura, Tevhid,* and *Hicret* and associations such as İlim ve Kültür Ocağı made attempts to formulate Islam as a political ideology entailing a lifestyle free from the problems of modern life, transcending sectarian and national boundaries, and offering a vision of the common good distinct from both capitalism and Communism.[40] Islamist activism, inspired by the Iranian Revolution and the Afghan resistance to the Soviet invasion, increasingly gained self-confidence.[41] The NSP, which remained ideologically more ambivalent than this Islamic activism, experienced tension with the Sufi orders, which were resentful of the policies of the NSP and fearful of state repression. The rise of Islamist parties created a class of religious politicians competing with the sheiks for prestige and influence. Religious identities did not directly foster political identities.[42] This inevitably limited the appeal of the party. Meanwhile, the NSP's relationship with democracy was characterized by ambiguities and uncertainties. Its participation in electoral politics reflected strategic interests rather than any democratic convictions of its leaders. The establishment of a moral society built on Islamic norms and laws dictated by the state remained the ultimate goal of the party until the very end. On several occasions, the party staged mass rallies advocating the establishment of sharia rule.[43] For the NSP, politics was a struggle between the faithful and everyone else that resembled the enemy/friend distinction of Carl Schmitt. Moderation theory would expect that political inclusion through the mechanisms of electoral opportunities and the threat of state repression would tame the NSP's ideological radicalism. Yet that did not happen in this instance. This indicates that ideological moderation is not an automatic consequence of political inclusion, as suggested by Proposition IV of moderation theory. Consistent with the expectations of Proposition IVr, the NSP did not make any systematic attempt to develop a centrist platform to enlarge its voting base in the absence of a permissible ideology.

Interregnum: The 1980 Military Coup

The 1980 military coup was the most critical event in Turkish politics since the introduction of multiparty democracy thirty years ago. All political parties and unions were closed; major politicians were banned from active politics; tens of thousands were imprisoned while dozens were hanged and thousands were subjected to periodic treatments in torture chambers.[45] The military rule was most repressive in Kurdish regions, which contributed to the popular appeal of the PKK.[46] The cultural rights of the Kurds were denied, and draconian antiterror laws highly curtailed freedom of speech and expression after the transition to civilian rule.[47] The military ordered a new constitution to be written in 1982 that severely curtailed the scope of political activity and individual freedom. The Constitution of 1982 gave enormous power to institutions that were insulated from popular politics. The TAF leadership carved out a very influential role for itself by assigning extraordinary powers to the National Security Council (NSC), which functioned as the body where the military dictated policies to governments. Public reactions to the 1980 military intervention were generally positive.[48] Actually, important political actors welcomed military interventions in 1960, 1971, 1980, and most recently in 1997.[49] In contrast, public reaction to the military's open interference in politics in spring 2007 tended to be more negative and restrained its influence. The JP collaborated with the army against the rising leftist movements in the aftermath of the 1971 military intervention.[50] In 1980 and 1997, the tacit or active approval of big business and the media was crucial for the legitimacy and impunity of the military interventions.

The Legacy of the Welfare Party

The Motherland Party (MP), which was founded by Turgut Özal (1927–1993), an ex-member of the NSP and a high-ranking bureaucrat, emerged triumphant from the 1983 elections. The MP, which positioned itself on the center-right of the political spectrum, ruled Turkey until the 1991 elections. The MP adopted liberal economic policies that replaced import subsidization with export orientation, privatization, and liberalization. These policies completely restructured the social relationships and were instrumental in the expansion of the pious middle class that formed the backbone of the Welfare politics in the 1990s.

The Welfare Party (WP), which was founded at the behest of Erbakan, was not allowed to participate in the 1983 elections. The party contested the municipal elections of 1984, receiving 4.4 percent of the vote and gaining control of two eastern towns.[51] A 1987 referendum ended the ban on leading politicians, and Erbakan was elected chairman of the WP. In the November 1987 parliamentary elections and the March 1989 municipal elections, the Welfare Party regained the constituency of the NSP. In 1987, its vote share rose to 7.2 percent; in 1989, it climbed to 10 percent. Consistent with its image as the party representing the segments of society most adversely affected by the socioeconomic modernization and secularization, the Welfare Party continued to articulate an antisecular and xenophobic discourse.[52] Nonetheless, the WP experienced momentous changes with the advent of the 1990s. The global prestige of democratic ideals following the collapse of the Socialist bloc freed Islamism from the shackles of the defensive and binary discourse of anti-Communism. At the same time, Islamist participation in an expanding public sphere (i.e., private media outlets, civil-society associations, and professional entities) contributed to ideological dynamism and pluralism among its adherents. The 1980s and 1990s witnessed the proliferation of Islamic public schools (İmam-Hatipler) and colleges, Islamic economic institutions that offered "interest-free profit," Islamic nongovernmental organizations and associations,[53] Islamic publications and media outlets, Islamic fashion trends, and Islamic-style vacations. These developments unintentionally undermined the Islamist claim to being an exclusive and superior alternative to the modernism represented by the West and the secular Turkish republic.[54] Instead of Islam with its universal message transforming modernity, Islamic norms and beliefs were adapted to the modern values of profit making, comfort, entertainment, the private sphere, pluralism, and electoral competition.[55] Meanwhile, a younger generation within the WP increasingly dissociated from the Cold War–era discourse of Erbakan.

The October 1991 parliamentary elections were a turning point for the Welfare Party in several ways. The party leadership decided to form an electoral alliance with the Nationalist Work Party (Milliyetçi Çalışma Partisi)[56] at the cost of alienating its Kurdish constituency.[57] Equally important, the party leadership decided to pursue an electoral platform that went beyond the confines of religious mobilization. Promising young technocrats joined the party ranks,[58] and later they played crucial roles in the formation of the JDP. In its electoral campaigning, the party incorporated a strong social-justice theme to its platform, which turned out to be quite appealing to the voters in the urban peripheries. In addition, women activists became an essential part of the party's canvassing. The lay Islamic intellectuals of the time made significant contributions to the preparation of the electoral platform. In the parliament, the WP condemned the U.S. attack against Iraq; called for the unity of Muslims in the face of the "Imperialist-Zionist" onslaughts in Bosnia, Chechnya, and Palestine; and advocated policies against practices deemed threatening to the Islamic morality of the society.[59] Meanwhile, the WP evolved from a marginal party into the most dynamic force in Turkish politics.[60] In this regard, the Fourth Congress of the WP in October 1993 signified a crucial development. The WP abandoned its espousal of the state-led economic development program in favor of policies that promoted private investment and entrepreneurship, put forward a bold critique of the Turkish state's repressive treatment of its Kurdish citizens, and developed a program of social justice.[61] The WP portrayed itself as the only force capable of providing a peaceful solution to the Kurdish problem at a time when the conflict had reached its peak. All these changes in the party's platform also reflected the growing influence of a younger generation of politicians who would later play pivotal roles in the foundation of the JDP.

As Proposition I of moderation theory suggests, the WP tried to broaden its electoral appeal and developed platforms that deviated from its ideological genesis in the early 1990s. Also consistent with the expectations of moderation theory, the WP's opening up translated into success at the ballot box. Conservative citizens who were disillusioned with the incompetent leadership

nter-right and center-left parties found a viable alternative in the dy-
/P with its fresh image. In the municipal elections of March 1994, the
Party gained the municipalities of Ankara and Istanbul in addition
e of twenty-three cities. The party's efficient grassroots organization
and social-justice platforms mobilized public support, especially in the urban
peripheries.[62] Tayyip Erdoğan (b. 1954),[63] who cultivated extensive support
among the party's local grassroots members, became the mayor of Istanbul.
The WP's electoral fortunes reached their peak in the December 1995 elections, when the party won a plurality of the votes. The success of the Welfare
Party came from its ability to mobilize urban peripheries, Anatolian conservative voters, and newly emerging pious middle classes with its platforms that
blended social-justice themes with espousal of economic entrepreneurship.

The WP and the center-right True Path Party (TPP) formed a coalition
government in summer 1996, and Erbakan became prime minister. Erbakan's
plan of creating an Islamic version of the G8 (Group of Eight), his open hostility to the ban on the headscarf on university campuses, his invitation to some
religious sheikhs to his official residence, and the activities and speeches of
some Welfare Party members that challenged Turkish secularism were the
apparent reasons for the increasing hostility of the guardians against the WP.
The NSC on February 28, 1997, declared political Islam (*irtica*) to be an existential threat to the Turkish republic. The measures dictated by the TAF
command entailed a complete reversal of its policies toward public Islam in
the 1980s.[64] The TAF command orchestrated a systematic campaign against
the WP and obtained the active support of media corporations, civil-society
associations, and the judiciary. The coalition government collapsed in summer 1997. Consistent with Propositions II and IIIr articulated in Table 2.1, the
WP leadership tried to appease the TAF and its allies. The WP discouraged
mass demonstrations or civil disobedience campaigns and did not even call
for early elections. Yet moderation did not save the party.[65]

In January 1998, the TCC dissolved the WP on the grounds that the party
had become a center of activities contrary to the principle of secularism. Erbakan and five of his close associates were temporarily banned from politics.
The Principal State Counsel argued that the party's advocacy of the headscarf
in state institutions and public schools and its members' speeches infringed
on the principle of secularism. Yet he did not provide any substantial evidence
to show how a party supported by just 22 percent of the population and lack-

ing paramilitary forces posed a significant threat to the secular-democratic order in a country with a highly developed and diversified economy, highly competitive politics, strong linkages with the West, a vibrant civil society, and a powerful guardianship.[66] The European Court of Human Rights (ECHR) concluded in February 2002 that the dissolution of a party supporting the application of divine laws was a measure necessary to protect the democratic order. In a separate case, Erdoğan, the mayor of Istanbul, was sentenced to four months in prison for a speech he delivered in Siirt in December 1997.

The WP's ideological stance defies facile conceptualizations, as it was the product of two distinct factions. In fact, its discourse and platforms were characterized by fluidity and ambiguity rather than ideological consistency and commitment to well-defined goals.[67] This ideological ambiguity initially brought success at the ballot box by allowing the party to secure the support of diverse social groups. A range of stances, from support for an Islamic state to relatively liberal versions of secularism, were represented in the party. For some voters, it was the only true alternative to the corrupt and unjust social order; for others, it was the harbinger of the Islamic state. On the one hand, the party never advocated violence or formed paramilitary organizations. Moreover, unlike most of the political Islamic movements elsewhere, the establishment of sharia rule had not been the central item in the party's agenda. The accusation that the party practiced dissimulation (taqiyya) was not very convincing, as the party's organization was too exposed and vast to sustain a hidden agenda.[68] On the other hand, there was always a trend within the party that demonstrated strong authoritarian tendencies. In his speeches, Erbakan asserted that all "true Muslims" had to vote for the WP.[69] The official ideology of the WP, the "Just Order," promised the elimination of social injustices and inequalities through the imposition of Islamic ethics.[70] The WP's espousal of a morally upright society inevitably involved intolerance of social diversity. In this regard, the relationship between the Welfare Party, Islamic social organizations, and the Sufi brotherhoods was far from harmonious and organic. For many brotherhoods, including the powerful Gülen community, the politicization of religion by the Welfare Party was counterproductive, and they had feared the state's overreaction, which, in fact, happened.[71] In summary, the WP espoused a majoritarian, but not a liberal and pluralistic, understanding of democracy.

Post-Islamism and the Split

The Virtue Party (VP), founded in December 1997, became the successor to the WP. Its platform and policies exhibited significant differences from its predecessor. Fearing another wave of repression, the VP downplayed the role of Islam in its public discourse.[72] It framed its opposition to the ban of the headscarf in public institutions and the dissolution of the WP in the language of rights. For the VP, secularism as practiced in Turkey was incompatible with religious freedom.[73] Completely abandoning its predecessors' anti-Western stance, the VP adopted a pro–European Union discourse.[74] The party argued that Turkey's prospective membership in the EU would limit the power of the guardians and contribute to religious freedom.[75] The adoption of a new discourse on rights, the complete reversal of the WP's opposition to the EU, and the constant references to democratic governance reflected the influence of the younger generation within the party. The party leadership applied to the ECHR, hoping that the court would condemn the dissolution of the WP. As suggested by Proposition IIIr of Table 2.1, organizational survival and lifting the ban on the movement's leader, Erbakan, became the new party's paramount priorities. Nonetheless, the party was stillborn. It had a precarious legal existence, and internal divisions completely paralyzed the party. A prominent figure of the VP provided a perceptive account of these challenges:

> It was clear that they [the guardians and their societal allies] were determined to neutralize our movement. In 1998, I sensed that the guardians had four options: (1) to dissolve the VP; (2) to divide the VP into weaker parts; (3) to make the VP denounce its core principles, that is, its domestication; and (4) to marginalize a VP that preserves its core principles. Actually, all these things have happened.[76]

The VP's poor performance in the 1999 parliamentary elections (receiving 15 percent of the national vote and coming in third) was another serious blow. The brief episode of the WP's coming to power, its subsequent repression by the guardians, and, finally, the dismal performance of the VP in the 1999 elections were critical for the crystallization of the internal divisions. The younger generation of party leaders (*yenilikçi*), who were mostly in their late forties and early fifties, became increasingly critical of Erbakan and his older associates' handling of the crisis with the guardians and their hegemonic control over the party organization. They were aware of the limits of the voter appeal of both the WP and VP and advocated more centrist platforms.[77] The conflict within the VP erupted into a head-on collision at the party convention in May 2000, which took the shape of a power struggle between younger reformists and Erbakan's old guard. The reformist candidate Abdullah Gül (b. 1950, elected president of Turkey in 2007) accused Erbakan and his entourage of being responsible for the electoral debacle of 1999. Furthermore, he expressed his appreciation for Western civilization and argued that Turkey could be a respected representative of the Muslim world in the European Union.[78] In his speech at the convention, Gül argued that the VP had to renovate itself as a "centrist" party to capitalize on the public disillusionment with the center-right and center-left parties.[79] As predicted by Proposition I of moderation theory, he was claiming that moderation would bring success at the ballot box. Although he narrowly lost the election, the rift was now irreparable. When the TCC dissolved the VP, mainly because of its advocacy of allowing the headscarf in public institutions, the reformists decided to go their own way.

The Justice and Development Party (JDP) was established in August 2001 under the chairmanship of Erdoğan. The timing was ideal, for Turkey had experienced its worst economic crisis in its post–World War II history in two subsequent crises in November 2000 and February 2001. Unemployment skyrocketed to unseen levels; the GDP decreased by 5.7 percent in 2001; and inflation reached three digits. The industrial production capacity of the country was seriously disrupted, and the private sector was in shatters.[80] The impunity of bank owners who deliberately misused public money further contributed to the resentment toward the government. Public confidence in major political parties and leaders was at a historic low. In 2001, according to a poll sponsored by the major business association, 84 percent of the public thought that the political party system was functioning improperly.[81] According to another poll conducted in early 2002, 85 percent of the public was unsatisfied with the economic management of the tripartite coalition government.[82] Surveys sponsored by Erdoğan and his associates demonstrated that large segments of the public would be very receptive to a new party that had an untarnished image.

As noted above, there had been significant internal debate and change among the Islamists since the early 1990s. A discourse based on inalienable rights and popular sovereignty became prevalent among Islamist cadres in response to the guardians' restrictions on the political and public roles of religion (i.e., ban on headscarf). Consequently, political exclusion did not generate a spiral of radicalization within the Islamist movement. State repression was not a *necessary* condition for ideological moderation of the Islamists.[83] In fact, state repression may radicalize Islamists when institutional incentives for moderation are completely blocked. This was the case in Nasser's Egypt, or after the military intervention in Algeria in the early 1990s. Besides, the VP cadres loyal to Erbakan regrouped in the Felicity Party (FP) and reproduced the discourse of the NSP and early WP days. The reformists, who had *already* had serious disagreements with the old guard, responded to the state repression by formally splintering off from the Islamist movement, pragmatically adopting centrist platforms, and carefully pursuing a strategy of behavioral moderation. In this sense, the JDP, the first post-Islamist political entity in Turkey, was a product of ideological moderation accompanied by changes in strategic interests.[84] The leaders of the JDP offered similar accounts of their ideological transformation. In many instances, Erdoğan frankly accepted that his views on Europe had changed since the early 1990s as a result of his foreign trips, interaction with European policymakers and influential Turkish actors, and administrative responsibility as the mayor of Istanbul.[85] After these trips, interactions, and professional engagements, he started to appreciate the economic system and political freedoms of Europe. According to Abdüllatif Şener (b. 1954):

> There are no more demands for sharia from the bottom as during the Welfare Party era. Political Islam was initiated with the aim of capturing the state. The main influence came from Mawdudi in Egypt and Sayyid Qutb in Pakistan. The Iranian Revolution was a great inspiration for a while but did not last. And look at the experiences in Algeria and Afghanistan. There is nothing appealing there. Political Islam is now discredited. . . . Its fashion expired. Now people come with bread-and-butter demands but not with sharia demands.[86]

Abdullah Gül offered a very similar picture:

> In the Welfare Party, there were groups demanding sharia rule. Welfare did not represent the local values we are now cultivating. The ideology of the party was partially shaped by alien imports. [He was referring to the impact of the Islamist ideology of the Iranian Revolution and Arab states on Welfare's ideol-

ogy.] Our vision was at odds with the rest of the party. The despotic rule of Erbakan Hoca made it impossible for us to realize our vision under the rubric of the National View. We believe that modernization and being Muslim complement each other. We accept the modern values of liberalism, human rights, and market economy.[87]

The founders of the JDP also realized that they had to act with restraint and not confront the guardians if they were to survive as a party.[88] Their adoption of a discourse of rights, accommodation, tolerance, and moderation was reinforced by a perception that polarization would ultimately undermine the centrist appeal of the JDP.[89] At the same time, they hoped Turkey's progress toward membership in the EU would ultimately dismantle the guardianship and contribute to the JDP's political survival and ascendancy. Thus, they reoriented their understanding of Europe from a Christian community to a union that has achieved high standards in political governance and economic prosperity.[90] This reorientation was coupled with downplaying references to the imagined glorious and authentic Islamic past. Erdoğan's understanding of Europe had completely evolved from 1994 to 2002. In 1994, he declared: "The real name of the European Community is the Catholic Christians Union."[91] In 2002, he reasoned, "We are advocating membership to the EU so as not to remain on the margins of civilization . . . Turkey does not have any models other than the EU to find effective solutions to its governability crisis stemming from lack of democratization."[92] In May 2003, in a public conversation with university students, Bülent Arınç (b. 1948), the Speaker of the Turkish parliament, candidly said, "I used to think that entrance to the European Union was treason to the nation." He explained how Turkey's pursuit of EU membership would offer full rights and freedoms to its citizens. Gül was not a strong advocate of joining the European Union when he was a minister without a portfolio in the Erbakan government of 1996–1997. In these speeches delivered in February 1997 in Washington, D.C., he maintained that his party stood for the incorporation of Islamic values with democratic governance and thereby distanced his position from that of his prime minister.[93] Yet he was deeply suspicious of Europe: "Will it [EU] become a 'Christians Only' Club? This is the real question." In sharp contrast, when he visited Washington, D.C., in 2003, his speeches were full of references to the JDP government's full commitment to EU-demanded reforms.

The JDP founders also developed a more realistic and sound understanding of electoral dynamics. It became crystal clear to them that an ambiguous Islamic discourse would have only limited appeal in Turkey. The voters' desertion of the VP in 1999 was a lesson taken seriously by the JDP leaders. Voters showed a great dislike for polarization and penalized the WP/VP for its inability to reconcile with the guardians, even if the dissolution of the WP was grossly unfair by democratic standards. The JDP founders came to the conclusion that electoral success required development of centrist platforms with cross-cutting appeals. According to Yaşar Yakış (b. 1938), a founding member of the JDP, the reformists had two options when the VP was banned: either to stay with the political tradition of the WP or to initiate a new political movement to fill the gap in the center of the political spectrum. The first option would confine the reformists to the core constituency of the Welfare Party, whereas the second option had the potential of making the reformists the predominant force in Turkish politics.[94] Hüseyin Çelik (b. 1959), the minister of education of the Fifty-ninth Cabinet, argued that he joined the JDP because of its difference from the legacy of the WP. The JDP's appeal was not confined to the mosque crowd. "[O]ur party advocates a political system in which neither state nor religion interferes with each other." He argued that Erdoğan's experience resembled Gorbachev's transformation from a Communist apparatchik to a democracy advocate.[95] Another JDP politician from Samsun explained that the JDP aimed to bring people from diverse backgrounds under the same rubric.[96]

From its first days, the JDP positioned itself as a center-right party. This was also reflected in the demographic characteristics of its founding members. Among the founders of the party are the fifty-two deputies who entered parliament on the VP ticket and seventy-three other individuals. Table 7.1 provides information about the latter group, which was composed of highly educated individuals with strong skills in communication, administration, and economics and who were in their late forties. Twenty-two of them had Ph.D.'s. In contrast to Islamic political movements in Turkey and elsewhere, doctors, engineers, or college graduates with degrees in natural sciences did not form a majority.[97] Erdoğan and his companions self-consciously selected individuals who were highly trained, educated, and experienced to address complex organizational, social, and economic problems.

Table 7.1. Demographics of the Seventy-three Nonparliamentarian JDP Founders

Gender	Male	Female				
	60	13				
Age	30–40	41–50	51–60	61–70	70+	Average
	15	28	22	8	0	48.5
Education	Primary School	High School	University	Masters	Ph.D.	
	1	3	34	13	22	
Profession*	Social Science	Economy	Law	Management	Engineering	Theology
	10	14	9	13	15	5
Occupation	Academy	Private Sector	Entrepreneur	Civil Society	Civil Servant	Politician
	16	19	14	11	9	4

Source: The booklet published by the JDP headquarters entitled *Founding Council.*

* These figures are only for individuals who are at least graduates of a university. Three individuals who were educated in dental and medical school are not reported in the table.

Moderates Rising

The JDP rapidly organized all around Turkey within a year. From the fall of 2001 to the summer of 2002, Erdoğan and his entourage visited around fifty provincial capitals and addressed large crowds. These rallies were quite instrumental in catapulting the JDP to the leading position in the public opinion polls in the early summer of 2002. A golden opportunity arose for the party when the tripartite coalition government that had been in power since the April 1999 elections started to crumble in summer 2002. The parliament eventually decided to hold early elections on November 3. The JDP conducted a campaign that was centered on the personal appeal of its chairman and built on mass rallies and one-to-one personal contact and persuasion. In September and October before the elections, Erdoğan spoke to crowds in around forty cities. Consequently, he visited all eighty-one provincial capitals of Turkey, except for the Alevi-Kurdish city of Tunceli, sometimes twice, in a year. The JDP campaigns generally avoided inflammatory discourse. Party leadership explicitly asked its candidates to shun religious and ethnic political rhetoric.

JDP supporters greeting Erdoğan on his campaign trail (Kastamonu, September 2002)

The main theme of Erdoğan's rally speeches in that period was the economic mismanagement of the tripartite coalition government. Wherever he talked, Erdoğan spoke about the economic crisis and corruption. His credibility came from his record as the former mayor of Istanbul who was competent and popular but unfairly prosecuted by the guardians. His folksy manners contributed to the image of an able but humble politician. While he argued that the JDP was the only party that could effectively cope with economic problems and widespread corruption, he skillfully refrained from any messages that could have been interpreted as "radical" by the guardians. The JDP was careful not to make unrealistic and binding commitments to voters. Realizing that the WP's confrontational strategy had brought about both its ban by the guardians and its penalization by the voters, the JDP aimed to portray itself as a central-right party. Erdoğan never publicly promised he would lift the ban on the headscarf, which was immensely unpopular among his supporters, or that he would reverse the legislation that limited religious public education. Meanwhile, the JDP leadership framed the ban on the headscarf and the limitations on religious education in terms of inviolable individual rights. This discourse served two purposes. It reminded conservative pious voters

that the JDP was attentive to their demands without polarizing t
landscape. More importantly, it signaled that the JDP would n
address Islamic topics but would pursue policies that would increas
of individual rights, as well as religious, ethnic, and political ones. The pa.
aimed to appear committed to the concerns of conservative religious voters,
not to scare off mainstream voters as the WP had, and to ease the anxiety of
the guardians and the voters who remained deeply skeptical of the JDP.

This approach confirms the expectations of Proposition IVr, which focuses on how ideological moderation facilitates behavioral moderation by expanding the boundaries of justifiable action and legitimizing new platforms.
Erdoğan was mostly free from the anti-Semitism that had historically characterized Turkish Islamist discourses. He also anchored his centrist and conciliatory discourse in the pluralistic and diverse Anatolian Sufi culture that had
experienced revitalization in the post-1980 period.[98] His emphasis on local
Sufi traditions decisively set the JDP apart from the politics of Erbakan, who
conceptualized Islam as the ruling ideology of the Ottoman Empire and the
anathema of Western civilization. Whereas for Erbakan, Islam was a holistic

A JDP politician participating in a village marriage celebration (Seyitgazi-Eskişehir,
October 2002)

ideology that had been in an epochal conflict with the West, it became a source of moderation and conciliation in the discourse of Erdoğan, who effectively communicated his party's novel stance to people from all walks of life. This discourse infused with Sufi themes set apart the JDP from the WP and demonstrated how Islamic traditions might beget moderate and conciliatory political platforms in the hands of ingenious politicians. It stands in contrast to neofundamentalist discourse that condemns Sufism and popular beliefs as un-Islamic or to Islamist discourse that explicitly articulates an ideological vision of Islam.[99] Meanwhile, Erdoğan very self-consciously argued that his party continued the legacy of Adnan Menderes' DP in the 1950s and Turgut Özal's MP in the 1980s. While the JDP espoused a permissive attitude toward the public expressions of Islam, it also tried to accommodate the guardians and secular voters like the previous center-right parties had. In many ways, the party's official ideology, "conservative democracy," was a continuation of platforms developed by Özal.[100]

The JDP leadership's centrist appeal and conciliatory electoral campaign paid off. The party emerged triumphant from the 2002 parliamentary elections by capturing a plurality of the national vote (34 percent), which translated into control of two-thirds of the parliament. The only other party that managed to pass the 10 percent threshold was the secularist RPP with 19 percent. A comparison between the WP vote share in 1995 and the JDP's performance in 2002 reveals how the latter expanded its constituency to regions and groups that had been hesitant to support Erbakan's parties. While the JDP received a greater percentage of votes than the WP in almost all regions, the upsurge of the JDP vote exhibited considerable geographical variation. In the Aegean counties where the WP had been a negligible force, the JDP received more than double the vote share of the WP. Likewise, in the Mediterranean and the Black Sea coastal provinces to the north, the JDP got twice the vote that Welfare had received in 1995. The JDP did clearly have a very strong presence in the regions that were not penetrated by the WP seven years previously. The JDP's voting support went beyond the confines of Central Anatolian provinces and urban peripheries, which formed the backbone of the WP's vote. One exception was the JDP's relatively poor performance in the predominantly Kurdish eastern regions. The party's attempts to reach Kurdish voters remained limited in 2002. Still, the JDP achieved huge success in the Kurdish-majority provinces in the 2004 local and 2007 parliamentary elections. From a purely electoral view, the JDP did not have much incentive to make a concentrated effort to capture the Kurdish vote. As long as the Kurdish nationalist parties were receiving less than 10 percent of the national vote, the JDP gained an absolute majority of the parliamentary seats representing the Kurds. For instance, the party controlled eight of ten seats in the province of Diyarbakir despite the fact that it captured barely 16 percent of the votes there.

Table 7.2 shows voter transitions among party blocs from the 1999 to the 2002 elections. The table was created by following Gary King's ecological inference method.[101] His method is based on several untestable assumptions, and the results would be misleading if these assumptions are not met.[102] Consequently, it is crucial to be cognizant of the trade-offs involved in making strong assumptions and the limits of the ecological inference.[103] The current analysis has a modest goal and does not aim for precision—whether or not a substantial number of center-right party supporters switched to the JDP in 2002. The analysis includes covariates that help alleviate the aggregation bias.[104] The figures in the table convey a good sense of the magnitude of voter transitions. The findings are also consistent with theoretical expectations and the author's qualitative knowledge of the history of Turkish elections and regional differences.[105]

A JDP politician pinning buttons on people joining the party (Van, June 2007)

Table 7.2. Voter Transitions among Party Blocs between 1999 and 2002

	CRO2*	CLO2†	JDP02	NAP	YP‡	FP	TOTALS
CR99*	49 (.00) (.00, .58)	07 (.00) (.00, .66)	34 (.02) (.00, .84)		05 (.00) (.00, .26)		25.2
CL99†		61 (.00) (.00, .69)	12 (.00) (.00, .75)		18 (.01) (.00, .23)		30.9
VP99			75 (.01) (.00, .98)		02 (.00) (.00, .33)	13 (.00) (.00, .16)	15.4
NAP99			61 (.02) (.00, .95)	32 (.00) (.00, .45)	11 (.01) (.00, .58)		18
TOTALS	14.7	21.8	34.3	8.4	7.3	2.5	

Notes: Figures that are not in parentheses show the percentage of row party supporters in 1999 who voted for a column party in 2002. The Kurdish vote is incalculable because of its extremely skewed geographical distribution. Summation of values in each row may be greater or less than 100 percent because of computational issues. Only major parties are included in the analysis. Only cells that are points of interest are filled in in the table. For example, there is no point in focusing on the voter transition from Virtue to NAP in 2002 because it may be nil.

* Central-right (CR) parties are the TPP and the MP.

† Central-left (CL) parties are the RPP and Democratic Left Party in 1999; and these two and the New Turkey Party in 2002.

‡ Youth Party (YP) was established by the business tycoon Cem Uzan and received around 7 percent of the national vote in 2002.

The fourth column in the table demonstrates voter transitions to the JDP. The JDP drew away a significant number of voters from all major party blocs, with the exception of the Kurdish nationalists. The ecological inference analysis suggests that three-fourths of the citizens who voted for the VP in 1999 voted for the JDP and more than three-fifths of the NAP voters defected to the JDP in the 2002 elections. Interestingly, around one-third of the center-right voters in 1999 transferred their allegiance to the JDP in 2002. The JDP managed to mobilize the moderate right-leaning voters who were beyond the reach of the WP. This clearly shows the ability of the JDP to portray itself as the new main center-right party and is consistent with the party leadership's moderate and centrist stance before the elections, as would be expected by moderation theory. In western provinces where the Welfare Party had hardly any significant presence, the JDP swept the elections in 2002 by successfully mobilizing the center-right voters. More than anything else, this pushed the center-right parties below the 10 percent threshold and paved the way for the JDP government.

Power with Moderation

When the JDP came to power in late 2002, Turkey was in the midst of an ambitious reform period induced by the prospects of EU membership. The JDP government enthusiastically pursued a very active pro-European policy and initiated many administrative, legal, and political reforms.[106] Political reforms offered broader rights to non-Muslim minorities and the Kurds, increased the scope of individual liberties, abolished the state security courts, and reduced the institutional role of the armed forces in policymaking. The JDP-controlled parliament passed the crucial seventh reform package in July 2003. The reform package drastically curbed the executive powers of the NSC and abolished many restrictive laws. In September of the same year, the government established the "Reform Observation Group" and "European Union Communication Group" to enforce the implementation of reforms and ensure a positive image of Turkey in the European public opinion. As a result of reform packages, Freedom House substantially improved Turkey's political rights and civil liberties score between 2002 and 2005.[107] Erdoğan also unequivocally criticized previous policies and signaled that the Cyprus issue should not block Turkey-EU relations. "We are never for concessionary politics in Cyprus, but we are saying that no progress can be achieved by the policies followed for the past forty years."[108] The JDP's pro-EU stance gained the support of big business, which had historically had a cozy relationship with the armed forces.[109] The Turkish Businessmen and Industrialists Association (Türk İşadamları ve Sanayicileri Derneği) has become a vocal critic of the armed forces' "excessive" involvement in politics. The JDP initiatives eventually bore fruit; the EU decided to initiate accession negotiations with Turkey in December 2004, and negotiations began in October 2005.

The government was also successful in achieving high and sustainable growth rates. Turkey experienced three of its most severe post–World War II economic crises between 1994 and 2001. As Figure 7.2 demonstrates, the Turkish economy has achieved sustainable yet declining growth rates since

2002 after a decade of erratic and highly volatile economic performance. The inflation rate, which had been in high double digits throughout the 1990s and had fostered economic uncertainty, was reduced to single digits in 2004. The JDP's ability to reduce governmental spending, its working relationship with the IMF, its overhaul of the banking system, and the atmosphere of political stability it ushered in, after eleven years of coalition governments and increasing foreign direct investments and exports, contributed to a robust and healthy economic performance.[110]

It can be argued that both the economic and the political reform processes started prior to the JDP coming to power and received additional impetus during Erdoğan's government. Voter confidence in the party remained high, and the JDP received another popular mandate in the 2007 elections. At the same

Figure 7.2. GDP Annual Percent Change in Turkey from 1980 to 2008 (in Constant Prices)

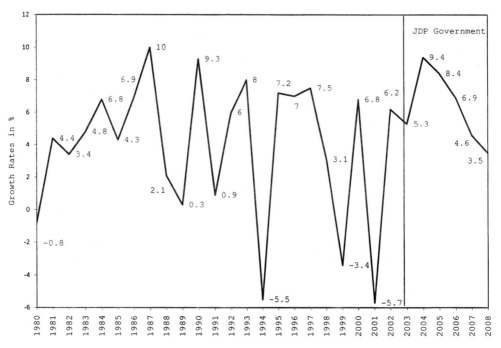

Note: The vertical line separates the period under the JDP government from previous periods.

Source: IMF World Economic Outlook, October 2008. Available at http://www.imf.org.

time, two factors seriously curtailed the JDP's reform agenda: (1) ⟨
tional characteristics of the party; (2) behavioral moderation pursu
party leadership. In a sense, the more the JDP was integrated into tɦ⟨
political system and emerged as the major center-right party, the more it lost
its reformist characteristics. The rest of this chapter focuses on these organizational and behavioral factors to argue how the experience of the JDP supports Propositions IIIr (organizational survival prevailing over programmatic
goals) and Vr (behavioral moderation curtailing democratization) elucidated
in Table 2.1.

Organizational Constraints

As described in Chapter 5, major Turkish political parties usually exhibit
strong authoritarian tendencies. They are dominated by long-serving leaders who often have unchallenged control over appointments and make key
decisions without being accountable to party cadres. Closed-list proportional
representation, used since the 1991 elections, reinforces a hierarchical power
structure within parties. Patronage distribution cultivates a culture of dependency in which lower-ranking party members are in constant expectation
of material inducements from higher-ranking members, especially when the
party controls the government. Careerist types of members have been predominant in party organizations.[111] The center-rightist parties such as the MP
and TPP became centers of patronage and pervasive corruption and generated
strong public apathy toward parties in the 1990s.

The JDP leadership promised to revive public confidence in political parties at a time when parties had a very negative public image. Erdoğan was
critical of rigid ideologies pursued by his ex-mentor Erbakan and by center-
right parties that institutionalized into corrupt entities by being incompatible
with evolving global conditions.[112] The party leadership declared that their
party would abandon authoritarian practices that characterized the WP and
the VP. The fight against corruption was a major theme of the JDP's platform.[113] A central theme in the JDP's electoral platform was its unspoiled
and uncorrupted image, which Erdoğan was determined to preserve. In May
2003, the JDP leadership issued a decree forbidding provincial party leaders
from running in local elections or taking administrative positions in public
enterprises and institutions, and their relatives from taking positions in lo-

cal party administrations.[114] Moreover, Erdoğan articulated a stance against populist demands in the electoral campaign and in the first year of the JDP's governance.[115] Immediately after the elections, he warned the newly elected members of parliament to serve their constituencies rather than personal demands and interests.

However, the very rapid rise of the JDP overwhelmed the party's nascent organizational structure along the lines suggested by Angelo Panebianco.[116] By late summer 2002, people from all walks of life were swarming party buildings with all sorts of demands. The unemployed demanded jobs; the poor and those who pretended to be poor asked for material assistance; public servants wanted promotions and political appointments; merchants sought to establish cozy relationships with men (very rarely women) of political power. Party membership and activism became a career in itself. The party had soon succumbed to corrupt practices and favoritism in bureaucratic appointments and allocation of public bids. Patronage distribution, which has been a defining characteristic of the Turkish political party system, is being reproduced in the JDP. Despite some structural reforms, the state continues to be the main employer in the economy, and access to state jobs often depends on good connections and networks.[117] Also, personal access to better health, education, welfare, and social security benefits are often mediated through party channels. Success in state and municipal bids is usually related to being a supporter of the party that controls the government. The JDP-controlled municipalities were hit with corruption scandals by 2005.[118] Local JDP politicians won bids that were nontransparent and unfair. The party leadership preferred to cover up these scandals by accusing the media and claiming conspiracy.[119] Despite its initial promises, it refused to revise the legislation on political ethics (legislation #3628) to make it more effective and implementable.[120]

The institutionalization of the JDP into a patronage-distributing party is also reflected in the composition of its grassroots. Even before the party became the government in fall 2002, a sense of idealism was mostly absent among party loyalists who were a motley group of individuals with diverse backgrounds. In this sense, the JDP was more of a party of careerists than believers. Although most of the JDP leadership and grassroots came from the WP tradition, the JDP became a magnet for individuals with various political affiliations in a short time. For JDP loyalists who also served in the WP and the VP, politics had become more mundane and less idealistic.[121] They no

unlike RF in Iran which was comprised of many groups, JDP started united, then lost power

longer felt that they were involved in a religious mission (*dava*). In a sense, the impacts of power that started with the Welfare Party's success in the municipal elections in 1994 reached their apex with the JDP's control of the government and municipalities.[122] A JDP politician in the northeastern city of Kars who had a long history of involvement in Islamist politics put it bluntly about two months before the 2002 elections:

> The politics in the Welfare Party was a mission of jihad. We were working as if we would go to heaven because of our political endeavor. Now everybody is working for his own interest. If I am not given my share, nobody can expect me to sacrifice. Days of mission (*dava*) are gone.

An ex-WP activist from the northern city of Samsun who joined the JDP concurred:

> In the early times of the Welfare Party, politics was unspoiled. Everybody was working for the common good with a zeal uncorrupted by personal concerns. Everybody had the afterlife in mind. Later on, politics became a race. Everybody started to grasp the biggest share of the pie.

An ex-WP activist from Sarayköy in the province of Denizli expressed a similar assessment:

> It is now so different from the Welfare Party. There, we were very conscious of our mission (*dava*), and we engaged in politics with zeal. This party is motley, without a common purpose and sense. Many came from Motherland, TPP, and NAP. They only have material expectations.

The nonsacred nature of political activism under the rubric of the JDP also set it apart from organizations such as the Egyptian Muslim Brotherhood that pursued an ambitious strategy of religious mobilization.[123] While the JDP grassroots are more open and representative of diverse social groups, the party organization has transformed into a giant entity whose primary function is providing access to state resources and implementing the directives of the headquarters. The prevailing "culture of patronage" was strongly related to the hierarchical structure of the party. The party's identity was built on the charismatic personality of its leader, Tayyip Erdoğan, who increasingly monopolized power over time.[124] He and his close circle had complete control over party positions and tickets. For instance, in 2002, in many of the provinces, candidates who were popular within the provincial branches did not make it to the actual list or only found places at the bottom of the list. Erdoğan reasoned that grassroots in their present situation would not choose the ablest individuals. He also underlined that citizens vote for leaders and the party, not candidates, in the Turkish electoral system. In fact, the JDP members often remarked that people voted for the JDP because of the appeal of its leader, regardless of who ran on the JDP ticket.[125] Nonetheless, some members who valued self-expression and political participation lamented the absence of democracy within the party. A veterinary surgeon in Samsun strongly objected after popular candidates did not make it onto the top of the party's candidate list in 2002:

> When we were in the Virtue Party, we were working for the *dava*. Then, we did not ask questions about the decisions of those at the top. But now, it is different. This party was founded by people who left Virtue because of the stubbornness of the top. Now they are doing the same thing we criticized in Virtue. Nobody, not even Tayyip Erdoğan, has a right to betray the people's will.

Despite his protests, the same person continued to be active within the party and was busy organizing the local campaigning before the 2007 elections. Apparently, benefits of party membership overwhelmed his objection to authoritarian practices over time. Party bylaws were progressively amended to increase the power of the leadership. Amendments in May 2002 made public "attacks" against the party, party leadership, and members a reason for permanent expulsion from the JDP and dropped the requirement that the party would choose at least half of its parliamentary candidates through free elections.[126] Two parliamentarians were later expelled from the party on this basis.[127] Amendments in February 2003 changed the voting system in party congresses to minimize the possibility of dissident voices being elected to administrative positions within the party hierarchy.[128] Delegates were now required to vote for lists instead of for individuals. In the first congress of the JDP in the fall of 2003, further amendments took the power to choose the members of the party's Central Executive Committee away from the Central Decision-Making and Governance Council and gave it to the party chairman.[129] In 2006, popularly elected provincial branch chairpersons who defeated the candidates favored by the party leadership were summarily dismissed and provincial congresses were annulled.[130] Amendments in November 2006 introduced more stringent rules to be nominated as a candidate for the party chairmanship and decreed disciplinary measures against public criticism of the party and its leadership.[131] There was no meaningful competition in party congresses at the county level that took place in fall 2008. Meanwhile, the JDP matured into a "leader party" in the sense that its viability and electoral success depends on the personality of its leader. The party could not provide an alternative avenue for more deliberative, autonomous, and broader public participation in politics. Once organized as a vote-maximizing party that came to government in a very short time span, the JDP leadership lost the opportunity to cultivate more democratic forms of representation. In the words of a JDP dissident, "A culture of obedience prevails in the party. The party does not have a democratic organization. The leader has all the say. Politicians owe their positions to the respect and esteem they showed to him."[132]

The JDP's rapid institutionalization into a patronage-distributing leader party had a broader implication. As suggested by Proposition IIIr, party leadership had no difficulty compromising their programmatic goals, for they were hardly accountable to the grassroots, and party members were primarily pursuing selective incentives. Careerists within party ranks who sought material inducements were in no position to hold the party leadership responsible for deviations from the party's declared goals of fighting corruption and introducing democracy to the party. Believer-type members who value ideological goals were a captive audience for the JDP leadership, as there was no other viable party that could sway them until the renaissance of the FP under new leadership in fall 2008. Additionally, these members often lacked the necessary information to monitor the actions of the leadership, along the lines suggested by the principal-agent problem.[133] Further, the JDP leadership convincingly argued that the survival of the party would be at stake if it pursued policies that would antagonize the guardians. For this reason, the leadership acted with great restraint regarding the ban on wearing the headscarf and restraints on religious education that were of great concern to believers until after the 2007 elections.

The Kurdish Unrest

The most important political issue in Turkey has been the unrest among the Kurdish citizens. The government failed to develop an independent and bold policy that would replace the armed forces' security-oriented strategy.[134] This was despite the fact that the party explicitly rejected all sorts of ethnic, religious, and regional discrimination. It also recognized Kurdishness as a sub-identity of Turkish citizenship.[135] The party hoped that the EU-related reforms would meet the Kurdish demands for greater cultural rights and political representation, restrain arbitrary state authority, and undermine the appeal of militant Kurdish nationalism. In fact, the EU-induced reform process generated considerable improvements in the human rights record of Turkey between 1999 and 2005 despite the imperfect implementation of reform packages concerning civil liberties and political rights. As Figure 7.3 demonstrates, there were significant reductions in the number of extrajudicial killings and deaths under custody and due to torture; banned and raided NGOs, political entities, cultural entities, and publishers; and banned and confiscated publications after 1999. Yet this trend came to an end by 2005, after the EU decided to initiate membership negotiations with Turkey. The PKK remobilized its forces on June 1, 2004, fearing political marginalization. The TAF demanded harsher measures to combat the insurgents and to pacify the rebellious Kurdish population in the southeastern cities. The growing assertiveness of Kurdish nationalism provoked xenophobic Turkish nationalism that translated into increasing intolerance toward Kurdish groups in mixed cities such as Mersin and Izmir. Once it had achieved its strategic goal of convincing the EU to open up negotiations, the JDP was unwilling to push the reform process further, fearing that it would aggravate the discontent of the guardians.

The JDP also faced strong criticism from the RPP and the NAP, which tried to ride the rising nationalist sentiments among the Turkish voters. In the 2007 elections, both the RPP and the NAP waged campaigns that charged the JDP of being "soft on terrorism" and giving concessions to the de-facto Kurdish state in northern Iraq. They hoped to undermine the JDP's support among nationalist and conservative Turkish voters, but that strategy failed to bear much fruit. The JDP successfully repelled this challenge by developing a discourse that simultaneously appears moderate and inclusive to the Kurds and nonconcessionary to the nationalistic Turkish voters. Consequently, the JDP established a

Figure 7.3. Selected Indicators of Human Rights Violations in Turkey (1994–2008)

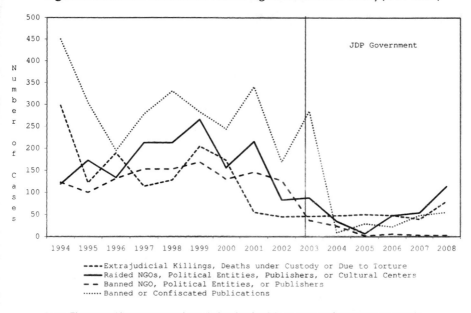

Note: The vertical line separates the period under the JDP government from previous periods.

Source: Data were compiled from the Human Rights Association of Turkey annual publications, which are available (in Turkish) at http://www.ihd.org.tr.

broad coalition that covers Central Anatolia and the Black Sea coast as well as eastern Kurdish provinces. Nonetheless, the rising nationalist tide among the Turks, the continuing violence between the Turkish army and the insurgents, and the increasing tensions between Kurdish migrants and Turkish residents severely restrict the JDP's ability to formulate a risky but promising policy that would offer full civic and political rights to the Kurdish minority and facilitate the integration of Kurdish nationalism into the political system.[136]

The JDP lacked a comprehensive and consistent policy toward the restless Kurdish citizens. A central reason for this is the lack of civilian control over the security forces. Turkey has a long history of extralegal killings by shadowy groups operating under the state's protection.[137] These groups were particularly active during the violent era leading to the 1980 coup. After a lull in the early postcoup years, assassinations again became routine in southeastern provinces where the Kurdish insurgents and the Turkish armed forces were fighting for control over the civilian population. Hundreds of civilians were gunned down, and their murderers were never caught. For years, Turkish dissidents and democracy activists suspected that the murders were part of a state strategy of intimidating and subduing Kurdish nationalists. In the last years, confessions from insurgent turncoats who were employed by the state corroborated these fears.[138] Extralegal killings were integral to the military's counterinsurgency tactics. Army personnel and civilians who operated under the rubric of a secret division within the Gendarme forces killed with impunity and enjoyed protection from high levels of the state bureaucracy and the armed forces. These individuals also engaged in organized crime, including drug trafficking. The nature of these activities and clandestine links between state officials, politicians, and killing squads were exposed to the view of the public in November 1996. The parliament formed an investigatory committee, the prime minister appointed a special inspector, and the journalists extensively documented these activities.[139] However, the civilian governments were unable and unwilling to root out the causes of these activities. Security forces remained unaccountable to civilian control. The existence of shadowy groups and a lack of accountability of the security forces have continued to hinder democratic consolidation.

Like the governments of previous center-right parties, the JDP government made little progress in disciplining and making the security forces publicly accountable. A series of events that took place in a Kurdish town demonstrated how the JDP failed to act with decision and vigor.[140] The province of Hakkari, deep in the southeastern corner of Turkey, has historically been one of the most underdeveloped provinces in Turkey, and it bore the brunt of warfare during the 1990s. Kurdish nationalism has a very strong appeal among the local population. The Kurdish nationalist party captured 45 percent of the votes in 2002 and gained control of the municipalities in the three urban centers of Hakkari, Yüksekova, and Şemdinli. The province was hit by a series of seventeen bombing assaults during July–November 2005. Although military personnel and buildings were the victims in several instances, the rest of the attacks targeted civilians. The perpetrators of these attacks were not discovered. Public opinion in the region tended to believe that clandestine forces linked to the armed forces were responsible for the attacks.[141] However, on November 9, the public caught two noncommissioned officers of the Turkish Gendarme forces and an insurgent turncoat after they staged a grenade attack against a bookstore in the town of Şemdinli. The attack resulted in the death of a civilian. In subsequent demonstrations, several more civilians were killed as a result of fire from the armed forces. The media covered the events in extensive detail, and the JDP government announced that it would thoroughly investigate the matter. Prime Minister Erdoğan personally promised that the forces behind the attacks would not remain undiscovered this time as they had on previous occasions.[142]

This turned out to be a hollow promise. The commander of the land forces publicly praised one of the officers involved in the bombing who had served under his command in the past. A public prosecutor prepared an indictment that accused the armed forces of engaging in illegal activities against the Kurdish insurgents and their sympathizers.[143] The prosecutor argued that gangs within the armed forces employed extralegal violent tactics to subdue the local population and pursue their private interests at the expense of public safety. The indictment caused a big uproar in the media and sustained the widespread fears that the armed forces act with impunity and violate legal boundaries under the pretext of war on terror. Yet the prosecutor was expelled from the legal profession. The Human Rights Commission of parliament made a visit to the province and produced a report that was highly criti-

The bookstore bombed by a counterinsurgency team. Scars from the explosion are visible on the ceiling and floor. (Şemdinli, June 2007)

rmed forces' antiterror strategy. The parliament later established
restigatory commission that conducted extensive interviews and a
bombings and killings in the province of Hakkari.[144] The conclu-
six-hundred-page report, which were announced in April 2006,
.... despite the overwhelming evidence that the higher echelons of the
armed forces coordinated the attacks. Three assailants were eventually found
guilty and sentenced to long prison sentences. The court decision reasoned
that the assailants could not have committed the crimes they were found
guilty of without the protection and involvement of their superiors. Still, the
court could not point to evidence that would lead to the trial of high-ranking
officers.[145] The case was later transferred to a military court that released all
the assailants. The issue gradually faded from public attention.

The passive stance on this issue taken by the JDP was the primary reason
why the judiciary failed to pursue the case vigorously. While legal mobilization stimulated judicial activism at lower courts, government protection was
necessary for the sustainability of this activism in the face of extensive pressures from the guardians. The JDP government failed to offer protection to the
members of the judiciary, who remained very vulnerable to pressure from the
TAF. The party leadership adopted a risk-aversive strategy and retreated from
its original promise that the case would be thoroughly investigated. It basically
tried to appease the TAF, which was determined to silence any public criticism
and scrutiny of its conduct in the counterinsurgency. While the JDP leadership
would have preferred to see the TAF's political influence reduced, it was too
concerned with its organizational interests to achieve that goal along with
democratization that would offer greater rights for politically discriminated
groups. The JDP's lack of will to confront the TAF and demand that it dismantle illegal counterinsurgency units was a serious blow to sustainable democratization. When the EU impetus for democratization weakened by 2006, the
JDP did not seek alliances with political actors seeking greater rights to revive
the reform process. As the Şemdinli incident vividly demonstrates, moderation that involved compromises and conciliation was not an agent of political
change. Successful democratization would have required decisive, risk-taking,
confrontational, and even radical action on the part of the JDP. These findings
are consistent with Proposition Vr, which argues that behavioral moderation
may actually harm democratic progress when it entails concessions to political
actors blocking reform and resisting the expansion of rights.

A Tale of
Two Elections

The Reform Front in Iran and the Justice and Development Party in Turkey have been the most prominent post-Islamist movements in the Middle East. Neither the RF nor the JDP shared a holistic ideological vision that left little room for pluralism and democratic governance. In fact, the birth of the RF and the JDP followed internal debates and criticism regarding the promises of the Islamist ideology. The Iranian Revolution resulted in authoritarian rule that suffered from chronic socioeconomic problems. The central theme of the RF's discourse was the increasing gap between revolutionary ideals and the reality of the Islamic Republic. The RF developed a powerful criticism of the state-centric nature of Islamist ideology and offered an alternative vision emphasizing civil society, rule of law, and societal rights and freedoms. Despite the broad appeal of its platform, it failed to become the dominant force in Iran for two reasons. Primarily, and consistent with Proposition IVr (see Table 2.1) that problematizes the relationship between behavioral moderation and democratic progress, the RF did not pursue a nonelectoral confrontational strategy of political change. Second, it did not have the means to implement policies of social welfare and to weaken the state's control over economic production and distribution. A central reason for the victory of Ahmedinejad in the June 2005 presidential election was widespread discontent caused by chronic inflation, unemployment, underemployment, corruption, and lack of economic opportunities. Ironically, broad segments of the Iranian society perceived Ahmedinejad as an "outsider" who would *reform* the corrupt and wasteful system and fulfill the social justice message of the revolution.

Turkish Islamists had a very unique trajectory, as they had regularly participated in elections since the early 1970s. A younger generation of Islamists, backed by liberals, developed a criticism of Islamism and of the secularist ruling ideology since the early 1990s. They took advantage of electoral opportunities and public discontent caused by socioeconomic downturn. The JDP, founded in 2001, was more successful than its Iranian counterpart in holding on to power and generating significant political change. Turkey's historical aspiration to join the European Union, the hegemony of the IMF-dictated neo-liberal economic policies, and the public discrediting of opposition parties facilitated the rise of the JDP. It also had superior organizational resources; its poverty-alleviation policies solidified its support among the working class and the poor; and its economic policies favoring the private sector cultivated support among businesspeople. Nonetheless, its ability and willingness to address the issues most critical for Turkish democratic consolidation—the recognition of the rights of historically discriminated-against groups and the containment of counterinsurgency-related groups operating beyond the rule of law—remained very limited despite historical opportunities.

A solid understanding of democratization and de-democratization in Iran and Turkey requires a systematic analysis of how state power is configured and exercised in these two countries. This implies focusing on darker aspects of state-society relations that rarely come into public and academic view. State power mostly remains beyond public accountability and transparency in both countries. Popularly elected governments do not have substantial control over violent and clandestine groups acting with impunity. These "internal security" organizations are principal agents that hinder political reform. Neither the RF nor the JDP managed to completely curb the influence of these organizations and establish partial control over their activities. Yet they achieved more success in this regard when they were willing to directly confront these organizations through legal and judicial channels at the risk of alienating the guardians, which often offered tacit or explicit protection to the clandestine organizations.

This chapter provides an empirically grounded discussion of the 2007 Turkish parliamentary and the 2008 Iranian parliamentary elections. It contributes to a better understanding of the limits of an electoral strategy of reform. While elections change the balance of governmental and legislative power, electoral victories do not necessarily diminish the political influence of the guardians. Constitutional amendments and widespread administrative and legal reform may be necessary but insufficient steps for dismantling guardianship. For instance, the EU reform process has substantially decreased the institutional power of the Turkish Armed Forces (TAF) and made the Turkish legal system more compatible with liberal-democratic principles. However,

the TAF and various security forces still remain beyond civilian control
reforms are not necessarily implemented, especially in the Kurdish-n
regions of Turkey. The de facto continuation of noncivilian prerogatives and
immunity naturally hinders democratic progress. Democratization requires
the mobilization of broad coalitions that would restrict the legal and practical
powers of the guardians. Yet neither the RF nor the JDP were willing to take
the bold steps necessary for the formation of these coalitions.

The Turkish Parliamentary Elections of 2007

From November 2002 to April 2007, the JDP governed Turkey without broad
opposition. The economy prospered; conflict in the Kurdish provinces was
mostly contained; Turkey enjoyed good relations with its neighbors and the
EU; the JDP swept the April 2004 municipal elections. The major challenge
confronting the JDP was the U.S. request to attack Saddam Hussein from
Turkish soil. On March 1, 2003, the Turkish parliament failed to approve legislation allowing U.S. soldiers to open a northern front. Even though the JDP
leadership sponsored the legislation, yes votes were just short of the two-thirds
majority required by the constitution. Other challenges included corruption
scandals in the JDP-controlled municipalities and state organs and occasional
skirmishes between the government and the guardians. Nonetheless, public
approval ratings of the JDP remained high and stable. It appeared that the
JDP would consolidate its rule by winning the November 2007 elections.

Meanwhile, political violence increased starting in 2005. A Catholic priest
was assassinated in Trabzon on the Black Sea coast in February 2005; offices
of the secularist *Cumhuriyet* newspaper were bombed in May 2006; a lawyer stormed the High Administrative Court and gunned down judges in May
2006; a bomb killed eleven civilians, including nine children, in the Kurdish-
majority city of Diyarbakır in September 2006; a juvenile assassinated the
Turkish-Armenian journalist Hrant Dink in Istanbul in broad daylight in January 2007; a group of youths cut the throats of three employees of a Christian
publisher in the Eastern city of Malatya in April 2007. A police investigation
that led to the discovery of a cache of grenades in June 2007 culminated in a
series of arrests that included former generals and well-known public figures
who were accused of forming a clandestine and violent organization with the
goal of overthrowing the JDP government. The investigation, which was in

progress at the time of writing, strongly suggested that these seemingly un-related violent events were coordinated by this organization to erode public confidence in the government, to generate political polarization, and to invite military intervention. It seemed that the generals decided to opt for this strat-egy because they had failed to convince the chief of staff to sponsor a coup in 2003 and 2004.

In spring 2007, the JDP was faced with the most severe political crisis since its establishment in 2001. According to the 1982 Constitution, the parliament elected a president every seven years. The term of President Ahmet Necdet Sezer (b. 1941) was ending, and the JDP-controlled parliament was about to elect the new president in May. Prime Minister Erdoğan had the ultimate say regarding the party's candidate. He waited until the last moment, April 24, to name Foreign Minister Abdullah Gül as the ruling party's candidate for president. Erdoğan calculated that the foreign minister's candidacy, which appeared to be a concession to the guardians, would ease tensions. However, the presidential elections turned into a crisis threatening the very foundation of Turkish democracy when secularist forces mobilized in opposition to the JDP's candidate.

The political atmosphere was tense even before the announcement of the candidacy of Gül. On April 12, the commander of the Turkish Armed Forces, Yaşsar Büyükanıt, in a thinly veiled warning to the JDP, declared that Tur-key's new president must have "sincere, not superficial, commitment" to the fundamental values of the Turkish Republic.[1] A day later, in an address to cadets at the War Academy, President Sezer stated:

> The Turkish political regime is under threat as never before. The laic republic's fundamental values are explicitly being challenged for the first time. Internal and external forces are united by common interests and have the same goal. External forces envision the transformation of the "laic republic" into a "mod-erate Islamic republic," under the pretext of a "democratic republic." Their goal is to make Turkey a model for Islamic countries. . . . Internal and external centers that are united to transform the Turkish Republic into a republic of moderate Islam are acting under the banner of democratization.[2]

According to the 1982 Constitution, the president wields substantial veto and appointment powers. The prospects of the new president coming from the JDP ranks greatly reinforced secularist fears that the JDP would undermine the guardianship system.[3] This fear was widely shared by a sizable segment of the society that continued to perceive the JDP as an agent of Islamization and a major threat to their lifestyles and social freedoms. From a Tocquevillian perspective, these citizens were anxious that majority rule would deteriorate into the tyranny of the religious majority. On April 14, hundreds of thousands participated in an anti-JDP rally in the capital city of Ankara.[4] A few days later, the Speaker of the Parliament, Bülent Arınç, argued that the main issue was whether Turkey would be able to elect a civilian, *pious,* and democratic president. He observed that people who were against the JDP simply could not accept such a president.[5] His remarks greatly exacerbated the secularist fears that piety would be a primary criterion in political decisions and allocations and thus further mobilized the opposition.

The showdown came on the day when parliament convened to vote on Gül's candidacy. According to one legal view, at least a two-thirds majority of the parliament (367 parliamentarians) should have been present during the presidential voting. The JDP initially dismissed this view, arguing that such a quorum had not been sought and had not been present during the election of presidents since 1989. In the first round of voting, 361 parliamentarians participated and Gül received 357 votes. He needed the votes of two-thirds of the legislators in the first two rounds and a simple majority (276) in the third round to be elected president. Members of the main opposition party, the RPP, and the MP and the TPP boycotted the voting. The RPP applied to the Constitutional Court, arguing that the voting was unconstitutional because the necessary quorum was not obtained. On the same night of voting, the TAF published a memorandum on its Web site:

> Certain groups, who have been intensely eroding the fundamental values of the Turkish Republic, primarily laicism, have been increasing their efforts in recent days. . . . In the last days, the debates surrounding the presidential elections revolve around the issue of laicism. The TAF follow this situation with anxiety. It should not be forgotten that the TAF are a party to these debates and the unwavering defenders of laicism. . . . The TAF reveal their stance and act accordingly whenever necessary.[6]

Gül's nomination, which was originally thought to be a compromise, failed to appease the secularist guardians. The memorandum was a shock to many people who had initially thought that Turkey's membership negotiations with the European Union and the accompanying reform process made an explicit military intervention in politics unthinkable. It can be argued that the TAF's decision to publish such a strongly worded memorandum was to make sure that the TCC would annul the first round of presidential voting. Just four days later, the court decided that the presidential voting in parliament was invalid because a quorum of 367 was missing. In response, the prime minister called for early elections and proposed that the president should be elected by popular vote for a term of five years. He also characterized the court's decision as a "bullet aiming at Turkish democracy."[7]

Mass protests continued unabated after the TAF's intervention. Huge mass rallies were held in Istanbul on April 29; in the western towns of Manisa, Marmaris, and Çanakkale on May 5; in the Aegean coast metropolis of İzmir on May 13; in the Black Sea coast city of Samsun on May 20; and in the western town of Denizli on May 26. These rallies galvanized the secularist opposition and showed how much an important if minority segment of the society disdained the JDP. A significant aspect of these rallies was their geographical concentration. No rallies took place in conservative Central and Eastern Anatolian towns or in Kurdish-majority areas. Erdoğan addressed large crowds in the eastern city of Erzurum on May 11, in the predominantly Kurdish city of Van on May 18, and in the Central Anatolian city of Sivas on May 27. Though the official reasons for Erdoğan's visits were the opening ceremonies for state-built housing units, he used these occasions to initiate the JDP's electoral campaign. The defining theme of his speeches was how bureaucratic forces violated popular sovereignty.

During the crisis, the JDP leadership repeatedly emphasized its commitment to laicism and rejected the accusations that the ruling party discriminates against nonpious citizens. Consistent with the expectations of Propositions I and II of moderation theory that assess the effects of state repression and electoral competition, the JDP acted with restraint while developing a new electoral strategy. On the one hand, the party leadership aimed to refresh the party's centrist image that had been tarnished during the mass protests. It realized that the polarization of the society into two camps would have dire consequences for the JDP government. Erdoğan and Büyükanıt, the chief of the general staff, met a few days after the court's decision. While the subject matter of the meeting was not disclosed, it appeared that the two figures reached a modus vivendi. Days later, the JDP orchestrated a comprehensive purge of its parliamentary group. In the new parliament, 160 of 342 in the JDP group were new faces that included prominent center-left politicians, liberals, technocrats, and locally influential centrist politicians. Erdoğan apparently aimed to dispel the fears among the guardians and their societal allies regarding the JDP's agenda. In the words of one of these politicians, who became the minister of culture after the elections:

> Our goal is to be a large mass party that embraces all segments of the society. Mass parties include people from all shades of the political spectrum. The JDP is the party of the progressive societal center. [However], until now, the JDP could not clearly explain itself to the elites. People like me can facilitate such communication.[8]

Moreover, liberal intellectuals and columnists threw their support behind the JDP in reaction to the TAF's memorandum. "The 27 April memorandum made me join the JDP," remarked a woman scholar specializing in international relations who was later elected to the parliament.[9] The alliance between liberals, who had considerable influence over public discourse, and the JDP was critical in preventing the latter's isolation. The JDP did not become a target of media assault, as the WP had in 1997. Media corporations and big business were clearly against the TAF's blatant involvement in politics and preferred the neoeconomic and business-friendly policies of the government despite the fact that the JDP was too religious for their taste.[10] They were also concerned that de-democratization would permanently jeopardize Turkey's EU ambitions.[11]

The JDP's call for elections was a well-calculated risk. Despite the secularist mass rallies, the party's support base remained stable. A series of public opinion polls showed that public support for the party was constantly over 40 percent between February and July 2007. The major factor in the JDP's popularity was the voters' satisfaction with the government's economic performance.[12] The JDP built its campaign on two themes: (1) economic stability and development, and (2) Gül's failed bid for presidency. Turkey's GDP per capita rose from 2,622 to 5,482 U.S. dollars between 2002 and 2006. Foreign direct investment in Turkey increased from 1,137 million U.S. dollars in 2002 to 20,106 million U.S. dollars in 2006.[13] Annual consumer price inflation dropped from 33 percent in November 2002 to 7 percent in July 2007.[14] Exports more than doubled in the same period. There were also some improvements in income inequality. While the richest quintile's share of total household income decreased from 50 to 44.4 percent, the poorest quintile's share increased from 5.3 to 6.1 percent.[15] The unemployment rate remained relatively high, though. A central message of the JDP's campaign was that economic accomplishments would be jeopardized should the party lose its parliamentary majority. In fact, survey data show that positive retrospective evaluations of the JDP government were a major factor in generating voter support for the party in the 2007 elections.[16] The party won the elections with a landslide by capturing 47 percent of the national vote and a majority of seats in the parliament.

The new middle-class and lower-income families in urban peripheries and rural areas formed the core supporters of the JDP. The ability of the party leadership to craft messages and policies appealing to both groups was crucial to its electoral success. The minimum wage increased more than the inflation rate between 2002 and 2007. The government distributed elementary and high school books free of charge, provided financial support to students from low-income families, and initiated a major campaign to increase female enrollment in elementary schools. It built around 140,000 housing units to accommodate low-income families. The JDP-controlled municipalities and state institutions periodically provided financial assistance, food, and coal to the poorer sections of the society.[17] The government inaugurated a major project that involved water provision and road construction to villages and small municipalities.[18] The project was highly instrumental in increasing the JDP's support in rural areas and small towns, especially in the less developed East. Another important aspect of the JDP's social policies was the extension of health services. All these social policies ensured the support of low-income and rural citizens for the JDP. The JDP also had the strong backing of the emerging middle class, distinguished by its pious and relatively conservative lifestyle. Members of this class were active in party branches and leadership. Given their influence and connections, their wealth increased after the JDP came to power.[19] They were the main beneficiaries of the JDP's pro-business and private sector–friendly policies.

The JDP's aborted attempt to elect Gül as the new president was another crucial factor that influenced the electoral results. The presidential crisis galvanized the JDP grassroots and silenced internal discontent.[20] Public opinion polls consistently showed that heavy majorities approved of Gül's presidency.

This was an important factor that discredited opposition parties that absented themselves from the parliamentary voting. In his election speeches, Erdoğan portrayed these opposition parties as violating the national will. He constantly argued that the "national will" should deliver the ultimate verdict. Members of the secularist RPP, the center-right Democratic Party (DP; Demokrat Parti),[21] and the NAP were complaining that people were not receptive to their messages because of Gül's failed presidential bid.[22] Pious citizens bitterly complained that Gül's presidency was blocked because of his religious orientation and his wife's headscarf. In a remote village of Central Anatolia, an old peasant woman put it tersely: "They did not allow a Muslim to be the president; I will vote for Tayyip [Erdoğan]." In summary, the presidential crisis rallied conservative and pious voters behind the JDP.

As in the 2002 elections, the personal charisma of Erdoğan was the driving force of the JDP electoral campaign. He addressed large crowds in fifty-five provincial centers and set the tone of the campaign. His approval ratings were the highest among all party leaders. Although they might have complaints regarding the JDP's performance, the voters generally had confidence in Erdoğan's leadership. This was a major reason why the opposition parties failed to capitalize on the JDP's inability to reduce unemployment levels, pro-

Erdoğan at a public rally during the 2007 campaign (Samsun, July 2007)

185

A JDP neighborhood meeting in a poor district of Ankara. A JDP politician is addressing the males in the background. (Mamak, July 2007)

tect small traders and farmers from ruinous competition, and fight against corruption. The JDP's major asset continued to be its leader.

Moreover, the JDP grassroots were the most organized and efficient among the Turkish parties. In a typical Anatolian town, citizens with good reputations and connections were often affiliated with the JDP. While the WP grassroots still formed the JDP's nucleus in many Anatolian towns, the party attracted politically ambitious people from all walks of life. The JDP leadership kept the grassroots' morale high; sponsored training programs about the party's principles, strategies, and goals; and provided the branches with ample funds. The grassroots were active beyond the election period; they built organic and patronage-based links with the population, and transmitted citizens' demands to the bureaucracy. As a result, the JDP grassroots were far more prepared for the elections than their opponents. In summer 2007, they pursued a highly systematic vote-canvassing operation and visited almost all villages and neighborhoods in their electoral districts. For instance, in a single day, several JDP provincial members attended the opening ceremony of a local supermarket and a farm machinery factory, a local public festival, as well as four weddings and a circumcision feast in the Black Sea coast province of Samsun. The factory and the circumcision feast were in a smaller town located 115 km away from Samsun's city center. One of the weddings was in a town 50 km from the city center, and the festival was held in a seaside town 85 km away from the center. On each occasion, an announcer introduced the JDP's provincial chief and his entourage to audiences. The chief delivered public speeches in the opening ceremonies and was the legal witness in the weddings. He praised the JDP's performance, made promises, and listened to personal demands. The fact that the JDP was in command of governmental and municipal resources gave credibility to his promises to the voters. Complaints were rare, and the public was highly receptive to the JDP members.[23] The benefits of such face-to-face communication and vote canvassing were tremendous during the campaign, especially in smaller towns and rural areas and among the lower socioeconomic segments of the society.

The JDP's huge support among the Kurdish-speaking citizens deserves special attention. The JDP's vote share in the Kurdish-majority provinces was well below its national average in the 2002 elections. In those provinces, the JDP's performance in 2007 turned out to be extraordinary. For instance, it increased its vote share from 7 to 34 percent in the province of Hakkari, from 16 to 41 percent in Diyarbakır, from 18 to 63 percent in Ağrı, and from 32 to 71 percent in Bingöl. In the county of Palu, the center of a Kurdish-Islamist rebellion in 1925, the JDP received 86 percent of the valid votes.[24] In addition to the nationwide factors, the JDP's appeal among the Kurds can be attributed to a combination of several unique factors: (a) the party's relatively inclusive stance toward the Kurds; (b) the party's social policies; (c) the backing of influential religious organizations and brotherhoods; (d) the ideological and organizational problems of the Kurdish nationalist party, the Democratic Society Party (DSP; Demokratik Toplum Partisi). First, the JDP seemed to be more inclusive of Kurdish political identity than its competitors. Although the JDP did not really develop a systematic and sustainable policy that would result in full recognition of the political and civil rights of the Kurdish-speaking population, it still remained the "most moderate Turkish party" in the eyes of many Kurds. For example, the JDP's refusal to authorize military incursions into Iraqi Kurdistan in pursuit of the militant Kurdish organization PKK before the elections contributed to its popularity among the Kurdish-speaking voters. According to a Kurdish ex-parliamentarian from the RPP, "Tayyip

[Erdoğan] is the most receptive and moderate face of the Turkish state in the eyes of the Kurds since the death of President Turgut Özal in 1993."[25] The RPP and the NAP tried to portray the JDP as being soft on "terrorism" and giving concessions to Kurdish nationalism during the elections. In response, the JDP leadership adopted a discourse that simultaneously highlighted the party's nationalistic credentials to the Turkish-speaking voters and its recognition of Turkey's ethnic diversity to the Kurdish-speaking voters. In his public addresses in Kurdish provinces, Erdoğan argued that the JDP was the only party that embraced all citizens regardless of their ethnic and religious identities. In conservative Turkish towns of Anatolia, he argued that the JDP was determined to fight against separatist terrorism. During a public rally in Bingöl, a poor Kurdish town, Erdoğan said:

> We do not join the ones who pursue ethnic nationalism in our country; we boo them. We do not join the ones who pursue regional nationalism in our country; we boo them. We do not join the ones who pursue religious nationalism in our country; we boo them too. We will be one; we will be in unity. We will be one nation, one flag, one homeland.[26]

In the Central Anatolian town of Niğde, he said:

> My citizens of Kurdish descent can never be represented by the terrorist organization PKK [insurgent Kurdish organization]. I say this with certainty. This is exploitation. We never accept any discrimination among our citizens . . . One nation, one flag, one homeland, one state [audience repeats his words].[27]

Interestingly, Erdoğan's campaign catch phrase, "One nation, one flag, one homeland, one state," was a slightly modified version of the TAF's motto of "One nation, one flag, *one language,* one homeland, one state."[28] Erdoğan deliberately did not mention "one language." His strategy that appeased both Turkish nationalists and Kurdish-speaking citizens turned out to be successful. The JDP emerged as the leading party in both provinces by receiving 71 percent of votes in Bingöl and 48 percent in Niğde. The JDP was the only party that could gather support among both Turkish nationalists and Kurdish-speaking voters. It competed with the NAP for the Turkish nationalist vote and with the DSP for the Kurdish vote. In fact, the JDP was the only party other than the Kurdish nationalist DSP that was effectively organized at the grassroots level in Kurdish-majority provinces.

The second factor that contributed to the huge appeal of the JDP amo[ng] Kurds was the party's poverty-alleviation programs that became very p[opular] among the impoverished urban and rural Kurdish-speaking citizens.[2] individuals in various Kurdish-dominated areas of eastern and southeastern Turkey, from taxi drivers to older women, expressed in personal communications with the author how the JDP cultivated popular support because of its services. A young pharmacist who supported the DSP in the town of Yüksekova, which bordered Iran and Iraq, perceptively observed this pattern:

> I think the JDP now has substantial support, especially among poor and older citizens. In Yüksekova, 76,000 individuals have a green card that enables them to have free treatment in hospitals and health centers . . . Mothers of each elementary school kid receive 10 to 15 YTL [New Turkish Lira] every month. School textbooks are now free. Poor families receive free coal and food. People have real sympathy for Tayyip [Erdoğan].[30]

According to two JDP members who were elected to parliament in July 2007, people were grateful to the party for its health and education services and poverty-alleviation programs.[31] Consequently, the JDP managed to break the hegemony of the DSP in urban ghettos of the predominantly Kurdish cities. For instance, the JDP increased its vote share from 15 to 36 percent in the poor Diyarbakır neighborhood on April 5.[32] In the neighborhood of Fatih, where the DSP had collected 68 percent of the valid votes in 2002, the JDP raised its vote share from 15 to 52 percent between 2002 and 2007. "Our efforts over several years greatly changed people's political perception and led them to vote for the JDP," said a leading woman member of the JDP who had also operated a health clinic and an NGO targeting women in the neighborhood for the last five years.[33] The JDP developed a pragmatic strategy that delivered concrete solutions to socioeconomic problems of the citizens while adopting a relatively inclusive discourse toward the Kurdish-speaking population.

A third factor that increased the JDP's Kurdish vote was religion. Previous studies have shown that religiosity was a significant determinant of voting behavior in Turkey in the 1980s and 1990s.[34] While the rise of Kurdish nationalism since the early 1990s curtailed the effects of religiosity on voting behavior, Islamic brotherhoods and NGOs recently intensified their activities and networking among the Kurdish-speaking population.[35] These networks and brotherhoods, including the well-organized Fethullah Gülen movement, lent their full support to the JDP in the July 2007 elections. According to a prominent Kurdish-Islamist intellectual, the JDP successfully attracted segments of the DSP constituency that were more pious and conservative than the DSP leadership.[36] Political crisis preceding the July 2007 elections also contributed to the JDP's appeal among the pious Kurds. When hundreds of thousands rallied in western cities against the JDP's presidential ambitions, Kurdish cities remained silent. The anti-JDP alliance between the guardians and the secular citizens mobilized many religious Kurdish-speaking citizens around the party. They were fearful that the fall of the JDP would lead to more authoritative and repressive policies toward the Kurds. In addition, many religiously oriented Kurds were angry that the army and the secular citizens would not permit a pious citizen to be president. The DSP cadres felt powerless to change that widespread perception. A PKK sympathizer complained after the elections that Kurdish people supported the JDP after watching the secular rallies on TV because they perceived that atheists would capture the government.[37]

The fourth important factor that led to the JDP's strong showing in the Kurdish regions was the organizational and ideological problems of the DSP.

A Kurdish electoral rally in the Mediterranean city of Mersin (Mersin, July 2007)

The DSP called for constitutional changes that would democratize Turkey and formally recognize the Kurdish cultural identity.[38] A young woman lawyer who was elected to the parliament from Batman identified her party's main goals as the official and full recognition of Kurdish culture and language, a ceasefire, and a general amnesty for PKK militants.[39] Yet other members of the party seemed to have more ambitious demands that involved self-governance. In a conference organized by a German foundation in Diyarbakır in September 2007, then DSP co-president Selahattin Demirtaş declared:

> We do not agree with solutions proposed by the EU and the JDP . . . The EU's approach is based on individual rights and freedoms. It does not accept the Kurds as a people; it does not recognize their collective rights; it has a just proposal that focuses on individuals. It envisions the solution as cultural rights. It does not offer solutions regarding political and social aspects.[40]

Other prominent members of the party expressed similar views that included demands for local self-governance and federalism. These contradictory messages from the party undermined its credibility in the view of Turkish public opinion and its ability to pursue a coherent and systematic parliamentary strategy. The party retained its separatist image in the eyes of many Turkish citizens. The party's postelection self-criticism recognized this problem and conceded that it failed to communicate its goals to the broader Turkish society.[41] Meanwhile, the DSP-controlled municipalities were targets of heavy public criticism because of their lack of a service-oriented approach. The DSP had already lost the control of many municipalities to the JDP in the 2004 local elections. In contrast to the Lebanese Hezbollah, which combined ideological cohesion with extensive welfare provision, the DSP failed to adequately address the socioeconomic needs of its constituency.

In addition, many Kurdish intellectuals criticized the DSP for replicating authoritarian, hierarchical, and secretive practices associated with the Turkish state.[42] "The DSP demands democracy, but its internal workings preclude democratic representation," claimed a Kurdish lawyer before the elections. The party had organic links and appealed to the same popular base as did the PKK. The PKK militants were highly influential in deciding the candidates to be supported by the party.[43] As a result, the DSP had great difficulty persuading the Turkish public opinion and its own supporters that its discourse of greater democratization that excluded demands for Kurdish self-governance was sincere. In the 2007 elections, the DSP threw its support behind fifty-three independent candidates. Twenty-two of these candidates eventually won parliamentary seats.

In summary, the JDP derived its support from different social groups and, with them, built a winning electoral coalition. Liberals and Kurds saw in the JDP an antidote against authoritarianism; pious citizens, an opportunity to increase the public visibility of Islam; poor citizens, a service-oriented government; business people, a guarantee of economic stability and neoliberalism. The opposition parties criticized the JDP for serving the interests of foreigners, being corrupt and partisan, pursuing a submissive foreign policy, and selling large state enterprises below their market value. Yet they failed to undermine the JDP's growing support base despite the rising nationalist tide among Turkish public opinion.[44]

An important consequence of the 2007 elections was the decreasing probability of a direct military intervention. The military's memorandum against Gül's candidacy failed to mobilize public opinion against the JDP. In the past, military interventions had had the active or passive support of important segments of the society. The TAF-led public campaign isolated the WP in 1997. Without the complicity of civil actors, the military would have had great difficulty toppling the WP-led coalition government. In summer 2007, political, economic, and international conditions were not ripe for direct military intervention. The TAF leadership was unwilling to face the political instability, economic chaos, and international isolation that would follow a military takeover. The JDP government remained the most popular party. Additionally, the business associations and the media sent clear signals that they disapproved of the military's direct political interference. Most importantly, the July 2007 elections gave the party a strong popular mandate. The Turkish economy's increasing linkages with international markets was an additional factor that disciplined the TAF's political ambitions. Finally, the European Union categorically condemned the memorandum of April 27.

The crucial question was whether the JDP would be able to translate its popular mandate into a systematic and consistent program of democratic reform. Immediately after its electoral victory, the JDP leadership decided to enact a new constitution and formed an academic committee that produced a new draft. However, the government did not make a sustained attempt to mobilize support for the draft constitution from various social groups or to systematically pursue an agenda of greater rights. Such a bold move would have built a large coalition in favor of a liberal constitution that would also have overwhelmed the opposition of the guardians. In any case, the debate on the constitution was overtaken by reactions to the JDP's exclusive focus on the ban on the headscarf in universities and increasing tensions between Turkey and the Iraqi Kurds. As the human rights situation deteriorated, the JDP preferred to shelve the draft constitution. At the same time, the government reached a common understanding with the TAF regarding the Kurdish policy.[45] In this regard, the measures reached on September 12, 2007, in the War on Terrorism High Council (Terörle Mücadele Yüksek Kurulu), which enabled key ministers and high-ranking soldiers to formulate a common policy toward the PKK insurgency, were highly informative.[46] These measures covered a wide range of policy issues, including agriculture, import-export, smuggling, board education, population control, marriage age, rural resettlement, broadcasting, Newroz celebrations, and Turkey's foreign image. Measure 1 involved guidelines that would be implemented to prevent the PKK from "exploiting the legal and administrative changes during the EU membership process." Measurement 30 delineated the state efforts to limit popular demand to make Kurdish a language of education. Measurement 41 recommended legal and administrative action against public figures who participated in programs in "media outlets that gave support to the PKK." Many other measurements suggested assimilative practices. The document was significant for demonstrating how the JDP failed to develop an independent Kurdish policy that would offer greater rights to this historically persecuted group. Instead, the party was content to implement the assimilative and regulative measures suggested by the TAF while it tried to preserve its moderate image in the eyes of Kurdish-speaking citizens.

As discussed earlier, the litmus test of democratic consolidation in Turkey remained the recognition of full rights of the Kurdish-speaking citizens. Yet the JDP government did not generate a sustainable strategy that would domesticate Kurdish nationalism and consolidate democratic achievements. Although the party recognized Kurdish ethnic identity, it did not take any initiatives that would institutionally guarantee Kurdish culture and language. The JDP was hesitant to implement the EU-demanded legal reforms. Subsequently, it lost the chance to use the EU reform process as a catalyst for securing freedom of Kurdish language and cultural rights. Legal harassment of nonviolent demands

iter recognition of Kurdish identity and language continued unabated.[47]
004, conflicts between the TAF and the PKK militants have rekindled.
hile, xenophobic nationalism and hate crimes against Kurdish-speaking
citizens were on the rise. Political polarization made it much harder for the
JDP to pursue a centrist strategy and to refuse the TAF's demands for pursuing
a more aggressive stance toward the Kurdish nationalists. The JDP's moderate
stance toward the guardians contained the tensions between these two actors
but hindered democratic progress. Consequently, moderation defined as willingness to make compromises and to negotiate and commitment to reconciliation with the powerful state elites was not an agent of democratic change.[48]
This finding is consistent with Proposition Vr, which emphasizes the negative
implications of behavioral moderation for democratization.

The year 2008 was very eventful for the JDP, which was faced with a
mortal danger. The Principal State Public Prosecutor applied to the TCC demanding the dissolution of the party on March 14, 2008. He argued that the
party had become a focal point of antisecular (*laiklik karşıtı*) activities. The
case against the party was more like a decapitation strike that aimed to ban
Erdoğan from political activity. The Constitutional Court agreed to consider
the indictment on March 31, 2008. Like its center-right and Islamist predecessors, and despite its electoral victories, the JDP was not immune from a judicial coup attempt. The JDP survived this judicial coup when risks associated
with its closure overwhelmed the benefits for the guardians. The TCC decided
not to ban the party in July 2008. Meanwhile, the investigation against the
clandestine organization named Ergenekon gained new impetus with the arrests of influential public figures, including former generals, in July 2008
and January 2009. Unlike in the Şemdinli case, when a counterinsurgency
unit reporting to the TAF high command violated human rights, this time
the JDP threw its support behind the police and the judicial investigation of
the organization that directly threatened its hold on power and seemed to
act independently of the TAF hierarchy. While the investigation was rightly
criticized for violating the rights of the defendants and focusing on opposition
figures with no involvement in Ergenekon, it was a significant step in ending
the culture of impunity enjoyed by violent units that had state protection. As
long as the JDP government, supported by a large section of the media and
organized civil society, actively backed the investigation, the investigation
promised to undermine groups who preferred undemocratic methods to deal

with governments they disliked. In this sense, the success of the investigation depended on coordinated, decisive, and unyielding action on the part of the JDP, not moderation.

The Iranian Parliamentary Elections of 2008

After eight years in government, the reformists in Iran were faced with another period of political marginalization after the victory of hard-liner Mahmoud Ahmedinejad in the 2005 presidential elections. Ahmedinejad initiated a purge of the state bureaucracy and rapidly dominated the Iranian domestic politics and foreign affairs with his eccentric speeches and actions. His statements regarding Israel and his rhetorically confrontational stance on Iran's nuclear energy program aggravated the tensions. In spite of his populist platform that was based on an Islamic sense of social justice, he failed to tackle inflation and unemployment. His unpredictable economic policies generated criticism from all shades of the political spectrum.[49] In addition, the restrictions on the press were intensified under his term. In the words of a journalist:

> Since 2005, the restrictions come step-by-step. There are certain guidelines that must be followed by the press. For example, the Security Council dictates the press coverage of the nuclear issue. We can deviate from the Council's line at the risk of losing our publication rights. Consequently, we prefer to be silent on issues we cannot write freely about.[50]

Meanwhile, Ahmedinejad managed to sustain a close relationship with Khamenei and the Pasdaran, which was crucial for his political survival.[51] Ahmedinejad also unveiled an innovative policy initiative that specifically targeted Iran's long-ignored provincial areas and rural poor. He constantly toured the provinces and held his cabinet meetings in small towns. His travels and rallies addressing the cheering local crowds were widely broadcast by state television.[52] His "provincial strategy" involved reaching out to the citizens at the periphery, extending patronage to wide segments of the population, and cultivating an image as the "people's president." Consequently, he seemed to enjoy substantial public support despite the fact that his rise and bombastic style created a strong sense of uneasiness not only among the reformists but also among some principalists.[53] In fact, Khatami and Karroubi started their own trips to provinces in 2007 to mobilize support.

Ahmedinejad's first public test was the local council and the AE elections held together in December 2006. The electoral results were generally interpreted as a setback for the president. His erstwhile presidential race opponent, Rafsanjani, received the highest number of votes in Tehran and later became the chairman of the AE. The principalists who were not closely affiliated with the president were also very successful. Mohammad Baqir Qalibaf, a politician who contested the 2005 presidential elections, became the mayor of Tehran. The reformists managed to participate in the elections with a single list and achieved some success.[54] Rafsanjani, Khatami, and Karroubi joined forces against what they perceived as Ahmedinejad's radicalism.[55] This axis aimed to contain the radical forces embodied by Ahmedinejad and isolate their influence in Iranian politics. The strategy they pursued involved extensive negotiations at the elite level and convincing key players of Iranian politics that Ahmedinejad should be restrained. An analyst close to Rafsanjani explained this strategy in the following words:

> There is now polarization between rationality and radicalism begetting violence. We should aim to ensure that the national institutions such as the leadership, the Revolutionary Guards, the Qom clerical establishment, and Friday prayer leaders are not parties to this polarization. They are very powerful, and if they oppose the reforms, that would be very bad. We should proceed with negotiations and convince the national institutions about the dangers of radicalism. If radicalism prevails, they would also be purged.[56]

It would be misleading to dismiss Mahmoud Ahmedinejad as an unsophisticated and fierce radical who came to power as a result of electoral manipulation. He represented a powerful and deeply pious trend in Iranian society that became disillusioned with the direction of the Islamic Republic. This trend espouses a puritan interpretation of the revolutionary goals and revolted against the Rafsanjani-era reconstruction and the Khatami-era reform policies. In the words of a young Ahmedinejad supporter who occupied an important position in the state bureaucracy:

> There are no big differences between Hashemi [Rafsanjani] and Khatami. They both pursued market economy, secular approaches, and rapprochement with the West and the U.S.A. The spirit of the revolution, martyrdom, is disregarded. Ahmedinejad represents the rebirth of the revolution and its ideals. He respects

the Imam [Khomeini], the system of *velayat-e faqih,* and the martyrs . . . Our fathers and brothers sacrificed themselves. Principalism follows their path and involves continuous revolution.[57]

Ahmedinejad supporters had little taste for pluralistic politics and included a large number of individuals who fought in the Iran-Iraq War and former members of the Pasdaran.[58] In alliance with other principalists, they controlled vast organizational networks and financial assets. Furthermore, they had privileged access to the core centers of institutionalized power and enjoyed preferential treatment from the GC in the elections. They accused their opponents of betraying the revolutionary heritage, sidestepping its achievements, and belittling the sacrifices of the martyrs against Iraq. The notion of martyrdom was central to their discourse that perceived politics as a constant struggle between the rightfully guided and the corrupted. The reformists were faced with the great challenge of countering this discourse with themes of human rights and pluralism. They also attempted to appropriate the notion of martyrdom and recast it to legitimize their position.

> Reform is returning to the revolutionary ideals and retaining the core of the revolution . . . I am twenty-eight years old. If I had been twenty-eight years old back then, I would have fought. The struggle I am waging at the moment is not different from fighting against the enemy. My father was killed in the war. He is a martyr. I am following his path. He would have participated in this struggle if he had been alive.[59]

The reformists also had to confront charges of disloyalty and of serving foreign interests. Since the U.S. invasions of Afghanistan and Iraq and the Bush administration's inclusion of Iran in the "Axis of Evil," a siege mentality had prevailed in Iran. The presence of U.S. troops across Iranian borders, the bellicose statements coming from Washington, D.C., and the U.S. funds for democracy promotion in Iran magnified the threat perception of the Islamic regime.[60] The guardians and their allies were increasingly concerned that the United States was pursuing a policy of regime change toward Iran that involved civil-society organizations and mass demonstrations inspired by the Color Revolutions that took place in Serbia in 2000, in Georgia in 2003, and in Ukraine in 2004. This was rather ironic because the RF neither had the willingness nor the capacity to undertake a Color Revolution in Iran. In any case, the Iranian regime increasingly restricted civil-society activism, including human rights advocacy and the women's movement, and detained Iranian citizens suspected of having contacts with the U.S. administration or organizations. Not incidentally, the influence of the Revolutionary Guards in Iranian politics significantly increased. For the hard-liners and their allies in the Guards, the reformist Khatami government and the reformist-controlled parliament that eschewed hawkish stances in foreign affairs appeared to be liabilities in the post-9/11 period. A typical hard-liner accusation against the RF was that the reformists did not self-confidently pursue Iran's legitimate nuclear energy program and were inclined to capitulate to the U.S. demands.[61] The 2004 parliamentary elections characterized by mass disqualification of the reformists and the 2005 presidential elections characterized by massive irregularities resulted in the elimination of the reformists and the formation of a unified government. Under these geopolitical circumstances, the reformists were experiencing a "crisis of legitimacy." In their own words:

> The U.S. actions undermine us. Our situation became worse off after the U.S. occupied Afghanistan and Iraq and unfairly labeled Iran as a member of the Axis of Evil. When we criticize the government policies, we are accused of serving the U.S. interests. The United States should not intervene in Iranian politics. When Bush says that the Iranian elections are uncompetitive, we are accused of sharing the same discourse with the United States. The U.S. pressure on Iran makes the position of the reformists more difficult to defend.[62]

In short, the prevailing geopolitical conditions had pernicious implications for the Iranian reformists. In contrast to their Turkish counterparts, the Iranian reformists lacked a consistent and powerful external backer. In Turkey, the European Union was a major force that unequivocally opposed undemocratic interventions in politics. Given Turkey's membership aspirations, the European Union had considerable leverage over Turkish politics. In contrast, the linkages between Iran and the Western countries were very weak and did not contribute to the formation of robust civic associations capable of challenging the regime's domination over the society. Consequently, the reformists were on the defensive on the eve of the 2008 parliamentary elections.

The elections for the Eighth Parliament of the Islamic Republic of Iran took place on March 14, 2008. In the first round, 208 candidates gained more than 25 percent of the valid vote and gained parliamentary seats. The remaining

Candidate advertisements exhibited in a newspaper office during the 2008 Iranian parliamentary elections (Tehran, March 2008)

82 seats were decided in a second round that was held on April 25. The RF participated in the elections and preserved its minority position in the parliament. Iran had thirty provinces (*ostan*), 207 electoral districts (*howze-ye entekhabat*), and 290 parliamentary seats.[63] The electoral district that included the cities of Tehran, Rey, Shemiranat, and Eslamshahr was the largest one and sent thirty representatives to parliament. As discussed earlier, the GC, in collaboration with the Interior Ministry (Vezarat-e Keshvar), prescreened the individuals who aspired to run in the elections. Khatami and his allies in the Sixth Parliament unsuccessfully attempted to take over this power from the GC in 2003. The ratio of disqualifications was 28 percent in 2008. In all, 7,597 Iranian citizens registered to run in the 2008 parliamentary elections. After several stages of prescreening, the GC endorsed the candidacy of about 5,500 individuals,[64] and 4,419 candidates ultimately ran in the elections.[65]

While some of the candidates were eliminated for technical reasons, the disqualifications specifically targeted the reformist candidates. The reformists bitterly complained that they were unable to contest two-thirds of the parliamentary seats. According to Dr. Abdollah Naseri, who was the spokesman of the Reformist Coalition (Etelaf-e Eslahtalaban or Yaran-e Khatami), the group was able to field only 102 candidates despite the fact that 909 reformist candidates registered to run in the elections. He indicated that around 90 percent of all the reformist candidates were disqualified. The most common reason given by the GC for the disqualification was the lack of belief in and practical commitment to Islam and the Islamic Republic of Iran, and the lack of loyalty to the constitution and the principle of *velayat-e faqih*.[66] The disqualifications affected even the ministers and governors of the Khatami presidency who had registered to be candidates. One of the disqualified reformist candidates was Tehran University sociology professor Hamidreza Jalaeipour, who lost three brothers during the war with Iraq. Jalaeipour himself served as the governor of the Kurdish city Mahabad during the war and was the publisher of some of the most prominent reformist newspapers in the late 1990s, including *Jamee*. Despite his impeccable revolutionary credentials, he was not approved by the GC.[67] The remaining reformist candidates were untested figures with little political experience and name recognition. The reformists attempted to rely on the public image of Khatami to attract voters. They did not have strong electoral expectations and were content to gain enough seats to establish a vocal minority in the new parliament.

Before the elections, the leading reformist figures contended that they would not participate in the elections in the absence of guarantees that the competition would be fair. Mohammad Reza Khatami, the ex-general secretary of the IIPF, declared: "If there are going to be elections in which the winner is predetermined, we won't waste our time or money. Without a strong showing by the reformists, the elections will not have any legitimacy."[68] Nonetheless, the reformist alliance decided to contest the elections, as it lacked an alternative strategy. The main party of the alliance justified this decision on the grounds that boycotting the elections would facilitate the authoritarian agenda of the hard-liners (*eqtedargaran*). The reformists participated in the elections to block this authoritarian scheme.[69] According to Mostafa Tajzadeh, a former deputy interior minister and a leading reformist candidate disqualified by the GC, the reformist participation in unfair and largely uncompetitive elections was necessary to maintain a public voice in the system and protest the hard-liners. Former president Khatami also encouraged people to vote despite the fact that "the individuals who supervise the elections are the ones who run for seats."[70] Besides, the reformists were fearful that boycotting the elections would result in their total marginalization. The demise of the FMI was still vivid in their minds. The FMI actively participated in the revolution and later occupied governmental posts and gained parliamentary representation in the initial stages of the new regime. However, after its falling-out with Khomeini, the movement lost its influence and power. The regime did not allow it to participate in subsequent elections. According to the reformists, Rafsanjani urged them to participate in the elections by arguing that an electoral boycott might bring irreversible political marginalization, giving the example of the FMI.[71]

Four of the foremost political groups participated in the elections: two from the principalist (*osulgaran*) camp and two from the reformist (*eslahtalaban*) camp. The divisions within the principalist camp surfaced long before the elections and reflected the competition between dominant political figures.[72] The United Front of Principalists (Jebhe-ye Mottahed-e Osulgaran) was closer to President Mahmoud Ahmedinejad, whereas the Broad Coalition of Principalists (Etelaf-e Faragir-e Osulgaran) distanced itself from the president and was affiliated with Ali Larijani, Mohammad Baqir Qalibaf, and Mohsen Rezai, the secretary of the EC. Larijani and Qalibaf had contested the 2005 presidential elections, and Rezai had withdrawn his candidacy at the last moment. Larijani later became the secretary of the powerful Supreme National Security Council (Shura-ye Ali-ye Amniyet-e Melli) and acted as the top negotiator on Iran's nuclear program until his resignation in October 2007. Larijani successfully ran for parliament from Qom Province in March 2008. While both principalist groups were content with the current distribution of institutional power and an absolutist interpretation of the *veluyat-e faqih* system, and were sharply critical of reformism, they differed in their stance toward Ahmedinejad's policies. The Broad Coalition of Principalists tended to be vocally critical of his populist economic policies and confrontational foreign policy. In any case, the two groups still maintained a working relationship, and boundaries were fluid. For instance, their candidate lists in Tehran had eight names in common, including the Speaker of the Seventh Parliament, Gholam-Ali Haddad-Adel. In addition to their full commitment to the *velayat-e faqih*, the principalist factions were also united in their concern with what they perceived as the Western cultural invasion and the urgency of addressing the needs of the Baby Boomer Generation.[73] In the words of a principalist activist who is in his late twenties:

We are victims of the Western cultural invasion. We have to increase our capacities to resist this invasion. We should rely on our strong religious and national culture [*sermaya-ye dini va melli*]. The cultural achievements of the Islamic Republic have been its most important legacy. We also need to address the needs of our young population. We should provide them with homes, marriage, and jobs.[74]

A prominent principalist analyst and columnist offered a slightly different perspective. According to him, the principalists should develop spaces of social freedoms and address the material needs of the younger generation without challenging the basic structure of political power.

The reform-minded people among the principalists pursue a different approach. The Baby Boomer Generation demands freedom in social affairs, not in politics, and social justice. They demand jobs, affordable housing, and opportunities for marriage. The groups who combine platforms of social freedom with social justice will be successful in Iranian politics.[75]

The reformists failed to produce a single united list, like the one they had in the December 2006 local council elections. In that election, the reformists fielded a united list of fifteen candidates running for the Tehran City Council. Four of these candidates won the elections, whereas just two Ahmedinejad supporters gained council seats.

Two major reformist groups contested in the 2008 parliamentary elections. The Reformist Coalition included about two dozen groups, the most powerful being the IIPF. This alliance carried the mantle of Khatami-era reforms. The other major reformist group was the NCP, led by the Speaker of the Third and Sixth Parliaments, Mehdi Karroubi. The party issued a newspaper carrying the same name and positioned itself as a reformist force, calling for a constitutional amendment that would limit absolute power. It also argued that the state should not dictate religion. Religion should be taught properly without the fear of state intervention that turned people away from religion.[76] At the same time, the party espoused a more centrist platform and seemed to endorse the *velayat-e faqih* system.[77] The candidate lists of the two reformist groups partially overlapped in Tehran and other electoral districts.

The campaigning period was seven days, and the candidates were not permitted to run television or radio ads. In practice, the state-controlled media favored the principalist candidates and offered negative coverage of the re-

The electoral office of a woman candidate affiliated with Karroubi's National Confidence Party (Tehran, March 2008)

formist candidates. This gave a considerable advantage to principalist candidates. Consequently, the lack of access to media was one of the main complaints of the reformists.[78] In the words of Khatami:

> The reformist trend does not have a public voice at the moment. We have no access to TV, which is the most effective media. We used to have daily circulation of more than three million; now we only have one hundred thousand. We cannot reach the people . . . In any case, we should encourage people to vote so that they can make their voices heard.[79]

Furthermore, the Seventh Parliament made several amendments in the electoral law that applied more restrictive regulations to the campaigns. The new law prohibited using photos of the candidates in posters and banners.[80] The parliament justified this amendment on the grounds that large-size photos created pollution and influenced voter choices. The candidates issued pamphlets and brochures with their pictures, and gave advertisements to newspapers that were sympathetic to their position. The principalist groups and candidates were at pains to demonstrate their allegiance to Khamenei, while

203

the reformists hoped to capitalize on the name of Khatami. The candidates also opened up electoral offices, sent SMS messages, advertised on the Web, and held public meetings in mosques after the prayers, at sports clubs, at universities, and in neighborhood halls. Nonetheless, citizens living in big cities tended to be very poorly informed about the candidates except for a few nationally known figures. The lesser-known candidates benefited when voters cast their ballots on the basis of the lists distributed by the electoral alliances.

In general, economic issues dominated the campaign, and political and cultural issues remained secondary. Ahmedinejad supporters built their campaigns around the theme of social justice, while the reformists promised to control inflation. The reformists were also critical of Ahmedinejad's confrontational and provocative foreign policies. They claimed that his policies brought about the isolation of Iran in the international community. They feared that Iran was on the brink of war with the United States because of Ahmedinejad's unnecessarily provocative foreign policy. In contrast, the supporters of Ahmedinejad portrayed the situation in very positive terms. According to them, the president's foreign policy elevated the international status of Iran, made

Khatami addressing reformers at a meeting (Tehran, March 2008)

the United States realize that it should enter into direct negotiations with Iran regarding the turmoil in Iraq, and advanced Iran's nuclear energy program.[81] Nonetheless, the competing platforms had many similar elements, such as the active role of the state in tackling poverty and promoting economic development. In the end, the two principalist groups clinched around 60 percent of the parliamentary seats. The two reformist groups gained control of around 16 percent of the seats, and the unaffiliated candidates picked up the rest. The GC annulled the races for three seats.[82]

One of the persistent problems regarding the Iranian elections was the unreliability of the official data and conflicting results issued by the different state agencies. The Interior Ministry announced that voter turnout was around 60 percent, significantly higher than the 51 percent for the 2004 parliamentary elections.[83] But there was some disagreement regarding the number of eligible numbers. The GC approved a parliamentary bill that raised the voting age from fifteen to eighteen in January 2007.[84] The justifications were that young people should focus on their education, and many other countries had the threshold of eighteen. This legislation considerably decreased the number of eligible voters. According to the GC, the number of eligible voters in the 2008 parliamentary elections was around 43,600,000. In the first round of the parliamentary elections, 24,484,273 citizens cast valid or invalid ballots. This ratio gave a turnout rate of 56 percent, which was still lower than the officially announced rate of 60 percent. Furthermore, according to other calculations based on figures issued by the Interior Ministry and the Statistical Center of Iran (Markaz-e Amar-e Iran), 47,733,051 Iranian citizens were eligible to vote in the 2008 elections.[85] On the basis of this number, the voter turnout dropped to 51 percent, as low as the turnout in 2004 when several reformist groups boycotted the elections.

In the 2004 parliamentary elections, the turnout was higher in provincial areas and small cities and towns, and lower in large cities and in provinces inhabited by ethnic minorities.[86] A similar pattern was observed in 2008.[87] The voter turnout was the weakest in Tehran Province, where public interest in the campaign was negligible. In that province, only around 30 percent of the eligible voters went to poll stations. Partially as a result of this low participation rate, the candidates affiliated with the two major principalist lists gained control of twenty-nine of the thirty seats in the Tehran city electoral district.[88] The United Front of Principalists list was very successful. Twenty-six of the thirty candidates on the list won parliamentary seats. Five of these candidates were women. Overall, women candidates won only eight seats in the new parliament.[89] The principalists also won thirty-three of the thirty-eight seats assigned to Tehran Province. Four of the remaining seats went to unaffiliated candidates (*mostaqel*), and a reformist candidate captured the remaining seat. The turnout was 40 percent in Isfahan Province, which had a very high rate of urbanization and included the second-biggest metropolitan area in Iran. In Kordestan Province, where ethnic discontent had been simmering since 2003, the turnout was 45 percent. In underdeveloped provinces, the turnout was well above the national average. It was 90 percent in Kohgilūyé and Boyer-Ahmad, 78 percent in South Khorasan, and 75 percent in Ilam.

It seems that Iranian citizens residing in small cities and rural areas had stronger incentives to participate in the parliamentary elections than Iranians living in big cities. The members of parliament, especially from the provincial areas, were important sources of patronage and connections. They also engaged in pork-barrel politics that favored their constituency. Material expectations, including employment opportunities and investments in the province, were strong factors that affected voting behavior. Additionally, factions fielded candidates with popular reputations in their constituencies. Finally, regional and ethnic solidarities also affected voting behavior.[90] In contrast, citizens in big cities had little material incentive to participate. This pattern was similar to voting behavior in parliamentary elections in authoritarian Arab regimes such as Jordan.[91] Parliamentary elections provided an institutionalized competition for influence and resources in a heavily state-regulated economy. Voters went to the polls with the expectation that they would materially benefit from their prospective representative. Concerns about patronage turned out to be more important than concerns about policy expectations.

The 2008 parliamentary elections did not result in any significant change in the institutional distribution of political power, which remains highly concentrated, unaccountable, and nontransparent. Instead, they served to perpetuate the authoritarian pluralism inherent in the Islamic Republic since the early revolutionary years. The elections did provide a mechanism that facilitated the rise of new factions and the formation and disbandment of fluid factional alliances, managed factional conflict, and introduced an element of uncertainty lacking in other authoritarian states in the Middle East. However, the elections by themselves were not catalysts of democratization or de-

democratization. Consequently, an electoral strategy of reform based on behavioral moderation had little chance of bringing political change in Iran. In this regard, the trajectory of the RF gives support to Proposition Vr, which states that behavioral moderation may not be conducive to democratic change.

Given the structure of political power in the Islamic Republic of Iran, the RF was faced with a harsh dilemma. On the one hand, the RF's electoral strategy reached a dead-end. The reformists failed to translate their electoral gains into a sustainable popular movement that would be the basis of political change toward democratization. The movement had been demoralized since the debacle in the 2004 parliamentary elections and unable to reenergize and mobilize its base. Electoral participation may not have been the best method for achieving political reform. On the other hand, the strategy of an electoral boycott was impractical and futile for two reasons.[92] First, a considerable number of Iranian citizens voted in the elections regardless of the restrictions and unfair practices. People went to the polls for many reasons, including material expectations, fear of retribution for not voting (ID cards were stamped at the polls), loyalty to the regime, or a sense of civic responsibility. The regime sought legitimacy in higher turnout rates and very actively encouraged voting. Second, even a successful boycott strategy would not necessarily empower the reformists in the absence of extensive grassroots-level organizations and popular networks. The hard-liners commanded superior mass-mobilization capacity and organizational resources. While the main reformist organizations, such as the IIPF and the NCP, opened up branches all over Iran, they still had little influence over public opinion, especially in small cities and rural areas, as they lacked the means to mobilize public opinion. The reformist press at the moment was a fraction of what it had been ten years ago in terms of circulation and influence. Unless the reformists developed new strategies to overcome this dilemma, they were in no position to initiate sustainable political change in the Islamic Republic.

The main driving force of the RF was the conviction that the sustainability of the Islamic regime depends on the satisfaction of the people. Mohammad Reza Khatami was very explicit when he asserted that the consent of the people was central to the continuation of the regime.[93] The problem was that the RF did not live up to its own promise. It failed to broaden its constituency and establish horizontal linkages with large segments of the society. The IIPF remained an urban middle-class movement with little substantial representation among the working class and peasants. As suggested by Proposition IIIr, which identifies the corrosive impacts of organizational institutionalization on programmatic goals, the RF did not prioritize the expansion of political participation and the empowerment of civic associations over the access to a legal political system under very restrictive circumstances. In the end, it even mostly lost that access. According to Saeed Hajjarian, the leading theoretician of political reform, the RF remained elitist. It attempted to solve all problems at the elite level and through bargaining within narrow circles. Hajjarian was also critical of the idea of contesting the elections in a system in which political power remained concentrated in the hands of nonelected figures.[94] An intellectual affiliated with the opposition group Alliance of the National Religious Forces (Melli Mazhabi) provided a perceptive criticism of the RF:[95]

> The reformists lacked a strategic plan and were unaware of the structure of political power in Iran. They thought that if they only controlled the parliament, they would be in a position to initiate democratic change. They failed to cultivate a strong civil society. When they were in power, they ignored civic institutions such as the union of teachers, the student movement, farmers associations, and human rights associations. Ultimately, the students, the supporters of Ayatollah Montazeri, and some intellectuals paid the price.[96]

It should be noted that neither the JDP in Turkey nor the RF in Iran paid a very heavy price for challenging the authoritarian aspects of the ruling regimes. The Turkish post-Islamists saw their party banned, suffered legal persecution, and served short prison sentences. The RF experienced mass disqualifications, legal persecution, and several assassination attempts targeting its key members. Yet they were spared waves of suppression that pulverized leftist and Kurdish groups in Turkey and open opponents of the *velayat-e faqih* in Iran. Both the JDP and the RF pursued relatively cautious strategies and refrained from directly and openly confronting the guardians. The RF was not willing to call for a campaign of civic disobedience as suggested by dissidents such as Akbar Ganji.[97] In the end, the reformists lacked any leverage over the guardians. They failed to gain any meaningful concessions while they gradually lost their ground. Perhaps a veteran of Iranian opposition was right when observing:

> You have to pay a price to achieve freedom. The groups that are unwilling to pay that price will not be the catalysts of democratic opening up. In contem-

porary Iran, people, including the reformists, are unwilling to pay that price. I believe the leaders should demonstrate to the younger generations that we are ready to pay the cost of freedom. Then they would be inspired.[98]

In conclusion, the 2007 Turkish and 2008 Iranian parliamentary elections revealed the limits of democratic reform through electoral means. In the Iranian context, elections institutionalized factional conflict without encouraging mass opposition, introduced an element of uncertainty to politics without threatening the authoritarian status quo, led to temporary alliances without contributing to the development of organized parties, and ensured citizen support for the regime without empowering popular control over power holders. When the U.S. occupations of Afghanistan and Iraq and the Color Revolutions in ex-Communist republics sharply aggravated the threat perception of the ruling elite, the regime simply bent the rules for elections to ensure hardliner control of government and parliament. That trend began with the 2004 parliamentary elections, continued with the 2005 presidential elections, and reached its zenith with the 2008 parliamentary elections. The electoral route to democratization in Iran proved to be an illusion.

The Turkish case was considerably different, although the similarities were significant. The JDP swept the elections, initiated unprecedented reforms stimulated by the EU negotiation process, achieved sustainable economic growth, attracted high levels of foreign investment, expanded Turkey's sphere of influence in foreign relations, and came to partially dominate the state institutions. Nonetheless, the party failed to convert its accomplishments into a resolute and steadfast drive toward democratic change. The party's electoral triumph in July 2007 was immediately followed by the intensification of violence between the TAF and the PKK, and the JDP leadership immediately backtracked from their preelection promise of a liberal constitution. And then the Constitutional Court decided not to ban the JDP but declared that the party had become a focal point of antisecular activities. This decision cast a strong shadow over the JDP's freedom of action.

CHAPTER 9

Conclusion

[handwritten marginalia: but the work doesn't demonstrate this — if or my own periods they were successful by avoiding full support & compromise... it shows... these issue...]

This study makes three contributions to the study of Muslim politics. First, it offers the first and only systematic analysis of Muslim reformers in two very important countries, Iran and Turkey. The comparative method adopted in this work clearly demonstrates that Muslim reformism embracing electoral democracy, political pluralism, and human rights can rise and mobilize substantial public support in very unexpected settings. Iran and Turkey greatly differ in terms of modern and recent history, sectarian affiliation, regime type, political economy, and foreign affairs. Yet both countries witnessed the rise of Muslim reformers in similar time periods. Muslim political actors, regardless of their sectarian orientation and political experience, are capable of responding to institutional incentives and constraints. Similar ideological and behavioral changes among Muslim political actors have also taken place in Egypt, Indonesia, Jordan, and Western Europe. At the same time, moderation theory does not apply to all Islamist parties participating in elections. Some Islamist parties have strong organizational foundations and operate in countries with weak states. These parties sponsor extensive welfare services, are well entrenched in communities, are financially autonomous, and control militias. Either they infiltrate the state apparatus or the state lacks the capacity to dismantle their grassroots networks and militias. In a sense, they are states within states. Hence, they are not faced with a trade-off between organizational survival and pursuit of revolutionary goals. They retain ideological goals while legally participating in the political system. Examples include Hamas in the Palestinian Authority, Hezbollah in Lebanon, and the Sadr Movement and the Islamic Supreme Council of Iraq (ISCI) in post-Saddam Iraq.[1] Moderation theory does not predict that these organizations will evolve in a manner similar to the RF and JDP.

Second, Muslim reformers harbor ambivalent attitudes toward societal pluralism. They espouse forms of secularism that are accommodative of public expressions of Islamic identity and display of Islamic symbols. That kind of secularism does not seek the marginalization of Islam and actually gives the religion a privileged role in informing public debates in Muslim-majority countries. However, societal pluralism in the twenty-first century also implies an unprecedented proliferation of a great variety of faiths and unfaiths. Like many other societies, Muslim societies have increasingly become more diverse and pluralistic in terms of lifestyles, religiosity, and societal practices. On the one hand, Muslim groups with varying orientations establish schools, commercial enterprises, media outlets, and political entities with outreach to non-Muslims in a deliberate effort to establish themselves as legitimate actors in global interactions. On the other hand, beliefs and practices that criticize and defy religious authorities and norms also enjoy a renaissance in Muslim societies. Dialogue between Muslim groups and their detractors, who often live side-by-side, is more relevant to the future of liberty and democratic governance in Muslim societies than dialogue between "civilizations." Without a common understanding, hegemonic interpretations of Islam may aim to stifle the individuality and societal spaces associated with this diversity and plurality. Consequently, the ways in which Muslim reformers come to terms with secularism understood as the condition of disbelief will have great repercussions on the prospects for individual liberties in Muslim societies in the twenty-first century.

Finally, the theoretical framework developed in this study aims to provide a comprehensive understanding of political change that delineates ideological and behavioral evolution as two separate but interrelated processes. The theory and empirical study mutually inform each other. On the one hand, moderation theory that focuses on the impact of state repression, electoral competition, and organizational resources on the behavior of political elites provides valuable insights when studying the phenomenon of Muslim reformism. It shows that Muslim political actors are not exceptional, in that they are likely to act quite predictably when faced with similar institutional structures and organizational capacities. On the other hand, the comparative study of Muslim reformers in Iran and Turkey leads to a more refined and sophisticated understanding of moderation theory in three ways.

First, the type of relationship between Muslim reformers and their followers at an organizational level needs to be carefully specified. Organizational frameworks that minimize Muslim reformers' accountability to their followers give the former considerable latitude in developing platforms at the expense of programmatic coherence and consistency. In both Iran and Turkey, civil-society activists, human rights defenders, and writers initially sympathetic to Muslim reformers increasingly became critical of them for not pursuing a rights-based political agenda and for their reluctance to take principled stances vis-à-vis the guardians.[2] Yet these criticisms did not have much effect on the Muslim reformist leadership that prioritized organizational stability and electoral goals over democratization. Neither the RF nor the JDP was able to establish sustainable and trust-based relationships with social actors with rights agendas. The RF gradually alienated the student, women's, and workers' movements, which initially gave their full backing to Khatami and his allies in the parliament. It did not really address the concerns and priorities of these important actors, who would have been able to prevent the isolation of the elected reformist politicians by 2004. The absence of a coordinated and sustained action between opposition political elites and social movements made the fall of the RF inevitable. In Turkey, the JDP established a well-run electoral machine with an extensive countrywide network. This network ensured that the party elites directly communicate with their base and sympathizers and reach the greatest number of voters during the election times. The electoral machine was effective and commanded resources far superior to those of its competitors. At the same time, it generated a culture of dependency that hampered participatory democracy and public accountability of leaders. Erdoğan gradually consolidated his undisputed authority over the party, which left no room for loyal opposition. The decision making was centralized in a small group of people with easy access to the prime minister. The party had little motivation to establish a common front with social movements seeking democratization and expansion of rights unless the guardians directly threatened the JDP's existence. In any case, the temporary alliance between the JDP and social movements unraveled whenever the JDP established a new modus vivendi with the guardians. Consequently, the party was unwilling to change political-opportunity structures in a way that would motivate and enable societal actors seeking democratic reform.[3] The most notable instance of such a behavior was the JDP's lukewarm and irresolute support for a new constitution that would replace the authoritarian 1982 Constitution in the aftermath of the 2007 elections. The party backtracked from its goal of enacting a new constitution several times when faced with strong opposition from the political establishment.

Second, moderation theory needs to provide more attention to the dynamics of ideological change. Change at the ideological level cannot be reduced to a byproduct of changes in strategic incentives. Ideological moderation needs to be thought of as a separate process that often facilitates, accommodates, or even hinders behavioral moderation.[4] Even tactical decisions may involve extensive debates among adherents of an antisystem political worldview. These debates can result in the formation of a new consensus, internal splits, or reaffirmation of the existing worldview. In neither Iran nor Turkey did ideological moderation automatically follow once radical Muslim activists were included in the political system. On the contrary, ideological transformations that resulted in the opening up of new horizons, engagement with democratic and liberal ideas that had previously been dismissed as un-Islamic, and often self-questioning took place in an expanding public sphere in the early 1990s. This public sphere consisted of magazines, journals, nongovernmental organizations, professional associations, and media outlets that addressed a growing stratum of a pious middle class. Ideological dynamism produced by participation in this public sphere outlived state repression that did not necessarily generate a process of reradicalization in both countries. At the same time, without such an ideological transformation, it would be unthinkable that Muslim reformers would capitalize on political opportunities and develop moderate platforms.

Third, behavioral moderation may actually hamper democratic progress in ways that are not anticipated by moderation theory. This point is especially relevant for studies of democratization in Muslim-majority countries with popular Islamic political movements. Many of the recent scholarly and journalistic studies on this subject have focused on two questions: (1) How moderate are Muslim political actors with sizable followings? and (2) Under what conditions do these actors come to espouse moderate platforms and renounce extremist behavior? Most of these works demonstrate that Muslim reformism successfully develops cross-fertilization between democratic ideas and Islamic norms. They persuasively refute the perceptions that Muslim beliefs and practices inherently foster authoritarian rule. Furthermore, it is usually argued that political inclusion of Muslim political groups would bring their moderation, a development that is usually assumed to be conducive to democratic progress. This study adopts a more critical view of the process of behavioral moderation that may translate into missed opportunities for political reform and perpetuation of the authoritarian political status quo. In this regard, it agrees with studies that critically examine how authoritarian regimes promote certain modes of political participation and activism among popular opposition groups that are more conducive to the sustainability of nondemocratic rule.[5] These regimes neutralize and co-opt opposition movements by institutionally shaping the political arena and reducing their mass-mobilization potential. The fact that Iranian and Turkish Muslim reformers actually came to occupy positions of political power independent of the guardians of the ruling regimes makes their cases different from similar movements in other countries. Hence, Muslim reformers in these two countries had room to politically maneuver that was not available to opposition movements in more authoritarian countries of the Muslim Middle East. However, in spite of their greater power and leverage vis-à-vis the regime elites than their counterparts elsewhere, the reformists in Turkey and Iran failed to dislodge authoritarian structures. Moderate strategies pursued by Muslim reformers that involved reconciliation, compromises, and electoralism actually impeded and delayed, if not undermined, democratic struggles in Iran and Turkey.

This does not mean that the democratic achievements of Muslim reformers in these two countries have been negligible. In Iran, the significant shifts in public discourse and the popularization of democratic ideas have been their greatest legacy.[6] In Turkey, the rise of the JDP restored public confidence in the electoral system and greatly facilitated the EU-induced political reform process. This study argues that the critical task for Muslim reformers is building institutions and developing the organizational capacity to make political power more accountable, more equally distributed, and less hegemonic. In this regard, Muslim reformers in Iran and Turkey have not been very successful. The challenge of building organizations that promote participatory forms of decision making and pursue rights-oriented agendas eluded the Iranian and Turkish Muslim reformers. The transformation of the Islamists into moderate groups with electoral purposes was not sufficient for democratization. Electoral victories did not automatically translate into political victories that made democratization sustainable and established public accountability of power and public participation in the political process. The RF was left without any viable strategies when the guardians blocked their access to the government and parliament. The JDP failed to develop a legal and institutional agenda of democratization that would decrease political polarization, mobilize the

214

unconditional support of the liberals, and effectively neutralize the political power of the guardians.

It can be objected that Iranian and Turkish Muslim reformers were faced with a hostile environment in which their survival was always at stake. They did not have any strong potential allies in pursuit of democratic reforms. One can point out that the JDP was confronted with an opposition that was more interested in sustaining the guardianship than in contributing to democratic reform. In view of that, strategic choices of the RPP, the main opposition party in Turkey, may seem puzzling. The RPP, representing Turkish secularist modernization, had an ambivalent attitude toward the EU-induced reform process. On the one hand, the RPP leadership espoused Turkey's integration with Europe as the fulfillment of the historical goal of the republic's founder, Mustafa Kemal Atatürk. On the other hand, it was fearful that the EU-induced reform process would work to the benefit of the JDP by increasing the latter's popularity and neutralizing the guardians. It seems that the RPP leadership was fearful that a JDP that achieved considerable progress toward Turkey's membership in the EU would become invincible in popular elections. The RPP would then remain a party of the electoral minority. The RPP was hoping that the guardians would block the JDP and bring about its ultimate downfall. That expectation came to naught after Gül, the JDP government foreign minister, became president in August 2007 and the Constitutional Court decided not to dissolve the JDP in July 2008. It became clear that the guardians could restrain and tame, but not overthrow, the JDP government. The RPP attempted to expand its electoral base by fall 2008 by increasingly focusing on corruption under the JDP government and signs of economic recession. It amended its program in its extraordinary convention in December 2008 to be more responsive to greater popular demands such as those of Alevi and Kurdish groups. The party leadership also made a halfhearted attempt to appeal to religious and Kurdish voters who had been captive audiences for the JDP before the 2009 local elections.

The 2009 local elections were a significant setback for the JDP. While the party again emerged from the ballot box as the predominant political force and retained its control of most of the large municipalities, its vote share dropped to 39 percent from 47 percent. The party lost votes not only to the Turkish nationalist NAP in coastal and central provinces but also to the Kurdish nationalist DSP in eastern provinces. Although the economic recession was a major factor in declining voter support for the JDP, the results also demonstrated the limits of the JDP's ambivalent Kurdish policy, which involved piecemeal policies such as the start of a Kurdish public television channel and plans for Kurdish language departments in public universities, but no comprehensive plan to expand the scope of rights. To put it bluntly, the JDP now appeared too soft on "PKK terrorism" in the eyes of Turkish voters who were discontented with continuing armed clashes, yet too uncompromising in the eyes of many Kurdish-speaking citizens who demand greater freedoms. Meanwhile, there were some strong indicators that some elements in the TAF were actively searching for ways to overthrow the government despite the disclosure of illegal cells since 2007.[7] Such attempts and the possibility of another legal case against the party put the JDP on the defensive and cast a huge shadow over its ability to govern. In fact, the JDP would have achieved more democratic progress if it had been willing to confront the guardians and had built strategic coalitions with groups pursuing rights agendas. These groups, organized as social movements excluded from the institutional distribution of power and with grassroots support, could have been important allies in challenging the authoritarian structures. In this sense, the increasing influence and self-confidence of social movements in Turkey (e.g., ethnic and sectarian groups seeking greater formal recognition and rights, human rights associations, unions, liberal media) is a promising development and may result in considerable reorientation of the priorities of the JDP government.

The June 2009 Uprising in Iran

The June 2009 presidential election quite unexpectedly brought an end to the charade of legal and moderate opposition in the Islamic Republic of Iran. The GC eventually approved four candidates to run in the election: President Ahmedinejad, ex–Prime Minister Mousavi, ex–Speaker of the Parliament Karroubi, and ex–Commander of the Pasdaran Rezai. Khatami announced his candidacy in February, only to withdraw in favor of Mousavi in March. Although Mousavi had been away from politics for twenty years and was mostly an uninspiring speaker, he quickly emerged as a serious contender who challenged Ahmedinejad's hegemony over Iranian politics. His campaign, which was supported by the major organizations and figures of the RF, capitalized on the widespread anti-Ahmedinejad sentiment that had built up among large segments of Iranian society. For the first time, Iranian state television staged one-on-one debates between presidential candidates. These debates significantly increased public interest in the election and brought sensitive issues into the limelight. The debate between Ahmedinejad and Mousavi on June 3 was particularly interesting, as the former accused the latter of colluding with ex-presidents Rafsanjani and Khatami. Most boldly, he explicitly named Rafsanjani and his family as being corrupt. This was a clever move on the part of Ahmedinejad to capture the working- and lower-middle-class vote by evoking the image of a humble outsider fighting against the corrupt order, symbolized by Rafsanjani. That strategy had actually worked very well in the 2005 election.

Unlike the previous election, the campaigning was intense and attracted enormous voter interest.[8] The Mousavi camp chose green as the color of their campaign. Green not only has Islamic connotations and refers to Mousavi's claim of being a descendent of Prophet Muhammad (hence the honorific title Mir preceding his first name), but it also symbolizes nature's rebirth in spring. Mousavi's rallies were well attended and galvanized segments of the population who felt excluded and discriminated against under the Ahmedinejad government, especially the young, urban, educated, and middle-class citizens. On June 8, Mousavi supporters formed a human chain that ran from the south of Tehran to the north. Two days later, they marched from Revolution Square to Freedom Square in the capital in a very symbolic act of defiance. At night, thousands of Ahmedinejad and Mousavi supporters poured into the streets and taunted each other in many parts of Iran. While emotions ran high during the campaign, demonstrations were mostly peaceful and did not involve any major clashes. As usual, the guardians, led by Khamenei, exhorted the public to participate in the election in an effort to claim popular legitimacy.

The officially announced results were surprising to many. Ahmedinejad was declared the winner in the first round.[9] He received about 24,600,000 of approximately 39,400,000 valid votes. Mousavi only won around 13,300,000 votes. The three "defeated" candidates immediately objected to the results and declared that the election was rigged. In fact, there were many problems with the way the election was conducted. First, according to official results announced by the Interior Ministry, the voter turnout rate was 85 percent. While anecdotal evidence suggested that participation in the election was high, there was no way to check the accuracy of the figure, as the ministry did not announce the number of eligible voters at the province and county levels. Furthermore, the ministry announced that there were 46,200,000 eligible voters in Iran. Yet this number did not make sense, since the number of eligible voters had been 43,600,000 in March 2008. Given Iran's annual population growth rate of 1.3 percent, an increase of 2,600,000 voters in fifteen months was simply impossible. Next, the opposition observers were expelled from polling stations, the SMS network was turned off to prevent communication among the opposition observers and election centers, plainclothes agents from the Intelligence Ministry stormed the Mousavi campaign headquarters in Tehran, and the way in which the results were publicly announced involved many irregularities. Besides, the Interior Ministry and the GC, which were in charge of conducting and supervising the election, were clearly not impartial institutions. The electoral system was vulnerable to organized fraud both at voting (e.g., voting twice or more, voting on behalf of others) and counting (e.g., manipulating the number of eligible voters, artificially increasing votes for a candidate) stages.[10]

Almost spontaneously, people started to protest the results in the streets a day after the election. Clashes with the security forces were reported in many cities. Demonstrations and clashes increased in the following days. Mousavi addressed a massive crowd on June 15 at Freedom Square in Tehran. On the same day, Basij forces opened fire at demonstrators and bystanders, and scores of people lost their lives or were injured. Demonstrations continued, and Mousavi supporters organized a massive rally on June 18 to commemorate those who were killed during Monday's protests. A day later, Khamenei delivered the Friday sermon in the compounds of Tehran University.[11] He confirmed the victory of Ahmedinejad by arguing that the accusations of vote rigging could not explain a difference of 11 million votes. In his opinion, citizens who voted showed their confidence in the political system. He also extended his support to Rafsanjani in an attempt to prevent him from completely siding with the opposition. Moreover, he demanded an end to street demonstrations, urged the "defeated" candidates to express their objections through legal channels, and warned that they would be responsible for any violence and rioting. Despite this uncompromising speech, people continued to demonstrate in the streets. The demonstrations gradually went beyond demands for the annulment of the election and involved broader calls for democratization. Not surprisingly, the security forces, including plainclothes Basij members, attacked protestors and killed dozens. Mass demonstrations temporarily faded away in the face of brutally violent repression. Nonetheless, in an open letter to the Iranian people, Mousavi insisted that the election should be annulled; challenged the neutrality of the GC, which supposedly would consider the objections to the electoral results; and declared that people had a right to peacefully protest against vote rigging. He also claimed that reformism entailed a return to the true principles of the Islamic Revolution.[12] In another letter, issued a day later, he defended protests as a constitutional right and criticized the violent reaction of the security forces.[13]

At the time of writing, the political situation was characterized by high levels of uncertainty and confusion. The guardians miscalculated not just the effects of a massive public participation in the election but also the buildup of widespread grievances, especially among the most resourceful and educated segments of the Iranian society. Khamenei's praise of the massive voter turnout as a testimony to the people's commitment to the political system rang hollow when countless Iranians poured out into the streets and declared that they did not have confidence in the electoral results. The only effective response the regime had in the face of such massive civil disobedience was violence. The guardians did not hesitate to use lethal force with impunity against their own citizens. Security forces arrested hundreds of reformist politicians, journalists, and activists and imposed draconian restrictions on the press in an effort to cripple the already weak organizational network of the opposition. State television accused "rioters" of attacking public property and being manipulated by foreign powers.

Yet it is also clear that the use of sheer force and the old tactic of blaming foreign plots and agent-provocateurs would not stabilize the political situation for several reasons. First, the crisis has its roots in the significant fractures within the ruling elite, who are engaged in an intense power struggle. The rise of Ahmedinejad has unnerved some important figures, including Rafsanjani, who perceive the former's populist-authoritarian stance as a threat to the limited pluralism that has characterized the Islamic Republic since its inception. These figures are too powerful to be silenced without any cost or compromises. Second, the segment of the population that is completely disenchanted with the political system is too large and influential to be permanently left without any political representation. Third, the fact that the Obama administration has completely abandoned regime-change discourse and policies toward the Islamic Republic has weakened the regime's attempts to associate all dissent with foreign-led conspiracies.[14] Fourth, the opposition seems to have learned some important lessons from the Khatami years, when the guardians simply isolated and marginalized the reformists, who were unwilling and incapable of going beyond "legal channels" to mobilize mass support. With the widespread allegations of electoral fraud and the guardians' uncompromising stance, it becomes clear that moderate strategies that involve legal procedures and negotiations will not bring about any effective political change. The reformists would achieve substantial political concessions from the guardians only if they could capitalize on and channel the massive public discontent into a sustainable civil-disobedience movement. Such a movement would be met with severe resistance from the guardians and involve many sacrifices, but it would also be the lasting legacy of the June 2009 uprising and would vindicate the memory of unarmed civilians who were beaten, wounded, and killed by security forces.

NOTES

1. In this book, Islamism is defined as a set of beliefs that aim to restructure societal relationships according to a particular interpretation of Islam by means of state power. Islamism, by definition, is illiberal (i.e., it does not recognize the inviolability of individual rights) but does not need to be undemocratic (i.e., not espouse the notion of popular rule). The adjective "Islamist" is used to label individuals and groups who adhere to Islamism.

2. Hence, the tendency to call them "Muslim democrats." See Nasr, "Rise of Muslim Democracy," 13–14. The term "Muslim democrats" signifies a strong normative meaning that is not always justified. It implies that these actors are agents of democratization and positive political change. I prefer "Muslim reformers" over "Islamic reformers" because the former implies plasticity of the religious identity and its coexistence with a variety of nonreligious identities and commitments. The adjective "Islamic" implies that religious identity and commitments always have priority.

3. Brown, Hamza, and Ottaway, "Islamist Movements."

4. This book follows Asef Bayat, who defines post-Islamism as both an exhaustion of Islamism and "an endeavor to fuse religiosity and rights, faith and freedom, Islam and liberty." Bayat, *Making Islam Democratic,* 10–11.

5. Personal interview with Mehmet Bekaroğlu, Ankara, September 11, 2007.

6. Hence this study is motivated by an empirical puzzle that emerges from the comparison of Iran and Turkey. Thelen, "Historical Institutionalism," 373.

7. Öniş and Türem, "Entrepreneurs, Democracy, and Citizenship," 452–453.

8. The most sophisticated presentation of this perspective is found in Philpott, "Explaining the Political Ambivalence of Religion."

9. Ibid., 516.

10. Ibid., 508.

11. For samples of a vast body of literature on the subject, see Roy, "The Crisis of Religious Legitimacy in Iran," and Arjomand, "The Reform Movement."

12. Brownlee, *Authoritarianism,* 13. Brownlee compares Egypt, Iran, Malaysia, and the Philippines to show how single-party rule contributes to authoritarian stability.

13. Ibid., 174.

14. For two similar arguments along these lines, see Keshavarzian, "Contestation without Democracy," and Tezcür, "Intra-Elite Struggles and Iranian Elections."

15. This view is based on the assumption that popular Islam is riddled with superstitions and falsities. See Tunaya, *Türkiye'de Siyasal Gelişmeler,* 141–145.

16. For an argument along these lines, see Öniş, "Globalization and Party Transformation."

17. This perspective is best articulated in Yavuz, *Islamic Political Identity in Turkey.*

18. For a historical analysis of Turkish Islam, see Ocak, *Türk Sufiliğine Bakışlar.*

19. Sufism is conceptualized as being antagonistic to political Islam elsewhere too. For Lebanon, see Kabha and Erlich, "Al-Ahbash and Wahhabiyya."

20. The democratizing impact of the EU on the JDP is argued in Öniş, "Political Economy of Turkey's Justice and Development Party."

21. The distinction between "necessary" and "sufficient" causes is elaborated in Brady and Collier, *Rethinking Social Inquiry,* 213–221.

22. Hence, this books follows the calls for greater social science and comparative breadth in Middle Eastern studies. Tessler, *Area Studies and Social Science.*

23. For a very similar definition, see Wickham, "Path to Moderation," 206.

24. The classic statement of this theory is found in Downs, *Economic Theory of Democracy.*

25. For a commonsense definition of "electoralist party," see Gunther and Diamond, "Species of Political Parties," 185–188.

26. This mechanism is similar to one of the four methods of moderation identified by Schwedler: "providing moderates with opportunities to increase their visibility and efficacy." Schwedler, *Faith in Moderation,* 13 and 194.

27. Political competition has a broader meaning than electoral competition. Schumpeter, who defines democracy as an "institutional arrangement for arriving at political decisions in which individuals acquire the power to decide by means of a competitive struggle for the people's vote," concedes that democratic method is related to individual freedom in most instances. He writes, "If everyone is free to compete for political leadership . . ., this will in most cases though not in all mean a considerable amount of freedom of discussion for all. In particular it will normally mean a considerable amount of freedom of the press." Schumpeter, *Capitalism, Socialism, and Democracy,* 169, 271–272.

28. Esping-Andersen, *Politics against Markets,* 6–9.

29. Ibid., 12.

30. Ibid., 17–26.

31. Furet's majestic study aims to explain the enigma of how Communism, despite its unprecedented cruelty and crudeness, appealed to so many individuals in twentieth-century Europe. Furet, *The Passing of an Illusion.* For the appeal of Communism in post–World War II France and Italy, see pages 383–394 and 415–423.

32. Panebianco, *Political Parties,* 11.

33. A similar point is made by Wickham when she notes that "Islamist opposition groups elsewhere in the Arab world demonstrate that participation does not inevitably induce ideological moderation." Wickham, "Path to Moderation," 225.

34. Ibid., 224. Despite its innovative approach, Wickham's work does not provide strong evidence to show that political learning, "change in core values and beliefs" (207), actually took place. First, her empirical evidence comes from interviews with only two individuals (Abu Ayla Madi Abu Ayla and Esam Sultan, the founders of the Wasat Party). Second, she qualifies her argument that political learning actually resulted in "substantive commitment to democratic principles" (206) by saying that "the *Wasat* party's conception of Islam is not elastic enough to permit a full reconciliation of religious and democratic values" (222). As political learning is thought to take place at the level of individual learning, its results may not be accepted as party doctrine.

35. Clark challenges the claim that cross-ideological cooperation leads to substantial ideological moderation—such as in core beliefs regarding human rights and women's political participation—on the basis of her study of the IAF's interaction with secular opposition in Jordan. Clark, "Conditions of Islamist Moderation," 555.

36. Schwedler, *Faith in Moderation,* 20.

37. Rajaee, *Islamism and Modernism,* 196–207.

38. Kamrava, *Iran's Intellectual Revolution,* 11.

39. Ibid., 29.

40. Metiner, *Bembeyaz Demokrasi Yemyeşil Şeriat,* especially 73–82, 175–181, 374–375, 416–418, 445–448. This very polemical autobiography offers some valuable insights into the ideological transformation of a generation of Islamists in the 1990s. Metiner was highly involved in Islamist circles as a publisher, adviser, writer, and politician.

41. The FP received around 2 percent of the total vote in the 2002 and 2007 elections. A much-needed leadership replacement in fall 2008 energized the party before the March 2009 local elections.

42. In this sense, they are "good Muslims" who do not threaten the Western interests in the strategically located Middle Eastern and South Asian countries. The distinction between "good Muslims" and "bad Muslims," the ones that confront the Western forces and their indigenous allies, has become central to the public, scholarly, and official discourse in the United States in the post–September 11 period.

43. See, for instance, Fuller, *Future of Political Islam.*

44. For example, see Benard, *Civil Democratic Islam.*

45. Nasr, "Rise of Muslim Democracy," 26.

46. Ottaway and Hamzawy, "Islamist in Politics," 22.

47. For instance, Islamist participation in Algeria and Morocco made the Islamists more pragmatic and willing to compromise. Werenfels, "Between Integration and Repression." However, it is not clear if this development contributed to the prospects of democratization.

48. In Eastern European revolutions, mass mobilization capacity of the opposition was crucial for regime breakdown. Bunce, "Rethinking Recent Democratization," 172.

49. Bermeo, "Myths of Moderation," 314.

50. As the case of Morocco shows, Islamist moderation actually brought a process of political repression in the first decade of the twenty-first century. See Wegner and Pellicer, "Islamist Moderation without Democratization," 167–169.

51. Tuğal, *Passive Revolution*, 4, 32, 246–250.

52. Schwedler, *Faith in Moderation*, 3.

53. Wickham, "The Path to Moderation," 206.

54. Migdal, in his *State in Society*, conceptualizes a state as a multilayered organization composed of multiple parts interacting with other social forces.

55. Panebianco, *Political Parties*, 69.

56. The "strategy of tension" aims to invite authoritarian rule by orchestrating violent campaigns, including bomb attacks and assassinations, that would erode public confidence in civilian governments and increase the appeal of military intervention. For the strategy of tension in Italy, see Ferraresi, *Threats to Democracy*, 86–89.

57. For a theoretical framework that emphasizes how variances in the composition of incentives (collective vs. selective) affect party strategies and pursuit of ideological goals, see Panebianco, *Political Parties*, 9–11 and 19–20. In contrast, "believers" who were interested in ideological purposes had a strong voice in the WP and the FP. The existence of a large number of believers naturally restricted the party leadership's ability to pursue an ideologically more flexible and electorally more expansionist strategy.

58. Six of the eleven members of the Court voted for the JDP's dissolution. This was one vote short of the seven votes required by the Constitution (Article 149). One member voted not to penalize the party, and the remaining four members voted to cut half of the state aid to the JDP. Before 2001, a simple majority vote was all that was needed to dissolve political parties.

59. The qualitative methods are particularly good for "process tracing," demonstrating *how* independent variables affect the dependent variables. Tarrow, "Bridging the Quantitative-Qualitative Divide," 472.

60. Johnson, "Consequences of Positivism," 241.

61. The value of qualitative research for generating theories, in contrast to simply verifying existing theories, is recognized in Glaser and Strauss, *Discovery of Grounded Theory*.

62. Bates, "Area Studies and the Discipline."

CHAPTER 2

1. Here, the definition of radical parties, which is used synonymously with antisystem parties, follows Sartori's original conceptualization. These parties exist in both democratic and authoritarian regimes, oppose the regime on principle, and consider several aspects of the regime illegitimate. In this sense, antisystem parties have a delegitimizing effect on the regime. Sartori, *Parties and Party Systems*, 132–133.

2. For a sophisticated analysis of the SDP in Germany, see Panebianco, *Political Parties,* 70–78.

3. Michels, *A Sociological Study,* 18.

4. Ibid., 334–335.

5. Ibid., 336.

6. Ibid.

7. Panebianco, *Political Parties,* 17–20.

8. Ibid., 16.

9. Schumpeter, *Capitalism, Socialism, and Democracy,* 283, 352–353.

10. Lipset, "Some Social Requisites of Democracy," 98–99.

11. Kirchheimer, "The Catch-all Party," 55.

12. Neumann, "Party of Democratic Integration."

13. Przeworski and Sprague, *Paper Stones,* 18.

14. For instance, see Esping-Andersen, *Politics against Markets.*

15. Przeworski and Sprague, *Paper Stones,* 184.

16. Ibid., 24.

17. Ibid., 183.

18. Lipset and Rokkan, "Cleavage Structures," 22.

19. Huntington, *The Third Wave,* 169.

20. Nasr, "Democracy and Islamic Revivalism," 285.

21. Mainwaring, "Party Objectives in Authoritarian Regimes."

22. This conceptualization of the effects of organization on behavior is similar to Paul Pierson's discussion of path dependency as increasing returns. Once organized as vote-maximizing, office-seeking parties, the strategic choices available to parties become very restricted over time. Pierson, "Increasing Returns, Path Dependence."

23. Kalyvas, "Commitment Problems in Emerging Democracies."

24. Kalyvas, "Democracy and Religious Politics," 317.

25. Waterbury, "Fortuitous By-products," 387–390.

26. Dahl, *Polyarchy,* 34.

27. Almond, "Christian Parties of Western Europe."

28. Almond, "Political Ideas of Christian Democracy," 762–763. He also speculated that a neoauthoritarian ideology could proceed from these parties.

29. Kalyvas, *Rise of Christian Democracy in Europe.*

30. Rokkan, *State Formation,* 234.

31. Kalyvas, "From Pulpit to Party," 304.

32. The Catholic Center Party's commitment to parliamentarism, inalienable human rights, freedom of religion, and welfare policies in imperial Germany proved to be the proto-model for the democratic stability of post-Nazi Germany. Cary, *Path to Christian Democracy.*

33. Grew, "Suspended Bridges to Democracy."

34. Hanley, *Christian Democracy in Europe,* 4.

35. William Hale argues that the JDP's policies regarding religious education mirror those adopted by Christian Democrats. Hale, "Christian Democracy and the AKP," 304.

36. They had initially tended to create integrationist and isolating organizations that encompassed all aspects of their supporters' lives. Rokkan, *State Formation,* 287.

37. Kalyvas, "Unsecular Politics and Religious Mobilization," 293–320.

38. Kalyvas, *Rise of Christian Democracy in Europe,* 264.

39. Panebianco, *Political Parties,* 11, 25–30.

40. Ibid., 10.

41. Barnard, *Functions of the Executive,* 92.

42. This also applies to corporate organizations, which are arguably more reliant on selective incentives to develop and sustain the motivation of their employees. Simon, "Organizations and Markets," 274–275.

43. Panebianco, *Political Parties,* 10, 30.

44. Hence, moderation of radical popular movements is not a prerequisite for democratization. Bermeo, "Myths of Moderation," 314.

45. For instance, the size and magnitude of electoral districts and the type of electoral system may strongly affect the incentives for moderation. See Kreuzer, "Electoral Institutions."

46. Schwedler, *Faith in Moderation,* 21.

47. Ibid., 193.

48. Sartori, "Politics, Ideology, and Belief Systems," 407, and Dahl, *Polyarchy,* 125–132.

49. North, *Understanding the Process of Economic Change,* 18.

50. A classic issue is the relationship between Christianity and modernity. The classic work that argues that the Enlightenment does not negate Christian faith and theology is Carl Lotus Becker's *Heavenly City of the Eighteenth-Century Philosophers.* Peter Gay describes the Enlightenment as a self-conscious alternative—taking its intellectual vigor from ancient classics—to the Christian worldview. Gay, *The Enlightenment.* For a recent rejoinder, see Taylor, *A Secular Age.* Also common is the question of whether Catholic and Protestant Christianity are intrinsically more hospitable to secularism and modernity than Islam. In this regard, Marshall G. S. Hodgson argues that how Islamic heritage is perceived and experienced by contemporary Muslims is critical for understanding the relationship between Islam and modernity. See Hodgson, *The Venture of Islam,* Vol. 3.

51. Weber, *Protestant Ethic and the Spirit of Capitalism.*

52. For a powerful critique of the idea that Islam is antithetical to secularism, see Ayubi, *Political Islam,* chap. 1. For the complex and fluid nature of the political visions of early Muslims, see Crone, *God's Rule: Government and Islam.*

53. Geertz, *Interpretation of Cultures,* 218.

54. The vast literature on ideology provides dozens of different definitions. For a comprehensive review of the literature, see Gerring, "Ideology." The current concep-

tualization follows Converse, "The Nature of Belief Systems in Mass Publics," and Sartori, "Politics, Ideology, and Belief Systems."

55. Elkins and Simeon, "A Cause in Search of Its Effects."

56. Swidler, "Culture in Action," and Geertz, *The Interpretation of Cultures,* 89.

57. March and Olsen, "The New Institutionalism."

58. Henry Eckstein attempts to provide a theoretical framework that conceptualizes political change consistent with culturalist assumptions. Actors adapt to social discontinuities and ruptures by developing new cultural patterns, being more flexible, retreating into smaller and more cohesive units (i.e., family), conforming with rituals in public, and behaving opportunistically. Eckstein, "Culturalist Theory of Political Change."

59. North, *Understanding the Process of Economic Change.*

60. Axelrod, "Evolutionary Approach to Norms," 1104.

61. Wedeen, "Conceptualizing Culture," 714.

62. Weber, *The Sociology of Religion,* 209.

63. For a majestic discussion of the rise of revisionist Islam in the twentieth century, see Hodgson, *The Venture of Islam,* 3:386–394.

64. In this regard, scholars of Islamic movements have recently started to conceptualize Islamists as rational actors responding to the limits and opportunities of the political system. For example, see Alexander, "Opportunities, Organizations, and Ideas"; and Wiktorowicz, *Islamic Activism.*

65. This insight is similar to Axelrod's argument that unsuccessful strategies are dropped in favor of successful strategies. Axelrod, *Evolution of Cooperation,* 56.

66. Hence, the theoretical model offered here is based on probabilistic thinking.

67. John H. Goldthorpe proposes causality as a generative process that assumes association between two or more variables is created by some mechanism operating at a micro level and characterized by methodological individualism. While this study follows this notion of causality, it underlines the importance of norms to human action in addition to strategic interests. Goldthorpe, "Causation, Statistics, and Sociology," 8–10. One of the unique strengths of case studies is their value in "clarifying previously obscure theoretical relationships." McKeown, "Case Studies and the Statistical Worldview," 174. The importance of the *how* question to causal analysis is articulated by Charles Tilly in "Mechanisms in Political Processes."

68. Mahoney and Rueschemeyer, *Comparative Historical Analysis.*

69. For a discussion of various types of comparative method, see Lijphart, "Comparative Politics and the Comparative Method"; Skocpol and Somers, "The Uses of Comparative History in Macrosocial Inquiry." The method of agreement was first articulated by John Stuart Mill. See Przeworski and Teune, *Logic of Comparative Social Inquiry,* chap. 2.

70. The comparative design also allows for variation in the dependent variable as it focuses on the evolution of Muslim democratic behavior. King, Keohane, and Verba, *Designing Social Inquiry,* 129–136.

71. The method of agreement is particularly suitable for evaluating necessary causal conditions. Dion, "Evidence and Inference," 139–140; Mahoney, "Qualitative Methodology and Comparative Politics," 134.

72. Gheissari and Nasr, *Democracy in Iran,* 127–136.

73. Ali Bulaç, Turkish daily *Zaman,* November 4, 2000.

74. Personal communication with Soudabeh Qaisari and Narges Sadat Amjad, women editors of the Iranian daily *Aftab-e Yazd,* Tehran, June 19, 2005.

75. Personal communication with Ertuğrul Yalçınbayır, Bursa, September 13, 2007. He was the general secretary when the party was established. The JDP leadership did not put him on the party ticket in the 2007 elections.

76. Personal communication with Saeed Asgharzadeh, editor of the Iranian daily *Saheb-e Kalam,* Tehran, June 18, 2005.

77. For instance, see the declarations of the RF figures supporting Rafsanjani in the Iranian daily *Sharq,* June 22, 2005.

78. Personal communication with the managers of Rafsanjani's electoral campaign, Tehran, June 21, 2005.

79. Mohammad Qouchani, "Are We Defeated?" *Sharq,* June 26, 2005.

80. In this sense, linkages between Turkey and the European Union that involve extensive political, economic, social, and cultural ties have been decisive in supporting and legitimizing pro-democracy domestic actors and generating a discourse based on rights and pluralism. For the role of linkages in democratization, see Levitsky and Way, "Linkage versus Leverage."

81. In this sense, the JDP did not engage in popular mobilization for nonelectoral purposes or sponsor mass protests. For an analytical discussion of the activities of the Muslim Brotherhood in Egypt, see Wickham, *Mobilizing Islam.*

82. Personal communication with Turhan Çömez, Ankara, September 8, 2007. He was Erdoğan's principal clerk before being elected to the parliament in November 2002. His vocal opposition to certain aspects of the party's policies brought about his marginalization within the JDP. At the time of writing, he was a fugitive accused of participating in an illegal scheme aimed to overthrow the JDP government.

CHAPTER 3

1. In academic forums, this view is mainly associated with Bernard Lewis and Samuel P. Huntington. For a recent argument along similar lines, see Lakoff, "Reality of Muslim Exceptionalism." Identifying Islam's unchanging core as the quest for conquest, Efraim Karsh claims that Islamic history can be read as cycles of imperialistic struggles and that Osama bin Laden is just the latest incarnation of this. Karsh, *Islamic Imperialism.*

2. For example, see Lewis, *What Went Wrong?*

3. Lewis, *Islam and the West,* 135–136. This implication is also pervasive in Gellner, *Muslim Society.*

4. For the historical origins of the concept, see Palmer, "Popular Democracy in the French Revolution."

5. Lewis' ideal figure for this role was the founder of the Turkish Republic, Mustafa Kemal Atatürk. It appears that the Bush administration's imposing of democracy was highly influenced by Lewis' notion of top-down Westernization. An obvious problem was that Atatürk had no Iraqi counterpart. For an interesting analysis of how Lewis' historical conceptualization of the relationship between Islam and democracy influenced the Bush vision of the Middle East, see Hirsh, "Bernard Lewis Revisited," available at www.washingtonmonthly.com/features/2004/0411.hirsh.html.

6. Zakaria, *The Future of Freedom,* 120. Zakaria does not offer a compelling account to disentangle the dynamics that bring more democracy on the one hand and freedom on the other, nor to explain how they clash with each other. Thomas Friedman makes a similar argument: "How do you get from here to there—how do you go from an authoritarian monarchy or a military regime to a more representative government—without ending up with a Khomeini-like theocracy à la Iran or a civil war à la Algeria?" Friedman, "God and Man in Baghdad," *New York Times,* December 4, 2003.

7. For an analysis of the second wave of democratization in the post-Communist countries, see Bunce and Wolchik, "Favorable Conditions and Electoral Revolutions." The Cedar Revolution in Lebanon in 2005 ultimately failed to overcome the country's deep ideological and sectarian divisions.

8. The monarchies and one-party regimes had different strategies in using limited parliamentarism to consolidate their grip over power. Lust-Okar and Jamal, "Rulers and Rules."

9. For the importance of personal and informal webs of relationships for the stability of Central Asian regimes, see Collins, "Logic of Clan Politics."

10. Fish, "Islam and Authoritarianism."

11. The Muslim world includes countries with a Muslim-majority population. By this criterion, there are forty-four sovereign countries in the Muslim world. Less than half of these countries are located in the Middle East.

12. For an optimistic assessment of Indonesia's democratic transition, see Rieffel, "Indonesia's Quiet Revolution."

13. Bratton and Van De Walle, "Popular Protest and Political Reform in Africa."

14. The introduction of free and competitive elections in Muslim-majority countries of Africa occurred as top-down decisions induced by interelite competition and external pressures for democratization. Van De Walle, "Africa's Range of Regimes."

15. Mahmood Mamdani directly confronts what he labels the "culture talk" of Lewis and Huntington. He argues that the roots of Islamic terror should not be searched out in the intricacies of Islamic belief or history, but in the Cold War policies of the United States. Mamdani, *Good Muslim, Bad Muslim.* Yahya Sadowski provides a lucid critique of the Islam-begets-authoritarianism thesis. Sadowski, "New Orientalism and the Democracy Debate." John Esposito has long been a famous advocate of

the idea that Islam by its nature is not hostile to modern and democratic values. See his *Islam and Politics*. Leonard Binder argues that the rise of liberal interpretations of Islam is crucial for the success of political liberalism. Binder, *Islamic Liberalism*. Khaled Abou El Fadl's *Islam and the Challenge of Democracy* contains opposing voices on the subject of Islamic belief and its relationship to democratic values.

16. For a survey of liberal Muslim thinkers, see Charles Kurzman's *Liberal Islam*. Abdou Filali-Ansary is critical of Kurzman's categorization of liberal Islam and instead suggests his own alternative categories. Filali-Ansary, "What Is Liberal Islam?"

17. For a comprehensive and comparative perspective on how the interpretation of religion is a major source of conflict among the faithful, see Hefner, "Multiple Modernities." Eickelman and Piscatori's *Muslim Politics* remains a classic source on the different political meanings of Islam in different historical and spatial settings.

18. For instance, see Moussalli, *Islamic Quest for Democracy*; Tamimi, "Renaissance of Islam."

19. For instance, see Shafiq, "Secularism and the Arab-Muslim Condition," 145.

20. Stepan and Robertson, "An 'Arab' More Than a 'Muslim' Democracy Gap"; Donno and Russett, "Islam, Authoritarianism, and Female Empowerment."

21. Bellin, "Robustness of Authoritarianism." For the pernicious influence of oil wealth on democracy, see Michael Ross, "Does Oil Hinder Democracy?"; Smith, "Oil Wealth and Regime Survival."

22. For an anthropological study of patrimonialism and its roots in Arab political culture, see Hammoudi, *Master and Disciple*.

23. For Iraq under Saddam Hussein, see Tripp, *A History of Iraq*; for the early years of the Palestinian Authority under Yasser Arafat, see Robinson, *Building a Palestinian State*; for Syria under Asad, see Van Dam, *Struggle for Power in Syria*.

24. Almond and Verba, *The Civic Culture*.

25. Granato, Inglehart, and Leblang, "Effect of Cultural Values on Economic Development."

26. Banfield, *Moral Basis of a Backward Society*.

27. Barro and McCleary, "Religion and Economic Growth across Countries."

28. Inglehart, *Modernization and Postmodernization*.

29. Putnam, *Making Democracy Work*.

30. Huntington, *Clash of Civilizations*.

31. Since their origins, political-culture explanations have been treated as secondary to "conventional explanations" (economic, institutional, rational, or societal) to explain political outcomes. See Pye, "Culture and Political Science." Also see Inglehart, "Renaissance of Political Culture."

32. Laitin, "Civic Culture at 30"; Marc Howard Ross, "Culture and Identity." Cultural explanations outside of the *"Civic Culture"* framework overcome these criticisms. Two classics are Scott, *Weapons of the Weak*; and Schaffer, *Democracy in Translation*.

33. A classic articulation of this criticism in found in MacIntyre, "Essential Contestability of Some Social Concepts." For a useful treatment of problems in concept

building, see Collier and Mahon, "Conceptual 'Stretching' Revisited"; Adcock and Collier, "Measurement Validity." It seems that the diagnoses of the measurement problems offered by Adcock and Collier and Mahon are not heeded in the political-culture literature where they are most needed.

34. Norris and Inglehart, "Islamic Culture and Democracy."

35. A theory of political culture needs to build on a theory of motivation "that specifies how and why people make choices that affect political life." Wilson, "Many Voices of Political Culture."

36. Elkins and Simeon, "A Cause in Search of Its Effects."

37. Ethnography-based works deal better with this diversity. A classic in this genre is Bulliet, *Islam*. Also valuable is Rosen, *The Culture of Islam*.

38. Seligson, "Renaissance of Political Culture."

39. For a similar critique of Putnam's and Inglehart's works, see Jackman and Miller, "Renaissance of Political Culture?"

40. For a bold criticism that mainly focuses on Putnam's and Inglehart's works, see Johnson, "Conceptual Problems."

41. The combination of different methods in a study is called triangulation. Jick, "Mixing Qualitative and Quantitative Methods." This is, in fact, done by Putnam in his study of Italian political reform.

42. One of the most eloquent critics of the notion of cultural inertia is Moore, *Social Origins of Dictatorship and Democracy*, especially pages 484–487.

43. For a survey of the trajectory of political-culture explanations from the perspective of a historian, see Formisano, "Concept of Political Culture."

44. The classic work on the topic remains Said, *Orientalism*. Lockman's critical historical survey of the development of Western knowledge of the Middle East, *Contending Visions of the Middle East*, is also noteworthy. For a critique of assigning Islam an unchanging core, see Mamdani, *Good Muslim, Bad Muslim*, 17–62.

45. For instance, see Tessler, "Islam and Democracy in the Middle East"; Meyer, Rizzo, and Ali, "Changed Political Attitudes in the Middle East"; Norris and Inglehart, *Sacred and Secular*, 154; Rose, "How Muslims View Democracy"; "Africa: Islam, Democracy and Public Opinion"; Hoffman, "Islam and Democracy"; Tessler and Gao, "Gauging Arab Support for Democracy"; Jamal and Tessler, "Attitudes in the Arab World."

46. Available at www.worldvaluessurvey.org.

47. For a sophisticated discussion of the evolving meaning of sharia, see Brown, "Sharia and State in the Modern Muslim Middle East."

48. For an insightful description of this phenomenon, see Hodgson, *The Venture of Islam*, 3:386–394.

49. Çarkoğlu and Toprak, *Türkiye'de Din, Toplum ve Siyaset*, 16–17.

50. Çarkoğlu, "Political Preferences of the Turkish Electorate."

51. For a balanced summary of the moderate Islamic position in the mid-1990s, refer to Kramer, "Islamist Notions of Democracy."

52. For a sweeping discussion of the decline of ideological commitments among Islamic political actors, see Kepel, *Jihad.*

53. For example, Langohr, "Of Islamists and Ballot Boxes"; Schwedler, "A Paradox of Democracy?" For a more skeptical view, see Al-Azmeh, "Populism Contra Democracy."

54. Mansoor Moaddel argues that the accommodative policies of Jordan resulted in the relatively moderate behavior of the Islamic movement in Jordan in contrast to the exclusive policies of Egypt, Syria, and monarchical Iran, which intensified the radicalization of Islamism; see Moaddel, *Jordanian Exceptionalism.*

55. For the origins of Islamism, see Türköne, *Siyasi İdeoloji Olarak İslamcılığın Doğuşu.* For a comprehensive study of the thought or work of the leading Muslim reformer of the nineteenth century, Jamal al-Din al-Afghani, see Keddie, *Islamic Response to Imperialism.*

56. The caliphate had been in the hands of the Ottoman dynasty since 1517. However, sultans had rarely highlighted their credentials as the heads of Sunni Islam until the late eighteenth century when Sultan Abdülhamid II (r. 1876–1909) propagated the notion of pan-Islamism. For Abdülhamid II's policies, see Deringil, "Legitimacy Structures in the Ottoman State."

57. Hamid Enayat shows that the abolition of the caliphate generated a vigorous debate and was a key factor in "stimulating the call for the Islamic state." Enayat, *Modern Islamic Political Thought,* 52.

58. ISI policies were not without their successes, especially in the earlier periods. For a balanced evaluation of ISI, see Owen and Pamuk, *History of Middle East Economies,* 95.

59. For a passionate and engaging study of Arab nationalism, see Dawisha, *Arab Nationalism in the 20th Century.*

60. For an analysis of Mawdudi's thought, see Nasr, *Mawdudi and the Making of Islamic Revivalism.*

61. For reasons for the failure of Mawdudi's Jamaat-e Islami to become a mass-based party in Pakistan, see Nasr, *Vanguard of the Islamic Revolution,* 220–223.

62. Qutb's usage of the concept of *jāhiliyya* was unprecedented and a major breakthrough. See Shepard, "Sayyid Qutb's Doctrine of Jāhiliyya."

63. Qutb, *Milestones,* 66–67. This book was published in 1964, after Qutb had suffered a long period under Nasser's repression. Qutb's earlier work, *Social Justice in Islam,* published in 1948, was less radical in its implications.

64. Qutb argued that jihad could not be thought of as only a defense mechanism, as this would do nothing to abolish injustice from earth. *Milestones,* 46–47. The purpose of jihad is to establish God's authority and to end the tyranny of man-made laws. Ibid., 57.

65. According to Euben, Mawdudi and Qutb selectively read canonical Islamic texts to generate an understanding of jihad that served the purpose of reestablishing God's sovereignty in the world. In her reading, jihad signifies a communal attempt

to bring justice, equality, and freedom to the world. This interpretation still begs the question of whether this notion of jihad can be incorporated into a pluralistic perception of politics. Euben, "Jihad, Martyrdom, and Political Action."

66. For militant Islamist groups that were heavily influenced by Qutb's ideology, see Kepel, *Muslim Extremism in Egypt.*

67. Khomeini, *Islam and Revolution,* 169–173.

68. Ibid., 27–150.

69. Khomeini clearly stated this point in an interview delivered after the revolution. Ibid., 337–338.

70. The only place where the export of the Iranian Revolution had some notable success was Lebanon, where civil-war conditions and the availability of a Shia constituency greatly contributed to the influence of Iranian revolutionaries. Norton, *Amal and the Shiʿa,* 99–106, 198. For a critical discussion of the construction of the "Iranian menace" and Arab support to Saddam Hussein's Iraq in the Iran-Iraq War, see Adib-Moghaddam, *Iran in World Politics,* 89–102.

71. For an analysis of the survival of the authoritarian Arab states, see Silvan, "Why Radical Muslims Aren't Taking Over Governments."

72. Even Omar al-Bashir, the soldier-ruler of the country who seized power in 1989, admitted that state-imposed Islamization resulted in a failure. *Al-Hayat* newspaper, February 7, 2001, quoted in Hassan, "Political Islam versus the Society in Sudan," available at http://www.sudanstudies.org/mhassan04.html.

73. For a remarkable study of the rise of the Taliban, see Ahmed Rashid, *Taliban.*

74. The most comprehensive sources in this regard are Kepel, *Jihad;* and Roy, *Failure of Political Islam.*

75. This argument is articulated in Gerges, *The Far Enemy.*

76. State repression was a factor in Turkish Islamists' eschewal of an anti-European stance in favor of their systematic advocacy of Turkey's membership in the European Union. They rightly sensed that the EU's insistence on democracy and liberal rights would protect them from the military's wrath. Dağı, "Transformation of Islamic Political Identity."

77. For an earlier typology of the different Islamic political orientations and an assessment of their relative strengths and weaknesses, see Shepard, "Islam and Ideology."

78. For two significant contributions based on ethnographic studies in this regard, see White, *Islamist Mobilization in Turkey;* and Wickham, *Mobilizing Islam.* A common fallacy of the modernization theory is the association of upward social mobility, education attainment, and entrepreneurship with lower levels of piety and "traditional values." This is evident in Lerner, *Passing of Traditional Society,* chaps. 1–2.

79. For instance, see Chhibber, "State Policy"; and Tessler, "Origins of Popular Support."

80. Kepel argues that this alliance cannot be sustainable. See Kepel, *Jihad,* 6, 365–366. He downplays the ability of Islamic populism, which combines messages of

social justice with economic liberalism, to bind these groups together. The success of the JDP stands as a testimony to the effectiveness of this strategy.

81. The notion of Islamic economics unifies the working class and the petty middle class against the perceived exploitation by big capitalists and regime cronies. See Kuran, "Discontents of Islamic Economic Morality." For the growing role of Islamic businesses, see Henry, *Mediterranean Debt Crescent*. For the critical role of the pious middle class in the Iranian Revolution, see Fischer, "Islam and the Revolt of the Petite Bourgeoisie."

82. Tuğal, "Appeals of Islamic Politics."

83. Janine Clark, in "Social Movement Theory and Patron-Clientelism," analyzes Islamic social networks in Egypt, Jordan, and Yemen.

84. For the formation of these new elites in Turkey, see Göle, "Secularism and Islamism in Turkey."

85. For a fresh analysis that describes the democratic Islamic trends in Egypt, see Baker, *Islam without Fear*. For a discussion of Wasat, see Olav, "*Hizb al-Wasat*."

86. According to former president Wahid, Indonesia demonstrates the compatibility of democracy and Islam. Wahid, "Indonesia's Mild Secularism."

87. Hefner, *Civil Islam*. According to Rais, Islamist ideology was not a marketable commodity in the pluralistic politics of Indonesia. Reported by Reuters, November 20, 2003.

88. Tamimi, *Rachid Ghannouchi*.

89. Many studies of varying quality make this argument. Anthony Shadid, in *Legacy of the Prophet,* covers a large terrain with the eye of an informed journalist. Bruce Lawrence, in *Shattering the Myth,* highlights the nonviolent dimensions of Islam. Graham Fuller, in *Future of Political Islam,* argues that Islamic movements are democratizing.

90. For a rich discussion of how democracy is perceived and constructed by Islamic actors in the Arab world, see Sadiki, *Search for Arab Democracy.*

91. For an engaging discussion of neofundamentalism, see Roy, *Globalized Islam,* 232–289.

CHAPTER 4

1. Taylor, *A Secular Age.*

2. Casanova, *Public Religions in the Modern World.* Casanova defines secularization as composed of three distinct but related elements: religious decline, differentiation, and privatization (7). He argues that differentiation in the West occurred as the result of the Protestant Reformation, the rise of the modern state, the rise of modern capitalism, and the rise of modern science (20–25). Although all these developments are specific to the West, the rapid diffusion of modern institutions, practices, and ideas resulted over time in the emergence of autonomous spheres of life in Muslim

countries. The notion of secularization as differentiation was first articulated by Max Weber. See Weber, *The Sociology of Religion*, 223–245.

3. Taylor, *A Secular Age*, 221.

4. Ibid., 18.

5. Ibid., 461.

6. One can reasonably argue that enchanted aspects of Islam are still vibrant and have a considerable number of adherents. For instance, the notion of the return of the Mahdi remains central to Shiite belief and is enshrined in the Iranian Constitution. In Iran, a culture of miracles and dreams continues to influence the public consciousness. Believers visit the shrines of imams and other holy figures with a variety of expectations ranging from cures for their illnesses to finding a suitable marriage partner. The Jamkaran Mosque, outside the city of Qom, has recently become a very popular pilgrimage destination. Some Shia believe that the Hidden Imam (*imam-e zaman*) will return to the world in Jamkaran. I visited the mosque in early March 2008 and found the place full of pilgrims from all around the country. People write their wishes for the Hidden Imam on a piece of paper and drop them in wells. It is widely believed that the Hidden Imam reads and fulfills people's wishes. According to Mohsen Kadivar, the regime promoted this belief after the death of Khomeini for political purposes. He observes that more Iranian pilgrims visit Jamkaran than either Mecca or Karbala. Personal communication with Mohsen Kadivar, Tehran, March 10, 2008.

7. These observations are based on World Values Surveys conducted in Muslim-majority countries.

8. Secularization theory of the 1950s and 1960s, which understood the decline of religious beliefs as the result of modernization, has now been widely challenged. For instance, see Stark, "Secularization, R.I.P." For recent defenses of secularism, see Bruce, *Religion in the Modern World*; Norris and Inglehart, *Sacred and Secular*. The latter argue that rising levels of existential security are conducive to secularization, although this trend is shaped by cultural traditions. Religiosity persists among people who are most vulnerable to survival-threatening risks. This argument can be criticized on two grounds. First, according to the logic of this argument, nomads should have been the most religious group, which is not the case. Also, the experience of Muslim countries in the twentieth century does not support the idea that industrialization and urbanization undermine the importance of religion.

9. Hefner pioneered the usage of the terms "civil Islam" and "public Islam." "Public Islam" entails public articulation of Muslim faith and expressions of Muslim identity without threatening societal and political pluralism. Hefner, *Remaking Muslim Politics*.

10. Taylor, *A Secular Age*, 21.

11. Ibid., 3.

12. Alan Wolfe observes that dogmatic beliefs are in decline and are being re-

placed by a pluralistic religious revival around the world. To him, this is an indicator of greater secularization. His observations are consistent with Charles Taylor's conceptual narrative. Wolfe, "And the Winner Is."

13. Talad Asad offers a penetrating critique of the hegemonic aspirations of secularism. He challenges the predominant view of secularism as the bulwark against religious despotism and protection of individual freedoms in West European history. He suggests that secularism cannot be thought of as separate from myth and violence. Asad, *Formations of the Secular.*

14. In this regard, Napoleon's landing in Egypt in the 1790s was a turning point in the relationship between Europe and the Islamic world. For a critical historical account of this encounter, see Cole, *Napoleon's Egypt.*

15. For an insightful critique of the Kemalist-led modernization and secularization in Turkey, see Şerif Mardin, *Religion, Society, and Modernity in Turkey.* The gist of his criticism is that Kemalism failed to replace Islam as a set of ideas and practices that offered a meaningful and rich experience to the masses.

16. In this regard, Wahhabism, which emerged in the center of the Arabian Peninsula in the eighteenth century, can be thought of as a reformist movement that sought to restore Islam's purity and return to original sources, the Qur'an and the Sunna. Associated with the ruling regime in Saudi Arabia, Wahhabism remains a controversial and widely criticized force in contemporary times. For a study that analyzes the original writings of the founder of the sect, Muhammad Ibn Abd al-Wahhab, and argues that contemporary Wahhabism sharply deviated from his original thought, see DeLong-Bas, *Wahhabi Islam.* For a commentary that denounces Wahhabism, see Algar, *Wahhabism.*

17. The pioneering figures in Muslim reformism include Jamal al-Din Afghani (1838–1897), Muhammad Abduh (1849–1905), and Rashid Rida (1865–1935). For classic studies of their thought, see Keddie, *Sayyid Jamāl ad-Dīn "al-Afghānī"*; Hourani, *Arabic Thought.*

18. Nasr correctly argues that secularism in the Muslim world has largely been associated with states' attempts to subdue and reshape the society. Nasr, "Lessons from the Muslim World."

19. A prominent example is the Turkish intellectual and poet İsmet Özel (b. 1944). For an analysis of his thought, see Morrison, "To Be a Believer in Republican Turkey."

20. The authoritative work on the subject is Michael Cook's *Commanding Right and Forbidding Wrong in Islamic Thought.* For his discussion of Shiite stances on and Khomeini's interpretation of the principle, see pages 530–548.

21. For an empirically rich discussion of the conflict between traditional and politicized Shiite clergy in Iraq in the 1950s and 1960s, see Jabar, *Shi'ite Movement in Iraq,* 84–89.

22. Zaman, *Ulama in Contemporary Islam,* 107. Mohsen Kadivar expressed similar concerns about their autonomy in a personal communication with the author. He indicated that the independence of scholars from state patronage and control is critical to

their authority and freedom. The Islamic Republic exerted control over the seminaries mainly through financial means. Yet many scholars were still not organically affiliated with the state. Tehran, March 10, 2008.

23. Ibid., 10.

24. Brown, "Sharia and State."

25. Zaman, *Ulama in Contemporary Islam,* 172.

26. Liberal democracy demands that religions curtail their hegemonic claims over the political sphere and the state, not secularization of beliefs and practices. This is a minimalistic requirement essential for the viability of liberal democracy and is much less demanding than metanarratives of secularization. For an eloquent articulation of this argument, see Bader, *Secularism or Democracy?* chap. 1.

27. This important point is aptly described and illustrated by examples in the preface of Salvatore and Eickelman, *Public Islam and the Common Good.*

28. For a comprehensive analysis of the evolution of Islamic political thought in Iran since the early twentieth century, see Rajaee, *Islamism and Modernism.*

29. Kadivar, "Introduction to the Public and Private Debate," 676–678. He also argues that freedom of opinion and religious belief are fully compatible in Islam. More importantly, nobody can be punished in the name of Islam for changing her/his religion or opinion. See Kadivar, "Freedom of Religion and Belief Islam."

30. An-Na'im, *Islam and the Secular State,* 4. By challenging the notion that the rule of the four caliphs in early Islamic history exemplifies an Islamic state in which religious and political authority are conflated (632–661), he follows Lapidus, "Separation of State and Religion." An-Na'im also argues that the rule of the Prophet that epitomizes the ideal regime is not suitable for replication and imitation.

31. An-Na'im, *Islam and the Secular State,* 268.

32. Ibid., 280.

33. Ibid., 29.

34. Ibid., 20.

35. Ibid., 38.

36. Personal communication with Tariq Ramadan, Rome, April 2, 2008. For his historically and culturally contextualized reading of sharia, see Ramadan, *Western Muslims and the Future of Islam,* 31–61.

37. Gutmann, *Identity in Democracy,* 166.

38. Feldman offers a different historical interpretation of the Islamic state and argues that "the call for an Islamic state is therefore first and foremost a call for law." Feldman, *Fall and Rise of the Islamic State,* 9. He suggests that "the system of scholarly control over law [which was prevalent for many centuries until the Ottoman reforms in the second half of the nineteenth century] encouraged stability, executive restraint, and legitimacy" (42). Consequently, he argues that repugnancy clauses in constitutions that give power to a body of jurists to review all legislation and decrees on grounds of compatibility with Islam may be a welcome development. If the Islamists are capable of developing new institutions, they may be capable of establishing the

rule of law. The problem with his analysis is that he does not provide any empirical evidence to sustain his bold and repeated claim that the Islamist demand for an Islamic state represents a popular demand for the rule of law. He offers no critical readings of the Islamist literature nor does he cite survey or qualitative data of Muslim public opinion.

39. Mirsepassi, *Intellectual Discourse*, 13.

40. Gheissari, *Iranian Intellectuals in the 20th Century*, 118–119.

41. Boroujerdi, *Iranian Intellectuals and the West*, 14.

42. Ibid., 12. Boroujerdi labels this intellectual stance as "Orientalism in reverse" (10–14).

43. There were notable exceptions of thinkers who articulated more pluralistic political visions. Mehdi Bazargan, the first prime minister of the Islamic Republic, espoused constitutionalism and democracy from an Islamic perspective. For an analysis of this thought, see Barzin, "Constitutionalism and Democracy."

44. His speech at the U.N.-sponsored Conference of Dialogue among Civilizations on September 5, 2000, in New York is available at http://www.iranian.com/Opinion/2000/September/Khatami/.

45. Personal communication with Mohsen Kadivar, Tehran, March 10, 2008.

46. Khosrokhavar, "New Religiosity in Iran."

47. In February 2008, the Religious Affairs Directory initiated a comprehensive project that aimed to screen the hadith (sayings of the Prophet). The project had two major components: (a) identifying false hadith and purging them from the canon, and (b) developing modernist interpretations of the authentic hadith. Reported by the BBC, February 26, 2008.

48. For sympathetic studies of Fethullah Gülen and his community, see Bulaç, *Din, Kent ve Cemaat*; Yavuz and Esposito, *Turkish Islam and the Secular State*; Özdalga, "Worldly Asceticism in Islamic Casting."

49. This approach is fully compatible with the requirements of liberal democracy. Gutmann, *Identity in Democracy*, 156.

50. The idea of Muslim reform became relevant to U.S. strategic interests as a way to contain and eradicate violent and radical Islamism. The key document in this regard is Benard, *Civil Democratic Islam*. Benard argues that the United States should promote secular and moderate understandings of Islam for strategic reasons. For an eloquent criticism of this approach and the notion of secularism it represents, see Mahmood, "Secularism, Hermeneutics, and Empire," 336.

51. For an analysis of the community, see Turam, *Between Islam and the State*. For the community's internal structure and perceptions of women see especially 60–61 and 130. Also useful is Başkan, "The Fethullah Gülen Community."

52. Arguments in favor of Islamic democracy tend to ignore this critical question. See Feldman, *After Jihad*.

53. The ultimate source for fundamentalist forms of religion is the Fundamentalist Project, sponsored by the American Academy of Arts and Sciences in the early 1990s,

which produced a series of five books. A summary of findings and theoretical conclusions is offered by Almond, Appleby, and Silvan in *Strong Religion.*

54. Gutmann, *Identity in Democracy,* 186.

55. For an elaboration of this argument, see Tezcür, "Constitutionalism, Judiciary, and Democracy."

56. Gutmann, *Identity in Democracy,* 188.

57. For a comparative and elaborate discussion of passive and alternative forms of secularism, see Kuru, "Passive and Assertive Secularism." Kuru is critical of the assertive forms of secularism institutionally implemented in France and Turkey.

58. Kadivar, "Introduction to the Public and Private Debate," 670.

59. Ibid., 672. In classic Islamic thought, the government is entitled to regulate public morals and commercial interactions and to deal with corruption, a practice known as *hisba.* The *muhtasib* is the agency that enforces *hisba.*

60. Ibid., 671.

61. An-Naʿim, *Islam and the Secular State,* 117.

62. Ibid., 283.

63. In this regard, the column of Hayrettin Karaman, a professor of Islamic law, in the Turkish daily *Yeni Şafak* is informative. For his views on the partiality of the secular state, see his column on January 2, 2009. Meanwhile, Karaman adopts a pragmatic attitude toward *hisba.* In his column published in *Yeni Şafak* on January 4, 2009, he argues that that practice should not be implemented by pious Muslims in a secular state if it leads to greater restrictions on Muslims' freedoms. This is a strategic adaptation to the reality of societal pluralism and secular political order.

64. Reported by www.ntvmsnbc.com on November 17, 2007.

65. It is often claimed that Nesin questioned the origins of the Qur'an in a speech he delivered on July 1, 1993. Hence, he is accused of provoking the crowd and being responsible for the massacre. Notwithstanding the absurdity of this claim, there was nothing in his speech that can be interpreted as an attack against Islam or an attempt at spreading atheism. The text of the speech is available in Turkish at http://www .nesinvakfi.org/aziz_nesin_sivas_konusmasi.html.

66. The party was uncomfortable with any public remembrances of the tragedy. The Ministry of Culture prevented the showing of video footage of the event during the public presentation of an oratorio composed by Fazıl Say in memory of the victims. The minister argued that the JDP would like to heal the wounds, not deepen them. Reported by the Turkish daily *Star,* July 5, 2003.

67. He was criticizing terrorist acts committed in the name of Islam. This segment of the interview is available in Turkish at http://www.zaman.com.tr/haber .do?haberno=29135. Interview with Fethullah Gülen, *Zaman,* March 23, 2004.

68. His explanatory remarks are available at http://tr.fgulen.com/content/view/ 7910/15.

69. For the role of the Catholic Church in democratizations in the late twentieth century, see Huntington, *The Third Wave.*

70. For a well-documented study of how the Second Vatican Council resulted in a major reform despite the preponderance of conservative forces, see Wilde, *Vatican II*.

71. Philpott, "The Catholic Wave."

72. In this sense, secularization can be conceptualized as the decline of religious authority. Chaves, "Secularization as Declining Religious Authority."

73. Shapiro, *State of Democratic Theory*, 3.

74. Tilly, *Democracy*, 23, 137.

75. It seems that several high-ranking military officers coordinated with rogue elements in security forces to destabilize the JDP government and invite authoritarian rule. For a journalistic discussion of these groups and their activities since 2003, see Tayyar, *Operasyon Ergenekon*. The Operation Ergenekon, which exposed these groups, targeted elements in clandestine groups that tried to topple the JDP government through extra-parliamentary means. It has involved arrests of many well-known public figures since January 2008. At the time of writing, the judicial case was in progress. The counterinsurgency in Turkey had its origins in the Cold War period when the NATO members formed clandestine units to counter a possible Communist takeover. These units are collectively known as Gladio, the code name for the Italian secret organization. For a history of Gladio, see Ganser, *NATO's Secret Army*. The section on Turkey has empirical inaccuracies. The Turkish leg of Gladio was not dissolved after the end of the Cold War but instead was transformed into a counterinsurgency fighting the Kurdish insurgents. For journalistic yet informative studies of the Turkish Gladio, see Kılıç, *Özel Harp Dairesi*; Yalçın and Yurdakul, *Reis*. It is now clear that the Turkish leg of Gladio was heavily involved in political violence before the 1980 coup, which destroyed the organizational base of the Turkish left.

76. For a recent application of the framework of "war of positions" to Egyptian and Iranian politics, see Bayat, *Making Islam Democratic*, 20–21.

77. For an insightful study of the center-right ideology in Turkey and its claims of being the victimized actors of Turkish politics, see Mert, *Merkez Sağın Kısa Tarihi*.

78. David Cook provides a rich discussion of the evolution of the notion of martyrdom in Islamic history. He argues that martyrdom became central to Islamist discourse only with the rise of Islamist ideology and after the Six-Day War in 1967. Cook, *Martyrdom in Islam*, 135–146. Ironically, most Muslims who were honored with the distinction of being martyrs were killed by their fellow coreligionists (167).

79. Varzi, *Warring Souls*, 19. Varzi offers an anthropologically grounded study of how the notion of martyrdom is socially and politically constructed in postrevolutionary Iran, and explores the growing alienation of the Baby Boomer Generation from this culture of self-denial.

80. The tension between the United States and Iran is closely related to the geopolitical competition between Israel and Iran in the aftermath of the Cold War and the Gulf War of 1991. Parsi, *Treacherous Alliance*.

81. Varzi, *Warring Souls*, 196.

82. For a pioneering book that presents unofficial and uncensored stories of the conscripts who fought against the PKK, see Mater, *Mehmed'in Kitabı*. The book is based on forty-two interviews and exposes the brutality and tragedy of the war experience in its barest details and challenges the official discourse. The book was initially banned for insulting the military.

83. Reported in the Turkish daily *Radikal,* May 28, 2008. The prosecutor asked that Ersoy be given a prison sentence of up to three years. At the time of writing, the case was pending. This was not the first time Ersoy had angered the authorities. The military junta banned her public performances after she had a sex change operation in 1981. Her new gender identity was officially recognized only in 1988, and she returned to public singing and acting with great success.

CHAPTER 5

1. Dahl, *Democracy and Its Critics,* 52.

2. Political parties that receive more than 7 percent of the national vote in the last elections are eligible for state aid.

3. An English translation of the Iranian constitution is available at http://www.oefre.unibe.ch/law/icl/ir00000_.html.

4. For a comprehensive introduction to Shiite Islam, see Momen, *Introduction to Shi'i Islam.*

5. Samii, "Dissent in Iranian Elections."

6. For discussions on the *velayat-e faqih,* see Saffari, "Legitimation of the Clergy's Right to Rule."

7. Sahifah-e-Nur, Vol. 21 (4/29/1989), 129. Stored at www.leader.ir/langs/EN/index.php?p=leader_imam.

8. Khomeini, *Islam and Revolution,* 59.

9. This was part of a process that marginalized the sharia on the grounds of state interests. Tamadonfar, "Islam, Law, and Political Control."

10. Sahifah-e-Nur, Vol. 20 (1/6/1988), 170. Available at www.leader.ir/langs/EN/index.php?p=leader_imam.

11. Kurzman, "Critics Within."

12. One of his main detractors has been Hossein Ali Montazeri, who questions his religious credentials and accuses him of abusing the power of the *faqih.* For instance, see his address to his supporters published by *Kayhan* (Persian newspaper published in London), December 4, 1997.

13. For Khamanei's official biography, see www.leader.ir/langs/EN/index.php?p=bio.

14. For a discussion of the regime's attempts to control religious seminaries, see Khalaji, *The Last Marja.*

15. Tezcür, Azadarmaki, and Bahar, "Religious Participation among Muslims."

16. Arjomand, "Civil Society and the Rule of Law."

17. Olivier Roy interprets clerical opposition to clerical rule as a sign of the IRI's legitimacy crisis. Roy, "Crisis of Religious Legitimacy in Iran."

18. For a description of clientelism in Iran, see Alamdari, "Power Structure of the Islamic Republic of Iran."

19. As a result, credit provided to the private sector by state-controlled banks remains very low. See Nicholas Birch, "In Iran, Clerics' Wealth Draws Ire," *Christian Science Monitor,* August 20, 2003.

20. See Buchta, *Who Rules Iran?* 73–78; Moslem, *Factional Politics,* 42–46.

21. Ansari, *Iran, Islam, and Democracy,* 52–81.

22. Esfahani and Taheripour, "Hidden Public Expenditures."

23. Abrahamian, *Tortured Confessions,* especially 138–167.

24. Ibid., 222–228.

25. For an argument along these lines applied to the end of Communism in Eastern Europe, see Kuran, "Now Out of Never."

26. Tezcür and Azadarmaki, "Religiosity and Islamic Rule."

27. For a sophisticated discussion of the rentier theory, see Michael Ross, "Does Oil Hinder Democracy?"

28. Farzanegan and Markwardt, "Effects of Oil Price Shocks."

29. For instance, in early 2009, the price of a gallon of rationed gasoline was less than forty cents in Tehran, well below actual production costs. The corresponding free-market price was around eighty cents.

30. Salefi-Isfahani, "Revolution and Distribution in Iran."

31. Smith, "Oil Wealth and Regime Survival."

32. Domestic gasoline consumption increased on average 8.14 percent annually from 1997 to 2005. About 33 percent of Iran's energy subsidy is allocated to the transportation sector and 31 percent to residential. For a comprehensive study of Iran's energy consumption, see Karbassi, Abduli, and Abdollazadeh, "Sustainability of Energy Production."

33. Stern, "Iranian Petroleum Crisis."

34. Bill Spindle, "Soaring Energy Use Puts Oil Squeeze on Iran," *Wall Street Journal,* February 20, 2007.

35. Marc Wolfensberger, "Iran's Threat to Cut Oil Flow in Nuclear Dispute May Backfire," Bloomberg, August 2, 2006.

36. Ahmedinejad was faced with stern criticism in the parliament over the governmental budget and inflation. Radio Free Europe/Radio Liberty (RFE/RL) Iran Report 10, January 22, 2007.

37. The most recent and comprehensive analysis of the Pasdaran is Wehrey et al., *Rise of the Pasdaran.*

38. Vali Nasr and Ali Gheissari, "Foxes in Iran's Henhouse," *New York Times,* December 13, 2004.

39. Wehrey et al., *Rise of the Pasdaran,* 55–75.

40. Ibid., 77.

41. The Basij was formally integrated into the command structure of the Pasdaran in 2007. Ibid., 32–33. Elected officials do not control the actions of Basij, which is entitled to enforce law. For an interview with its commander, General Hejazi, see the Iranian daily *Kayhan,* November 25, 2002.

42. For a not-very-objective analysis of these groups, see Rubin, *Into the Shadows.*

43. For an informative interpretation of the Turkish Revolution, see Mardin, "Ideology and Religion in the Turkish Revolution."

44. An English translation of the Turkish Constitution is available at http://www .hri.org/docs/turkey.

45. For a historical account along these lines, see Cizre, "Parameters and Strategies of Islam-State Interaction."

46. The classic work that narrates the evolution of defensive modernization is Berkes, *Türkiye'de Çağdaşlaşma.*

47. Max Weber's "differentiation thesis" provides the tools to conceptualize this dimension of secularization. Weber, *Sociology of Religion,* chap. 14.

48. M. Şükrü Hanioğlu argues that the official ideology of the Turkish Republic was shaped in the period from 1889 to 1902. Hanioğlu, *Young Turks in Opposition.*

49. Tunaya, *İslamcılık Akımı,* 250.

50. For an elaboration of the concept of the military's political autonomy, see Pion-Berlin, "Military Autonomy."

51. For an analysis of the civilian-military relations after the coup, see Cizre, "Anatomy of the Turkish Military's Political Autonomy."

52. Most of the military interventions in the twentieth century were preceded by demands from civilians for military involvement in politics. Powell, *Contemporary Democracies,* 173–174.

53. Personal communication with Dr. Ümit Kardaş, retired military judge and prosecutor, Istanbul, June 21, 2007.

54. For a critical assessment of the AMAI, see Parla, "Mercantile Militarism in Turkey." For a more recent critical treatment, see Akça, "Kolektif Bir Sermayeder."

55. This information is obtained from the Gendarmerie's official Web site. See http://www.jandarma.tsk.mil.tr/redirect.htm?url=/genel/goreviic.htm.

56. This organization is better known as JİTEM, its Turkish acronym.

57. See, especially, Şahan and Balık, *İtirafçı;* Ertan Beşe, "Intelligence Activities of the Gendarmerie Corps"; Ağaşe, *Cem Ersever ve JİTEM Gerçeği.* The author had the opportunity to visit a GIAU branch in an eastern city in February 2003.

58. Many Kurdish-majority provinces remained under the State of Emergency from 1984 to 2002.

59. Ahmet Şık, "Genelkurmay Memorandum," Turkish magazine *Nokta* 19, March 8–14, 2007, 10–14. Two weeks later, the magazine published the diary of a top general that revealed that several generals had attempted to overthrow the JDP government in 2004. Chief of Staff Hilmi Özkök resisted these attempts. The offices of *Nokta* were

raided by the police shortly thereafter, and the magazine ceased to be published under intense pressure from the TAF.

60. This article was amended in October 2001.

61. For a summary of the NSCSG's powers, see "İşte en gizli yönetmelik," *Radikal,* August 27, 2003.

62. The current law regulating the NSC and its Secretariat General is available at http://www.mgk.gov.tr/Ingilizce/Kanun/kanun_en.htm. It was most recently amended as part of the EU-demanded reforms.

63. Hilal Köylü, "MGK'da Sivil Dönem Başlıyor," *Radikal,* August 2, 2004.

64. This is argued in Cizre, "Problems of Democratic Governance"; Michaud-Emin, "Restructuring of the Military High Command."

65. For instance, see "İşte o Belge," Turkish daily *Hürriyet,* August 9, 2001. The last known update was in fall 2005. A copy of the document in Turkish is available at http://www.savaskarsitlari.org/arsiv.asp?ArsivTipID=6&ArsivAnaID=29284.

66. For a comprehensive study of the history of the RAD, see Tarhanlı, *Müslüman Toplum, "Laik" Devlet.*

67. In 1996, the Turkish Constitutional Court ruled that the Alevi Democratic Peace Movement's (Demokratik Barış Hareketi's) call for the dissolution of the RAD did not violate the secularism principle. Akbulut, "State of Political Participation."

68. Çakır and Bozan, *Sivil, Şeffaf ve Demokratik, . . .?* 24.

69. Ibid., 22.

70. Sunni Islam has four legal schools (*madhhab*): Hanbali, Hanafi, Maliki, and Shafiʻi. While a majority of Sunni Muslims in Turkey belong to the Hanafi school, the Kurds usually adhere to the Shafiʻi school. For a history of how these schools were formed, see Hodgson, *The Venture of Islam,* 2:448.

71. Alevis are a heterodox Islamic sect that combines devotion to Ali, the son-in-law of the Prophet, with esoteric beliefs and practices. For an empirically well-grounded and conceptually strong article on the formation of Alevi political identities, see Dressler, "Turkish Alevi Poetry in the Twentieth Century."

72. For a critical assessment of the court's decisions, see Koğacıoğlu, "Progress, Unity, and Democracy."

73. The European Court of Human Rights, *Case of Refah Partisi and Others v. Turkey*: Judgment, Strasbourg: February 13, 2003. Available at http://www.echr.coe.int/echr.

74. The decisions of the court partially depend on the nature of its alliances with other state institutions and civil-society organizations. See Belge, "Friends of the Court."

75. Hirschl, *Towards Juristocracy.*

76. Hirschl, "Constitutional Courts vs. Religious Fundamentalism."

77. Turkish News Agency, Anadolu Ajansı, February 8, 2006.

78. The paragraph was amended in October 2001. The earlier version stated "no views and opinions that contradict."

79. The European Court of Human Rights, *Case of Leyla Şahin v. Turkey*: Judgment, Strasbourg: November 10, 2005. Available at http://www.echr.coe.int/echr.

80. For a critical analysis of the GC's role in elections, see Samii, "Iran's Guardians Council."

81. For an officially sanctioned English translation of the law, see the Iranian embassy in South Africa's Web site: http://www.iranembassy-sa.org.za/E/Iran%20Info/Parties%20Law.htm.

82. This information was obtained from the Interior Ministry: http://www.moi.ir/Portal/Home/Default.aspx?CategoryID=0589d5b1-4f2f-4e4e-90c0-fc80ae138404.

83. Reform-oriented Iranian politicians complain about the regime's unwillingness to encourage party politics. Vahid Sepehri, "Politicians React to Government's Disrespect for Parties," RFL/RF Iran Report 10 (February 2007). Available at http://www.rferl.org/featuresarticle/2007/01/526b5203-ca44-422e-95a9-d45badae0076.html.

84. An English copy of the election law is available at http://www.parstimes.com/law/election_law.html.

85. For a discussion of the nascent Iranian party structure, see Fairbanks, "Theocracy Versus Democracy."

86. *Kayhan*, February 25, 2000.

87. Samii, "Iran's 2000 Elections."

88. The figures come from Tezcür, "Intra-Elite Struggles in Iranian Elections."

89. This fact contradicts Samii, "Dissent in Iranian Elections."

90. Some citizens seem to vote just because they want the stamp. See interviews in *The Independent*, February 21, 2004, and reporting by Reuters, June 15, 2005.

91. Robert Tait, "Iran Poll Challenger Accused of Ballot Fraud," *The Guardian*, June 20, 2005.

92. For recent regime changes in the post-Communist world, see McFaul, "Transitions from Postcommunism."

93. Keshavarzian, "Contestation without Democracy," 74.

94. For a critical analysis of Turkish party politics, see Çarkoğlu et al., *Türkiye'de Yeni Bir Parti Sistemine Doğru*.

95. Akarca and Tansel, "Economic Performance and Political Outcomes."

96. Adaman, Şenatalar, and Çarkoğlu, *Hanehalkı Gözünden Türkiye'de Yolsuzluğun Nedenleri*.

97. TÜSİAD, *Seçim Sistemi ve Siyasi Partiler Araştırması*.

98. Protest voting and the center-periphery paradigm are the major themes in Sayarı and Esmer, *Politics, Parties, and Elections in Turkey*.

99. This classic statement is found in Mardin, "Center-Periphery Relations."

100. Kalaycıoğlu, "Elections and Party Preferences in Turkey." In the 1990s, ethnicity emerged as a major determinant of vote choice. Çarkoğlu and Toprak, *Türkiye'de Din, Toplum ve Siyaset*.

101. For a systematic analysis that shows that religious and ethnic cleavages have strong geographical components, see West, "Regional Cleavages in Turkish Politics."

102. The most regionally contained parties in Turkish politics have been those of the Kurdish nationalists.

103. For an elaboration of this argument supported by electoral data and maps, see Tezcür, "Political Cleavages in Turkey."

CHAPTER 6

1. For the growth of the Middle Eastern states, see Owen, *State, Power and Politics,* chaps. 2–3.

2. Arendt, as always, is perceptive: "We can hardly avoid the paradoxical fact that it was precisely the revolutions . . . which drove the very 'enlightened' men of the eighteenth century to plead for some religious sanction at the very moment when they were about to emancipate the secular realm fully from the influences of the churches and to separate politics and religion once and for all." Arendt, *On Revolution,* 185–186.

3. For his activities in Lebanon from 1959 on, see Ajami, *The Vanished Imam*; and Norton, *Amal and the Shiʿa,* chap. 3.

4. Aziz, "Role of Muhammad Baqir al-Sadr."

5. Halm, *Shiism,* 67, 96, 107, 117.

6. Arjomand, "Crisis of the Imamate."

7. Arjomand, *Shadow of God.*

8. For the events of 1905–1906, see Afary, *Iranian Constitutional Revolution.*

9. Algar, *Roots of the Islamic Revolution.*

10. Fischer, *Iran,* 235.

11. Skocpol, "Rentier State and Shiʿa Islam," 272.

12. Arjomand, "Iran's Islamic Revolution."

13. Akhavi, "Ideology and Praxis of Shiʿism."

14. Moaddel, "Ideology as Episodic Discourse."

15. For a succinct summary of such theoretical arguments, see Keddie, "Iranian Revolutions in Comparative Perspective."

16. Burke and Lubeck, "Explaining Social Movements."

17. Shambayati, "The Rentier State"; Parsa, "Entrepreneurs and Democratization."

18. For peasants, see Arjomand, *Turban for the Crown,* 107; for workers, see Bayat, *Workers and Revolution in Iran.*

19. Parsa, *States, Ideologies, and Social Revolutions.*

20. Ibid., 144.

21. Keddie, *Modern Iran.*

22. Abrahamian, *Khomeinism,* 17, 53.

23. Arjomand, "Ideological Revolution in Shiʿism."

24. Keddie, *Modern Iran,* 188–213. Also see Keddie, "Iran."

25. Inevitably, some histories of the Iranian Revolution mention cultural, socioeco-

nomic, and political factors as causes of the revolution without clearly specifying the causal mechanism at play. For example, see Bakhash, *Reign of the Ayatollahs.*

26. Kurzman, *Unthinkable Revolution in Iran.*

27. Ibid., 33–49.

28. Ibid., 50–76.

29. Wolfe, *Three Who Made a Revolution.* The critical role played by Lenin at the most decisive moments of the November 1917 revolution is well captured by Reed, *Ten Days That Shook the World.*

30. The definitive scholarly work on the Freedom Movement of Iran is Chehabi, *Iranian Politics and Religious Modernism,* 53–60. With some reservation, H. E. Chehabi characterizes the FMI as a democratic party.

31. Keddie, *Modern Iran,* 197.

32. In this sense, the parallels between Bazargan and Alexander Kerensky, whose provincial government confronted the powerful Soviets, are striking. Trotsky describes this situation as "double sovereignty." Trotsky, *The Russian Revolution,* 199–209.

33. Perhaps Conrad was prophetic. "In a real revolution, the best characters do not come to the front. A violent revolution falls into the hands of narrow-minded fanatics and of tyrannical hypocrites at first. Afterwards comes the turn of all the pretentious intellectual failures of the time." Conrad, *Under Western Eyes,* 101.

34. For a comprehensive discussion of the factional politics in Iran in the 1980s, see Moslem, *Factional Politics in Post-Khomeini Iran,* 47–82. Also informative are Vakili-Zad, "Conflict among the Ruling Revolutionary Elite," and an article in the Iranian daily *Salam,* May 3, 1997.

35. In 1986, Rafsanjani, then Speaker of the Parliament, acknowledged that revolutionary elites were divided into two opposing camps with regard to the state's role in the economy. Quoted in Akhavi, "Elite Factionalism."

36. Writing in 1993, Abrahamian defined the leftists as radicals and the rightists as moderates. *Khomeinism,* 133. Factional conflict in the parliament is extensively documented and analyzed in Baktiari, *Parliamentary Politics in Revolutionary Iran.*

37. Sohrab Behdad reaches the conclusion that early revolutionary economic policies contributed to the social status of the middle and lower-middle classes while having no serious effect on the well-being of the unemployed and underemployed urban poor and landless peasants. Behdad, "Winners and Losers of the Iranian Revolution."

38. Behdad and Nomani, "Workers, Peasants, and Peddlers."

39. Moaddel, "Class Struggle in Post-Revolutionary Iran."

40. From 1981 to 1989, Mousavi served as the prime minister. He was the favorite candidate of the reformist groups for the 2005 presidential elections, but he preferred not to run. Mahan Abedin, "Iran's Reformists Lie in Wait," *Asia Times,* November 24, 2004.

41. For an analysis of the elections, see Sarabi, "Post-Khomeini Era in Iran."

42. These numbers were obtained from Baktiari, *Parliamentary Politics,* 113, 148.

43. Iranian daily *Kayhan,* February 25, 2000.

44. Brumberg, *Reinventing Khomeini,* 185–230.

45. Vahdat, *God and Juggernaut,* 182, 212–213.

46. This is a central argument of Brumberg, *Reinventing Khomeini.*

47. This view was recently expressed by a close companion of Khomeini, Mohammed Reza Tavassoli, who continues to serve on the Expediency Council. See the interview with him in the Iranian daily *Iran,* June 2, 2004.

48. This information and details of Khoeiniha's career were obtained from the Iranian monthly *Hamshahri* 1 (December 2001): 11–13. Also informative is Elaine Sciolino, "Some of the Top People in Iran," *New York Times,* November 20, 1986.

49. The party's official Web site is http://www.etemademelli.ir.

50. Rajaee, "A Thermidor of Islamic Yuppies?" It remains debatable whether their notion of modernity is completely inclusive of the sanctity of individual rights and unfettered political pluralism.

51. For an overview of the reformist thinkers, see Arjomand, "The Reform Movement."

52. For a succinct discussion of post-Islamist thinkers, see Khosrokhavar, "New Intellectuals in Iran."

53. These intellectuals were affiliated with various newspapers and journals and were highly influential among educated Iranians. For an insightful description of them, see Jalaeipour, "Religious Intellectuals."

54. Al-e Ahmad, *Gharbzadegi.*

55. Shariati relies on binary distinctions to criticize traditional and historical religion: religion of legitimation vs. religion of revolution, Black Shiite Islam vs. Red Shiite Islam. Many of his works are translated into English. For instance, see Shariati, *On the Sociology of Islam.* For an insightful reading of Shariati's thought, see Fischer, *Iran,* 154–156, 165–170.

56. Some of his writings have been translated into English. Soroush, *Reason, Freedom and Democracy in Islam.* Vahdat characterizes Soroush's thought as conducive to democratic individualism. Vahdat, "Post-Revolutionary Discourses."

57. Soroush, *Reason, Freedom and Democracy in Islam,* 33–34.

58. Ibid., 56–57.

59. Ibid., 142.

60. Ibid., 131.

61. He is also critical of the rule of clergy on the grounds that it deviates from the historical patterns of the clergy's political interactions in Iran. *Iran-e Farda,* February 1, 1995.

62. Some of his writings are translated into and published in English. Mir-Hosseini and Tapper, *Islam and Democracy in Iran,* 73–100.

63. For his eloquent discussion of these nine types, see Kadivar, *Nazariyet-e Dowlat dar Fiqh-e Shia.*

64. Kadivar's political theology is extensively analyzed in Sadri, "Sacral Defense of Secularism"; Vahdat, "Post-revolutionary Discourses, Part 2." Also informative is an interview with Mohsen Kadivar, *Al-Sharq al-Awsat,* April 8, 2007. Available at http://www.asharq-e.com/news.asp?section=3&id=8575.

65. Personal communication with Mohsen Kadivar, Tehran, March 10, 2008. For his interpretation of Mulla Khurasani, see Kadivar, "Innovative Political Ideas."

66. For analyses of his political thought, see Sadri, "Sacral Defense of Secularism"; Vahdat, "Post-revolutionary Discourses"; and Roman Seidel, "Mohammed Shabestari: Faith, Freedom, and Reason," *Qantara.de Dialogue with the Islamic World,* February 14, 2004. Available at http://www.qantara.de/webcom/show_article.php/_c-575/_nr-3/_p-1/i.html?PHPSESSID=5869.

67. The adjective "hard-liner" indicates commitment to the *velayat-e faqih* and support for the current distribution of institutional power in the Islamic Republic.

68. For a discussion of the socioeconomic developments during Rafsanjani's presidency that facilitated the rise of the reform movement, see Gheissari and Nasr, *Democracy in Iran,* 119–126.

69. Iranian daily *Abrar,* April 27, 1997. On April 21, *Salam* reported results from another poll that showed Khatami receiving 62 percent of the vote. Neither newspaper gave any information about how the polls were conducted or their reliability. The information about *Salam* is quoted in Wells, "Thermidor in the Islamic Republic of Iran."

70. Bakhash, "Iran's Remarkable Election."

71. Cited in Rebai, *Jameeshenasi-ye Tahavvolet-e Arzeshi,* 165.

72. For an analysis of Khatami's views on politics and the West based on his writings, see Milani, "Reform and Resistance."

73. In an interview in January 1980, Khomeini argued that as a political system, Islam is superior to all other political systems, including democracy. For Khomeini, Islam has nothing to borrow or learn from democracy. Khomeini, *Islam and Revolution,* 329–343.

74. Eighty percent found Khatami's praise of American civilization and people in his interview with CNN in January 1998 to be a positive gesture. The survey, with 1,869 respondents, was conducted a week after the president's interview with CNN in Tehran. Iranian daily *Farda,* February 16, 1998.

75. In a press conference delivered in New York on September 7, 2000, he implicitly argued that Iran would be fully democratic only when a majority of Iranian people who were deeply religious came to realize that democratic values stemmed from the foundations of their faith.

76. Khatami, in a speech delivered to an audience on the fifteenth anniversary of the passing of Khomeini on May 27, 2004.

77. Khatami interview with the Iranian daily *Entekhab,* September 5, 1999.

78. These themes were prevalent in his speeches broadcast by the Vision of the Islamic Republic of Iran Network 1 on May 28 and June 14, 2001, and May 27, 2004.

79. For an analysis that points to the nondemocratic nature of the Khomeini regime, see Chehabi, "Political Regime."

80. "The political is the most intense and extreme antagonism, every concrete antagonism becomes that much more political the closer it approaches the most extreme point, that of the friend-enemy grouping." Schmitt, *The Concept of the Political,* 29.

81. Vahdat, "Religious Modernity in Iran."

82. The most informative English source on political events during Khatami's tenure is found in Ansari, *Iran, Islam and Democracy,* 82–244.

83. Ganji was arrested on separate charges in 2000 and stayed in prison for six years. He was on a hunger strike for several months in 2005.

84. For a critical discussion of the judiciary's role in curtailing freedom of the press and suppressing political opposition, see Tabari, "Rule of Law."

85. Shambayati, "A Tale of Two Mayors." His sentence was later reduced to two years, and he was pardoned by Khamenei just before the 2000 elections.

86. Like Kadivar, Hashem Aghajari, a disabled veteran of the Iran-Iraq War and a professor of history, was an open critic of the notion of *velayat-e faqih.* He supported the idea that public officials should be elected by popular vote. See his interview in the Iranian bimonthly, *Asr-e Maa* 7 (August 9, 2000). Aghajari was condemned to death in 2002 for a speech he delivered in the city of Hamadan in which he condemned the clerics for forming a new oppressive ruling class. He was set free in July 2004.

87. Fairbanks, "Theocracy versus Democracy."

88. In this work, "hard-liners" and "principalists" are often used synonymously, unless stated otherwise.

89. "Second Khordad" (Dovom Khordad) in the Iranian calendar stands for May 23, the date of the 1997 presidential elections.

90. Important differences exist between these groups. For example, the OEIR charter explicitly states that those who are in politics must be pious; the guardianship of the jurists is the best system of governance during the occultation. Available at http://mojahedi-enghelab.org/print.aspx?ID=19.

91. Samii, "Iran's 2000 Elections." In 1996, the GC disqualified around 44 percent of all aspirants. See "Parliamentary Elections in Iran," *Human Rights Watch,* February 15, 2000.

92. Iranian daily *Asr-e Azadegan,* Vol. 115, February 24, 2000.

93. This information was obtained from "Youth Employment in Islamic Republic of Iran," a document prepared by the IRI Presidency National Youth Organization in 2004. The document is available at http://www.ilo.ch/public/english/employment/strat/yen/download/iranict.pdf.

94. The outgoing parliament raised the voting age from fifteen to sixteen in 2000. The reformist parliament promptly revoked that bill. In 2007, the parliamentary law increasing the voting age was approved by the GC despite the opposition of the Ahmedinejad government. *USA Today,* January 13, 2007.

95. Iranian daily *Hamshahri,* September 9, 2000.

96. This information about the 2000 parliamentary elections was obtained from the Iranian daily *Bayan,* April 8, 2000. The SCC ordered the closure of that newspaper a few months later, in June.

97. Interview with Hashemi Rafsanjani, *Hamshahri,* January 9–10, 2000.

98. Reuters, February 2, 2000.

99. Mohsen Heyderian, "Participation Party and the Third Congress," September 22, 2002. Available at http://archiv.iran-emrooz.net/heydarian/1381/heydar810631.html.

100. Humiliated by his defeat, Rafsanjani decided not to serve in the parliament. The GC validated the results only after Khamenei's intervention. AFP, May 18, 2000.

101. Some reformists were expecting that the hard-liners would opt for violence immediately after the elections. Iranian daily *Fath,* March 2, 2000.

102. Reuters, March 11, 2000.

103. Hajjarian was very influential in the formation of the IIPF and worked on the institutionalization of the reform movement at the grassroots level. Ehsani, "Existing Political Vessels."

104. Editorial in *Sobh-e Emrooz,* March 13, 2000.

105. Voice of the Islamic Republic of Iran Radio 1, April 14, 2000. Khamenei delivered an even more stringent speech on April 20. It was also common among the hard-liners to condemn reformers by likening them to Gorbachev in the last years of the Soviet Union. For a criticism of this analogy, see the interview with former parliamentarian Elaleh Koulaei in the Iranian monthly *Ayeen,* August 1, 2004.

106. In the previous Iranian year (1378), the courts revoked the licenses of 135 publications. The Persian year 1378 started in March 1999. *Fath,* April 3, 2000.

107. Reported by AFP, July 1, 2000.

108. See http://www.cpj.org/attacks00/mideast00/Iran.html. An unintended consequence of the crackdown on the press was the explosion in demand for the number of satellite dishes. Interview with Ali Hekmat, a reformist journalist, in Iranian daily *Yas-e No,* August 12, 2003.

109. Reported in Ansari, *Iran, Islam and Democracy,* 225.

110. *International Herald Tribune,* August 8, 2000.

111. Personal communication with Abbas Salimi Namin, the director of the Office for Contemporary Iranian History Studies, Tehran, March 6, 2008.

112. For example, see Iranian daily *Nowruz,* June 12, 2001.

113. This information was obtained from Kalantari, "Iranian Voting Behavior."

114. See, for instance, an interview with Sohrab Razzaqi, professor of political science, in *Yas-e No,* May 3, 2003; and an interview with Ali Shakoori Rad, senior member of the IIPF and director of Moin's presidential campaign in 2005, in the Iranian daily *Nasimesaba,* November 23, 2003.

115. The survey questionnaire was administered to 412 respondents. Multistage area probability sampling with randomized household selection and random selection of respondents within households was used.

116. In contrast, in the immediate aftermath of the 2000 elections, around 60

percent of the respondents were content with Khatami's performance. Reported in the Iranian daily *Iran,* May 21, 2000.

117. "Iranian Hardliners Block Reform Bill," *Washington Post,* June 4, 2003.

118. It is interesting to note that the reformist-controlled parliament gave more negative votes to Khatami's cabinet than the previous principalist-controlled parliament had. IRNA, August 21, 2003; cited in Boroujerdi, "Reformist Movement in Iran."

119. *Hamshahri,* June 1, 2003.

120. Reuters, April 14, 2004.

121. RFE/RL, January 12, 2004.

122. BBC, January 11, 2004.

123. IRNA, January 17, 2004.

124. *Yas-e No,* January 26, 2004.

125. IRNA, January 26, 2004.

126. IRNA, January 31, 2004.

127. IRNA, February 2, 2004.

128. IRNA, February 4, 2004.

129. BBC, February 17, 2004. The reformist newspapers *Yas-e No* and *Sharq,* which published this letter, were temporarily closed. Reuters, February 19, 2004.

130. BBC, February 18, 2004.

131. Samii, "Dissent in Iranian Elections." Voter turnout was around 33 percent in Tehran.

132. *Aftab-e Yazd,* February 29, 2004.

133. For instance, Karroubi, the Speaker of the Parliament, could not win a seat in the first round. He withdrew in the second round. Interview with Karroubi, *Aftab-e Yazd,* February 29, 2004.

134. The charter, dated April 25, 2005, is available at the official Web site of the IIDC: http://www.abadgaran.ir.

135. *Sharq,* April 13, 2004.

136. According to Amir Mohebian, a columnist for the conservative daily *Resalat,* the hard-liners were also changing by being accommodative of social freedoms and economic liberalization. AP, October 13, 2003.

137. *Iran,* February 24, 2004.

138. Personal communication with Farshad Mahdipour, Tehran, March 8, 2008. Mahdipour is the political editor of the Iranian daily *Hamshahri* and a close observer of the principalist politics.

139. Khatami's address to a youth organization; BBC, April 7, 2004. See also the statement by the OEIR on the fifteenth anniversary of Khomeini's death in the Iranian daily *Vaqa-ye Ettefaqieh,* June 29, 2004.

140. The leaders of the RF repeatedly emphasized that they were seeking gradual change through legal means. See the interview with Mohammad Reza Khatami in *Sharq,* April 24, 2004; and the interviews with leading reformers in *Aftab-e Yazd,* May 22, 2004.

141. *Iran,* July 22, 2004. Some opted for conspiracy theories by arguing that the West had helped the hard-liners to repress the reformists because it did not want a strong Iran. *Sharq,* July 11, 2004.

142. "What will remain if we forsake reforms? Inaction and isolation or riot and revolution." Interview with Mohammad Reza Khatami in *Sharq,* April 24, 2004. Interview with Rasoul Montajabnia, member of the MCL, *Sharq,* September 16, 2004.

143. Interview with Ahmad Shirzad, former parliamentarian from Isfahan; Iranian daily *Etemad,* October 10, 2004.

144. The fact that ex-prime minister Mousavi and Khoeiniha refused to run left the RF without a unifying figure. Iranian daily *Farhang-e Ashti,* December 4, 2004.

145. One can speculate that the possibility that a multiplicity of hard-liners would result in disunity worried the GC. "Abundance of Candidates Worries Hard-Liners in Iran," RFE/RL, June 15, 2005.

146. BBC, May 23, 2005.

147. Preelection surveys were notoriously unreliable and usually underestimated the appeal of Ahmedinejad, who came in second.

148. Rafsanjani's supporters were praising his statesmanlike qualities and unique ability to overcome the institutional gridlock of Iranian politics through his vast connections and informal influence. Personal correspondence with a Rafsanjani campaign manager in Tehran, June 21, 2005.

149. Voter turnout and results of the 2005 elections were obtained from the Web site of the Interior Ministry at www.moi.ir several days after the election.

150. Ahmedinejad was a member of the Islamic Revolution Devotees Society (IRDS), a party of younger-generation hard-liners who were veterans of the Iran-Iraq War. Founded in 1997, the party repeatedly accused Khatami of ignoring the increasing socioeconomic gap and sharply criticized the RF. Samii, "Changing Landscape of Party Politics."

151. Personal communication with managers of Ahmedinejad's campaign, Tehran, June 20, 2005.

152. *Iran,* June 19, 2005.

153. IRNA, June 20, 2005. The banned newspapers were *Aftab-e Yazd* and *Eqbal.*

154. The IIPF ironically declared that international supervision of the elections was unnecessary two months before the elections. IRNA, December 13, 2003.

155. Personal communication with Ebrahim Zerger, a former Basij member, at the University of Tehran, Tehran, March 7, 2008.

156. *Washington Post,* June 21, 2005.

157. For a sophisticated discussion of the characteristics of valid counterfactuals, see Lebow, "What's So Different about Counterfactual?"

158. For an analysis of the multiple and informal centers of power in the Islamic Republic, see Kamrava and Hassan-Yari, "Suspended Equilibrium."

159. The hard-liners equated loyalty to the constitution with unconditional accep-

tance of the *velayat-e faqih*. Interview with cleric Mahdavi Kani, the secretary general of the MCA, in *Hamshahri,* May 2, 2004.

160. Statement delivered by Mohammad Reza Khatami at the Fifth Congress of the IIPF. Reported by IRNA, October 17, 2003.

161. IRNA, March 4, 2004. Also, *Iran,* July 22, 2004.

162. Fairbanks, "Theocracy versus Democracy."

163. For instance, interview with Behzad Nabavi in the Iranian daily *Towsee,* July 8, 2003.

164. According to Mohebian, a columnist of the conservative daily *Resalat,* the reformists sacrificed the students and journalists. Interview with Amir Mohebian, *Hamshahri,* September 25, 2004. For different types of women's activism during the Khatami years, see Sedghi, *Women and Politics in Iran,* 245–271.

165. The main student organization, the Office for Consolidating Unity (Daftar-e Tahkim-e Vahdat), mostly kept a low profile during the sit-in. BBC, January 29, 2004.

166. This is the author's impression based on his talks to Iranians from different walks of life in 2005 and 2006.

167. For example, Mohammad Reza Tabesh, a leading member of the IIPF, did not take part in the sit-in. Interview with Mohammad Reza Tabesh in *Hamshahri,* July 5, 2004.

168. For the IIPF's decision, see *New York Times,* February 2, 2004. For MCL's decision, see AFP, February 9, 2004.

169. Interview with Mohammad Reza Khatami in *Al-Ahram Weekly,* Vol. 679, March 2004. Available at http://weekly.ahram.org.eg/2004/680/re121.htm.

170. Interview with Mehdi Karroubi in *Al-Sharq al-Awsat,* April 11, 2007. Available at http://www.asharq-e.com/news.asp?section=3&id=8613.

171. His speech is available at http://emruz.info/ShowItem.aspx?ID=584&p=1.

172. For the declaration of his candidacy, see http://www.norooznews.ir/news/10545.php.

CHAPTER 7

1. Mitchell, *Society of the Muslim Brothers*; Jabar, *Shiʿite Movement in Iraq.* The main exception will be the Kurdish Hezbollah that was active throughout the 1990s. That terrorist organization was responsible for hundreds of murders in southeastern Turkey and received state support for a while because it countered the influence of Kurdish militant nationalism. It was decapitated in 2000. Çiçek, *Hangi Hizbullah?*

2. For an empirically rich analysis of this diversity, see Kara, *Cumhuriyet Türkiyesi'nde bir Mesele Olarak İslam,* 181–221.

3. Mardin, "Center-Periphery Relations." Recent studies have shown that this cleavage continues to be very important in Turkish politics. Çarkoğlu and Hinich, "A Spatial Analysis."

4. The RPP was founded by Mustafa Kemal Pasha in 1922. For a critical perspec-

tive on the RPP's formulation of secularist nationalism, see Parla, *Türkiye'de Siyasi Kültürün Resmi Kaynakları,* Vol. 3.

5. The classic work on the relationship between the Turkish state and the evolution of the bourgeoisie is Keyder, *Türkiye'de Devlet ve Sınıflar.*

6. For a critical review of the DP leadership, see Sayarı, "Adnan Menderes."

7. See Başgil, *Din ve Laiklik.*

8. One important reason for the increasing fragmentation of political space is the modification of the electoral law from winner-take-all to proportional representation after the military intervention of 1960.

9. The only times when center-left-oriented parties gained a plurality of votes were in 1961, 1974, 1977, and 1999. In all other elections, with the exception of 1995, center-right parties were victorious.

10. Since 1950, the religious issues that have divided the two camps include: calls to prayer in Turkish instead of Arabic, the religious curriculum in public schools, the headscarf controversy, the state's relationship with Sufi brotherhoods, and relations with other Muslim countries.

11. The center-right DP, which was in power from 1950 to 1960, was often accused of making important concessions to "religious reactionaries." The irony is that none of the accusations against the DP included violations of the principle of secularism when DP leaders were put on trial in 1961. Yücel, *Demokrat Parti,* 163–165. For the organization of a conspiracy within the military, see Fidel, "Military Organization and Conspiracy." For a balanced summary of the events that led to the intervention, see Kasaba, "Populism and Democracy in Turkey."

12. For a dated but useful analysis of the JP, see Sherwood, "Rise of the Justice Party." For a solid analysis of the JP's secularism, see Demirel, *Adalet Partisi.*

13. For example, Douglas Frantz, in his article "Turkey, on Road to Secularism, Fears Detour," *New York Times,* January 8, 2002, repeated the fear that the growing role of Islam in public life and in politics is likely to threaten the freedom of religion in Turkey.

14. See Hale, *Turkish Politics and the Military,* 110–113, for a vacillating position on the question of whether intervention in 1960 was justified; see Ahmad, *The Making of Modern Turkey,* and Zurcher, *Turkey,* 213–214, for uncritical analyses of the army's intervention in 1980. For an article that exempts the Turkish army from comparison with its counterparts in Third World countries and praises its supposedly suprapolitical stance, see Tachau and Heper, "The State, Politics, and the Military."

15. According to conventional studies of democratization, the tasks of convincing the military to relinquish political power and changing their preoccupation with so-called internal security threats are central to every successful democratic transition. O'Donnell and Schmitter, *Transitions from Authoritarian Rule.*

16. For an ethnographic study of the school curriculum in a small town between 1989 and 1991, see Kaplan, "*Din-u Devlet* All Over Again?"

17. For the argument that the Turkish model of secularism is the necessary condi-

tion for the development of democracy in a Muslim country, see Lewis, *Emergence of Modern Turkey*. The works of two prominent Turkish scholars are also important: Berkes, *Türkiye'de Çağdaşlaşma*, and Kongar, *21. Yüzyılda Türkiye*. The dualistic view of the secularist elites vs. the traditional masses is also reproduced by Huntington, in *Clash of Civilizations*, who considers Turkey a primary example of a divided society. All these works downplay the pivotal role played by center-right parties in Turkey.

18. Kara, *İslamcıların Siyasi Görüşleri*, 19.

19. Ibid., 24.

20. According to a very influential and widely read article by Turkish nationalist intellectual Yusuf Akçura in the early twentieth century, the biggest impediment to Islamic unity is the power of imperialistic states with vast Muslim populations, such as Russia and Great Britain. Yusuf Akçura, *Üç Tarz-ı Siyaset*.

21. These parties were the National Development Party, founded in 1945; the Nation Party, founded in 1948; and the Islamic Democracy Party, founded in 1951. Only the Nation Party had some electoral success. Yet this party has little affinity with the ideology of Islamism, according to Tunaya, *İslamcılık Akımı*, 191. Nonetheless, in 1954 a court in Ankara banned the party on grounds that it was based on religious principles. Prime Minister Menderes supported the decision because he perceived the Nation Party as threatening to his hegemony over the votes of religious citizens.

22. A leading Islamist journal of the time was *Sebilürreşad*, which was published between 1905 and 1925, and 1948 and 1966. Gün, *Sebilürreşad Dergisi*, 88, 343–351, 387–390.

23. For a journalistic biography of Erbakan, see Yalçın, *Hangi Erbakan?*

24. The state, allied with the United States, actively encouraged "anti-Communism" among the Islamists, followers of brotherhoods, and other rights groups. For an insightful and self-critical analysis, see Türkmen, *Türkiye'de İslâmcılık ve Özeleştiri*, 32, 47–50. Türkmen, advocating an internationalist Islamist position, was a central figure in the Islamist circles as a publisher, activist, and writer.

25. For a good introduction to the evolution of the Nakshis and other brotherhoods in the Republic of Turkey, see Zarcone, *La Turquie Moderne et l'Islam*, 272–303.

26. Yaşar, "Dergah'tan Parti'ye"; Çakır, *Ayet ve Slogan*, 22–24.

27. Özdalga, "Necmettin Erbakan."

28. Yavuz, *Islamic Political Identity in Turkey*, 141–144, 207–208.

29. This discussion of the ideology of the NOP and its successor, the National Salvation Party (NSP), was based on party documents, issues of the daily *Milli Görüş*, and books and speeches by the party leadership. Erbakan's *Milli Görüş* is a manifesto of his party's ideological orientation. The party program in Turkish is available at http://www.belgenet.com/parti/program/mnp.html.

30. The theme of authenticity is central to the thinking of Islamist movements. Göle, "Snapshots of Islamic Modernities."

31. For Jamaat-e Islami, see Nasr, *Vanguard of the Islamic Revolution*.

32. Eickelman and Piscatori, *Muslim Politics*, 38.

33. Anti-Zionism was actually a thinly veiled anti-Semitism that identified Jews as being responsible for problems of the Ottoman Empire and the Islamic world. An anti-Semitic stance was widespread among the Turkish Islamists, including Necip Fazıl Kısakürek, a leading intellectual who heavily influenced the leadership cadres of the WP and the JDP.

34. For an extended discussion of Erbakan-led parties' opposition to Turkish secularism, see Tepe, *Beyond Sacred and Secular,* 188–194.

35. The prosecutor presented speeches delivered by Erbakan and leading members of the party as evidence of the party's antiregime stance. These speeches included announcements that claimed they were going to reconvert St. Sophia from a museum to a mosque after the NOP came to power, portrayed the NOP as the party that would bring order and faith to the nation, criticized the seminudity of girls in official celebrations, equated ballet with prostitution, and defined the party as the harbinger of truth and other parties as representing falsity, among other things. *Milli Nizam Partisi Kapatılma Davası: Cumhuriyet Başssavcılığının İddianamesi,* available at http://www .belgenet.com/dava/mnp_01.html.

36. For a detailed analysis of the NSP, see Sarıbay, *Türkiye'de Modernleşme, Din ve Parti Politikasi.*

37. Okutan, *Bozkurt'tan Kur'an'a Milli Türk Talebe Birliği,* 164, 168, 174–184, 197–200.

38. For an informed discussion of the NAP in the 1970s, see Landau, "Nationalist Action Party in Turkey."

39. Türkmen, *Türkiye'de İslâmcılık ve Özeleştiri,* 64, 73–95.

40. Yenigün, *Bir Şehidin Notları,* 151–152, 185–190, 197–203. Yenigün, who was an influential Islamist intellectual and activist, was murdered in July 1980.

41. A central debate among the Turkish Islamists regarding the Iranian Revolution was whether it pursued sectarian goals. Many Islamists provided only lukewarm support to the Iranian Revolution, disliking its Shiite orientation and emphasis on the Imamate. At the same time, writers such as Türkmen and Yenigün focused on its messages and appeal to all Muslims. The debate remained important until the early 1990s. See the articles of Süleyman Uluğ, Hamza Türkmen, and Hayreddin Karaman in *İran İzlenimleri*; Çakir, *Ayet ve Slogan,* 155–163.

42. Ayata, "Patronage, Party, and State."

43. The NSP rally in Konya on September 6, 1980, just six days before the military intervention, quickly evolved into a demonstration for the establishment of the Islamic state.

44. Schmitt, *Concept of the Political.*

45. According to a 1986 report by Amnesty International, 61,200 people were convicted. Fifty individuals were executed as a result of trials, and 299 people died under suspicious conditions in prisons.

46. The Turkish state's repressive policies and its refusal to recognize the distinct Kurdish identity were major reasons for the local support for the PKK. A 1995 report

that was based on a survey conducted with 1,267 respondents living in the Kurdish regions provides some valuable insights. Ergil, *Doğu Sorunu.* Also, see Ergil, "The Kurdish Question in Turkey."

47. See the Human Rights Watch reports between 1991 and 1997, available at http://www.hrw.org/doc?t=europe&c=turkey. Larry Diamond labels Turkey an "illiberal democracy" in the 1980s and 1990s in his analysis of the strategic swing states for the future of democratization. See Diamond, "Is Pakistan the Future?"

48. Before the coup, the public was disappointed with the inability of major political parties and politicians to agree and to form a grand coalition. See Birand, Bila, and Akar, *12 Eylül.*

49. This is consistent with the observation that most military interventions are preceded by calls for the same from at least some civilian political forces. Powell, *Contemporary Democracies,* 173–174.

50. This argument is articulated in Cizre, *AP-Ordu İlişkileri.*

51. These cities were Urfa and Van.

52. The Welfare Party's electoral rally in the Sultanahmet Square of Istanbul in 1987 is very telling in this regard. While Erbakan condemned the Christian invasion of Turko-Islamic culture as a result of tourism, a group of Western tourists were taking pictures of the rally. Documented in Özkan, *Türkiye ve Dünyadan Örneklerle Seçim Kazandıran Kampanyalar.*

53. These include human rights associations founded by Islamic activists, such as Mazlum-Der (e. 1991) and Özgür-Der (e. 1999).

54. For a study that analyzes how the dominant themes in Islamic novels were transformed from the 1980s to the 1990s along these lines, see Çayır, *Türkiye'de İslamcılık ve İslami Edebiyat.*

55. For an eloquent criticism of these developments, see Arslan, *Modern Dünyada Müslümanlar,* 186–197.

56. This party was founded in 1983 in place of the Nationalist Action Party (NAP), which was closed after the 1980 intervention. It later retook the name Nationalist Action Party.

57. Çalmuk, *Erbakan'ın Kürtleri,* 37–59; Tan, *Kürt Sorunu,* 463–470.

58. For the importance of secular education on the formation of religious political elites, see Göle, "Secularism and Islamism in Turkey."

59. Members of the Welfare Party proposed bills to prohibit gambling (February 28, 1992), to abolish the ban of the headscarf (January 16, 1992), to authorize the reconversion of St. Sophia from a museum to a mosque (February 14, 1992), and to prohibit interest from being a tax-deductible item (January 16, 1992); they also suggested a general discussion on the hazards of alcohol consumption (April 30, 1992).

60. For this period, see Çakır, *Ne Şeriat Ne Demokrasi,* which has rich descriptions. For a more analytical treatment, see Gülalp, "Political Islam in Turkey."

61. For an extended discussion of these changes, see Şen, *Refah Partisi'nin Teori ve Pratiği.*

62. Jenny White's ethnographic work in Ümraniye, Istanbul, highlights effective grassroots organizing and framing of sociopolitical issues in Islamic moral terms to explain the WP's success. White, *Islamist Mobilization in Turkey.*

63. For his biography, see Çakır and Çalmuk, *Recep Tayyip Erdoğan.*

64. These measures included legislation bringing Koran teaching under state control, assigning supervision of all mosques to the RAD, enforcing the ban on the headscarf, and reducing the number of students attending religious schools (İmam-Hatip Okulları). These schools were accused of producing militants for the party. The official documents related to the "February 28 process" are available in Yıldız, *28 Şubat: Belgeler.*

65. Islamist writers also criticize Erbakan for his timid stance. Türkmen, *Türkiye'de İslâmcılık ve Özeleştiri,* 69–70; Kaya, *Değişim Sürecinde AK Parti ve Müslümanlar,* 15, 38.

66. Court documents are available in Turkish at http://www.belgenet.com/dava/rpdava_idd.html. For an internal criticism of the TCC's decision, see Tezcür, "Constitutionalism, Judiciary, and Democracy"; Bader, "Secularism and Militant Democracy." For a criticism of the dissolution of political parties, see Koğacıoğlu, "Progress, Unity, and Democracy."

67. For a more extensive discussion, see Şen, *Refah Partisi'nin Teori ve Pratiği,* 79–81, 154.

68. *Taqiyya* has a long tradition in Islamic history and was widely practiced by Muslim groups (i.e., Imami Shia) that had a precarious existence. See Crone, *God's Rule,* 123, 317.

69. For example, see Çakır, *Ne Şeriat Ne Demokrasi,* 124.

70. The Just Order recognized the inviolability of private property and private enterprises. Although the program was never defined precisely, it was widely criticized for threatening individual freedoms. See Şen, *Refah Partisi'nin Teori ve Pratiği,* 103–114.

71. The relationship between the WP and the brotherhoods is analyzed in Çakır, *Ne Şeriat Ne Demokrasi,* 60–69. See also Akdoğan, *Siyasal İslam.*

72. Mehmet Bekaroğlu, who was a VP parliamentarian at that time, provides an insightful and down-to-earth account of the VP's strategic moves and the demoralizing effects of the constant threat of dissolution. See his *"Adil Düzen" den "Dünya Gerçekleri" ne,* 146–153, 176–180.

73. This liberal criticism of Turkish secularism was also a part of the WP's defense against the charges of the Principal State Counsel. Refah Partisi, *Ön Savunma.*

74. In 1991, Erbakan wrote: "Our history is the history of one thousand and five hundred years of conflict between the European and Islamic cultures. We are not Westerners, not Europeans." Erbakan, *Türkiye'nin Temel Meseleleri,* 135.

75. For a narrative of how the VP discourse on Europe has differed from that of the WP, see Tanıyıcı, "Transformation of Political Islam."

76. Personal communication with Numan Kurtulmuş, Istanbul, September 21, 2007.

77. See the interviews with Bülent Arınç in the Turkish daily *Milliyet,* October 15,

1999, and with Abdullah Gül in the Turkish daily *Hürriyet,* February 8, 2000. Gül criticized the notion of a religious party and argued that religious parties neither succeed in elections nor produce anything for the common good.

78. Interviews with Gül in the Turkish dailies *Radikal,* June 5, 2000, and *Yeni Şafak,* March 26–27, 2000.

79. Gül expressed these ideas when he announced his candidacy on March 8, 2000, and during his convention speech on May 14, 2000.

80. The impact of the crises on industrial and commercial centers in Anatolia was described in an extensive report by Türkiye Odalar ve Borsalar Birliği (TOBB; Union of Chambers and Commodity Exchanges of Turkey) in *Hürriyet,* August 2, 2001.

81. TÜSİAD, *Seçim Sistemi ve Siyasi Partiler Araştırması.*

82. Strateji Mori, *Türkiye'nin Nabzı* [Pulse of Turkey] (February 2002) [Public Opinion Survey].

83. In this regard, for an analysis of Islamic responses to the state repression, see Özipek, "28 Şubat ve İslamcılar."

84. For a comparative discussion of post-Islamism, see Roy, *Globalized Islam,* 72–92.

85. For instance, see Yılmaz, *Tayyip,* 268–283.

86. Personal communication with Abdüllatif Şener, one of the vice prime ministers in the Erdoğan government, Ankara, July 4, 2002. He left the party and established a new party in May 2009.

87. Personal communication with Abdullah Gül (Turkish president since 2007), Ankara, June 26, 2002.

88. For a critical account of how the reformers internalized the guardians' limits on political reform and hence were co-opted by the regime, see Bekaroğlu, *"Adil Düzen" den "Dünya Gerçekleri" ne,* 125–130, 384–393.

89. For a semiofficial expression of the JDP's moderation, see Akdoğan, "Adalet ve Kalkınma Partisi."

90. Personal communication with Murat Mercan, a vice-chair of the JDP, Ankara, June 26, 2002.

91. Excerpt from a speech delivered by Erdoğan, then the newly elected mayor of Istanbul, during the opening ceremony of the Welfare Party's Ümraniye District Building in 1994.

92. Excerpt from the speech delivered by Erdoğan in the JDP parliamentary group meeting on June 5, 2002.

93. These are the speeches he delivered at the Council of Foreign Relations (February 26, 1997), the American-Turkish Council Annual Conference (February 20, 1997), the ATAS Conference on Science and Education (February 22, 1997), the American Turkish Society (February 25, 1997), the Bear Stearns Business Luncheon (February 25, 1997), and the Business Council for International Understanding (February 25, 1997). I obtained the transcripts of these speeches from Gül himself in June 2002.

94. The author personally obtained the pamphlet entitled "The Identity of the JDP" and dated February 21, 2002, from Yakış.

95. Personal communication with Hüseyin Çelik, Ankara, July 2, 2002.

96. Personal communication with Mustafa Demir, Samsun, July 7, 2007.

97. For rich discussions on the relationship between professions and Islamic activism, see Ibrahim, "Anatomy of Egypt's Militant Islamic Groups"; and Eickelman and Piscatori, *Muslim Politics,* 72.

98. References to historical Anatolian Sufi figures such as Mawlana Rumi, Yunus Emre, Sheik Edibali, and Pir Sultan Abdal were common in Erdoğan's speeches.

99. For engaging discussions of neofundamentalism and Islamism, see Roy, *Globalized Islam,* chaps. 2 and 6.

100. Akdoğan, *Ak Parti ve Muhafazakar Demokrasi.*

101. King, *Solution to the Ecological Inference Problem.*

102. For instance, see Tam-Cho, "Iff the Assumption Fits. . ."; Gelman et al., "Models, Assumptions and Model Checking"; Tam-Cho and Manski, "Cross-Level/Ecological Inference."

103. Tam-Cho and Manski, "Cross-Level/Ecological Inference."

104. Following Ferree, "Iterative Approaches to R x C Ecological Inference Problems."

105. King emphasizes the importance of contextual knowledge for the ability of making ecological inference more valid. King, *Solution to the Ecological Inference Problem,* 21.

106. For a discussion of these reforms, see Tepe, "Turkey's AKP."

107. Freedom House scores range from one to seven, one being most free and seven the least free. Despite improvements in its score under the JDP government, Turkey was still classified as partially free by 2006. Scores are available at http://www .freedomhouse.org.

108. Erdoğan's address to the chairmen of party provincial organizations on January 5, 2003.

109. Öniş and Türem, "Entrepreneurs, Democracy, and Citizenship."

110. For a critical assessment of the JDP's economic policies, see Patton, "AKP Government."

111. This conceptual approach follows Panebianco, *Political Parties.*

112. *Radikal,* April 1, 2004.

113. For example, see Erdoğan's speech at the party's first congress on October 12, 2003; transcript of same is in author's possession.

114. *Radikal,* May 27, 2003.

115. He repeatedly claimed that he would not be one of those prime ministers who allocated public sources for inefficient and dead-end investments.

116. Panebianco, *Political Parties,* 69.

117. Through the end of 2003, more than 35,000 individuals, most having party connections, were given public employment through the consent of ministers. *Radikal,* March 12, 2004.

118. The scandals were widely and extensively covered in the press. See, for example, the front pages of *Radikal* on June 28 and 29, and September 27, 2006.

119. For instance, see *Radikal,* August 26, 2006.

120. Personal communication with Ertuğrul Yalçınbayır, September 13, 2007.

121. For grassroots political activism in the WP, see White, *Islamist Mobilization.*

122. Several politicians who were involved in the WP told me that corruption started with the WP's capture of municipalities in 1994.

123. Wickham, *Mobilizing Islam,* 125–149.

124. The party has established charismatic linkages with the citizens. For various types of linkages parties build with their constituencies, see Kitschelt, "Linkages between Citizens and Politicians."

125. This observation is based on conversations with JDP politicians and grassroots during the 2002 and 2007 electoral campaigns.

126. Changes in JDP Bylaws Articles 117 and 124; available at http://web.akparti .org.tr/parti_tuzugu_80.html.

127. *Hürriyet,* June 7, 2006.

128. Changes in Bylaws Articles 46 and 69.

129. Changes in Bylaws Article 79. In this congress, Erdoğan was uncontested and reelected as the party chairman by 1,600 participating delegates. The congress atmosphere was that of a leader party with strong discipline. Ironically, the RPP convention in December 2008 enabled the chairman to choose the members of the Central Executive Committee. Despite their ideological differences, the JDP and RPP had allocated more power to the leader over time.

130. *Milliyet,* August 16, 2006.

131. Bylaws Articles 69, 114, and 116.

132. Personal communication with ex-JDP parliamentarian Turhan Çömez, Ankara, September 8, 2007.

133. Simon, "Organizations and Markets."

134. For a strategic analysis of the Turkish military's campaigns against the Kurdish insurgents, see Özdağ, *Türk Ordusunun PKK Operasyonları.*

135. Erdoğan's speech in Diyarbakır, reported by *Milliyet,* August 12, 2005.

136. A majority of Turks perceived the United States as the greatest threat. The possible explanations for this include the U.S. invasion of Iraq and support to the Iraqi Kurds that is perceived as being hostile to Turkish interests. See http://www .worldpublicopinion.org/pipa/articles/home_page/393php?lb=hmpg2&pnt=393&nid =&id=.

Around two dozen lynch attempts targeting Kurdish citizens occurred in various parts of Turkey in 2005 and 2006. See *Radikal,* September 1, 2006, and the Turkish daily *Özgür Gündem,* September 10, 2006.

137. These activities are aptly documented in Yalçın and Yurdakul, *Reis.*

138. For instance, see Kalkan, *Katille Buluşma.*

139. The illegal and murderous state-sponsored activities are widely documented in the inspector's report: Savaş, *Susurluk Raporu.* An informative journalistic work is Berberoğlu, *Kod Adı Yüksekova.*

140. This section draws from Tezcür, "Judicial Activism in Perilous Times."

141. This evaluation is based on conversations with citizens in Hakkari, Yüksekova, and Şemdinli, June 24–26, 2007.

142. Erdoğan's address to the JDP parliamentary group, November 22, 2005.

143. A hard copy of the indictment is in the possession of the author. It is also available at http://www.milliyet.com.tr/sabitimg/06/gazete/siyaset/semdinli _iddianame.pdf.

144. Hard copies of both of these reports are in the author's possession. A copy of the Human Rights Commission report is available at http://www.tbmm.gov.tr/ komisyon/insanhak/insanhaklari.htm.

145. A hard copy of the court decision dated February 2007 regarding the sentencing of the insurgent turncoat Veysel Ateş is in the possession of the author.

CHAPTER 8

1. A detailed text of the commander's speech is available at http://www.ntvmsnbc .com/news/405466.asp. In the same press conference, the commander sharply criticized the accusations made against the Turkish Armed Forces by a public prosecutor after the bombing of a bookstore in the Kurdish town of Şemdinli on November 9, 2005. This was an explicit attempt to influence the court's decision.

2. The full text of his speech is available at http://www.cankaya.gov.tr/tr_html/ KONUSMALAR/13.04.2007-3652.html.

3. This was not the first time the civilian politicians did not comply with the TAF's preferences during the presidential elections. Since the 1960 coup, the TAF had tried to make sure that its favorite candidate was elected president. Similar to the behavior of the JDP in 2007, major parties refused to comply with the TAF's preferences in the 1973 presidential elections. Nye, "Civil-Military Confrontation in Turkey."

4. On March 31, a smaller rally under the banner of "defending our republic" was held in the Mediterranean coast town of Antalya.

5. He made these comments at an award ceremony sponsored by an association dedicated to the legacy of ex-president Turgut Özal on April 15. See *Radikal,* April 16, 2007.

6. The memorandum is available on the TAF's official Web site: http://www.tsk .mil.tr/10_ARSIV/10_1_Basin_Yayin_Faaliyetleri/10_1_Basin_Aciklamalari/2007/ BA_08.html. An interesting aspect of this memorandum is the problems with its language. It seemed that the memorandum was drafted in haste.

7. Reported by *Milliyet,* May 2, 2007.

8. Personal communication with Ertuğrul Günay, Ankara, July 3, 2007.

9. Personal communication with Zeynep Dağı, Ankara, July 5, 2007.

10. Güneri Civaoğlu, "İşadamları ve AKP" [Businessmen and JDP], *Milliyet,* July 19, 2007.

11. For an analysis of the media's and big business positions, see "Siyasetin

Üzerinde Yeni Hayalet: Darbe Korkusu" [New Ghost of Politics: Fear of Coup], Turkish weekly magazine *Aksiyon,* May 14, 2007.

12. Tarhan Erdem, "AKP %48'e Dayandı, CHP %20'nin Altında" [JDP Close to 48 Percent, RPP below 20 Percent], *Radikal,* July 19, 2007.

13. Statistics are available at the Turkish Treasury's Web site: http://www.hazine .gov.tr/stat/yabser_ist.htm.

14. Data on inflation are available at http://www.yaklasim.com/malibilgiler/ pratikbilgiler/maddeler/039.htm.

15. Data are available on the Turkish Statistical Institution's Web site at http:// www.tuik.gov.tr.

16. Kalaycıoğlu, "Three Styles of Politics." Also see Çarkoğlu and Toprak, *Değişen Türkiye'de Din, Toplum ve Siyaset,* 84–86.

17. For an insightful analysis of how the JDP's poverty-alleviation policies generate extensive patronage, see Meral Tamer, "AKP'nin Yoksula Yardım Çarkı Nasıl İşliyor?" [How Does JDP's Poverty Alleviation Work?], *Milliyet,* July 1, 2007. For electoral purposes, the JDP delivered coal to citizens in spring and summer. "1.8 Milyon Aileye Kömür" [Coal to 1.8 Million Families], *Radikal,* July 30, 2007.

18. Tolga Şardan, "KÖYDES ile BELDES AKP'ye Kazandırdı" [JDP Won with KÖYDES and BELDES], *Milliyet,* August 7, 2007.

19. For an analysis of the new middle class in the Central Anatolian province of Kayseri, see European Stability Initiative, *Islamic Calvinists: Change and Conservatism in Central Anatolia,* Berlin and Istanbul, September 19, 2005. Available at http://www .esiweb.org/pdf/esi_document_id_69.pdf.

20. Several high-ranking JDP politicians expressed this view in interviews with the author in June and July 2007. The JDP's grassroots members were also very active in making the presidential election central to the campaign.

21. The DP was established in May 2007 after the self-dissolution of the TPP. It aspired to represent the legacy of Menderes' DP of the 1950s.

22. Personal communication with party activists in the provinces of Tokat, Sivas, and Mersin in July 2007.

23. The author was a participant observant of the JDP's electoral activities in Samsun on July 7, 2007, and witnessed similarly intense and well-organized vote-canvassing efforts in Ankara, Istanbul, İzmir, and Van.

24. A scholarly analysis of this important rebellion that led to Turkey's subsequent repressive and assimilative policies toward the Kurds is Olson, *Emergence of Kurdish Nationalism.*

25. Personal communication with Esat Canan, who was an RPP parliamentarian between 2002 and 2007 from the province of Hakkari, on October 11, 2007, Ankara.

26. June 16, 2007. This was Erdoğan's second electoral rally. Available at http:// www.akparti.org.tr/haber.asp?haber_id=17824&kategori=1.

27. Erdoğan electoral rally, June 26, 2007. Available at http://www.akparti.org .tr/haber.asp?haber_id=18020&kategori=1.

28. This motto is inscribed in army barracks and offices all over the country.

29. It should be mentioned that predominantly Kurdish areas in the east have historically been the most underdeveloped and backward regions of Turkey. For example, in some neighborhoods of Diyarbakır, the largest city in the east, GNP per capita is fourteen times less than the national average. "Diyarbakır'da 20.000 Aç" [20.000 Hungry People in Diyarbakir], *Radikal,* August 5, 2007. According to many politicians and intellectuals, this huge regional disparity has been the root cause of discontent among the Kurds. For a pioneering work that identifies the dynamics of poverty and underdevelopment in eastern Turkey, see Bozarslan, *Doğu'nun Sorunları,* first published in 1966.

30. Personal communication, June 24, 2007, Yüksekova.

31. *Milliyet,* July 30, 2007.

32. For a journalist's discussion and analysis of the JDP's rise in Diyarbakır, see "AKP Diyarbakır'da DTP'yi Yakaladı" [JDP Caught DSP in Diyarbakir], *Milliyet,* August 2, 2007.

33. Personal communication with Necla Hattapoğlu, October 20, 2007, Diyarbakır.

34. For instance, see Kalaycıoğlu, "Elections and Party Preferences."

35. For example, see "The Real Challenge to Secular Turkey," *Economist,* August 31, 2006.

36. "Kürtler AKP'ye Sadece Kredi Açtı" [Kurds Conditionally Give JDP Credit], *Milliyet,* July 30, 2007.

37. Personal communication, October 15, 2007, Yüksekova.

38. Ahmet Türk's first address to the DSP parliamentary group, *Özgür Gündem,* August 21, 2007.

39. Personal communication with Ayla Akat Ata, June 28, 2007, Batman.

40. The speech was delivered in Diyarbakır on September 30, 2007.

41. "DTP öz Eleştiri Yaptı" [DSP-Generated Self-criticism] *Hürriyet,* August 10, 2007.

42. Personal communications in the provinces of Batman, Diyarbakır, and Van in June 2007.

43. Personal communication with DTP sympathizers in Diyarbakır, Van, and Ankara in summer and fall 2007.

44. For rising nationalism in Turkey, see http://www.worldpublicopinion.org/pipa/articles/home_page/393.php?nid=&id=&pnt=393&lb=hmpg2.

45. Kurdish-Islamic intellectuals were also critical of the JDP's Kurdish policy after the 2007 elections. See Tan, *Kürt Sorunu,* 510–514.

46. The official document that described the measures was published by the pro-Kurdish nationalist daily *Özgür Gündem* on June 28, 2008. A hard copy of the document is in the possession of the author.

47. For example, the Sur municipality in Diyarbakır was dissolved in June 2007 because of its attempt to communicate with its constituency in languages other than Turkish. An overwhelming majority of the citizens living in that municipality have

Kurdish as their mother language. Many citizens, especially women, do not speak Turkish at all. Personal communication with Abdullah Demirbaş, former mayor of Sur, October 21, 2007, Diyarbakır.

48. For a similar criticism of the JDP's moderation from an Islamist perspective, see Kaya, *Değişim Sürecinde AK Parti ve Müslümanlar.*

49. For a journalistic yet informative analysis of Ahmedinejad's presidency, see Naji, *Ahmedinejad.* For his economic policies, see pages 229–238.

50. Personal communication with Badrossadat Mofidi, general secretary of the Association of Iranian Journalists, March 10, 2008.

51. For his relationship with Khamenei and other centers of power in Iran, see Naji, *Ahmedinejad,* 256–266.

52. Naji also provides a useful overview of Ahmedinejad's provincial tours. Ibid., 213–219.

53. Personal communication with Farshad Mahdipour, editor of the political service of the Iranian daily *Hamshahri,* Tehran, March 8, 2008.

54. Gareth Smyth and Najmeh Bozorgmehr, "Ahmedi-Nejad Suffers Vote Setback in Iran," *Financial Times,* December 17, 2006.

55. "The Year of Union," Iranian daily *Etemad,* March 15, 2007.

56. Personal communication with Mohammed Atrianfar, Tehran, March 9, 2008. He used to be the editor of the Iranian dailies *Hamshahri* and *Sharq.* He also contributed to the Iranian daily *Kargozaran.*

57. Personal communication with Vahed Khavei, Tehran, March 10, 2008.

58. The commander of the Revolutionary Guards openly called on citizens to support the principalists in the elections. "Iran Revolutionary Guards Back Conservatives," Agence France-Presse, February 9, 2008.

59. Personal communication with a young reformist, Tehran, March 5, 2008.

60. For an original analysis of the evolution of the U.S.-Iran relations on the basis of interviews with decision makers in Iran, Israel, and the United States, see Parsi, *Treacherous Alliance,* especially chapters 17–20.

61. Personal communication with Abbas Salimi Namin, the director of the Office for Contemporary Iranian History Studies, and a prominent political analyst affiliated with principalists, Tehran, March 6, 2008.

62. Personal communication with several reformist politicians, Tehran, March 5, 2008.

63. For a detailed analysis of the elections, see Tezcür, "Intra-Elite Struggles and Iranian Elections."

64. There are conflicting reports of the disqualification rate. This information was obtained from the Web site of the Islamic Republic of Iran Broadcasting. Available at http://www.iribnews.ir/Full_en.asp?news_id=251400.

65. For election results, see http://www.presstv.ir/Detail.aspx?id=46127&sectionid =351020101.

66. Speech delivered in a reformist meeting in Tehran on March 9, 2008. Also see

the Iranian daily *Etemad-e Melli,* January 24, 2008. For a province-by-province report of the qualified reformist candidates, see the Iranian daily *Farhang-e Ashti,* February 17, 2008.

67. Personal communication with Hamidreza Jalaeipour, Tehran, March 10, 2008.

68. *Aftab News,* May 13, 2007. Available at http://aftab.ir/news/2007/may/13/c1c1179071693_politics_iran.php.

69. The electoral manifesto of the IIPF was entitled "Why Do We Participate in the Unfair Elections for the Eighth Parliament?" The author obtained this document in Tehran on March 9, 2008.

70. Khatami speech delivered at a reformist meeting in Tehran, March 9, 2008.

71. Personal communication with several members of the Islamic Iran Participation Front, Tehran, March 5, 2008.

72. For an extended discussion, see editorials in the Iranian daily *Aftab-e Yazd* on March 6, 2007, and October 23, 2007.

73. The average annual population growth rate in Iran was 3.30 percent between 1975 and 1980. It skyrocketed to 4.16 between 1980 and 1985 before dropping to 0.97 between 2000 and 2005. The Iranian citizens who were born in the first decade of the Revolution form the Baby Boomer Generation. The data on population growth rate are available at http://data.un.org.

74. Personal communication with Malek Shariati Niasar, a member of the Central Council of the Basij, Tehran, March 7, 2008. He was active in the campaigns of principalist candidates.

75. Personal communication with Amir Mohebbian, managing director of Arya News Agency, Tehran, March 11, 2008. Mohebbian, a prominent political analyst, contributed to the Iranian daily *Resalat.*

76. This information was obtained from the charter of the NCP at http://etemademelli.ir/about/manshour.

77. *Etemad-e Melli,* February 9, 2008.

78. Personal communication with members of the Reformist Coalition in Tehran, March 5, 2008.

79. Khatami speech delivered at a reformist meeting in Tehran, March 9, 2008.

80. For a criticism of the amendment, see the Iranian daily *Etemad,* February 2, 2008.

81. In a statement of the United Front of Principalists, reported by *Iran,* December 31, 2007.

82. Ali Akbar Dareini, "Conservatives Dominate after Iran Parliament Runoffs," Associated Press, April 26, 2008.

83. Nazila Fathi, "Reformers Gain in Iran Vote despite Being Barred," *New York Times,* March 16, 2008. The Interior Ministry announced the participation rate as 26 percent in the second round.

84. Reported in *USA Today,* January 13, 2007.

85. The calculations are from an Iranian Web site that provides comprehensive

and detailed information on electoral results. See http://www.mardomak.org. Also see, "Back to First Principles," *Economist,* March 19, 2008.

86. Kazemzadeh, "Intra-Elite Factionalism."

87. Turnout rates in provinces are available at http://www.mardomak.org/news/participation_elections86_per_provnc.

88. See electoral results at http://www.mardomak.org/news/final_comb_tehran.

89. All eight were affiliated with the principalist groups. This was a significant drop from previous elections. The Fifth Parliament had fourteen women members; the reformist-dominated Sixth Parliament, fourteen; and the Seventh Parliament, thirteen. The Fourth Parliament had nine women members, and the first three parliaments had four each.

90. Personal communication with the assistant editor of the *Kargozaran* newspaper, Badrosadat Mofidi, Tehran, March 10, 2008.

91. See Lust-Okar, "Competing for Resources in Jordanian Elections."

92. Iran did not have international electoral observers. The presence of international observers who are entrusted with making sure elections are fair increases the probability of an electoral boycott by the opposition, who fear losing internationally certified but still manipulated elections. Beaulieu and Hyde, "In the Shadow of Democracy Promotion."

93. Mohammad Reza Khatami's address at Sharif University, Tehran, June 22, 2007. Available at http://emruz.info/ShowItem.aspx?ID=7540&p=1.

94. "Interview with Saeed Hajjarian," *Vaqa-ye Ettefaqieh,* July 17, 2004.

95. Melli Mazhabi is composed of several parties and groups of intellectuals and political activists who are against the *velayat-e faqih.* It claims to carry the mantle of Mohammed Mosaddeq, Ali Shariati, Mehdi Bazargan, and Mahmoud Taleqani. The regime tolerates the existence of the Alliance as long they are not very active politically and abide by the strict regulations.

96. Personal communication with Taqi Rahmani, Melli Mazhabi intellectual, Tehran, March 10, 2008.

97. "Khamenei must go," Akbar Ganji's letter to Abdolkarim Soroush, July 28, 2005. An English translation is available at http://freeganji.blogspot.com/2005/07/letter-to-dr-abdolkarim-soroush.html.

98. Personal communication with Kayvan Samimi, a prominent member of the Melli Mazhabi, Tehran, March 8, 2008.

CHAPTER 9

1. For Hamas, see Mishal and Sela, *The Palestinian Hamas*; for Hezbollah, see Norton, *Hezbollah*; for Shiite movements in Iraq, see Cole, "United States and Shi'ite Religious Factions."

2. In Turkey, see Türkmen, *Türkiye'de İslâmcılık ve Özeleştiri,* 151–168; Kaya, *Değişim Sürecinde AK Parti ve Müslümanlar,* 111–116, 159–166, 189–196. In Iran,

prominent human rights activists such as the Nobel Peace Laureate Shirin Ebadi and Akbar Ganji criticized reformist participation in the 2004 parliamentary and 2005 presidential elections and advocated a boycott.

3. This conceptualization of the relationship between social movements and political-opportunity structures follows the discussion of Campbell, "Where Do We Stand?"

4. Yavuz argues that behavioral change precedes ideological change. Yet he does not offer a theoretical framework to support this argument. See his *Secularism and Muslim Democracy in Turkey,* 11.

5. For instance, see Lust-Okar, *Structuring Conflict in the Arab World,* and Brownlee, *Authoritarianism in an Age of Democratization.*

6. In fact, women became politically more engaged and exhibited a higher consciousness and assertiveness in seeking their rights through legal means and making claims on state institutions during the presidency of Khatami. Osanloo, *The Politics of Women's Rights in Iran,* 38–41.

7. For example, see the headline article in the Turkish daily *Taraf,* June 12, 2009.

8. This section is based on my personal on-the-ground observations during the electoral period.

9. Official results were posted at the province and county level on the Web site of the Interior Ministry at www.moi.ir.

10. At the same time, a direct comparison between the 2005 and 2009 presidential election results at the province and county level would not lead to any conclusive evidence that elections are rigged for two methodological reasons: (1) the voting age was raised from fifteen to eighteen in January 2007, and (2) to make inferences about individual-level behavior on the basis of aggregate data results in ecological fallacy.

11. A complete English translation of his speech is available at http://www.presstv.com/detail.aspx?id=98610.

12. This information comes from a letter signed by Mousavi and posted on a Web site affiliated with his movement. Mousavi's fifth letter to the Iranian people, June 20, 2009, available at http://www.kalemeh.ir/vdcf.cd1iw6dexgiaw.txt.

13. Mousavi's sixth letter to the Iranian people, June 20, 2009, available at http://kalemeh.ir/vdcc.4qoa2bqmmla82.html.

14. An article that appeared in a Pasdaran weekly publication two days before the election actually accused the Mousavi campaign of attempting a "velvet revolution" to overthrow the regime. See http://www.bbc.co.uk/persian/iran/2009/06/090610_si_ir88_sepah_velvetrevolution.shtml.

BIBLIOGRAPHY

Note: Citation information for interviews and Web sources is provided in endnotes and is not included in this bibliography. To accommodate the additional letters in Turkish, alphabetization follows this order: C, Ç, G, Ğ, I, İ, O, Ö, S, Ş, U, Ü.

Abrahamian, Ervand. *Khomeinism: Essays on the Islamic Republic.* Berkeley and Los Angeles: University of California Press, 1993.
———. *Tortured Confessions: Prisons and Public Recantations in Modern Iran.* Berkeley and Los Angeles: University of California Press, 1999.
Adaman, Fikret, Burhan Şenatalar, and Ali Çarkoğlu. *Hanehalkı Gözünden Türkiye'de Yolsuzluğun Nedenleri ve Önlenmesine İlişkin Öneriler* [The Causes of Corruption from Household Perceptions and Suggestions for Its Prevention in Turkey]. Istanbul: TESEV, 2001.
Adcock, Robert, and David Collier. "Measurement Validity: A Shared Standard for Qualitative and Quantitative Research." *American Political Science Review* 95 (September 2001): 529–546.
Adib-Moghaddam, Arshin. *Iran in World Politics: The Question of the Islamic Republic.* London: Hurst, 2007.
Afary, Janet. *The Iranian Constitutional Revolution, 1906–1911.* New York: Columbia University, 1996.
"Africa: Islam, Democracy and Public Opinion." *Afrobarometer Briefing Paper* 3 (September 2002). Available at http://www.africaaction.org/docs02/ab0209.htm.
Ağaşe, Çetin. *Cem Ersever ve JİTEM Gerçeği* [Cem Ersever and the Truth about JITEM]. Istanbul: Bilge Karınca Yayınları, 2003.
Ahmad, Feroz. *The Making of Modern Turkey.* London and New York: Routledge, 1993.
Ajami, Fouad. *The Vanished Imam: Musa Sadr and the Shia of Lebanon.* Ithaca, NY: Cornell University Press, 1992.
Akarca, Ali T., and Aysit Tansel. "Economic Performance and Political Outcomes: An Analysis of the Turkish Parliamentary Elections and Local Election Results between 1950 and 2004." *Public Choice* 129 (October 2006): 77–105.

Akbulut, Olgun. "The State of Political Participation of Minorities in Turkey—An Analysis under the ECHR and ICCPR." *International Journal on Minority and Group Rights* 12 (2005): 375–395.

Akça, İsmet. "Kolektif Bir Sermayeder Olarak Turk Silahlı Kuvvetleri" [Turkish Armed Forces as a Collective Capitalist]. *Birikim* 160–161 (August–September 2002).

Akçura, Yusuf. *Üç Tarz-ı Siyaset* [Three Political Approaches]. Ankara: Türk Tarih Kurumu, 1987.

Akdoğan, Yalçın. "Adalet ve Kalkınma Partisi" [Justice and Development Party]. In *Modern Türkiye'de Siyasi Düşünce: İslamcılık* [Political Thought in Modern Turkey: Islamism], ed. Yasin Aktay, 620–631. Istanbul: İletişim, 2004.

———. *Ak Parti ve Muhafazakar Demokrasi* [Justice and Development Party and Conservative Democracy]. Istanbul: Alfa, 2004.

———. *Siyasal İslam: Refah Partisi'nin Anatomisi* [Political Islam: The Anatomy of the Welfare Party]. Istanbul: Şehir, 2000.

Akhavi, Shahrough. "Elite Factionalism in the Islamic Republic of Iran." *The Middle East Journal* 41 (Spring 1987): 181–201.

———. "The Ideology and Praxis of Shi'ism in the Iranian Revolution." *Comparative Studies in Society and History* 25 (April 1983): 195–221.

Alamdari, Kazem. "The Power Structure of the Islamic Republic of Iran." *Third World Quarterly* 26 (December 2005): 1285–1301.

Al-Azmeh, Aziz. "Populism Contra Democracy: Recent Democratist Discourse in the Arab World." In *Democracy without Democrats: The Renewal of Politics in the Muslim World,* ed. Ghassan Salame, pp. 112–129. London: I. B. Tauris, 1994.

Al-e Ahmad, Jalal. *Gharbzadegi.* Translated from the Persian by John Green and Ahmad Alizadeh. Lexington, KY: Mazda Publishers, 1982.

Alexander, Christopher. "Opportunities, Organizations, and Ideas: Islamists and Workers in Tunisia and Algeria." *International Journal of Middle East Studies* 32 (November 2000): 465–490.

Algar, Hamid. *Roots of the Islamic Revolution in Iran.* Revised and expanded edition. Oneonta, NY: Islamic Publications International, 2001.

———. *Wahhabism: A Critical Essay.* Oneonta, NY: Islamic Publications International, 2002.

Almond, Gabriel. "The Christian Parties of Western Europe." *World Politics* 1 (October 1948): 30–58.

———. "The Political Ideas of Christian Democracy." *The Journal of Politics* 10 (November 1948): 734–763.

Almond, Gabriel, and Sidney Verba. *The Civic Culture: Political Attitudes and Democracy in Five Nations.* New ed. Newbury Park, CA: Sage Publications, 1989.

Almond, Gabriel A., Scott R. Appleby, and Emmanuel Silvan. *Strong Religion: The Rise of Fundamentalisms around the World*. Chicago and London: University of Chicago Press, 2003.

An-Na'im, Abdullahi Ahmed. *Islam and the Secular State: Negotiating the Future of Shari'a*. Cambridge: Harvard University Press, 2008.

Ansari, Ali M. *Iran, Islam and Democracy: The Politics of Managing Change*. 2nd ed. London: Royal Institute of International Affairs, 2006.

Arendt, Hannah. *On Revolution*. New York: Penguin Books, 1990.

Arjomand, Said Amir. "Civil Society and the Rule of Law in the Constitutional Politics of Iran under Khatami." *Social Research* 67 (Summer 2000): 283–301.

———. "Crisis of the Imamate and the Institution of Occultation in Twelver Shi'ism: A Sociohistorical Perspective." *International Journal of Middle Eastern Studies* 28 (November 1996): 491–515.

———. "Ideological Revolution in Shi'ism." In *Authority and Political Culture in Shi'ism*, ed. Said Amir Arjomand, 191–203. New York: State University of New York, 1988.

———. "Iran's Islamic Revolution in Comparative Perspective." *World Politics* 38 (April 1986): 383–414.

———. "The Reform Movement and the Debate on Modernity and Tradition in Contemporary Iran." *International Journal of Middle East Studies* 34 (November 2002): 719–731.

———. *The Shadow of God and the Hidden Imam*. Chicago: University of Chicago Press, 1984.

———. *The Turban for the Crown: The Islamic Revolution in Iran*. New York: Oxford University Press, 1988.

Arslan, Abdurrahman. *Modern Dünyada Müslümanlar* [Muslims in the Modern World]. Istanbul: İletişim, 2000.

Asad, Talad. *Formations of the Secular: Christianity, Islam, and Modernity*. Stanford, CA: Stanford University Press, 2003.

Axelrod, Robert. "An Evolutionary Approach to Norms." *The American Political Science Review* 80 (December 1986): 1095–1111.

———. *The Evolution of Cooperation*. New York: Basic Books, 1984.

Ayata, Sencer. "Patronage, Party, and State: The Politicization of Islam in Turkey." *Middle East Journal* 50 (Winter 1996): 40–56.

Ayubi, Nazih. *Political Islam: Religion and Politics in the Arab World*. London and New York: Routledge, 1991.

Aziz, T. M. "The Role of Muhammad Baqir al-Sadr in Shi'i Political Activism in Iraq from 1958 to 1980." *International Journal of Middle Eastern Studies* 29 (Spring 1993): 1–31.

Bader, Veit. "Secularism and Militant Democracy: The Pitfalls of 'Secularism' in

Turkish and Indian Constitutional Debates." Paper presented at Religion, Secularism and Democracy Conference, New Delhi, January 4–7, 2009.

———. *Secularism or Democracy? Associational Governance of Religious Diversity.* Amsterdam: Amsterdam University Press, 2007.

Baker, Raymond William. *Islam without Fear: Egypt and the New Islamists.* Cambridge: Harvard University Press, 2003.

Bakhash, Shaul. "Iran's Remarkable Election." *Journal of Democracy* 9 (January 1998): 80–94.

———. *The Reign of the Ayatollahs: Iran and the Islamic Revolution.* New York: Basic Books, 1984.

Baktiari, Bahman. *Parliamentary Politics in Revolutionary Iran: The Institutionalization of Factional Politics.* Gainesville: University Press of Florida, 1996.

Banfield, Edward C. *Moral Basis of a Backward Society.* Chicago: Free Press, 1958.

Barnard, Chester. *Functions of the Executive.* Cambridge: Harvard University Press, 1968. [Originally published in 1938.]

Barro, Robert J., and Rachel M. McCleary. "Religion and Economic Growth across Countries." *American Sociological Review* 68 (October 2003): 760–781.

Barzin, Saeed. "Constitutionalism and Democracy in the Religious Ideology of Mehdi Bazargan." *British Journal of Middle Eastern Studies* 21 (May 1994): 85–101.

Başgil, Ali Fuat. *Din ve Laiklik* [Religion and Laicism]. Istanbul: Kubbealtı Neşriyatı, 1998.

Başkan, Filiz. "The Fethullah Gülen Community: Contribution or Barrier to the Consolidation of Democracy in Turkey?" *Middle Eastern Studies* 41 (November 2005): 849–861.

Bates, Robert H. "Area Studies and the Discipline: A Useful Controversy?" *PS: Political Science and Politics* 30 (June 1997): 166–170.

Bayat, Asef. *Making Islam Democratic: Social Movements and the Post-Islamist Turn.* Stanford, CA: Stanford University Press, 2007.

———. *Workers and Revolution in Iran.* London and New Jersey: Zed Books, 1987.

Beaulieu, Emily, and Susan D. Hyde. "In the Shadow of Democracy Promotion: Strategic Manipulation, International Observers, and Election Boycotts." *Comparative Political Studies* 42 (March 2009): 392–415.

Becker, Carl Lotus. *Heavenly City of the Eighteenth-Century Philosophers.* New Haven: Yale University Press, 1932.

Behdad, Sohrab. "Winners and Losers of the Iranian Revolution: A Study in Income Redistribution." *International Journal of Middle Eastern Studies* 21 (August 1989): 327–358.

Behdad, Sohrab, and Farhad Nomani. "Workers, Peasants, and Peddlers: A Study of Labor Stratification in the Post-Revolutionary Iran." *International Journal of Middle Eastern Studies* 34 (November 2002): 667–690.

Bekaroğlu, Mehmet. *"Adil Düzen" den "Dünya Gerçekleri" ne: Siyasetin Sonu* [From "Just Order" to "World Realities": End of Politics]. Ankara: Elips, 2007.

Belge, Ceren. "Friends of the Court: The Republican Alliance and Selective Activism of the Constitutional Court of Turkey." *Law and Society Review* 40 (September 2006): 653–692.

Bellin, Eva. "The Robustness of Authoritarianism in the Middle East: Exceptionalism in Comparative Perspective." *Comparative Politics* 36 (January 2004): 139–157.

Benard, Cheryl. *Civil Democratic Islam: Partners, Resources, and Strategies*. Pittsburgh: Rand Corporation, 2003.

Berberoğlu, Enis. *Kod Adı Yüksekova: Susurluk, Ankara, Bodrum, Yüksekova Fay Hattı* [Code Name Is Yüksekova: Susurluk, Ankara, Bodrum, Yüksekova Fault Line]. Istanbul: Milliyet, 1999.

Berkes, Niyazi. *Türkiye'de Çağdaşlaşma* [Modernization in Turkey]. Istanbul: Yapı Kredi Yayınları, 2002.

Bermeo, Nancy. "Myths of Moderation: Confrontation and Conflict during Democratic Transitions." *Comparative Politics* 29 (April 1997): 305–322.

Beşe, Ertan. "Intelligence Activities of the Gendarmerie Corps." In *Almanac 2005: Security Sector and Democratic Oversight*, ed. Ümit Cizre, 172–189. Istanbul: TESEV, 2006.

Binder, Leonard. *Islamic Liberalism: A Critique of Development Ideologies*. Chicago: University of Chicago Press, 1988.

Birand, Mehmet Ali, Hikmet Bila, and Rıdvan Akar. *12 Eylül: Türkiye'nin Miladi* [September 12: Turkey's Milestone]. Istanbul: Doğan Kitabçılık, 1999.

Boroujerdi, Mehrzad. *Iranian Intellectuals and the West: The Tormented Triumph of Nativism*. Syracuse, NY: Syracuse University Press, 1996.

———. "The Reformist Movement in Iran." In *Oil in the Gulf: Obstacles to Democracy and Development*, ed. Daniel Heradstvcit and Helge Hveem, 63–71. Aldershot, England: Ashgate, 2004.

Bozarslan, Mehmet Emin. *Doğu'nun Sorunları* [Problems of the East]. Istanbul: Avesta, 2002. [Originally published in 1966.]

Brady, Henry E., and David Collier, eds. *Rethinking Social Inquiry: Diverse Tools, Shared Standards*. Lanham, MD: Rowman and Littlefield, 2004.

Bratton, Michael, and Nicolas Van De Walle. "Popular Protest and Political Reform in Africa." *Comparative Politics* 24 (July 1992): 419–442.

Brown, Nathan J. "Sharia and State in the Modern Muslim Middle East." *International Journal of Middle East Studies* 29 (August 1997): 359–376.

Brown, Nathan J., Amr Hamza, and Marina Ottaway. "Islamist Movements and the Democratic Process in the Arab World: Exploring the Gray Zones." *Carnegie Working Papers* 67 (March 2006): 5–19.

Brownlee, Jason. *Authoritarianism in an Age of Democratization.* New York: Cambridge University Press, 2007.

Bruce, Steve. *Religion in the Modern World: From Cathedrals to Cults.* Oxford: Oxford University Press, 1996.

Brumberg, Daniel. *Reinventing Khomeini: The Struggle for Reform in Iran.* Chicago and London: University of Chicago Press, 2001.

Buchta, Wilfried. Who Rules Iran? The Structure of Power in the Islamic Republic. Washington, D.C.: Washington Institute for Near East Policy, 2000.

Bulaç, Ali. *Din, Kent ve Cemaat: Fethullah Gülen Örneği* [Religion, City, and Community: The Case of Fethullah Gülen]. Istanbul: Ufuk, 2007.

Bulliet, Richard W. *Islam: The View from the Edge.* New York: Columbia University Press, 1994.

Bunce, Valerie J. "Rethinking Recent Democratization: Lessons from the Postcommunist Experience." *World Politics* 55 (January 2003): 167–192.

Bunce, Valerie J., and Sharon L. Wolchik. "Favorable Conditions and Electoral Revolutions." *Journal of Democracy* 17 (October 2006): 5–18.

Burke, Edmund III, and Paul Lubeck. "Explaining Social Movements in Two Oil-Exporting States: Divergent Outcomes in Nigeria and Iran." *Comparative Studies in Society and History* 29 (October 1987): 643–665.

Campbell, John L. "Where Do We Stand? Common Mechanisms in Organizations and Social Movements Research." In *Social Movements and Organization Theory,* ed. Gerald F. Davis, Doug McAdam, W. Richard Scott, and Mayer N. Zald, 41–68. New York: Cambridge University Press, 2003.

Cary, Noel D. *The Path to Christian Democracy: German Catholics and the Party System from Windthorst to Adenauer.* Cambridge: Harvard University Press, 1996.

Casanova, Jose. *Public Religions in the Modern World.* Chicago: University of Chicago Press, 1994.

Chaves, Mark. "Secularization as Declining Religious Authority." *Social Forces* 72 (March 1994): 749–774.

Chehabi, H. E. *Iranian Politics and Religious Modernism: The Liberation Movement of Iran under the Shah and Khomeini.* Ithaca, NY: Cornell University Press, 1990.

———. "The Political Regime of the Islamic Republic of Iran in Comparative Perspective." *Government and Opposition* 36 (Winter 2001): 48–70.

Chhibber, Pradeep K. "State Policy, Rent Seeking, and the Electoral Success of a Religious Party in Algeria." *The Journal of Politics* 58 (February 1996): 126–148.

Cizre (Sakallıoğlu), Ümit. "The Anatomy of the Turkish Military's Political Autonomy." *Comparative Politics* 29 (January 1997): 151–166.

———. *AP-Ordu İlişkileri: Bir İkilemin Anatomisi* [JP-Army Relations: An Anatomy of a Dilemma]. Istanbul: İletişim Yayinlari, 1993.

———. "Parameters and Strategies of Islam-State Interaction in Republican Turkey." *International Journal of Middle East Studies* 28 (May 1996): 231–251.

———. "Problems of Democratic Governance of Civil-Military Relations in Turkey and the European Union Enlargement Zone." *European Journal of Political Research* 43 (January 2004): 107–125.

Clark, Janine. "The Conditions of Islamist Moderation: Unpacking Cross-Ideological Cooperation in Jordan." *International Journal of Middle East Studies* 38 (November 2006): 539–560.

———. "Social Movement Theory and Patron-Clientelism." *Comparative Political Studies* 37 (October 2004): 941–968.

Cole, Juan. *Napoleon's Egypt: Invading the Middle East.* New York: Palgrave Macmillan, 2007.

———. "The United States and Shi'ite Religious Factions in Post-Ba'thist Iraq." *Middle East Journal* 57 (October 2003): 543–566.

Collier, David, and James E. Mahon, Jr. "Conceptual 'Stretching' Revisited: Adapting Categories in Comparative Analysis." *American Political Science Review* 87 (December 1993): 845–855.

Collins, Kathleen. "The Logic of Clan Politics: Evidence from the Central Asian Trajectories." *World Politics* 56 (January 2004): 224–261.

Conrad, Joseph. *Under Western Eyes.* New York: The Modern Library, 2001.

Converse, Philip. "The Nature of Belief Systems in Mass Publics." In *Ideology and Discontent,* ed. David Apter, 206–261. New York: Free Press, 1964.

Cook, David. *Martyrdom in Islam.* New York: Cambridge University Press, 2007.

Cook, Michael. *Commanding Right and Forbidding Wrong in Islamic Thought.* New York: Cambridge University Press, 2001.

Crone, Patricia. *God's Rule: Government and Islam.* New ed. New York: Columbia University Press, 2005.

Çakır, Ruşen. *Ayet ve Slogan* [Verse and Slogan]. Istanbul: Metis, 1990.

———. *Ne Şeriat Ne Demokrasi* [Neither Shari'a nor Democracy]. Istanbul: Metis, 1994.

Çakır, Ruşen, and İrfan Bozan. *Sivil, Şeffaf ve Demokratik bir Diyanet İşleri Başkanlığı Mümkün mü?* [Is a Civil, Transparent, and Democratic Religious Affairs Directory Possible?]. Istanbul: TESEV Yayınları, 2005.

Çakır, Ruşen, and Fehmi Çalmuk. *Recep Tayyip Erdoğan: Bir Dönüşüm Öyküsü* [Recep Tayyip Erdoğan: A Story of Transformation]. Istanbul: Metis, 2001.

Çalmuk, Fehmi. *Erbakan'ın Kürtleri: Milli Görüş'ün Güneydoğu Politikası* [Erbakan's Kurds: The National View's Southeast Policy]. Istanbul: Metis, 2001.

Çarkoğlu, Ali. "Political Preferences of the Turkish Electorate: Reflections on an Alevi-Sunni Cleavage." *Turkish Studies* 6 (June 2005): 273–292.

Çarkoğlu, Ali, Tarhan Erdem, Ömer Faruk Gençkaya, and Mehmet Kabasakal. *Türkiye'de Yeni Bir Parti Sistemine Doğru: Siyasi Partilerde Reform* [Toward a New Party System in Turkey: Reform of Political Parties]. Istanbul: TESEV, 2000.

Çarkoğlu, Ali, and Melvin J. Hinich. "A Spatial Analysis of Turkish Party Preferences." *Electoral Studies* 25 (June 2006): 369–392.

Çarkoğlu, Ali, and Binnaz Toprak. *Değişen Türkiye'de Din, Toplum ve Siyaset* [Religion, Society and Politics in Changing Turkey]. Istanbul: TESEV, 2006.

———. *Türkiye'de Din, Toplum ve Siyaset* [Religion, Society and Politics in Turkey]. Istanbul: TESEV, 2000.

Çayır, Kenan. *Türkiye'de İslamcılık ve İslami Edebiyat* [Islamism and Islamic Literature in Turkey]. Istanbul: Bilgi Üniversitesi, 2008.

Çiçek, Hikmet. *Hangi Hizbullah?* [Which Hizbullah?]. Istanbul: Kaynak, 2000.

Dağı, İhsan M. "Transformation of Islamic Political Identity in Turkey: Rethinking the West and Westernization." *Turkish Studies* 6 (March 2005): 21–37.

Dahl, Robert A. *Democracy and Its Critics.* New Haven: Yale University Press, 1989.

———. *Polyarchy: Participation and Opposition.* New Haven: Yale University Press, 1971.

Dawisha, Adeed. *Arab Nationalism in the Twentieth Century: From Triumph to Despair.* Princeton, NJ: Princeton University Press, 2002.

DeLong-Bas, Natana. *Wahhabi Islam: From Revival and Reform to Global Jihad.* New York: Oxford University Press, 2004.

Demirel, Tanel. *Adalet Partisi: İdeoloji ve Politika* [The Justice Party: Ideology and Politics]. Istanbul: İletişim, 2004.

Deringil, Selim. "Legitimacy Structures in the Ottoman State: The Reign of Abdülhamid II (1876–1909)." *International Journal of Middle Eastern Studies* 23 (August 1991): 345–359.

Diamond, Larry. "Is Pakistan the Future (Reverse) Wave of the Future?" *Journal of Democracy* 11 (July 2000): 91–106.

Dion, Douglas. "Evidence and Inference in the Comparative Case Study." *Comparative Politics* 30 (January 1998): 127–145.

Donno, Daniela, and Bruce M. Russett. "Islam, Authoritarianism, and Female Empowerment: What Are the Linkages?" *World Politics* 56 (July 2004): 582–607.

Downs, Anthony. *An Economic Theory of Democracy.* New York: Harper and Brothers, 1957.

Dressler, Markus. "Turkish Alevi Poetry in the Twentieth Century: The Fusion of Political and Religious Identities." *Alif: Journal of Comparative Poetics* 23 (January 2003): 109–153.

Eckstein, Henry. "A Culturalist Theory of Political Change." *American Political Science Review* 82 (September 1988): 789–804.

Ehsani, Kaveh. "Existing Political Vessels Cannot Contain the Reform Movement: A Conversation with Sai'id Hajjarian." *Middle East Report* 212 (Spring 1999): 40–42.

Eickelman, Dale F., and James Piscatori. *Muslim Politics.* 2nd ed. Princeton, N.J: Princeton University Press, 2004.

El Fadl, Khaled Abou. *Islam and the Challenge of Democracy.* Princeton, NJ, and Oxford, England: Princeton University Press, 2004.

Elkins, David J., and Richard E. B. Simeon. "A Cause in Search of Its Effects, or What Does Political Culture Explain?" *Comparative Politics* 11 (January 1979): 127–145.

Enayat, Hamid. *Modern Islamic Political Thought.* Austin: University of Texas Press, 1982.

Erbakan, Necmettin. *Milli Görüş* [National View]. Istanbul: Dergah, 1975.

———. *Türkiye'nin Temel Meseleleri* [Fundamental Issues of Turkey]. Ankara: Rehber, 1991.

Ergil, Doğu. *Doğu Sorunu: Teşhisler ve Tesbitler* Özel Araştırma Raporu [Eastern Problem: Diagnoses and Analyses Special Research Report]. Istanbul: Türkiye Odalar ve Borsalar Birliği, 1995.

———. "The Kurdish Question in Turkey." *Journal of Democracy* 11 (July 2000): 122–135.

Esfahani, Hadi Salehi, and Farzad Taheripour. "Hidden Public Expenditures and the Economy in Iran." *International Journal of Middle Eastern Studies* 34 (November 2002): 691–718.

Esping-Andersen, Gøsta. *Politics against Markets: The Social Democratic Road to Power.* Princeton, NJ: Princeton University Press, 1985.

Esposito, John. *Islam and Politics.* 4th ed. Syracuse, NY: Syracuse University Press, 1998.

Euben, Roxanne. "Killing for Politics: Jihad, Martyrdom, and Political Action." *Political Theory* 30 (February 2002): 4–35.

Fairbanks, Stephen C. "Theocracy versus Democracy: Iran Considers Political Parties." *Middle East Journal* 52 (Winter 1998): 17–31.

Farzanegan, Mohammad Reza, and Gunther Markwardt. "The Effects of Oil Price Shocks on the Iranian Economy." *Energy Economics* 31 (January 2009): 134–151.

Feldman, Noah. *After Jihad: America and the Struggle for Islamic Democracy.* New York: Farrar, Straus, and Giroux, 2003.

———. *The Fall and Rise of the Islamic State*. Princeton, NJ: Princeton University Press, 2008.

Ferraresi, Franco. *Threats to Democracy: The Radical Right in Italy after the War*. Princeton, NJ: Princeton University Press, 1996.

Ferree, Karen E. "Iterative Approaches to R x C Ecological Inference Problems: Where They Go Wrong and One Quick Fix." *Political Analysis* 12 (Spring 2004): 143–159.

Fidel, Kenneth. "Military Organization and Conspiracy in Turkey." *Studies in Comparative International Development* 6 (February 1970): 19–43.

Filali-Ansary, Abdou. "What Is Liberal Islam? The Sources of Enlightened Muslim Thought." *Journal of Democracy* 14 (April 2003): 19–33.

Fischer, Michael. *Iran: From Religious Dispute to Revolution*. Cambridge: Harvard University Press, 1980.

———. "Islam and the Revolt of the Petite Bourgeoisie." *Daedalus* 111 (Winter 1982): 101–125.

Fish, Steven. "Islam and Authoritarianism." *World Politics* 55 (October 2002): 4–37.

Formisano, Ronald P. "The Concept of Political Culture." *Journal of Interdisciplinary History* 3 (Winter 2001): 393–426.

Fuller, Graham. *The Future of Political Islam*. New York: Palgrave Macmillan, 2003.

Furet, François. *The Passing of an Illusion: The Idea of Communism in the Twentieth Century*. Trans. Deborah Furet. Chicago: University of Chicago Press, 1999.

Ganser, Daniele. *NATO's Secret Army: Operation Gladio and Terrorism in Western Europe*. New York: Routledge, 2005.

Gay, Peter. *The Enlightenment: An Interpretation, The Rise of Modern Paganism*. New York: Alfred A. Knopf, 1966.

Geertz, Clifford. *The Interpretation of Cultures*. New York: Basic Books, 1973.

Gellner, Ernest. *Muslim Society*. Cambridge: Cambridge University Press, 1981.

Gelman, Andrew, David K. Park, Stephen Ansolabehere, Phillip N. Price, and Lorraine C. Minnite. "Models, Assumptions and Model Checking in Ecological Regression." *Journal of the Royal Statistical Society* 164 (January 2001): 101–118.

Gerges, Fawaz A. *The Far Enemy: Why Jihad Went Global*. New York: Cambridge University Press, 2005.

Gerring, John. "Ideology: A Definitional Analysis." *Political Research Quarterly* 50 (December 1997): 957–994.

Gheissari, Ali. *Iranian Intellectuals in the Twentieth Century*. Austin: University of Texas Press, 1998.

Gheissari, Ali, and Vali Nasr. *Democracy in Iran: History and the Quest for Liberty*. New York: Oxford University Press, 2006.

Glaser, Barney G., and Anselm L. Strauss. *The Discovery of Grounded Theory: Strategies for Qualitative Research.* New York: Aldinede Gruyter, 1999.

Goldthorpe, John H. "Causation, Statistics, and Sociology." *European Sociological Review* 17 (March 2001): 1–20.

Göle, Nilufer. "Secularism and Islamism in Turkey: The Making of Elites and Counter-Elites." *Middle East Journal* 51 (Winter 1997): 46–58.

———. "Snapshots of Islamic Modernities." *Daedalus* 129 (Winter 2000): 91–117.

Granato, Jim, Ronald Inglehart, and David Leblang. "The Effect of Cultural Values on Economic Development: Theory, Hypotheses, and Some Empirical Tests." *American Journal of Political Science* 40 (August 1996): 607–631.

Grew, Raymond. "Suspended Bridges to Democracy." In *European Christian Democracy: Historical Legacies and Comparative Perspectives,* ed. Thomas Kselman and Joseph A. Buttigieg, 11–42. Notre Dame, IN: Notre Dame University Press, 2003.

Gunther, Richard, and Larry Diamond. "Species of Political Parties: A New Typology." *Party Politics* 9 (March 2003): 167–199.

Gutmann, Amy. *Identity in Democracy.* Princeton, NJ: Princeton University Press, 2003.

Gülalp, Haldun. "Political Islam in Turkey: The Rise and Fall of the Refah Party." *The Muslim World* 89 (January 1999): 22–41.

Gün, Fahrettin. *Sebilürreşad Dergisi Ekseninde Çok Partili Hayata Geçerken İslamcılara Göre Din, Siyaset ve Laiklik (1948–1954)* [Religion, Politics, and Laicism according to Islamists during the Transition to Multiparty Democracy: A Study of Sebilürreşad Magazine]. Istanbul: Beyan, 2001.

Hale, William. "Christian Democracy and the AKP: Parallels and Contrasts." *Turkish Studies* 6 (June 2005): 293–310.

———. *Turkish Politics and the Military.* London and New York: Routledge, 1994.

Halm, Heinz. *Shiʿism.* 2nd ed. New York: Columbia University Press, 2004.

Hammoudi, Abdellah. *Master and Disciple: The Cultural Foundations of Moroccan Authoritarianism.* Chicago: University of Chicago Press, 1997.

Hanioğlu, M. Şükrü. *The Young Turks in Opposition.* New York: Oxford University Press, 1995.

Hanley, David, ed. *Christian Democracy in Europe.* London and New York: Pinter, 1994.

Hassan, Mohammed S. "Political Islam versus the Society in Sudan: How the Islamic Project for Renewal Failed." Paper presented at the Sudanese Society Meeting, Santa Clara University, May 2004. Available at http://www.sudanstudies.org/mhassan04.html.

Hefner, Robert W. *Civil Islam: Muslims and Democratization in Indonesia.* Princeton, NJ, and Oxford, England: Princeton University Press, 2000.

———. "Multiple Modernities: Christianity, Islam, and Hinduism in a Globalizing Age." *Annual Review of Anthropology* 27 (October 1998): 83–104.

———. *Remaking Muslim Politics: Pluralism, Contestation, Democratization.* Princeton, NJ: Princeton University Press, 2004.

Henry, Clement M. *The Mediterranean Debt Crescent: Money and Power in Algeria, Egypt, Morocco, Tunisia, and Turkey.* Gainesville: University Press of Florida, 1996.

Hirschl, Ran. "Constitutional Courts vs. Religious Fundamentalism: Three Middle Eastern Tales." *Texas Law Review* 82 (June 2004): 1819–1860.

———. *Towards Juristocracy: The Origins and Consequences of the New Constitutionalism.* Cambridge: Harvard University Press, 2004.

Hirsh, Michael. "Bernard Lewis Revisited: What if Islam Isn't an Obstacle to Democracy in the Middle East but the Secret to Achieving It?" *Washington Monthly* (November 2004). Available at www.washingtonmonthly.com/features/2004/0411.hirsh.html.

Hodgson, Marshall G. S. *The Venture of Islam: Conscience and History in a World Civilization.* Vol. 2.: *The Expansion of Islam in the Middle Periods.* Chicago: University of Chicago Press, 1977.

———. *The Venture of Islam: Conscience and History in a World Civilization.* Vol. 3: *The Gunpowder Empires and Modern Times.* Chicago: University of Chicago Press, 1977.

Hoffman, Steven Ryan. "Islam and Democracy: Micro-Level Indicators of Compatibility." *Comparative Political Studies* 37 (August 2004): 652–676.

Hourani, Albert. *Arabic Thought in the Liberal Age 1789–1939.* Cambridge: Cambridge University Press, 1983. [Originally published in 1962.]

Huntington, Samuel P. *The Clash of Civilizations and the Remaking of New World Order.* New York: Simon and Schuster, 1996.

———. *The Third Wave: Democratization in the Late Twentieth Century.* Norman: University of Oklahoma Press, 1991.

Ibrahim, Said E. "Anatomy of Egypt's Militant Islamic Groups: Methodological Notes and Preliminary Findings." *International Journal of Middle Eastern Studies* 12 (December 1980): 423–453.

Inglehart, Ronald F. *Modernization and Postmodernization.* Princeton, NJ: Princeton University Press, 1997.

———. "A Renaissance of Political Culture." *American Political Science Review* 82 (September 1988): 632–659.

İran İzlenimleri [Observations in Iran]. Istanbul: Objektif, 1992.

Jabar, Faleh A. *The Shi'ite Movement in Iraq.* London: Saqi Books, 2003.

Jackman, Robert, and Ross Miller. "A Renaissance of Political Culture?" *American Journal of Political Science* 40 (May 1996): 632–659.

Jalaeipour, Hamidreza. "Religious Intellectuals and Political Action in the Reform Movement." In *Intellectual Trends in Twentieth Century Iran: A Critical Survey*, ed. Negin Nabavi. Gainesville: University Press of Florida, 2003.

Jamal, Amaney, and Mark Tessler. "Attitudes in the Arab World." *Journal of Democracy* 19 (January 2008): 97–100.

Jick, Todd D. "Mixing Qualitative and Quantitative Methods: Triangulation in Action." *Administrative Science Quarterly* 24 (December 1979): 602–611.

Johnson, James. "Conceptual Problems as Obstacles to Progress in Political Science: Four Decades of Political Culture Research." *Journal of Theoretical Politics* 15 (January 2003): 87–115.

———. "Consequences of Positivism: A Pragmatist Assessment." *Comparative Political Studies* 39 (March 2006): 224–252.

Kabha, Mustafa, and Haggai Erlich. "Al-Ahbash and Wahhabiyya: Interpretations of Islam." *International Journal of Middle Eastern Studies* 38 (November 2006): 519–538.

Kadivar, Mohsen. "Freedom of Religion and Belief Islam." In *The New Voices of Islam: Reforming Politics and Modernity: A Reader,* ed. Mehran Kamrava, 119–142. London: I. B. Tauris, 2006.

———. "The Innovative Political Ideas and Influence of Mulla Muhammad Kazim Khurasani." *Annals of Japan Association for Middle East Studies* 21 (2005): 59–73.

———. "An Introduction to the Public and Private Debate in Islam." *Social Research* 70 (Fall 2003): 659–680.

———. *Nazariyet-e Dowlat dar Fiqh-e Shia* [Theories of State in Shi'i Legal Thought]. 5th ed. Tehran: Ney, 2001.

Kalantari, Samad. "Iranian Voting Behavior in the 7th and 8th Presidential Elections." *Discourse* 3 (Winter 2002): 243–251.

Kalaycıoğlu, Ersin. "Elections and Party Preferences in Turkey: Changes and Continuities in the 1990s." *Comparative Political Studies* 27 (October 1994): 402–424.

———. "Three Styles of Politics: Conservatism, Liberalism, and Nationalism in Turkish Politics." Paper presented at the annual meeting of the Middle East Studies Association (MESA), Washington, D.C., November 22–25, 2008.

Kalkan, Ersin. *Katille Buluşma: Bir Jitem Dosyası, Musa Anter Cinayeti* [Meeting with the Murderer: A JITEM Dossier, the Murder of Musa Anter]. Istanbul: Güncel, 2006.

Kalyvas, Stathis N. "Commitment Problems in Emerging Democracies: The Case of Religious Parties." *Comparative Politics* 22 (July 2000): 379–398.

———. "Democracy and Religious Politics: Evidence from Belgium." *Comparative Political Studies* 31 (June 1998): 292–320.

———. "From Pulpit to Party: Party Formation and the Christian Democratic Phenomenon." *Comparative Politics* 30 (April 1998): 293–312.

———. *The Rise of Christian Democracy in Europe.* Ithaca, NY, and London: Cornell University Press, 1996.

———. "Unsecular Politics and Religious Mobilization." In *European Christian Democrats,* ed. Thomas Kselman and Joseph A. Buttigieg, 293–320. Notre Dame, IN: University of Notre Dame Press, 2003.

Kamrava, Mehran. *Iran's Intellectual Revolution.* New York: Cambridge University Press, 2008.

Kamrava, Mehran, and Houchang Hassan-Yari. "Suspended Equilibrium in Iran's Political System." *The Muslim World* 94 (October 2004): 495–524.

Kaplan, Sam. "*Din-u Devlet* All Over Again? The Politics of Military Secularism and Religious Militarism in Turkey Following the 1980 Coup." *International Journal of Middle East Studies* 34 (May 2002): 113–127.

Kara, İsmail. *Cumhuriyet Türkiyesi'nde bir Mesele Olarak İslam* [Islam as a Question in Republican Turkey]. Istanbul: Dergah, 2008.

———. *İslamcıların Siyasi Görüşleri* [Political Views of Islamists]. Istanbul: İz Yayıncılık, 1994.

Karbassi, A. R., M. A. Abduli, and E. Mahin Abdollazadeh. "Sustainability of Energy Production and Use in Iran." *Energy Policy* 35 (October 2007): 5171–5180.

Karsh, Efraim. *Islamic Imperialism: A History.* New Haven: Yale University Press, 2006.

Kasaba, Reşat. "Populism and Democracy in Turkey, 1946–1961." In *Rules and Rights in the Middle East: Democracy, Law, and Society,* ed. Ellis Goldberg, Reşat Kasaba, and Joel Migdal, 43–68. Seattle: University of Washington Press, 1993.

Kaya, Rıdvan. *Değişim Sürecinde AK Parti ve Müslümanlar* [The JDP and Muslims during Transition]. Istanbul: Ekin, 2007.

Kazemzadeh, Masoud. "Intra-Elite Factionalism and the 2004 Majles Elections in Iran." *Middle Eastern Studies* 44 (March 2008): 189–214.

Keddie, Nikki R. "Iran: Change in Islam; Islam in Change." *International Journal of Middle East Studies* 11 (July 1980): 527–542.

———. "Iranian Revolutions in Comparative Perspective." *American Historical Review* 88 (June 1983): 579–598.

———. *An Islamic Response to Imperialism: Political and Religious Writings of Sayyid Jamāl ad-Dīn "al-Afghānī,"* including a translation of the "Refutation of the Materialists" from the original Persian by Nikki R. Keddie and Hamid Algar. Berkeley: University of California Press, 1983.

———. *Modern Iran: Roots and Results of the Revolution*. New Haven and London: Yale University Press, 2003.

———. *Sayyid Jamāl ad-Dīn "al-Afghāni"; A Political Biography*. Berkeley: University of California Press, 1972.

Kepel, Gilles. *Jihad: The Trail of Political Islam*. Cambridge: Harvard University Press, 2002.

———. *Muslim Extremism in Egypt*. Los Angeles: University of California Press, 1993.

Keshavarzian, Arang. *Bazaar and State in Iran: The Politics of the Tehran Marketplace*. New York: Cambridge University Press, 2007.

———. "Contestation without Democracy: Elite Fragmentation in Iran." In *Authoritarianism in the Middle East: Regime and Resistance*, ed. Marsha Pripstein Posusney and Michele Penner Angrist, 63–88. Boulder, CO: Lynne Reinner, 2005.

Keyder, Çağlar. *Türkiye'de Devlet ve Sınıflar* [State and Classes in Turkey]. Istanbul: İletişim, 1989.

Khalaji, Mehdi. *The Last Marja: Sistani and the End of Traditional Religious Authority in Shiism*. Washington, D.C.: Washington Institute for Near East Policy, 2006.

Khomeini, Ruhollah. *Islam and Revolution: Writings and Declarations of Imam Khomeini*. Translated and annotated by Hamid Algar. Berkeley, CA: Mizan Press, 1981.

Khosrokhavar, Farhad. "The New Religiosity in Iran." *Social Compass* 54 (September 2007): 453–463.

———. "The New Intellectuals in Iran." *Social Compass* 51 (June 2004): 191–202.

Kılıç, Ecevit. *Özel Harp Dairesi: Türkiye'nin Gizli Tarihi* [Special War Bureau: The Secret History of Turkey]. Istanbul: Güncel Yayıncılık, 2007.

King, Gary. *A Solution to the Ecological Inference Problem*. Princeton, NJ: Princeton University Press, 1997.

King, Gary, Robert O. Keohane, and Sidney Verba. *Designing Social Inquiry: Scientific Interference in Qualitative Research*. Princeton, NJ: Princeton University Press, 1994.

Kirchheimer, Otto. "The Catch-all Party." In *The West European Party System*, ed. Peter Mair, 50–60. New York: Oxford University Press, 1990.

Kitschelt, Herbert. "Linkages between Citizens and Politicians in Democratic Polities." *Comparative Political Studies* 33 (August-September 2000): 845–879.

Koğacıoğlu, Dicle. "Progress, Unity, and Democracy: Dissolving Political Parties in Turkey." *Law and Society Review* 38 (September 2004): 433–461.

Kongar, Emre. *21. Yüzyilda Türkiye: 2000'li Yıllarda, Türkiye'nin Toplumsal Yapısı*

[Turkey in the Twenty-first Century: Turkey's Social Structure in the Twenty-first Century]. Istanbul: Remzi Kitabevi, 1998.

Kramer, Gudrun. "Islamist Notions of Democracy." In *Political Islam: Essays from Middle East Report*, ed. Joel Beinin and Joe Stork, 71–82. Berkeley and Los Angeles: University of California Press, 1997.

Kreuzer, Marcus. "Electoral Institutions, Political Organization, and Party Development: French and German Socialists and Mass Politics." *Comparative Politics* 30 (April 1998): 273–292.

Kuran, Timur. "The Discontents of Islamic Economic Morality." *American Economic Review* 86 (May 1996): 438–442.

———. "Now Out of Never: The Element of Surprise in the East European Revolution of 1989." *World Politics* 44 (October 1991): 7–48.

Kuru, Ahmet T. "Passive and Assertive Secularism: Historical Conditions, Ideological Struggles, and State Policies toward Religion." *World Politics* 59 (July 2007): 568–594.

Kurzman, Charles. "Critics Within: Islamic Scholars' Protests against the Islamic State in Iran." *International Journal of Politics, Culture, and Society* 15 (Winter 2001): 341–359.

———, ed. *Liberal Islam: A Source-Book*. New York: Oxford University Press, 1988.

———. *The Unthinkable Revolution in Iran*. Cambridge: Harvard University Press, 2004.

Laitin, David. "The Civic Culture at 30." *American Political Science Review* 89 (March 1995): 168–173.

Lakoff, Sanford. "The Reality of Muslim Exceptionalism." *Journal of Democracy* 15 (October 2004): 133–139.

Landau, Jacob M. "The Nationalist Action Party in Turkey." *Journal of Contemporary History* 17 (October 1982): 587–606.

Langohr, Vickie. "Of Islamists and Ballot Boxes: Rethinking the Relationship between Islamisms and Electoral Politics." *International Journal of Middle East Studies* 33 (November 2001): 591–610.

Lapidus, Ira. "The Separation of State and Religion in the Development of Early Islamic Society." *International Journal of Middle Eastern Studies* 6 (October 1975): 363–385.

Lawrence, Bruce. *Shattering the Myth: Islam beyond Violence*. Princeton, NJ: Princeton University Press, 1998.

Lebow, Richard Ned. "What's So Different about Counterfactual?" *World Politics* 52 (July 2000): 550–585.

Lerner, Daniel. *The Passing of Traditional Society: Modernizing the Middle East*. Glencoe, IL: Free Press, 1958.

Levitsky, Steven, and Lucan A. Way. "Linkage versus Leverage: Rethinking the

International Dimension of Regime Change." *Comparative Politics* 38 (July 2006): 379–400.

Lewis, Bernard. *The Emergence of Modern Turkey.* London and New York: Oxford University Press, 2002. [Originally published in 1961.]

———. *Islam and the West.* New York: Oxford University Press, 1993.

———. *What Went Wrong? The Clash between Islam and Modernity in the Middle East.* New York: Oxford University Press, 2002.

Lijphart, Arendt. "Comparative Politics and the Comparative Method." *American Political Science Review* 65 (September 1971): 682–693.

Lipset, Seymour Martin. "Some Social Requisites of Democracy: Economic Development and Political Legitimacy." *American Political Science Review* 53 (March 1959): 69–105.

Lipset, Seymour Martin, and Stein Rokkan. "Cleavage Structures, Party Systems, and Voter Alignments: An Introduction." In *Party Systems and Voter Alignments: Cross-National Perspectives,* ed. Seymour Martin Lipset and Stein Rokkan, 1–64. New York: Free Press, 1967.

Lockman, Zachary. *Contending Visions of the Middle East: The History and Politics of Orientalism.* New York: Cambridge University Press, 2004.

Lust-Okar, Ellen. "Competing for Resources in Jordanian Elections." In *Political Participation in the Middle East,* ed. Ellen Lust-Okar and Saloua Zerhouni, 75–94. Boulder, CO: Lynne Rienner, 2008.

———. *Structuring Conflict in the Arab World: Incumbents, Opponents, and Institutions.* New York: Cambridge University Press, 2007.

Lust-Okar, Ellen, and Amaney Jamal. "Rulers and Rules: Reassessing the Influence of Regime Type on Electoral Law Formation." *Comparative Political Studies* 35 (April 2002): 337–366.

MacIntyre, Alasdair. "The Essential Contestability of Some Social Concepts." *Ethics* 84 (October 1973): 1–9.

Mahmood, Saba. "Secularism, Hermeneutics, and Empire: The Politics of Islamic Reformation." *Public Culture* 18 (Spring 2006): 323–347.

Mahoney, James. "Qualitative Methodology and Comparative Politics." *Comparative Political Studies* 40 (February 2007): 122–144.

Mahoney, James, and Dietrich Rueschemeyer, eds. *Comparative Historical Analysis in the Social Sciences.* New York: Cambridge University Press, 2003.

Mainwaring, Scott. "Party Objectives in Authoritarian Regimes with Elections or Fragile Democracies: A Dual Game." In *Christian Democracy in Latin America: Electoral Competition and Regime Conflicts,* ed. Scott Mainwaring and Timothy R. Scully, 3–29. Stanford, CA: Stanford University Press, 2003.

Mamdani, Mahmood. *Good Muslim, Bad Muslim: America, the Cold War, and the Roots of Terror.* New York: Pantheon Books, 2004.

March, James G., and Johan P. Olsen. "The New Institutionalism: Organizational Factors in Political Life." *The American Political Science Review* 78 (September 1984): 734–749.

Mardin, Şerif A. "Center-Periphery Relations: The Key to Turkish Politics." *Daedalus* (Winter 1973): 169–190.

———. "Ideology and Religion in the Turkish Revolution." *International Journal of Middle Eastern Studies* 2 (July 1971): 197–211.

———. *Religion, Society, and Modernity in Turkey.* Syracuse, NY: Syracuse University Press, 2006.

Mater, Nadire. *Mehmed'in Kitabı: Güneydoğu'da Savaşmış Askerler Anlatıyor* [Mehmed's Book: Soldiers Who Fought in the Southeast Talk]. Istanbul: Metis Yayınları, 1998.

McFaul, Michael. "Transitions from Postcommunism." *Journal of Democracy* 16 (July 2005): 5–19.

McKeown, Timothy J. "Case Studies and the Statistical Worldview: Review of King, Keohane, and Verba's *Designing Social Inquiry: Scientific Inference in Qualitative Research.*" *International Organization* 53 (Winter 1999): 161–190.

Mert, Nuray. *Merkez Sağın Kısa Tarihi* [A Short History of the Center-Right]. Istanbul: Selis Kitapları, 2007.

Metiner, Mehmet. *Bembeyaz Demokrasi Yemyeşil Şeriat* [Snow White Democracy Very Green Shariat]. Istanbul: Doğan, 2004.

Meyer, Katherine, Helen Rizzo, and Yousef Ali. "Changed Political Attitudes in the Middle East: The Case of Kuwait." *International Sociology* 22 (June 2007): 289–324.

Michaud-Emin, Linda. "The Restructuring of the Military High Command in the Seventh Harmonization Package and Its Ramifications for Civil-Military Relations in Turkey." *Turkish Studies* (March 2007): 25–42.

Michels, Robert. *A Sociological Study of the Oligarchical Tendencies of Modern Democracy.* New York: Free Press, 1962. [Originally published in 1915.]

Migdal, Joel S. *The State in Society: Studying How States and Societies Transform and Constitute One Another.* New York: Cambridge University Press, 2001.

Milani, Mohsen. "Reform and Resistance in the Islamic Republic of Iran." In *Iran at the Crossroads,* ed. John L. Esposito and R. K. Ramazani, 29–56. New York: Palgrave, 2001.

Mir-Hosseini, Ziba, and Richard Tapper. *Islam and Democracy in Iran: Eshkevari and the Quest for Reform.* London: I. B. Tauris, 2006.

Mirsepassi, Ali. *Intellectual Discourse and the Politics of Modernization: Negotiating Modernity in Iran.* Cambridge: Cambridge University Press, 2000.

Mishal, Shaul, and Avraham Sela. *The Palestinian Hamas: Vision, Violence, and Coexistence.* New ed. New York: Columbia University Press, 2006.

Mitchell, Richard P. *The Society of the Muslim Brothers.* Reprint ed. New York: Oxford University Press, 1993.

Moaddel, Mansoor. "Class Struggle in Post-Revolutionary Iran." *International Journal of Middle East Studies* 23 (August 1991): 317–343.

———. "Ideology as Episodic Discourse: The Case of the Iranian Revolution." *American Sociological Review* 57 (June 1992): 353–379.

———. *Jordanian Exceptionalism: A Comparative Analysis of State-Religion Relationships in Egypt, Iran, Jordan, and Syria.* New York: Palgrave, 2002.

Momen, Moojan. *An Introduction to Shiʿi Islam.* New Haven: Yale University Press, 1987.

Moore, Barrington, Jr. *Social Origins of Dictatorship and Democracy: Lord and Peasant in the Making of the Modern World.* Boston: Beacon Press, 1966.

Mori, Strateji. *Türkiye'nin Nabzı* [Pulse of Turkey]. February 2002. [Public Opinion Survey.]

Morrison, Scott. "To Be a Believer in Republican Turkey: Three Allegories of İsmet Özel." *The Muslim World* 96 (July 2006): 507–521.

Moslem, Mehdi. *Factional Politics in Post-Khomeini Iran.* Syracuse, NY: Syracuse University Press, 2002.

Moussalli, Ahmad S. *The Islamic Quest for Democracy, Pluralism, and Human Rights.* Gainesville: University Press of Florida, 2001.

Naji, Kasra. *Ahmedinejad: The Secret History of Iran's Radical Leader.* London: I. B. Tauris, 2008.

Nasr, Seyyed Vali Reza. "Democracy and Islamic Revivalism." *Political Science Quarterly* 110 (Summer 1995): 261–285.

———. "Lessons from the Muslim World." *Daedalus* 132 (Summer 2003): 67–72.

———. *Mawdudi and the Making of Islamic Revivalism.* Oxford: Oxford University Press, 1996.

———. "The Rise of Muslim Democracy." *Journal of Democracy* 16 (April 2005): 13–27.

———. *The Vanguard of the Islamic Revolution: The Jamaʿat-i Islami of Pakistan.* Berkeley: University of California Press, 1994.

Neumann, Sigmund. "The Party of Democratic Integration." In *The West European Party System,* ed. Peter Mair, 46–49. New York: Oxford University Press, 1990.

Norris, Pippa, and Ronald F. Inglehart. "Islamic Culture and Democracy: Testing the 'Clash of Civilizations' Thesis." *Comparative Sociology* 1 (December 2002): 235–263.

———. *Sacred and Secular: Religion and Politics Worldwide.* New York: Cambridge University Press, 2004.

North, Douglass C. *Understanding the Process of Economic Change.* Princeton, NJ: Princeton University Press, 2005.

Norton, Augustus Richard. *Amal and the Shiʿa: Struggle for the Soul of Lebanon*. Austin: University of Texas Press, 1987.

———. *Hezbollah: A Short History*. Princeton, NJ: Princeton University Press, 2007.

Nye, Roger P. "Civil-Military Confrontation in Turkey: The 1973 Presidential Elections." *International Journal of Middle East Studies* 8 (April 1977): 209–228.

Ocak, Ahmet Yaşar. *Türk Sufiliğine Bakışlar* [Perspectives on Turkish Sufism]. Istanbul: İletişim, 1996.

O'Donnell, Guillermo, and Phillippe C. Schmitter. *Transitions from Authoritarian Rule: Tentative Conclusions about Uncertain Democracies*. Baltimore and London: Johns Hopkins University Press, 1986.

Okutan, Çağatay M. *Bozkurt'tan Kur'an'a Milli Türk Talebe Birliği (MTTB) 1916–1980* [From Gray Wolf to Koran: National Turkish Student Union (MTTB) 1916–1980]. Istanbul: Bilgi Üniversitesi Yayınları, 2004.

Olav, Utvik Bjorn. *"Hizb al-Wasat* and the Potential for Change in Egyptian Islamism." *Critique: Critical Middle Eastern Studies* 14 (Autumn 2005): 293–306.

Olson, Robert. *The Emergence of Kurdish Nationalism and the Sheikh Said Rebellion, 1880–1925*. Austin: University of Texas Press, 1989.

Osanloo, Arzoo. *The Politics of Women's Rights in Iran*. Princeton, NJ: Princeton University Press, 2009.

Ottaway, Marina, and Amr Hamzawy. "Islamist in Politics: The Dynamics of Participation." *Carnegie Papers* 98 (November 2008): 3–22.

Owen, Roger. *State, Power and Politics in the Making of the Modern Middle East*. 3rd ed. London and New York: Routledge, 2004.

Owen, Roger, and Şevket Pamuk. *A History of Middle East Economies in the Twentieth Century*. Cambridge: Harvard University Press, 1999.

Öniş, Ziya. "Globalization and Party Transformation: Turkey's Justice and Development Party in Perspective." In *Globalizing Democracy: Party Politics in Emerging Democracies*, ed. Peter Burnell. London: Routledge, 2006.

———. "The Political Economy of Turkey's Justice and Development Party." In *The Emergence of a New Turkey: Democracy and the AK Party*, ed. Hakan Yavuz, 207–234. Salt Lake City: University of Utah Press, 2006.

Öniş, Ziya, and Umut Türem. "Entrepreneurs, Democracy, and Citizenship in Turkey." *Comparative Politics* 34 (July 2002): 439–456.

Özdağ, Ümit. *Türk Ordusunun PKK Operasyonları* [Turkish Military Operations against the PKK]. Istanbul: Pegasus, 2005.

Özdalga, Elisabeth. "Necmettin Erbakan: Democracy for the Sake of Power." In *Political Leaders and Democracy in Turkey*, ed. Metin Heper and Sabri Sayarı, 127–147. Lanham, MD: Lexington Books, 2002.

———. "Worldly Asceticism in Islamic Casting: Fethullah Gülen's Inspired Piety and Activism." *Critique: Critical Middle Eastern Studies* 9 (Autumn 2000): 83–104.

Özipek, Bekir Berat. "28 Şubat ve İslamcılar" [February 28 and Islamists]. In *Modern Türkiye'de Siyasi Düşünce: İslamcılık,* ed. Yasin Aktay, 640–651. Istanbul: İletişim, 2004.

Özkan, Necati. *Türkiye ve Dünyadan Örneklerle Seçim Kazandıran Kampanyalar* [Winning Campaigns from Turkey and the World]. Istanbul: Mediacat, 2002.

Palmer, Robert R. "Popular Democracy in the French Revolution: Review Article." *French Historical Studies* 1 (Autumn 1960): 445–469.

Panebianco, Angelo. *Political Parties: Organization and Power.* New York: Cambridge University Press, 1988.

Parla, Taha. "Mercantile Militarism in Turkey, 1960–1998." *New Perspectives on Turkey* 19 (Fall 1998): 29–52.

———. *Türkiye'de Siyasi Kültürün Resmi Kaynakları: Kemalist Tek-Parti İdeolojisi ve CHP'nin Altı Ok'u* [Official Sources of Political Culture in Turkey: Kemalist One-Party Ideology and the RPP's Six Arrows]. Vol. 3. Istanbul: İletişim Yayınları, 1991.

Parsa, Misagh. "Entrepreneurs and Democratization: Iran and the Philippines." *Comparative Studies in Society and History* 37 (October 1995): 803–830.

———. *States, Ideologies, and Social Revolutions.* Cambridge: Cambridge University Press, 2000.

Parsi, Trita. *Treacherous Alliance: The Secret Dealings of Israel, Iran, and the United States.* New Haven: Yale University Press, 2007.

Patton, Marcia J. "AKP Government: Rabbits from a Hat?" *Middle East Journal* 60 (Fall 2006): 513–536.

Philpott, Daniel. "The Catholic Wave." *Journal of Democracy* 15 (April 2004): 32–46.

———. "Explaining the Political Ambivalence of Religion." *American Political Science Review* 101 (August 2007): 505–525.

Pierson, Paul. "Increasing Returns, Path Dependence, and the Study of Politics." *American Political Science Review* 94 (June 2000): 251–267.

Pion-Berlin, David. "Military Autonomy and Emerging Democracies in South America." *Comparative Politics* 25 (October 2002): 83–102.

Powell, G. Bingham, Jr. *Contemporary Democracies: Participation, Stability, and Violence.* Cambridge: Harvard University Press, 1982.

Przeworski, Adam, and John Sprague. *Paper Stones: A History of Electoral Socialism.* Chicago: University of Chicago Press, 1986.

Przeworski, Adam, and Henry Teune. *The Logic of Comparative Social Inquiry.* New York: Wiley-Interscience, 1970.

Putnam, Robert D. *Making Democracy Work: Civic Traditions in Modern Italy.* Princeton, NJ: Princeton University Press, 1993.

Pye, Lucian. "Culture and Political Science: Problems in the Evaluation of the Concept of the Political Culture." *Social Science Quarterly* 53 (September 1972): 285–296.

Qutb, Sayyid. *Milestones.* Indianapolis, IN: American Trust Publications, 1990.

———. *Social Justice in Islam.* Revised ed. Oneonta, NY: Islamic Publications International, 2000. [Originally published in 1948.]

Rajaee, Farhang. *Islamism and Modernism: The Changing Discourse in Iran.* Austin: University of Texas Press, 2007.

———. "A Thermidor of Islamic Yuppies? Conflict and Compromise in Iran's Politics." Middle East Journal 53 (Spring 1999): 217–231.

Ramadan, Tariq. *Western Muslims and the Future of Islam.* New York: Oxford University Press, 2003.

Rashid, Ahmed. *Taliban.* New Haven: Yale University Press, 2000.

Rebai, Ali. *Jameeshenasi-ye Tahavvolet-e Arzeshi: Negahe be Raftarshinasi-ye Ray Dahnedgah der Dovom Khordad 1376* [Sociology of Value Change: A Look at the Behavioral Science of Voting on Dovom Khordad 1376]. Tehran: Farhang va Andisheh, 2001.

Reed, John. *Ten Days That Shook the World.* New York: Penguin, 1990.

Refah Partisi. *Ön Savunma.* Ankara: Refah Partisi, 1997.

Rieffel, Lex. "Indonesia's Quiet Revolution." *Foreign Affairs* 83 (September/October 2004): 98–111.

Robinson, Glenn. *Building a Palestinian State: The Incomplete Revolution.* Bloomington: Indiana University Press, 1997.

Rokkan, Stein. *State Formation, Nation-building, and Mass Politics in Europe: The Theory of Stein Rokkan.* Selected and rearranged by Peter Flora, Stein Kuhnle, and Derek Urwin. New York: Oxford University Press, 1999.

Rose, Richard. "How Muslims View Democracy: Evidence from Central Asia." *Journal of Democracy* 13 (October 2002): 102–111.

Rosen, Lawrence. *The Culture of Islam: Changing Aspects of Contemporary Muslim Life.* Chicago and London: University of Chicago Press, 2004.

Ross, Marc Howard. "Culture and Identity in Comparative Political Analysis." In *Comparative Politics: Rationality, Culture, and Structure,* ed. Mark Irving Lichbach and Alan S. Zuckerman, 42–80. New York: Cambridge University Press, 1997.

Ross, Michael. "Does Oil Hinder Democracy?" *World Politics* 53 (April 2001): 325–361.

Roy, Olivier. "The Crisis of Religious Legitimacy in Iran." *The Middle East Journal* 53 (Spring 1999): 201–217.

———. *The Failure of Political Islam.* Cambridge: Harvard University Press, 1994.

———. *Globalized Islam: The Search for a New Ummah.* New York: Columbia University Press, 2004.

Rubin, Michael. *Into the Shadows: Radical Vigilantes in Khatami's Iran.* Washington, D.C.: Washington Institute for Near East Policy, 2001.

Sadiki, Larbi. *The Search for Arab Democracy: Discourses and Counter-Discourses.* New York: Columbia University Press, 2004.

Sadowski, Yahya. "The New Orientalism and the Democracy Debate." In *Political Islam: Essays from Middle East Report,* ed. Joel Benin and Joe Stork, 33–50. Berkeley and Los Angeles: University of California Press, 1997.

Sadri, Mahmoud. "Sacral Defense of Secularism: The Political Theologies of Soroush, Shabestari, and Kadivar." *International Journal of Politics, Culture and Society* 15 (Winter 2001): 257–270.

Saffari, Said. "The Legitimation of the Clergy's Right to Rule in the Iranian Constitution of 1979." *British Journal of Middle Eastern Studies* 20 (May 1993): 64–82.

Said, Edward W. *Orientalism.* New York: Vintage Books, 1979.

Salefi-Isfahani, Djavad. "Revolution and Distribution in Iran: Poverty and Inequality." Unpublished paper, 2006.

Salvatore, Armando, and Dale F. Eickelman, eds. *Public Islam and the Common Good.* Leiden and Boston: Brill, 2004.

Samii, Abbas W. "The Changing Landscape of Party Politics in Iran—A Case Study." *Journal of the European Society for Iranian Studies* 1 (Winter 2005): 53–62.

———. "Dissent in Iranian Elections: Reasons and Implications." *Middle East Journal* 58 (Summer 2004): 403–423.

———. "Iran's Guardians Council as an Obstacle to Democracy." *Middle East Journal* 55 (Autumn 2001): 642–663.

———. "Iran's 2000 Elections." *Middle East Review of International Affairs* 4 (March 2000): 1–15.

Sarabi, Farzin. "The Post-Khomeini Era in Iran: The Elections of the Fourth Islamic Majlis." *Middle East Journal* 48 (Winter 1994): 89–107.

Sarıbay, Ali Yaşar. *Türkiye'de Modernleşme, Din ve Parti Politikası: MSP Örnek Olayı* [Modernization, Religion and Party Politics in Turkey: The Case of NSP]. Istanbul: Alan, 1985.

Sartori, Giovanni. *Parties and Party Systems: A Framework for Analysis.* New York: Cambridge University Press, 1976.

———. "Politics, Ideology, and Belief Systems." *The American Political Science Review* 63 (June 1969): 398–411.

Savaş, Kutlu. *Susurluk Raporu* [Susurluk Report]. Ankara: Başbakanlık, 1999.

Sayarı, Sabri. "Adnan Menderes: Between Democratic and Authoritarian Populism." In *Political Leaders and Democracy in Turkey,* ed. Metin Heper and Sabri Sayarı, 65–87. Lanham, MD: Lexington Books, 2002.

Sayarı, Sabri, and Yılmaz Esmer, eds. *Politics, Parties, and Elections in Turkey.* Boulder, CO, and London: Lynne Rienner, 2002.

Schaffer, Frederic C. *Democracy in Translation.* Ithaca, NY: Cornell University Press, 2000.

Schmitt, Carl. *The Concept of the Political.* Trans. George Schwab. Chicago: University of Chicago Press, 1996.

Schumpeter, Joseph. *Capitalism, Socialism, and Democracy.* New York: Harper Perennial, 1975 [1950].

Schwedler, Jillian. *Faith in Moderation: Islamist Parties in Yemen and Jordan.* New York: Cambridge University Press, 2006.

———. "A Paradox of Democracy? Islamist Participation in Elections." *Middle East Report* 209 (Winter 1998): 25–29, 41.

Scott, James C. *Weapons of the Weak: Everyday Forms of Peasant Resistance.* New Haven: Yale University Press, 1985.

Sedghi, Hamideh. *Women and Politics in Iran: Veiling, Unveiling, and Reveiling.* Cambridge: Cambridge University Press, 2007.

Seligson, Mitchell. "The Renaissance of Political Culture or the Renaissance of the Ecological Fallacy?" *Comparative Politics* 34 (April 2002): 273–292.

Shadid, Anthony. *The Legacy of the Prophet: Despots, Democrats, and the New Politics of Islam.* Boulder, CO: Westview Press, 2001.

Shafiq, Munir. "Secularism and the Arab-Muslim Condition." In *Islam and Secularism in the Middle East,* ed. Azzam Tamimi and John Esposito, 139–150. London: Hurst Publishers, 2000.

Shambayati, Hootan. "The Rentier State, Interest Groups, and the Paradox of Autonomy: State and Business in Turkey and Iran." *Comparative Politics* 26 (April 1994): 307–331.

———. "A Tale of Two Mayors: Courts and Politics in Iran and Turkey." *International Journal of Middle East Studies* 36 (May 2004): 253–275.

Shapiro, Ian. *The State of Democratic Theory.* New Haven: Yale University Press, 2003.

Shariati, Ali. *On the Sociology of Islam.* Trans. Hamid Algar. Berkeley: Mizan Press, 1979.

Shepard, William E. "Islam and Ideology: Towards a Typology." *International Journal of Middle East Studies* 19 (August 1987): 307–335.

———. "Sayyid Qutb's Doctrine of *Jāhiliyya.*" *International Journal of Middle East Studies* 35 (November 2003): 521–545.

Sherwood, W. B. "The Rise of the Justice Party in Turkey." *World Politics* 20 (October 1967): 54–65.

Silvan, Emmanuel. "Why Radical Muslims Aren't Taking Over Governments." *Middle East Review of International Affairs* 2 (May 1998): 9–16.

Simon, Herbert. "Organizations and Markets." *Journal of Economic Perspectives* 5 (Spring 1991): 25–44.

Skocpol, Theda. "Rentier State and Shi'a Islam in the Iranian Revolution." *Theory and Society* 11 (May 1982): 265–283.

Skocpol, Theda, and Margaret Somers. "The Uses of Comparative History in Macrosocial Inquiry." *Comparative Studies in Society and History* 22 (April 1980): 174–197.

Smith, Benjamin. "Oil Wealth and Regime Survival in the Developing World, 1960–1999." *American Journal of Political Science* 48 (April 2004): 232–246.

Soroush, Abdolkarim. *Reason, Freedom and Democracy in Islam: Essential Writings of Abdolkarim Soroush.* Trans. and ed. Mahmoud Sadri and Ahmad Sadri. New York: Oxford University Press, 2000.

Stark, Rodney. "Secularization, R.I.P—Rest in Peace." *Sociology of Religion* 60 (Fall 1999): 249–273.

Stepan, Alfread, and Graeme B. Robertson. "An 'Arab' More Than a 'Muslim' Democracy Gap." *Journal of Democracy* 14 (July 2003): 30–44.

Stern, Roger. "The Iranian Petroleum Crisis and United States National Security." *Proceedings of the National Academy of Sciences of the United States of America* 104 (January 2007): 377–382.

Swidler, Ann. "Culture in Action: Symbols and Strategies." *American Sociological Review* 51 (April 1986): 273–286.

Şahan, Timur, and Uğur Balık. *İtirafçı: Bir JITEM'ci Anlattı* [Confessionist: A JITEM Member Spoke]. Istanbul: Aram, 2004.

Şen, Serdar. *Refah Partisi'nin Teori ve Pratiği: Refah Partisi, Adil Düzen ve Kapitalizm* [The Welfare Party's Theory and Practice: The Welfare Party, Just Order, and Capitalism]. Istanbul: Sarmal, 1995.

Tabari Keyvan. "The Rule of Law and the Politics of Reform in Iran." *International Sociology* 18 (March 2003): 96–113.

Tachau, Frank, and Metin Heper. "The State, Politics, and the Military in Turkey." *Comparative Politics* 16 (October 1983): 17–33.

Tamadonfar, Mehran. "Islam, Law, and Political Control in Contemporary Iran." *Journal for the Scientific Study of Religion* 40 (June 2001): 205–220.

Tam-Cho, Wendy K. "Iff the Assumption Fits . . .: A Comment on the King Ecological Inference Solution." *Political Analysis* 7 (Winter 1998): 143–163.

Tam-Cho, Wendy K., and Charles F. Manski. "Cross-Level/Ecological Inference."

In *Oxford Handbook of Political Methodology,* ed. Janet M. Box-Steffensmeier, Henry Brady, and David Collier, 547–569. New York: Oxford University Press, 2008.

Tamimi, Azzam S. *Rachid Ghannouchi: A Democrat within Islamism.* New York: Oxford University Press, 2001.

———. "The Renaissance of Islam." *Daedalus* 132 (Summer 2003): 51–58.

Tan, Altan. *Kürt Sorunu: Ya Tam Kardeşlik ya da Hep Birlikte Kölelik* [The Kurdish Question: Either Togetherness or Enslavement]. Istanbul: Timaş, 2009.

Tanıyıcı, Şaban. "Transformation of Political Islam in Turkey." *Party Politics* 9 (July 2003): 463–483.

Tarhanlı, İştar B. *Müslüman Toplum, "Laik" Devlet: Türkiye'de Diyanet İşleri Başkanlığı* [Muslim Society, "Laic" State: Religious Affairs Directory in Turkey]. Istanbul: AFA, 1993.

Tarrow, Sidney. "Bridging the Quantitative-Qualitative Divide." In *Rethinking Social Inquiry: Diverse Tools, Shared Standards,* ed. Henry E. Brady and David Collier, 171–181. Lanham, MD: Rowman and Littlefield, 2004.

Taylor, Charles. *A Secular Age.* Cambridge: The Belknap Press of Harvard University Press, 2007.

Tayyar, Şamil. *Operasyon Ergenekon* [Operation Ergenekon]. Istanbul: Timaş Yayınları, 2008.

Tepe, Sultan. *Beyond Sacred and Secular: Politics of Religion in Israel and Turkey.* Stanford, CA: Stanford University Press, 2008.

———. "Turkey's AKP: A Model 'Muslim-Democratic' Party." *Journal of Democracy* 16 (October 2005): 69–82.

Tessler, Mark, ed. *Area Studies and Social Science: Strategies for Understanding Middle East Politics.* Bloomington: Indiana University Press, 1999.

———. "Islam and Democracy in the Middle East: The Impact of Religious Orientations on Attitudes toward Democracy in Four Arab Countries." *Comparative Politics* 3 (April 2002): 237–254.

———. "The Origins of Popular Support for Islamist Movements: A Political Movement Analysis." In *Islam, Democracy, and the State in North Africa,* ed. John Entelis, 93–126. Bloomington: Indiana University Press, 1997.

Tessler, Mark, and Eleanor Gao. "Gauging Arab Support for Democracy." *Journal of Democracy* 16 (July 2005): 83–97.

Tezcür, Güneş Murat. "Constitutionalism, Judiciary, and Democracy in Islamic Societies." *Polity* 39 (October 2007): 479–501.

———. "Intra-Elite Struggles in Iranian Elections." In *Political Participation in the Middle East,* ed. Ellen Lust-Okar and Saloua Zerhouni, 51–74. Boulder, CO: Lynne Rienner, 2008.

———. "Judicial Activism in Perilous Times: The Turkish Case." *Law and Society Review* 43 (June 2009): 305–336.

———. "Political Cleavages in Turkey: A Geographical Perspective." Paper presented at Workshop 19, "Politicizing Socio-Cultural Structures: Elite and Mass Perspectives on Cleavages," of the European Consortium on Political Research (ECPR) Joint Session of Workshops, Helsinki, Finland, May 7–12, 2007.

Tezcür, Güneş Murat, and Taghi Azadarmaki. "Religiosity and Islamic Rule." *Journal for the Scientific Study of Religion* 47 (June 2008): 211–224.

Tezcür, Güneş Murat, Taghi Azadarmaki, and Mehri Bahar. "Religious Participation among Muslims: Iranian Exceptionalism." *Critique: Critical Middle Eastern Studies* 15 (Fall 2006): 17–32.

Thelen, Kathleen. "Historical Institutionalism in Comparative Politics." *Annual Review of Political Science* 2 (1999): 369–404.

Tilly, Charles. *Democracy.* New York: Cambridge University Press, 2007.

———. "Mechanisms in Political Processes." *Annual Review of Political Science* 4 (June 2001): 21–41.

Tripp, Charles. *A History of Iraq.* New York: Cambridge University Press, 2005.

Trotsky, Leon. *The Russian Revolution: The Overthrow of Tzarism and the Triumph of the Soviets.* Selected and edited by F. W. Dupee, from *The History of the Russian Revolution.* New York: Anchor Books, 1959.

Tuğal, Cihan. "The Appeal of Islamic Politics: Ritual and Dialogue in a Poor District of Turkey." *Sociological Quarterly* 47 (May 2006): 245–273.

———. *Passive Revolution: Absorbing the Islamic Challenge to Capitalism.* Stanford, CA: Stanford University Press, 2009.

Tunaya, Zafer Tarık. *İslamcılık Akımı* [Islamist Movement]. Istanbul: Bilgi Üniversitesi, 2003.

———. *Türkiye'de Siyasal Gelişmeler [1876–1938]* [Political Developments in Turkey (1876–1938)]. Istanbul: Bilgi Üniversitesi, 2002.

Turam, Berna. *Between Islam and the State: The Politics of Engagement.* Stanford, CA: Stanford University Press, 2006.

Türkmen, Hamza. *Türkiye'de İslâmcılık ve Özeleştiri* [Islamism in Turkey and a Self-Criticism]. Istanbul: Ekin, 2008.

Türköne, Mümtazer. *Siyasi İdeoloji Olarak İslamcılığın Doğuşu* [The Birth of Islamism as Political Ideology]. Istanbul: İletişim, 1991.

TÜSİAD. *Seçim Sistemi ve Siyasi Partiler Araştırması* [Electoral System and Political Parties Study]. Istanbul: TÜSİAD, 2001.

Vahdat, Farzin. *God and Juggernaut: Iran's Intellectual Encounter with Modernity.* Syracuse, NY: Syracuse University Press, 2002.

———. "Post-revolutionary Discourses of Mohammad Mojtahed Shabestari and

Mohsen Kadivar: Reconciling the Terms of Mediated Subjectivity. Part 1: Mojtahed Shabestari." *Critique: Journal for Critical Studies of the Middle East* 16 (Spring 2000): 31–54.

———. "Post-revolutionary Discourses of Mohammad Mojtahed Shabestari and Mohsen Kadivar: Reconciling the Terms of Mediated Subjectivity. Part 2: Mohsen Kadivar." *Critique: Journal for Critical Studies of the Middle East* 17 (Fall 2000): 135–157.

———. "Post-revolutionary Discourses on Modernity in Iran: Expansion and Contraction of Human Subjectivity." *International Journal of Middle East Studies* 35 (November 2003): 599–631.

———. "Religious Modernity in Iran: Dilemmas of Islamic Democracy in the Discourse of Mohammad Khatami." *Comparative Studies of South Asia, Africa, and the Middle East* 25 (2005): 650–664.

Vakili-Zad, Cyrus. "Conflict among the Ruling Revolutionary Elite in Iran." *Middle Eastern Studies* 30 (July 1994): 618–631.

Van Dam, Nikolaos. *The Struggle for Power in Syria: Politics and Society under Asad and the Ba'th Party.* London: I. B. Tauris, 1996.

Van de Walle, Nicolas. "Africa's Range of Regimes." *Journal of Democracy* 13 (April 2002): 66–80.

Varzi, Roxanne. *Warring Souls: Youth, Media, and Martyrdom in Post-Revolution Iran.* Durham: Duke University Press, 2006.

Wahid, K. H. Abdurrahman. "Indonesia's Mild Secularism." *SAIS Review* 21 (Fall 2001): 25–28.

Waterbury, John. "Fortuitous By-products." *Comparative Politics* 29 (April 1997): 383–402.

Weber, Max. *Protestant Ethic and the Spirit of Capitalism.* Los Angeles: Roxbury, 2002.

———. *The Sociology of Religion.* Introduction by Talcott Parsons. Boston: Beacon Press, 1993.

Wedeen, Lisa. "Conceptualizing Culture: Possibilities for Political Science." *American Political Science Review* 96 (December 2002): 713–728.

Wegner, Eva, and Miquel Pellicer. "Islamist Moderation without Democratization: The Coming of Age of the Moroccan Party of Justice and Development." *Democratization* 16 (February 2009): 157–175.

Wehrey, Frederic, Jerrold D. Green, Brian Nichiporuk, Alireza Nader, Lydia Hansell, Rasool Nafisi, and S. R. Bohandy. *The Rise of the Pasdaran.* Santa Monica, CA: RAND, 2009.

Wells, Matthew C. "Thermidor in the Islamic Republic of Iran: The Rise of Muhammad Khatami." *British Journal of Middle Eastern Studies* 26 (May 1999): 27–39.

Werenfels, Isabelle. "Between Integration and Repression: Government Responses to Islamism in the Maghreb." *SWP Research Paper* S 39 (December 2005): 5–33.

West, W. Jefferson II. "Regional Cleavages in Turkish Politics: An Electoral Geography of the 1999 and 2002 National Elections." *Political Geography* 24 (May 2005): 499–523.

White, Jenny B. *Islamist Mobilization in Turkey: A Study in Vernacular Politics.* Seattle: University of Washington Press, 2002.

Wickham, Carrie Rosefsky. *Mobilizing Islam: Religion, Activism, and Political Change in Egypt.* New York: Columbia University Press, 2002.

———. "The Path to Moderation: Strategy and Learning in the Formation of Egypt's *Wasat* Party." *Comparative Politics* 36 (January 2004): 205–228.

Wiktorowicz, Quintan, ed. *Islamic Activism: A Social Movement Theory Approach.* Bloomington: Indiana University Press, 2004.

Wilde, Melissa J. *Vatican II: A Sociological Analysis of Religious Change.* Princeton, NJ: Princeton University Press, 2007.

Wilson, Richard W. "The Many Voices of Political Culture: Assessing Different Approaches." *World Politics* 52 (January 2000): 246–273.

Wolfe, Alan. "And the Winner Is." *Atlantic Monthly,* March 2008.

Wolfe, Bertram D. *Three Who Made a Revolution.* New York: Stein and Day, 1984.

Yalçın, Soner. *Hangi Erbakan?* [Which Erbakan?]. 5th ed. Istanbul: Öteki Yayınevi, 1994.

Yalçın, Soner, and Doğan Yurdakul. *Reis: Gladio'nun Türk Tetikçisi* [The Chief: The Turkish Triggerman of Gladio]. Istanbul: Doğan Yayıncılık, 2003.

Yaşar, Emin M. "Dergah'tan Parti'ye, Vakıf'tan Şirkete Bir Kimliğin Oluşumu ve Dönüşümü: İskenderpaşa Cemaati [From Dervish Lodge to Political Party, Foundation to Company: The Evolution of the Iskenderpasa Order]." In *Modern Türkiye'de Siyasi Düşünce: İslamcılık,* ed. Yasin Aktay, 321–340. Istanbul: İletişim, 2004.

Yavuz, M. Hakan. *Islamic Political Identity in Turkey.* Oxford and New York: Oxford University Press, 2003.

———. *Secularism and Muslim Democracy in Turkey.* New York: Cambridge University Press, 2009.

Yavuz, M. Hakan, and John L. Esposito, eds. *Turkish Islam and the Secular State: The Gülen Movement.* Syracuse, NY: Syracuse University Press, 2003.

Yenigün, Sedat. *Bir Şehidin Notları* [Notes of a Martyr]. Istanbul: İnkılâb, 1998.

Yıldız, Abdullah. *28 Şubat: Belgeler* [February 28: Documents]. Istanbul: Pınar Yayınları, 2000.

Yılmaz, Turan. *Tayyip: Kasımpaşa'dan Siyasetin Ön Saflarına* [Tayyip: From Kasimpasa to Political Limelight]. Ankara: Ümit, 2001.

Yücel, M. Serhan. *Demokrat Parti.* Istanbul: Ülke Kitaplari, 2001.

Zakaria, Fareed. *The Future of Freedom: Illiberal Democracy at Home and Abroad.* New York and London: W. W. Norton, 2003.

Zaman, Muhammad Qasim. *The Ulama in Contemporary Islam: Custodians of Change.* Princeton, NJ: Princeton University Press, 2002.

Zarcone, Thierry. *La Turquie Moderne et l'Islam.* Mayenne, France: Flammarion, 2004.

Zurcher, Erich. *Turkey: A Modern History.* London: I. B. Tauris, 1993.

NEWSPAPERS AND MAGAZINES

Abrar (Persian)

Aftab-e Yazd (Persian)

Aksiyon (Turkish)

Al-Ahram

Al-Sharq al-Awsat

Asia Times

Asr-e Azadegan (Persian)

Asr-e Maa (Persian)

Ayeen (Persian)

Bayan (Persian)

Bloomberg

Christian Science Monitor

Economist

Entekhab (Persian)

Etemad (Persian)

Etemad-e Melli (Persian)

Farda (Persian)

Farhang-e Ashti (Persian)

Fath (Persian)

Financial Times

Guardian

Hamshahri (Persian)

Hürriyet (Turkish)

Independent

International Herald Tribune

Iran (Persian)

Iran-e Farda (Persian)

Kayhan (Persian, based in London)

Kayhan (Persian, based in Tehran)

Milliyet (Turkish)

Nasimesaba (Persian)

New York Times

Nokta (Turkish)

Nowruz (Persian)

Özgür Gündem (Turkish)

Radikal (Turkish)

Resalat (Persian)

Salam (Persian)

Sharq (Persian)

Sobh-e Emrooz (Persian)

Star (Turkish)

Taraf (Turkish)

Towsee (Persian)

USA Today

Vaqa-ye Ettefaqieh (Persian)

Wall Street Journal

Washington Post

Yas-e No (Persian)

Yeni Şafak (Turkish)

Zaman (Turkish)

INDEX

CPSIA information can be obtained at www.ICGtesting.com
Printed in the USA
BVOW08s0146040913

330042BV00001B/69/P